# EMBODIED GROUNDING

How do the accomplishments that make us most deeply human – our capacity to think, to use language, to experience emotions, and to relate to one another – depend on our bodies? Exploring these issues involves laying aside an ancient Western tradition that placed body and mind in opposition, as well as more recent scientific understanding of thought as abstract, disembodied information processing. The chapters in this volume review current work on relations of the body to thought, language use, emotion, and social relationships, as presented by internationally recognized experts in these areas.

Gün R. Semin is Academy Professor, Royal Netherlands Academy of Arts and Sciences, Utrecht University, Faculty of Social Sciences.

Eliot R. Smith is Professor of Psychological and Brain Sciences, Indiana University, Bloomington, Indiana.

# Embodied Grounding

*Social, Cognitive, Affective, and Neuroscientific Approaches*

Edited by

**GÜN R. SEMIN**
*Utrecht University*

**ELIOT R. SMITH**
*Indiana University, Bloomington*

CAMBRIDGE
UNIVERSITY PRESS

CAMBRIDGE UNIVERSITY PRESS
Cambridge, New York, Melbourne, Madrid, Cape Town, Singapore, São Paulo, Delhi

Cambridge University Press
32 Avenue of the Americas, New York, NY 10013-2473, USA

www.cambridge.org
Information on this title: www.cambridge.org/9780521706155

First published 2008

Printed in the United States of America

*A catalog record for this publication is available from the British Library.*

*Library of Congress Cataloging in Publication Data*

Embodied grounding : social, cognitive, affective, and neuroscientific approaches /
[edited by] Gün R. Semin, Eliot R. Smith.
   p.   cm.
Includes bibliographical references and index.
ISBN 978-0-521-88019-0 (hardback) – ISBN 978-0-521-70615-5 (pbk.)
1. Mind and body.   2. Semiotics.   3. Language and languages – Philosophy.   4. Social
psychology.   5. Emotions.   I. Semin, G. R.   II. Smith, Eliot R.   III. Title.
BF161.E425   2008
150.19′8–dc22        2007029339

ISBN   978-0-521-88019-0 hardback
ISBN   978-0-521-70615-5 paperback

# Contents

# Contributors

**Lisa Feldman Barrett**  Boston College, MA, USA

**Lawrence W. Barsalou**  Emory University, GA, USA

**Lera Boroditsky**  Stanford University, CA, USA

**Pablo Briñol**  Universidad Autónoma de Madrid, Spain

**John T. Cacioppo**  University of Chicago, IL, USA

**Gerald L. Clore**  University of Virginia, VA, USA

**Jens Förster**  International University, Bremen, Germany, and University of Amsterdam, The Netherlands

**Ronald S. Friedman**  University of Albany, State University of New York, NY, USA

**Arthur M. Glenberg**  University of Wisconsin at Madison, WI, USA

**Kristen A. Lindquist**  Boston College, MA, USA

**Paula M. Niedenthal**  Centre National de la Recherche Scientifique (CNRS) and University of Clermont-Ferrand

**Lindsay Oberman**  University of California, San Diego, CA, USA

**Richard E. Petty**  Ohio State University, OH, USA

**Jesse Prinz**  University of North Carolina, Chapel Hill, NC, USA

**Friedemann Pulvermüller**  Medical Research Council, Cognition and Brain Sciences Unit, Cambridge, UK

**Simone Schnall**  University of Plymouth

**Thomas W. Schubert**  Utrecht University

**Beate Seibt**  Utrecht University

**Gün R. Semin**  Utrecht University

**Eliot R. Smith**  Indiana University, Bloomington, IN, USA

**Sven Waldzus**  ISCTE, Lisbon

**Piotr Winkielman**  University of California, San Diego, CA, USA

# Introducing Embodied Grounding

## Gün R. Semin and Eliot R. Smith

In just the last two decades, the embodiment perspective has inspired research and new theoretical ideas across a wide swath of the behavioral and cognitive sciences. Much of the appeal underlying this impact arises from the simple insight upon which the core ideas of embodiment rest: that nervous systems evolved for the adaptive control of action – not for abstract cogitation (chess-playing, in Brooks's memorable 1991 statement of this insight). This idea immediately has several significant implications.

First, minds co-evolved with bodies, especially sensory-motor systems. There are now many examples illustrating the importance of this fact. One is the way organisms use the physical properties of bodies to reduce the need for costly central computation (Thelen & Smith, 1994; Pfeifer & Scheier, 1999). Another is the "active vision" idea that when agents move, far from introducing problematic variation into sensory inputs, they actually create the conditions for discovering cross-modal associations, facilitating under-standing of the environment and the adaptive shaping of action (Edelman, 1987; Pfeifer & Scheier, 1999).

Second, the embodiment approach suggests a renewed focus on the whole behaving organism in its natural context as the object of study. Seen from this perspective, either the isolation of specific "slices" such as central information-processing systems, or the study of organisms in environments vastly different from those in which they evolved, seem less than optimal research approaches.

Third, the context in which organisms behave is very often a social context. In the case of humans, the very capabilities that make us human – to elaborate philosophical ideas, build cities, sing, and dance – are usually collective acts or, even if performed by an individual, depend absolutely on a multitude of social products (not the least of which is language). The embodiment approach should shed light not only on the functioning of individual humans but also on the ways they cooperate, compete, and otherwise relate to each other, in groups and as individuals.

Fourth, a focus on the whole behaving organism in its context breaks down traditional disciplinary boundaries as well as distinctions between topics like cognition and motivation. The recognition of this basic fact has driven psychological theory and research to focus increasingly on the interdependences among cognition, motivation, affect, and action as they are all influenced by the body. An embodied approach is taking root not only in psychology but across a variety of disciplines ranging from the neurosciences to developmental processes to cognitive sciences and robotics with an increasingly powerful synergy between these different approaches. In this situation, fresh discoveries in one "field" lead to reformulations of the very same issues in a different "field."

The impetus to cross boundaries is also the inspiration for this volume, the foundations of which were laid during a four-day conference including the majority of the contributors in May 2006. This meeting gave rise to a unique synergy because the participants came from quite different specialties ranging from neuroscience to cognitive psychology, social psychology, affective sciences, and psycholinguistics. The discussions and exchanges resulted in the current volume, which follows a tripartite organization. The contributions that make the first part of this volume address the *embodied grounding of concepts and language*. Whereas the disciplinary breadth of the material in these contributions is considerable, ranging from neuroscience to experimental cognitive psychology, the authors of the different chapters are not only informed about each other's work but also influenced by it. These contributions examine the central issues in this field from complementary perspectives because interaction at the conference helped them build bridges across traditional boundaries. The driving theme for these four chapters is that our representations of the social world are fundamentally connected with the actions that our bodies perform, so that these actions inform our concepts, language, and thinking.

- The opening chapter by Barsalou presents an embodied account of symbolic operations, proceeding from the neural simulation of concrete concepts to how these relate to abstract concepts and symbols. He reviews the most recent research in this area, which come from a variety of different methods ranging from experimental behavioral work to neuroscientific findings. In concluding his contribution, Barsalou examines the link between language and perceptual symbols systems, arguing for links between, for instance, syntax and the role it may play in psychological processes such as retrieval, how simulations are assembled, and the nature of recursively embedded structures.

- The next contribution by Glenberg is based on his Indexical Hypothesis, a model that is designed to interface bodily states with language and action. His chapter outlines this hypothesis and the processes underlying how meaning is understood.
- Indeed, there is considerable intellectual cross-fertilization not only between Glenberg's Indexical Hypothesis and Barsalou's perceptual symbol systems model but also with the third chapter of this section, namely, Pulvermüller's examination of the cortical mechanisms responsible for semantic grounding and embodiment concepts.
- The final chapter in this part by Boroditsky and Prinz examines the sources contributing to human knowledge and thinking. They argue for two input streams to the complex human knowledge system and thinking. The first stream they refer to is the use of stored records of sensory and motor states, inspired by Barsalou's (Chapter 1) perceptual symbols systems model. The second source that they elaborate upon is the contribution of language – treated not as an abstract inner mental "code" but as a rich store of sensorimotor regularities in the real world, whose statistical properties offer important evidence for the construction and constitution of thought.

The second part of the volume focuses on the *embodiment of social cognition and relationships*.

- Semin and Cacioppo outline a model of social cognition that breaks away from a traditional individual-centered analysis of social cognition and treats social cognition as grounded by neurophysiological processes that are distributed across brains and bodies and is manifested in the co-regulation of behaviors. The theoretical framework they introduce is an attempt to model the processes involved from joint perception to co-regulation in social interaction.
- Smith describes how social relationships that link people to other individuals or social groups are both expressed and regulated by bodily processes. Drawing on Alan Fiske's Relational Models Theory, research described in this chapter tests hypotheses that both synchronized movements and interpersonal touch operate as embodied cues to close relationships (communal sharing relationships, in Fiske's terminology).
- A related chapter by Schubert, Waldzus, and Seibt also draws upon Fiske's model, relating it to Barsalou's fundamental point that abstract concepts (such as interpersonal closeness or differences in power or authority) are

understood in terms of bodily metaphors. For example, research finds that authority differences are expressed in differences in size, height, or vertical position; the powerful literally do "lord it over" the rest of us.

- Briñol and Petty deal with a different aspect of social cognition: the effects of embodiment on processes involved in social influence, especially those leading to changes in attitudes or evaluations of particular objects. Their discussion is based on the Elaboration Likelihood Model, one of the best-supported and most far-reaching theoretical accounts of attitude change, showing how it organizes findings about the effects of bodily movements on attitudes, as well as generating new and intriguing predictions.

The third part has as its topic the *embodiment of affective processes*.

- Clore and Schnall take the viewpoint that affective reactions provide embodied evidence that people can use to validate or invalidate their evaluative beliefs about objects. In particular, affective reactions are sometimes found to have limited effects unless preexisting beliefs exist that are congruent with the affective reactions. The authors describe provocative research suggesting that holding incongruent beliefs and affective reactions has cognitive costs for the individual.
- Barrett and Lindquist address the embodiment of emotional responses. Noting that traditional theories hold that body and mind make separate and independent contributions to an emotional episode, they apply the embodiment perspective to generate the novel suggestion that the body helps constitute the mind in shaping an emotional response. That is, the conceptual knowledge that we use to categorize and understand our own (and other people's) emotions is itself represented in sensorimotor terms.
- Winkielman, Niedenthal, and Oberman similarly take an embodied approach to emotional processes in which such processes are grounded in modality-specific systems. They describe studies directly testing the hypothesis that manipulating bodily resources will influence the perception and understanding of emotional events. The chapter ranges widely, covering the role of embodiment in the formation of attitudes as well as in the representation of abstract emotion concepts.
- The chapter by Förster and Friedman presents a new conceptual model of the effects of bodily movements, facial expressions, and other embodied cues on attitudes as well as on cognitive processing styles (such as creativity and flexibility). Guided by Higgins's Regulatory Focus Theory, they show how effects of embodied cues can be accommodated and also how paradoxes in existing evidence may be resolved.

Taken together, these chapters illustrate the extraordinarily broad range of topics upon which research has been influenced by the embodiment perspective. As we observed at the beginning of this introduction, embodiment calls for a focus on the entire organism rather than on isolated slices of information-processing or behavioral systems. As a group, these chapters reflect this breadth of focus, as researchers and theorists grapple with the implications of embodiment for levels and topics ranging from neuroscience to language comprehension, social relationships to attitude change, and affect to cognition. We hope that this volume will inspire and excite still more boundary-crossing research and theory, faithful to the true underlying message of the embodiment perspective.

PART ONE

EMBODIED LANGUAGE AND CONCEPTS

# 1    Grounding Symbolic Operations in the Brain's Modal Systems

Lawrence W. Barsalou

A central theme of modern cognitive science is that symbolic interpretation underlies human intelligence. The human brain does not simply register images, as do cameras or other recording devices. A collection of images or recordings does not make a system intelligent. Instead, symbolic interpretation of image content is essential for intelligent activity.

What cognitive operations underlie symbolic interpretation? Across decades of analysis, a consistent set of symbolic operations has arisen repeatedly in logic and knowledge engineering: binding types to tokens; binding arguments to values; drawing inductive inferences from category knowledge; predicating properties and relations of individuals; combining symbols to form complex symbolic expressions; representing abstract concepts that interpret metacognitive states. It is difficult to imagine performing intelligent computation without these operations. For this reason, many theorists have argued that symbolic operations are central, not only to artificial intelligence but to human intelligence (e.g., Fodor, 1975; Pylyshyn, 1973).

Symbolic operations provide an intelligent system with considerable power for interpreting its experience. Using type-token binding, an intelligent system can place individual components of an image into familiar categories (e.g., categorizing components of an image as people and cars). Operations on these categories then provide rich inferential knowledge that allows the perceiver to predict how categorized individuals will behave, and to select effective actions that can be taken (e.g., a perceived person may talk, cars can be driven). Symbolic knowledge further allows a perceiver to analyze individuals in an image, predicating properties and relations that apply to them (e.g., identifying a person as an adult male, or two people as having a family resemblance). Such predications further support high-level cognitive operations, such as decision making (e.g., purchasing a gas, hybrid, or electric car), planning (e.g., finding electricity to charge an electric car while driving around town), and problem solving (e.g., how to get in if the keys are locked in the car). Symbolic operations also include a variety of operations for combining symbols, such that an intelligent system can construct complex symbolic expressions (e.g., combining word meanings during language comprehension). Finally, by establishing abstract concepts about mental states and mental operations, an intelligent system can categorize its mental life in a metacognitive manner and reason about it (e.g., evaluating one's planning and decision making strategies).

What mechanisms implement symbolic operations? Since the cognitive revolution, language-like symbols and operations have been widely assumed to be responsible. Numerous theoretical approaches have been derived from predicate calculus and propositional logic. Not only have these approaches been central in artificial intelligence (e.g., Charniak & McDermott, 1985), they have also been central throughout accounts of human cognition (e.g., Barsalou, 1992; Barsalou & Hale, 1993; Anderson, 1983; Newell, 1990).

Although classic symbolic approaches are still widely accepted as accounts of human intelligence, and also as the engine for artificial intelligence, they have come increasingly under attack for two reasons. First, classic symbolic approaches have been widely criticized for not being sufficiently statistical. As a result, neural net approaches have developed to remedy this deficiency (e.g., Rumelhart & McClelland, 1986; O'Reilly & Munakata, 2000). Second, classic symbolic approaches have been criticized for not being grounded in perception, action, and introspection. As a result, researchers have argued that higher-order cognition is grounded in the brain's modal systems.

As statistical and embodied approaches are increasingly embraced, the tendency to "throw the baby out with the bath water" has often been embraced as well. Some researchers have suggested that classic symbolic operations are irrelevant to higher cognition, especially researchers associated with neural nets and dynamical systems (e.g., van Gelder, 1990; but see Prinz & Barsalou, 2000). Notably, some neural net researchers have realized that symbolic operations are essential for implementing higher cognitive phenomena in knowledge, language, and thought. The problem in classic theories is not their inclusion of symbolic operations but *how* they implement them. For this reason, neural net researchers have developed neural net accounts of symbolic operations (e.g., Pollack, 1990; Smolensky, 1990). Interestingly, these approaches have not caught on widely, either with psychologists or with knowledge engineers. For psychologists, neural net accounts of symbolic processes have little psychological plausibility; for knowledge engineers, they are difficult and inefficient to implement. As a result, both groups continue to typically use classic approaches when symbolic operations must be implemented.

An alternative account of symbolic operations has arisen in grounded theories of cognition (e.g., Barsalou, 1999, 2003a, 2005a). Not only does this account have psychological and neural plausibility, it suggests a new approach to image analysis. Essentially, this approach develops symbols whose content is extracted from images. As a result, symbols can be bound to regions of images, thereby establishing type-token mappings. Inferences drawn from category knowledge also take the form of images, such that they can be mapped back into perception. Analysis of an individual in an image proceeds by processing its perceived regions and assessing whether perceptually grounded properties and relations can be predicated of them. Symbol combination involves the manipulation and integration of image components to construct structured images that, in effect, implement complex symbolic propositions. Abstract concepts result from situated introspection, namely, the process of perceiving internal mental and bodily states in the context of external situations and developing image-based representations of them for later use in reasoning.

The remaining sections present this framework in greater detail. The next section illustrates how symbolic operations could arise from simulation. The following section presents current empirical evidence for this account. The final section addresses the role of language in symbolic operations.

## GROUNDING COGNITION IN THE BRAIN'S MODAL SYSTEMS

Standard architectures assume that amodal symbols are transduced from experience to represent knowledge. Figure 1.1 illustrates this general approach. On experiencing a member of a category (e.g., *dogs*), modal states arise in the visual system, auditory system, motor system, somatosensory system, and so on (i.e., the solid arrows in Figure 1.1a). These states represent sensory-motor information about the perceived category member, with some (but not all) of this information producing conscious experience. Although modal states are shown only for sensory-motor systems, we assume that modal states also arise in motivational systems, affective systems, and cognitive systems. The perception of these internal systems will be referred to as *introspection* from here forward. Once modal states arise in all relevant modal systems for a category, amodal symbols that stand for conceptual content in these states are then transduced elsewhere in the brain to represent knowledge about the category (e.g., *legs, tail, barks, pat, soft* in Panel B for

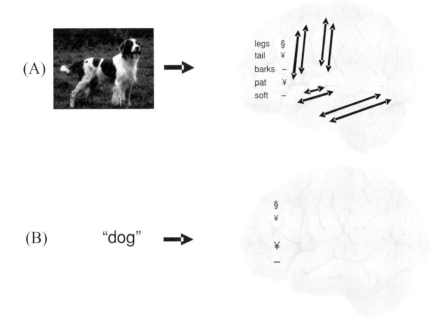

Figure 1.1. The transduction of amodal symbols from modal states in standard cognitive architectures (Panel A). Use of transduced symbols to represent the meaning of a word (Panel B). See the text for further description.

the experience of a dog). Although words often stand for transduced amodal symbols (e.g., *leg*), most theories assume that sub-linguistic symbols, often corresponding closely to words, are actually the symbols transduced (e.g., in Figure 1.1).

Once established in the brain, amodal symbols later represent knowledge about the category across a wide range of cognitive tasks (Figure 1.1, Panel B). During language comprehension, hearing the word for a category (e.g., "dog") activates amodal symbols transduced from modal states on previous occasions. Subsequent cognitive operations on category knowledge, such as inference, are assumed to operate on these symbols. Note that none of the modal states originally active when amodal symbols were transduced (Figure 1.1, Panel A) are active during knowledge representation (Figure 1.1, Panel B). Instead, amodal symbols are assumed to be sufficient, with modal states being irrelevant.

The architecture in Figure 1.1 underlies a wide variety of standard approaches to representing knowledge, such as feature lists, semantic networks, and frames. This architecture also underlies those neural net architectures where the hidden layers that represent knowledge are related arbitrarily to perceptual input layers. The architecture in Figure 1.1 does not underlie neural nets in which input units play roles in knowledge representation.

### The Capture and Simulation of Modal States in Embodied Architectures

A very different approach to representing knowledge has arisen recently in theories of grounded cognition. Actually, this approach has deep roots in philosophical treatments of knowledge going back over 2000 years (e.g., Epicurus, 341–270BC/1987). Modern theories can be viewed as reinventions of these older theories in the contexts of psychology, cognitive science, and cognitive neuroscience (e.g., Barsalou, 1999, 2008; Prinz, 2002). Interestingly, the amodal architectures that currently dominate the field constitute a relatively recent and short presence in a historical context where theories grounded in the modalities have dominated.

Figure 1.2 illustrates the grounded approach to representing knowledge. On experiencing a member of a category (e.g., *dogs*), modal states are again represented as activations in the visual system, auditory system, motor system, somatosensory system, and so on (Panel A). As for Figure 1.1, modal states are only shown for sensory-motor systems, but this approach assumes that such states are also captured during the introspection of those motivational states, affective states, and cognitive states available to consciousness. Local association areas then partially capture these modality-specific states (shown in Panel A as asterisks). Higher-order cross-modal associations (also shown as asterisks) then integrate conjunctive neurons in lower-order association areas to establish a multimodal representation of the experience.

Once established in the brain, these multimodal associative structures represent knowledge about the category across a wide range of cognitive tasks (Figure 1.2, Panel B). During language comprehension, for example, hearing the word for a category (e.g., "dog") activates conjunctive neurons in higher-order cross-model association areas that have previously encoded experiences of the respective category. In turn, these conjunctive neurons activate lower-order conjunctive neurons that partially reactivate modal states experienced previously for the category. These neural reenactments attempt to simulate the modal states likely to occur when actually encountering category members. As the dashed arrows in Panel B illustrate, the modal states are only partially reenacted, not fully reenacted. For the remainder of this chapter, these reenactments will be referred to as *simulations*, given that they result from the brain attempting to simulate previous experience.

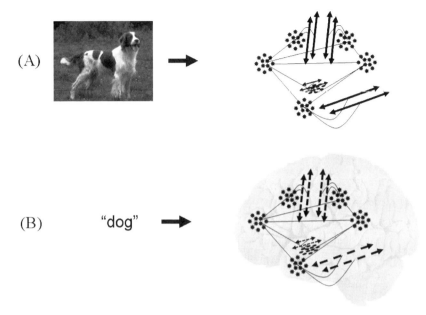

Figure 1.2. Conjunctive units in hierarchically organized association areas capture modal states across modalities in grounded theories of knowledge (Panel A). Captured multimodal states are simulated to represent the meaning of a word (Panel B). See the text for further description.

The capture-and-simulate architecture in Figure 1.2 underlies a wide variety of traditional and modern approaches to representing knowledge. Whereas some of these approaches focus on mental images, others focus on neural reenactments of modal states in the brain, which may often be unconscious. All share the common assumption that the representation of knowledge is grounded in modal states rather than in amodal symbols transduced from them. All share the common assumption that simulations of previous experience are central to cognition.

### Additional Assumptions

Several misunderstandings often arise about the simulation architecture in Figure 1.2. First, this architecture is often viewed as an instantiation of classic empiricist theories. Second, this architecture is often viewed as a recording system incapable of interpretation. Third, this architecture is often viewed as capturing knowledge only from perception of the external world. Each of these misunderstandings will be addressed in turn.

First, the architecture in Figure 1.2 need not be a classic empiricist theory. In principle, specific simulations could be genetically determined rather than being acquired from experience. If particular simulations had evolutionary significance, they could be genetically encoded into the brain such that they are ready to become active in relevant situations. A more likely possibility is that strong genetic constraints determine the feature systems and association areas that exist in the brain. Because certain categories of objects, events, and introspective states were important over evolution, a neural architecture evolved that is optimally prepared to represent and process these particular categories (cf. Caramazza & Shelton, 1998). Although experience with categories is necessary to establish representations of them in memory, the feature systems relevant for representing these categories originate genetically, as do the associative systems for integrating them. Indeed, nativists have often assumed that images are central to cognition (e.g., Kant, 1787/1965; Reid, 1785/1969). There is no a priori reason why a system that uses simulation to represent knowledge cannot have strong genetic constraints as well.

Second, the architecture in Figure 1.2 need not be a recording system. Unlike a camera or video recorder, this architecture is not limited to capturing holistic bit-mapped records of experience. Instead, the interpretation of experience lies at the heart of this account, where interpretation arises from the application of symbolic operations (Barsalou, 1999, 2003a, 2005a). Because this account is the focus of this chapter, it is not described further. As will become clear, this architecture is highly capable of implementing interpretation.

Third, the architecture in Figure 1.2 need not only acquire knowledge from perception of the external world. Instead, it can capture extensive amounts of knowledge from introspection, namely, from the internal perception of affect, motivation, proprioception, pain, pleasure, cognitive states, cognitive operations, and so on. Because the human brain is capable of perceiving internal states (to some extent), it captures these states and simulates them on subsequent occasions, just as it captures and simulates the perception of external states. As described later, the capture and simulation of internal states appears central to the representation of abstract concepts, specifically, and to human cognition, more generally. Thus, the architecture in Figure 1.2 can be applied to the capture and simulation of both external and internal states.

### The Status of Empirical Evidence for Grounded Knowledge

Accumulating empirical evidence supports the simulation architecture in Figure 1.2. Many findings indicate that the brain's modal systems for perception, action, and introspection are active during the higher cognitive activities of memory, knowledge, language, and thought. For reviews of the evidence from cognitive psychology, see Barsalou (2003b, 2008) and Barsalou, Simmons, Barbey, and Wilson (2003). For reviews of evidence from social psychology, see Barsalou, Niedenthal, Barbey, and Rupport (2003) and Niedenthal, Barsalou, Winkielman, Krauth-Gruber, and Ric (2005). For reviews of evidence from cognitive neuroscience, see Martin (2001, 2007), Pulvermüller (1999), and Thompson-Schill (2003). For reviews of developmental evidence, see Smith (2005), Smith and Gasser (2005), and Thelen (2000). The rapidly accumulating findings across these diverse literatures indicate that the higher cognitive processes engage modal systems frequently and robustly.

### The Importance of Going beyond Demonstration Experiments

Problematically, these findings do not indicate what roles the modalities play in higher cognition. When these findings were acquired, it was not accepted widely that modal systems participated in higher cognition at all. Researchers holding this hypothesis therefore attempted to evaluate it primarily using demonstration experiments. Typically, these researchers did not attempt to establish the roles that modal processing played in the experimental phenomena studied. Instead, the primary goal was simply to demonstrate that the brain's modal systems become active during cognitive processes. Now that the presence of modal processing is becoming well established in higher cognition, however, demonstration experiments are likely to have diminishing returns. Instead, it is becoming increasingly important to establish the specific roles that modal processing plays.

One possibility is that the brain's modal systems play relatively peripheral, or even epiphenomenal, roles in higher cognition. Although these systems become active, other systems that operate on amodal symbols implement basic cognitive operations (Figure 1.1). Alternatively, the brain's modal systems may provide the core computational engine in higher cognition (Figure 1.2). In particular, modal systems may implement fundamental symbolic operations, such as binding types to tokens, binding arguments to values, drawing inductive inferences from category knowledge, predicating properties and relations of individuals, combining symbols to form complex symbolic expressions, and representing abstract concepts that interpret introspective states metacognitively.

### An Example

The following experiment illustrates both the utility and limitations of demonstration experiments. Simmons, Martin, and Barsalou (2005) assessed the neural representation of food categories. Participants lay passively in a functional magnetic resonance imaging (fMRI) scanner while briefly viewing food pictures and evaluating whether the picture currently present physically matched the previous picture. Participants were not asked to categorize the foods, to think about how they taste, or to conceptualize them in any manner. Nevertheless, the pictures activated brain areas that represent how foods taste and how rewarding they are to consume. Although participants did not actually taste anything, category knowledge about foods became active and produced activations in the brain's gustatory and reward systems.

This experiment offers a demonstration that the brain's modal systems become active during cognitive processing. When participants looked at visual pictures, their gustatory systems became active, even though they were not tasting anything. Nevertheless, it is not clear what role these gustatory activations play in higher cognition. Are they epiphenomenal? Or are they implementing symbolic operations associated with drawing taste and reward inferences about the perceived visual objects? Although this experiment, and many others like it, demonstrate that modal systems become active during higher cognition – a possibility that seemed unlikely until recently – this experiment does not shed any light on the specific role that these activations play.

## Symbolic Operations

One possibility is that activations in modal systems underlie symbolic operations. Rather than amodal symbols implementing these operations, simulations implement them. The following subsections describe how simulations could, in principle, implement the symbolic operations of predication, conceptual combination, and abstract concepts. Later subsections summarize preliminary evidence for these accounts and their limitations to date.

### Representing Concepts and Instances: Simulators and Simulations
To implement symbolic operations, it is essential for an intelligent system to have some means of learning and representing concepts. The lack of concepts is what prevents many recording devices, such as cameras and video recorders, from implementing the symbolic operations that would allow them to interpret the images they capture. The central innovation of Perceptual Symbol Systems theory (PSS) is its ability to implement concepts and their interpretive functions using image content as basic building blocks (Barsalou, 1999, 2003a, 2005a).

According to PSS, concepts develop in the brain as follows. Much research has shown that categories have statistically correlated features (e.g., *wheels, steering wheel*, and *engine* for *cars*; McRae, de Sa, & Seidenberg, 1997). Thus, encountering different instances of the same category should activate similar neural patterns in feature systems (cf. Farah & McClelland, 1991; Cree & McRae, 2003). Furthermore, similar populations of conjunctive neurons in the brain's association areas – tuned to these particular conjunctions of features – should tend to capture these similar patterns (Damasio, 1989; Simmons & Barsalou, 2003). Across experiences of a category's instances, this population of conjunctive neurons integrates the modal features of a category, establishing a distributed multimodal representation of it (Figure 1.2).

PSS refers to these distributed multimodal representations as *simulators*. Conceptually, a simulator functions as a type and is roughly equivalent to a concept in standard theories. Specifically, a simulator integrates the multimodal content of a category across instances and provides the ability to interpret later individuals as tokens of the type. Consider the simulator for the category of *cars*. Across learning, visual information about how cars look becomes integrated in the simulator along with auditory information about how they sound, somatosensory information about how they feel, motor programs for interacting with them, emotional responses to experiencing them, and so on. The result is a distributed system throughout the brain's feature and association areas that accumulates modal representations of the category.

In principle, an indefinitely large number of simulators can develop in memory for all forms of knowledge, including objects, properties, settings, events, actions, introspections, and so forth. Specifically, a simulator develops for any component of experience that attention selects repeatedly. When attention focuses repeatedly on a type of object in experience, such as *cars*, a simulator develops for it. Analogously, if attention focuses on a type of action (*driving*) or on a type of introspection (*fear*), simulators develop to represent it as well. Such flexibility is consistent with Schyns, Goldstone, and Thibaut's (1998) proposal that the cognitive system acquires new properties as they become relevant for categorization. Because selective attention is flexible and open-ended, a simulator develops for any component of experience that attention selects repeatedly.

Once a simulator becomes established for a category, it reenacts small subsets of its content as specific *simulations*. All the content in a simulator never becomes active at once. Instead, only a small subset becomes active to represent the category on a particular occasion (cf. Barsalou, 1987, 1989, 1993, 2003b). For example, the *car* simulator might simulate a sedan on one occasion but simulate a sports car or off-road vehicle on others. Because all the experienced content for cars resides implicitly in the *car* simulator, many different subsets can be reenacted as simulations.

The presence of simulators in the brain makes the implementation of symbolic operations possible. Indeed, symbolic operations follow naturally from the presence of simulators. Because simulators are roughly equivalent to concepts, the symbolic functions made possible by concepts are also made possible by simulators. The next three subsections illustrate how simulators enable three classic symbolic functions: predication, conceptual combination, and the representation of abstract concepts. For further details, see Barsalou (1999, 2003a, 2005a).

### Implementing the Symbolic Function of Predication in PSS

To implement predication, an intelligent system must first distinguish types from tokens. In PSS, simulators implement types because they aggregate multimodal information across category members (e.g., cars). Conversely, simulations implement tokens because they represent category members (e.g., individual cars). Thus, the simulator-simulation distinction in PSS naturally implements the type-token distinction essential for predication.

This distinction further allows PSS to explain a wide variety of phenomena related to predication, including type-token predication, true versus false propositions, and interpretive spin. Type-token predication results from binding simulators to simulations (or perceptions). For example, binding the *car* simulator to a simulated (or perceived) car produces the predication that the individual is an instance of the *car* category. These type-token bindings essentially implement propositions, where binding the simulator to the individual represents a claim about the individual, namely, that the individual is a *car*. Notably, such propositions can be false, as when the *car* simulator is applied mistakenly to a small truck. Furthermore, the potential predications of an individual are infinite, thereby producing interpretative spin. Because indefinitely many simulators (and combinations of simulators) can be used to interpret an individual, indefinitely many true and false interpretations are possible. For example an individual car could be interpreted as a *car*, *vehicle*, *artifact*, *sedan*, *junked sedan*, *truck* (false), and so on. Thus, the simulator-simulation distinction allows PSS to implement classic symbolic functions related to predication.

### Implementing Conceptual Combination in PSS

To see how PSS implements conceptual combination, first consider a simulator for the spatial relation, *above*. An *above* simulator could result from having pairs of objects pointed out in perception where the focal object always has a higher vertical position than the other object (e.g., a helicopter above a hospital). As each *above* relation is pointed out, selective attention focuses on the spatial regions containing the two objects, filters out the objects, and captures modal information about the shapes and sizes of the regions, the vertical distance between them, their horizontal offset, and so on (the parietal lobe and parahippocampal place areas are plausible regions where the *above* simulator might be represented in the brain). Over time, the *above* simulator captures many such pairs of regions and the spatial relations between them. On later occasions, this simulator can produce a wide variety of *above* simulations, each containing a pair of spatial regions not containing objects. An *above* simulation could represent two round regions of equal size, nearly touching vertically, with no horizontal offset; it could represent two rectangular regions of different size, distant vertically, with a large horizontal offset; and so on.

The *above* simulator lends itself to producing conceptual combinations. Imagine that this simulator produces one particular *above* simulation. Next, imagine that the *helicopter* simulator runs a simulation in the upper region of this *above* simulation, and that the *hospital* simulator runs a simulation in the lower region. The resulting simulation represents a helicopter above a hospital, thereby implementing a conceptual combination that expresses the proposition *ABOVE (helicopter, hospital)*. The individual simulators for *above, helicopter,* and *hospital* remain bound to their respective regions of the complex simulation, thereby continuing to interpret them symbolically in embedded type-token propositions.

Infinitely many other conceptual combinations can be implemented by simulating different types of objects or events in the regions of the *above* simulation, thereby expressing related propositions, such as *ABOVE (jet, cloud)*, *ABOVE (lamp, table)*, and so on. In general, this is how PSS implements conceptual combination. Because simulators represent components of situations and relations between components, their simulations can be combined into complex, multicomponent simulations. Much like an object-oriented drawing program, PSS extracts components of situations so that it can later combine them to represent either previously experienced situations or novel ones.

### Representing Abstract Concepts in PSS

Relatively little is known about abstract concepts (e.g., *truth, thought*), given that most research has addressed concrete concepts (e.g., *car, bird*). Abstract concepts however, are likely to provide deep insights into the nature of human cognition, and to help produce increasingly sophisticated forms of intelligent computation, given the metacognitive capabilities that they enable.

Recent theory suggests that one central function of abstract concepts is to represent introspective states (e.g., Barsalou, 1999). In an exploratory study, more content about introspective states was observed in abstract concepts than in concrete concepts (Barsalou & Wiemer-Hastings, 2005). In another exploratory study, the abstractness of a concept increased with the amount of introspective content that it contained (Wiemer-Hastings, Krug, & Xu, 2001). These studies further found that abstract concepts typically relate introspective states to situations and events. For example, *intend* relates introspective states about goals to events in the world that follow from these states causally (intending to seek information, which then leads to asking someone a question and receiving an answer).

Because abstract concepts focus on introspective states to a large extent, they provide a window on metacognition. Similar to how people perceive the external world through vision and audition, people perceive their internal worlds through introspection. During introspection, people perceive motivations, affective states, cognitive states, and cognitive operations. Clearly, only a small subset of brain activity is perceived introspectively, but this subset supports impressive understanding and control of internal mechanisms.

According to PSS, simulators develop to represent the internal world, just as they develop to represent the external world. As people perceive the internal world, they focus attention on salient regions of it repeatedly, such that simulators develop for these regions. Thus, simulators develop for cognitive states, such as *image* and *belief*, cognitive operations such as *retrieve* and *compare*, affective states such as *happiness* and *fear*, and motivational states such as *hunger* and *ambition*. Once these simulators exist, they support symbolic operations in the introspective domain, thereby establishing metacognition. Type-token propositions result when simulators for introspective content become bound to regions of introspective activity. These categorizations then license associated inferences and support symbolic analyses of introspective activity. Predications result from mapping relevant simulators into regions of introspective activity. Novel conceptualizations of how to organize introspective processing to achieve goals result from combining relevant simulators.

## EMPIRICAL EVIDENCE FOR THE PSS ACCOUNT OF SYMBOLIC OPERATIONS

The next three subsections describe preliminary evidence for the PSS accounts of predication, conceptual combination, and abstract concepts, respectively. The final subsection discusses limitations of the current evidence.

## Predication

### The Property Verification Task

One way to study predication is with the property verification task. In one version of this task, the word for a concept appears (e.g., "pony"), followed by the word for a property (e.g., "mane"), and the participant indicates as quickly as possible whether the property is true or false of the concept (e.g., "pony–mane" versus "pony–horns"). This task assesses predication because participants are asked whether a property predication is true of a concept (i.e., can the property *mane* be predicated of the concept *pony*?). By manipulating and measuring variables potentially related to simulation, this task can be used to assess whether simulation underlies predication.

The experiments to be reviewed next assess three specific predictions about predication that follow from the PSS account. First, if simulations represent the properties predicated of objects during property verification, then different types of properties should activate different modal systems in the brain. For example, verifying visual properties should activate visual areas, whereas verifying auditory properties should activate auditory areas. Second, when the modality of the property being verified changes, verification should take longer than when the modality remains the same. Third, perceptual aspects of the properties being verified, such as their size and shape, should affect the time to verify them.

### Evidence from Brain Activation

Earlier we saw that viewing pictures of food activated the brain's gustatory system. Because gustatory processing was not relevant for the task that participants had to perform (one-back perceptual matching), it is not clear what role the gustatory activations were playing, although a plausible interpretation is that they were representing taste inferences.

Similar activations for properties were observed in the next two studies described. In these studies however, participants were asked to predicate properties as the modality of the properties varied. If modal activations represent the properties being predicated in these experiments, then as different types of properties are predicated (e.g., visual versus auditory), different corresponding brain areas should become active (e.g., visual versus auditory). If the brain represents these properties with simulations, activations across modal systems would be expected to vary in this manner.

In a positron emission tomography (PET) experiment by Kellenbach, Brett, and Patterson (2001), participants received the names of animate and inanimate objects in blocks of 24 names each. At the start of each block, participants received a property and had to decide whether it could be predicated of each object in the block or not (e.g., was each object in the block *colorful*). Across blocks, three different properties were tested. One property was whether the object is *colorful* (e.g., *banana*), not *monochrome* (e.g., *skunk*). The second property was whether the object is *loud* (e.g., *drill*), not *silent* (e.g., *pillow*). The third property was whether the object is *small* (e.g., *coin*), not *large* (e.g., *bus*). In a control condition, participants determined whether a letter string had an "X" in it or not. In half the trials, the object possessed the property; in the other half, it did not. The objects assessed for each property were controlled carefully.

Of interest was how brain activations across the block for a particular property (e.g., *colorful*) differed from activations for blocks in the control condition. Kellenbach et al. found that relevant modal activations became active for each property relative to the control. Color judgments activated color processing areas in the fusiform gyrus. Sound judgments activated auditory processing areas in the superior temporal gyrus. Size judgments activated parietal areas associated with processing space. Other brain areas were also active in each property condition, but the areas just mentioned were most relevant to the simulation hypothesis.

These findings suggest that participants simulated the property being assessed on each block (e.g., *loud*). As each name of an object in the subsequent block was read (e.g., "drill"), participants simulated the object and assessed whether it contained the simulated property (e.g., is a drill loud). If the property simulation matched a modal region of the simulated object, participants responded "true;" if not, they responded "false."

If this account is correct, then it follows that the symbolic operation of predication is grounded in simulation. To assess whether a property can be predicated of an object, participants simulate the property and then assess whether it can be found in a simulation of the object. Kellenbach et al.'s results do not show definitively that this account is correct but their results are highly consistent with it. As the property being predicated changes, so do the modal areas active for it.

Goldberg, Perfetti, and Schneider (2006) found similar results in an fMRI experiment. As in Kellenbach et al., participants received a property name prior to a block of object names and had to assess whether the property could be predicated of each object. Goldberg et al. assessed four properties: *green* (color), *loud* (sound), *soft* (touch), and *sweet* (taste). Analogous to Kellenbach et al.'s results, Goldberg et al. observed relevant modal activation for each property. Predicating the color property activated object processing regions in the temporal lobe. Predicating the sound property activated the superior temporal sulcus near auditory processing areas. Predicating the touch property activated post-central gyrus areas for processing somatosensory information. Predicating the taste property activated orbitofrontal areas associated with gustatory processing. As the predication changed, so did the relevant modal activation, again suggesting that the properties being predicated were grounded in simulation.

In another fMRI experiment, Kan, Barsalou, Solomon, Minor, and Thompson-Schill (2003) found that participants recruited simulation to represent the visual properties of objects during property verification. Specifically, they found that the fusiform gyrus became active when participants verified visual properties of objects. Interestingly, this activation only occurred when task conditions required deep conceptual representation of the properties. When task conditions allowed the use of a superficial word-association strategy, participants did not use simulation (i.e., the fusiform area was not active). This pattern suggests that predication can be performed using different strategies, and that predication only relies on simulation when deep processing of properties is required (also see Solomon & Barsalou, 2004). For reviews of possible strategies available during conceptual processing, see Glaser (1992) and Barsalou, Santos, Simmon, and Wilson (in press).

Because the previous studies all used blocked designs, the brain activations measured for a block were aggregates across many trials and events within trials. Although neural activations for the properties being verified were of primary interest, these activations were combined with activations for the objects. Furthermore, activations across many trials were combined.

In an fMRI experiment that used an event-related design, Simmons, Ramjay, Beauchamp, McRae, Martin, and Barsalou (2007) isolated the activations associated with individual properties on particular trials. On each trial, participants received an object name followed by a color property or a motor property (e.g., *banana–yellow, frisbee–thrown*). Unlike the previous experiments, the property changed from trial to trial together with the object, rather than a single property being presented before a block of objects. Furthermore, the design of the experiment made it possible to deconvolve the activation for the concept on each trial from the activation for the property. As a result, it was possible to isolate brain areas associated with processing the properties, with activations for the objects excluded.

Similar to the previous studies, Simmons et al. found that color and motor properties activated relevant modal areas. Color properties activated a fusiform area that is often active ·during the perception of actual color. Motor properties activated a medial temporal area associated with viewing the motions of objects. Because this study isolated activations for predicates, it offers even stronger evidence that participants represented predicates with modal activations.

### Evidence from Property Switching

We just saw evidence from multiple experiments that changing the modality of a predication changes the brain areas that become active. This next set of studies explores a behavioral implication of these findings: If predicating properties in different modalities activates different modal systems, then switching between two modal systems to verify two consecutive properties should take longer than staying within the same modal system.

Imagine first verifying *television–noisy* and then verifying *microwave–beeping*. Because *noisy* and *beeping* are both auditory properties, attention can stay within the auditory modality to simulate *beeping* after previously simulating *noisy*. Now imagine first verifying *eggplant–purple* and then verifying *microwave–beeping*. Because *purple* is a visual property, attention must switch from the visual system to subsequently simulate *beeping* in the auditory system. As a result, there should be a switching cost associated with changing modalities, and verifying the second property should take longer.

Pecher, Zeelenberg, and Barsalou (2003, 2004) assessed this hypothesis. In their studies, verification trials sampled properties from four to six modalities: vision, audition, action, touch, taste, and smell. Across experiments, properties were presented in either Dutch or English. As just described, the key manipulation across studies was whether the modalities of two consecutive properties – a context property followed by a target property – were the same or different. In one experiment, the stimulus onset asynchrony (SOA) from the concept to the property was manipulated between participants (0 ms versus 260 ms). At both SOAs, participants were slower to verify properties when they had to switch modalities across consecutive trials than when they did not. When the SOA was 0 ms, the switching cost was 29 ms; when the SOA was 260 ms, the switching cost was 20 ms. The lack of an effect for SOA is consistent with previous findings showing that modal effects occur across SOAs that range from 0 ms to 1600 ms (Solomon, 1997; Solomon & Barsalou, 2001, 2004).

Marques (2006) replicated the presence of switching costs in Portuguese, observing a similar switching effect of 36 ms. Marques further showed that this switching effect occurred for both natural kind categories (41 ms) and for artifact categories (31 ms). More importantly, he showed that the switching effect is not the result of shifting from one conceptual domain to another. Unlike the Pecher et al. studies, Marques held the conceptual domain constant between two target trials. Whenever a target property belonged to a natural kind (e.g., *dog–bark*), the same and different context properties also belonged to natural kinds (e.g., *bee–buzz* versus *lobster–rough*). Conceptual domains were similarly held constant for artifacts (for the target property *telephone–ring*, the same versus different context properties were *clock–tick tock* versus *mirror–reflect*). Under these conditions, Marques still observed a switching effect, indicating that uncontrolled shifts in conceptual domains are not responsible.

Another experiment in Marques (2006) offers further support. This experiment manipulated the conceptual domain across two consecutive trials while holding the modality of the property constant. For example, participants verified the auditory property, *dog–bark*, either after verifying an auditory property for another natural type (*lion–roar*) or after verifying an auditory property for an artifact (*clock–tick tock*). This manipulation had no effect on the time to verify target properties. Participants were equally fast regardless of whether the conceptual domain changed or remained constant. Solomon and Barsalou (2001) similarly found that concept similarity had little impact on property verification. Thus, the basic switching effect is not the result of changing the conceptual domain but instead appears to be the result of changing the property modality.

Vermeulen, Niedenthal, and Luminet (in press) offer further evidence for switching costs, showing that they occur between affective and sensory domains, not just between sensory domains. Specifically, participants verified affective properties (e.g., *triumph–exhilarating*) faster when preceded by another affective property (e.g., *couple–happy*) than by a sensory property (e.g., *victory–sung*). Thus, switching costs not only implicate simulations of properties on sensory modalities, but they also implicate simulations on introspective modalities, which is consistent with the proposal that simulators develop for components of both external and internal experience.

Finally, Pecher et al.'s (2003) Experiment 2 ruled out the alternative explanation that associative strength is responsible for switching costs, namely, that switching costs occur because properties within a modality are more highly related than properties between modalities. Pecher et al. presented participants with pairs of trials that contained either two highly associated properties, such *spotless* and *clean* (e.g., *sheet–spotless*, *air–clean*), or two unassociated properties, such as *polyester* and *clean* (e.g., *shirt–polyester*, *air–clean*). If associative strength was responsible for the switching effects in earlier experiments, then verifying *clean* should be faster after verifying *spotless* than after verifying *polyester*. However, associated pairs of properties were verified 1 ms slower than unassociated pairs. If associative strength had been responsible for the previous results, this strong manipulation of associative strength should have produced a large effect. Thus, the most likely account of the effects observed in previous experiments is that shifting modalities slowed the time to simulate properties.

In summary, switching costs provide further evidence that predication is grounded in simulation. Indeed, switching costs offer stronger evidence than the neural evidence cited in the previous section, which is largely correlational. Although neural activations in modal systems are consistent with properties being simulated, these activations could simply accompany amodal symbols that lie at the heart of symbolic processing (i.e., these activations are epiphenomenal). Although this is not a parsimonious account, it is nevertheless possible.

Switching costs suggest that these modal activations are not merely epiphenomenal but underlie the symbolic process of predication itself. Because switching modalities induces a cost in predication, it appears that modal processing plays a causal role in predication. If modal processing were epiphenomenal, the amodal symbolic operations central to predication should be unaffected by a change in modality. These amodal operations should only be affected when variables central to representing and processing amodal symbols are manipulated. Because many known factors believed to affect amodal symbol processing have been controlled in the switching costs literature, it is unlikely that these factors could have produced the switching costs observed. Instead, the most obvious and natural explanation is that the core processes underlying predication are grounded in modal simulation. For further discussion of the switching cost literature, see Barsalou, Pecher, Zeelenberg, Simmons, and Hamann (2005).

### Evidence from Matching Property Simulations to Object Regions

Two further lines of research show that perceptual variables affect predication. Similar to the switching cost experiments, these experiments show that the ease of predication is affected by the ease of modal processing, again implicating simulation as a core symbolic mechanism.

Across several experiments, Solomon and Barsalou (2001) showed that the detailed shape of a property affected property verification. Because the subtle shape properties that affected verification are difficult to verbalize, the results suggest that simulation contributed to the predication process directly, not epiphenomenally. Specifically, verifying a property on an earlier trial facilitated verifying the same property later if the detailed shape was similar. Thus, verifying *mane* for *pony* was facilitated by previously verifying *mane* for *horse* (same detailed shape) but not by verifying *mane* for *lion* (different detailed shape).

This effect did not result from greater overall similarity between *horse* and *pony* than between *horse* and *lion*. When the property was highly similar for all three concepts, facilitation occurred from both the high and low similarity concepts. For example, verifying *belly* for *pony* was facilitated as much by verifying *belly* for *lion* as by verifying *belly* for *horse* (where *belly* is equally similar for all three concepts, as indicated by independent scaling). Thus, the detailed perceptual similarity of the properties across trials was the critical factor, not the similarity between concepts. When the detailed shape of the critical property matched across two trials, facilitation occurred. When the detailed shapes differed, it did not. This pattern supports the conclusion that participants simulated properties when predicating them of concepts, and that the shapes affected the predication process rather than being epiphenomenal.

If participants match simulated properties to simulated objects during property predication, the size of a property might similarly affect processing. As a property simulation becomes larger, more work must be performed to simulate it and to match it against increasingly large regions of object simulations. For example, verifying a large property of *dog* (e.g., *back*) should take longer than verifying a small property (e.g., *nose*), all other factors being equal. Research on verifying properties during the perception of actual objects shows that verification can become more difficult as properties become larger (Morrison & Tversky, 1997). If verifying properties conceptually depends on similar mechanisms as verifying properties perceptually, then verifying large properties should be more difficult than verifying small properties both conceptually and perceptually.

To assess this hypothesis, Solomon and Barsalou (2004) had participants perform 200 property verification trials, half true and half false. Of primary interest was explaining the variance in reaction times (RT) and error rates across the 100 true trials. Why were some concept-property pairs verified faster and more accurately than others? To assess this issue, the true concept-property pairs were scaled for perceptual, linguistic, and expectancy variables that might explain this variance. The linguistic variables included the associative strength between the concept and property words in both directions, the word frequency of the properties, their length, and so on. The perceptual variables included the size and position of the properties, whether they were occluded, whether they would be handled during situated action, and so on. The expectancy variables assessed the polysemy of the property words (i.e., some property words have many different senses across objects; consider the variability in *legs* across *human*, *dog*, *caterpillar*, and *table*).

The RTs and error rates for the 100 true trials were regressed onto the three groups of variables in hierarchical regression. Most notably, the perceptual variables explained significant amounts of unique variance after variance attributable to the linguistic and expectancy variables was removed. Within the perceptual variables, the variable of size explained the most unique variance. As properties became larger, they took longer to verify. This finding suggests that people predicate properties by binding simulations of them to regions of object simulations. As the regions that must be processed become larger, more time is required to process them. Kan et al. (2003) provided an fMRI replication of this experiment.

*Summary*

We began with neural evidence showing that relevant modal brain activations occur as people predicate properties from different modalities. As people predicate taste, visual, auditory, size, and motor properties, areas in the brain that process gustatory, visual, auditory, location, and motor information become active, respectively. Thus, particular types of properties are correlated with brain activations in the respective modal systems. Although these activations could be epiphenomenal – simply accompanying operations on amodal symbols that actually perform predication – behavioral experiments suggest that these activations affect the process of predication. When a predicated property shifts to a new modality, relative to staying on the same modality, a switching cost ensues. The shape and size of predicated properties similarly affect the time to verify properties (and also the accuracy). Because perceptual variables affect predication performance, this suggests that modal activations are not epiphenomenal but play central roles in implementing predication.

## Conceptual Combination

As we just saw, many experiments address the role of simulation in predication. Because these experiments generally implicate simulation in predication, this implication can be held with some confidence, although much further work remains to be done. In contrast, only one line of research has addressed predication in the symbolic operation of conceptual combination. Thus, conclusions about the importance of simulation in conceptual combination must remain much more tentative until further research is performed.

Wu and Barsalou (submitted) tested the following hypothesis: If people combine simulations to combine concepts, then perceptual variables such as occlusion should affect the combination process. Wu and Barsalou manipulated occlusion by asking half the participants to generate properties for isolated noun concepts (e.g., *lawn*) and by asking the other half to generate properties for the same concepts preceded by revealing modifiers (e.g., *rolled-up lawn*). Wu and Barsalou predicted that if people simulate *lawn* to generate its properties, they should rarely produce its occluded properties, such as *dirt* and *roots*. As in actual perception, occluded properties should not receive much attention because they are hidden behind an object's surface. Conversely, Wu and Barsalou predicted that when people combine *rolled-up* and *lawn*, previously occluded properties would become salient in simulations and be produced more often.

Amodal theories of conceptual combination do not readily make this prediction, given that they do not anticipate effects of perceptual variables like occlusion. To the contrary, these theories typically assume that conceptual representations abstract over perceptual variation associated with occlusion, size, shape, and orientation. Furthermore, amodal theories are relatively compositional in nature (e.g., Smith, Osherson, Rips, & Keane, 1988). When people combine *rolled-up* with *lawn*, for example, the meaning of the conceptual combination should be roughly the union of the individual meanings. Unless additional post hoc assumptions are added that produce interactions between nouns and modifiers, the properties for *lawn* are not obviously changed by *rolled-up* (e.g., the accessibility of *dirt* and *roots* does not vary). As Wu and Barsalou predicted, internal properties were produced relatively infrequently for isolated nouns. Conversely, internal properties increased significantly when revealing modifiers were present during conceptual combination. Internal properties were also produced earlier in the protocols and in larger clusters.

In a second experiment, Wu and Barsalou showed that occlusion affected conceptual combination in both familiar and novel noun phrases. One possibility is that people store amodal descriptions of familiar conceptual combinations based on past experience with their referents. When people encounter instances of *half watermelon* and see the properties of *red* and *seeds*, amodal symbols for *red* and *seeds* are activated and stored with *half watermelon*. On later occasions, *red* and *seeds* become active when *half watermelon* is processed. In contrast, *red* and *seeds* become active much less often when *half* and *watermelon* are processed in isolation, given that *red* and *seeds* are less relevant for the *half* and *watermelon* when processed individually.

If this account is correct, then occlusion effects should be less likely to occur for novel noun phrases, given that people have not seen their instances and so

would not have had the opportunity to store properties associated with them. Instead, people would have to rely on their existing amodal representations of *half* and *watermelon* to represent the combination. Occlusion effects should not occur, given that the rate of producing internal properties of a noun should be the same for the noun in isolation as when combined with a novel modifier. For example, the rate of producing *engine* should be approximately equal when producing properties for *car* and for the novel combination, *glass car*.

Wu and Barsalou however, observed occlusion effects for novel combinations, suggesting that participants simulated their referents to perform conceptual combination. Because occluded properties (e.g., *engine*) were produced more often for novel combinations (e.g., *glass car*) than for isolated noun concepts (e.g., *car*), participants appeared to be simulating the novel combinations, such that internal properties of the head nouns became unoccluded.

In a third experiment, Wu and Barsalou assessed another amodal account of the occlusion effect. Perhaps rules stored with the modifiers are responsible for the increase in occluded properties. Whenever participants encounter a revealing modifier, a rule becomes active that increases the weight of the amodal symbols that represent internal properties of the following head noun. For example, when *rolled-up* is combined with *lawn*, the rule associated with *rolled-up* increases the activation of internal features of *lawn*, such as *dirt* and *roots*. As a result, these properties are produced at higher rates than when properties are produced for the head noun in isolation.

If such rules are responsible for occlusion effects, a given modifier should generally increase the salience of occluded properties, regardless of the head noun. Wu and Barsalou showed however, that for many noun phrases, the presence of a revealing modifier did not increase the salience of internal properties. When *rolled-up* was combined with *snake* to create *rolled-up snake*, internal properties were not generated more often than for *snake* in isolation. Thus, a rule associated with *rolled-up* does not increase the salience of the internal properties for whatever head noun is modified. Instead, internal properties only become more salient when a revealing modifier becomes combined with only those entities whose internal parts become unoccluded when the modifier is combined with them.

This finding further implicates simulation in conceptual combination. Because internal properties do not become unoccluded in a simulation of a rolled-up snake, participants do not produce them more often during property generation. Because internal properties do become unoccluded in a simulation of a rolled-up lawn, participants produce them more often.

Across Wu and Barsalou's experiments, the results support the conclusion that people manipulate simulations to represent conceptual combinations. When a simulation reveals occluded properties, they are produced more often than when they remain occluded. Occlusion affects conceptual combination even for novel combinations, suggesting that simulations are being constructed online to represent them. Occlusion effects do not occur when combining a revealing modifier with a head noun does not refer to something whose internal properties become unoccluded. Clearly, much more evidence is required to establish that simulation plays a central role in conceptual combination. Nevertheless, the initial evidence suggests that this possibility has some likelihood of being correct.

### Abstract Concepts

Similar to conceptual combination, very little research has addressed the role of simulation in abstract concepts. Again, the initial evidence suggests that simulation may be important.

The proposal that simulation represents abstract concepts runs counter to most current views, which have their roots in Paivio's (1971, 1986) Dual Code Theory. Based on the finding that memory tends to be better for concrete concepts than for abstract concepts, Paivio proposed that only the language system represents abstract concepts. Because both the language and simulation systems represent concrete concepts (two systems), memory for concrete concepts is good. Because only the language system represents abstract concepts (one system), memory for abstract concepts is inferior. Based on a wide variety of related findings, many researchers have since echoed this view. In particular, nearly all neuroimaging researchers who have assessed the neural bases of concrete and abstract concepts have concurred with Dual Code Theory (for a review, see Sabsevitz, Medler, Seidenberg, & Binder, 2005). Because these studies have generally found left-hemisphere language areas to be more active for abstract than for concrete concepts (especially Broca's area), they have concluded that language represents abstract concepts.

A logical problem with this account is that language per se cannot represent a concept. If people use an unfamiliar foreign language to describe the meaning of an abstract concept, they do not understand the concept (cf. Searle, 1980). They only understand the concept once they can ground the language in experience (also see Schwanenflugel, 1991). This suggests that simulations of situations should be central to the representations of abstract concepts. Thus, Barsalou (1999) proposed that abstract concepts refer to distributed focal content within a background situation, where the focal content often includes introspective states, events, and the relations between them. Furthermore, when people are asked to represent an abstract concept when a physical situation is not mentioned explicitly, they simulate a relevant situation and focus on regions of the simulation relevant to the concept.

Consider how an everyday sense of *truth* might be represented from this perspective. Imagine that a speaker makes a claim about a situation, such as, "It is snowing outside." Further imagine that a listener represents the claim (perhaps as a simulation), compares it to perception of the actual situation, and decides if the claim interprets the situation accurately. If the simulated claim represents the perceived situation accurately, the claim is interpreted as true. Thus, this sense of *truth* is grounded in a complex multimodal situation extended over time.

According to the PSS account, people simulate complex situations like these to represent abstract concepts in the absence of actual situations and focus attention on relevant content within these simulations. For this sense of *truth*, people focus on the speaker's claim, the listener's representation of its meaning, the listener's perception of the corresponding situation, the listener's comparison of the represented claim to the perceived situation, and the listener's conclusion about whether the two match. Although the rest of the situation is backgrounded, it frames the focal content.

Besides offering this simulation-based account of *truth*, Barsalou (1999) also offered similar accounts of *negation* and *disjunction*, and suggested similar approaches for implementing mathematical and logical reasoning. In general, many abstract concepts, such as *freedom* and *invention*, can be viewed as being grounded in complex simulations of multimodal situations, with simulated content about events, introspective states, and the relations between them being foregrounded against backgrounded situational content.

### Evidence from Property Generation

Barsalou and Wiemer-Hastings (2005) offered preliminary support for this account. When participants generated properties of concrete and abstract concepts, they generated distributions of properties that contained more similarities than differences. For each type of concept, participants tended to describe the situations in which a concept occurred, including relevant information about agents, objects, settings, events, and mental states. Participants produced all these different types of properties for both concrete and abstract concepts, and produced them in comparable distributions. This finding strongly suggests that participants represented both concrete and abstract concepts in situations.

Although strong similarities existed between these distributions for concrete and abstract concepts, differences existed in content and complexity as well. Regarding content, concrete concepts focused more on objects and settings than did abstract concepts, whereas abstract concepts focused more on mental states and events. Regarding complexity, abstract concepts included more information, deeper hierarchical structures, and more contingency relations than did concrete concepts.

Overall, these findings are consistent with the view that people situate concepts when they represent them, regardless of whether they are concrete or abstract. Although people focus on different content within situations, situations remain present as background. Importantly, these results do not indicate whether people simulate these situations or represent them using amodal symbols. However, much indirect evidence is consistent with the view that people use simulation to represent background situations (for reviews, see Barsalou, 2003b, 2005b; Barsalou, Niedenthal, Barbey, & Ruppert, 2003; Yeh & Barsalou, 2006). The next experiment offers direct evidence that people use simulation to represent the situations that underlie abstract concepts.

### Evidence from Brain Activation

As mentioned earlier, neuroimaging research on abstract concepts has largely adopted Paivio's (1971, 1986) view that abstract concepts rely on the brain's language system, not on the simulation system. Wilson, Simmons, Martin, and Barsalou (in preparation) argue however, that previous neuroimaging experiments have primarily observed activations in language areas because they used tasks that encourage superficial linguistic processing (e.g., lexical decision, synonym judgment). Because information from the language system was sufficient for performing the tasks in these experiments, the simulation system was not engaged (Barsalou, Santos, Simmons, & Wilson, in press; Glaser, 1992; Solomon & Barsalou, 2004; Kan et al., 2003).

To engage the simulation system, Wilson et al. presented the name of an abstract concept to participants in an fMRI scanner for 5 sec, and then had them verify whether the concept applied to a subsequent picture. For example, participants received the word "convince" for 5 sec and assessed whether the concept *convince* applied to a subsequent picture of a politician speaking to a crowd (or did not apply to a picture of a park). Wilson et al. argued that participants had to activate a deep conceptual representation of the abstract concept during the 5-sec priming period to determine whether the concept applied to the subsequent picture. If so, then areas involved in simulation should become active as participants prime conceptual representations of the abstract concept.

Wilson et al. confirmed this prediction. When participants received the abstract concept *convince* and prepared to assess whether it applied to a subsequent picture, they activated brain areas involved in representing mental states and social interaction. Similarly, when people prepared to assess whether the abstract concept *arithmetic* applied to a subsequent picture, they activated brain areas involved in performing arithmetic operations. For both concepts, participants simulated relevant situations to represent the respective concept during the priming period prior to receiving a picture. Notably, the language system was not more active for abstract concepts than for concrete concepts under these task conditions, suggesting that the priming task activated deep conceptual representations for the abstract concepts.

These findings suggest that people use simulation to represent abstract concepts. When given the word for an abstract concept, people simulate the situations in which the concept occurs. Clearly, much further evidence is required to confirm this finding. Combined with previous evidence that people use simulations to represent situations, however, it is reasonable to assume that future evidence will show that people represent abstract concepts with simulated situations as well.

### Limitations of the Current Evidence

The findings that support the PSS accounts of symbolic operations are clearly limited. At this point in time, very little research has addressed these accounts. Although the greatest amount of research performed so far has addressed predication, much further work is clearly required to conclude decisively that simulation implements this symbolic operation. Given that even less research has addressed conceptual combination and abstract concepts, even greater caution is necessary in drawing conclusions about how these symbolic operations arise. Nevertheless, the initial evidence suggests that the PSS accounts of these operations are plausible.

Beside the lack of evidence, a lack of process models and formal models also currently characterizes research on these issues. Clearly, models must be developed that describe in detail how simulation mechanisms implement symbolic operations. The descriptive accounts offered so far in Barsalou (1999, 2003a, 2005a) outline architectures and mechanisms that could certainly structure these models. Nevertheless, such architectures and mechanisms must be specified in detail and implemented computationally to ensure that they produce symbolic operations.

Once such models have been specified, they are likely to generate increasingly sophisticated empirical research that goes beyond demonstration experiments. Rather than simply demonstrating the presence of modal activity, later generations of experiments should attempt to isolate specific mechanisms in these models and the coordination between them (cf. Barsalou, Breazeal, & Smith, 2007).

### SYMBOLIC OPERATIONS ARISE FROM INTERACTIONS BETWEEN LANGUAGE AND SIMULATION

In addressing the nature of symbolic operations, the focus has been on simulation. It is highly likely however, that symbolic operations in humans do not result from simulation alone but instead reflect interactions between language and simulation.

To see this point, first consider the possible presence of simulation mechanisms in nonhumans who lack linguistic systems. Following evolutionary theorists, the basic architecture of the human conceptual system may have existed in previous species (e.g., Donald, 1993). From this perspective, the simulation system existed long before humans, so that multimodal experience could be captured to inform situated action (e.g., Barsalou, 2005b). Much like humans, nonhumans have attentional systems that could allow them to isolate regions of experience and store categorical knowledge about these regions in simulators. By establishing simulators in this manner and organizing them situationally, nonhumans could simulate anticipatory inferences that support feeding, reproduction, and so on.

If nonhumans have simulators that correspond to regions of experience, then nonhumans have simple symbolic abilities. Nonhumans can bind tokens to types (i.e., categorize entities and events in perception). Nonhumans can combine concepts to recognize novel combinations of familiar concepts (e.g., a familiar food appearing in a familiar location where the food has not been perceived previously). On hearing a communicative call, nonhumans simulate an associated referent (e.g., Gil-da-Costa, Braun, Lopes, Hauser, Carson, Herscovitch, & Martin, 2004). Clearly, these symbolic capabilities are simpler than those of humans, yet they are symbolic abilities that link conceptual knowledge (simulators) with experience.

Consistent with evolutionary theorists (e.g., Donald, 1993), symbolic capabilities could have increased dramatically once language evolved to control the simulation system in humans. Adding language increased the ability of the simulation system to represent non-present situations (past, future, counterfactual). Adding language increased the ability to reference introspective states, thereby increasing the ability to represent abstract concepts and perform metacognition. Adding language increased the ability to coordinate simulations between agents, yielding more powerful forms of social organization.

The language system appears to play central roles in producing the compositional structure of simulations (Barsalou, 1999, 2003a, 2005a). For example, the syntactic structure of sentences could control the retrieval, assembly, and transformation of the componential simulations that are combined to represent sentences and texts. Similarly, interactions between language and simulation could produce the complex compositional structures that underlie the conceptual combinations, productively produced phrases, and recursively embedded structures that characterize human cognition.

A variety of other complex symbolic interactions may also arise from interactions between the language and simulation systems. When a speaker has something to say, a simulation represents it initially (e.g., a speaker simulating an anticipated hike around a lake at sunset). Putting the simulation into words requires control of attention across the simulation. When attention focuses on a region, a simulator categorizes it. Linguistic forms associated with the simulator, such as words and syntactic structures, become active, which are then integrated into the evolving motor program for an utterance (e.g., the speaker stating, "I'm looking forward to hiking around the lake at sunset"). In turn, when a listener comprehends the utterance, its words and syntactic structures function as instructions to assemble a simulation compositionally that should – ideally – correspond to the speaker's simulation (e.g., simulating the speaker's anticipated hike around the lake).

Complex symbolic interactions also occur extensively during reasoning. As people try to figure things out during decision making, planning, and problem solving, they simulate the relevant situation and verbalize about it simultaneously (e.g., deciding whether it would be better to work at home or at the office later in the afternoon). Whereas simulations represent the content of thought, words manipulate and modify these simulations, as possibilities are evaluated and decisions made.

In general, language provides a powerful system for indexing regions of simulations (via simulators) and for manipulating simulations in language and thought. As the two systems interact, one may dominate momentarily, followed by the other, perhaps cycling many times, with both systems active simultaneously at many points. Most importantly, both systems may be essential for achieving the powerful symbolic abilities of the human cognitive system (Barsalou, Santos, Simmons, & Wilson, in press). Neither system alone is likely to be sufficient. Instead, the two systems work together to produce human symbolic capabilities. Much remains to be learned about interactions between the language and simulation systems and the impressive capabilities that these interactions achieve.

AUTHOR NOTES

This work was supported by National Science Foundation Grants SBR-9421326, SBR-9796200, and BCS-0212134 and by DARPA contract BICA FA8650–05-C-7256 to Lawrence W. Barsalou. Address correspondence to Lawrence W. Barsalou, Department of Psychology, Emory University, Atlanta, GA 30322 (barsalou@emory.edu, http://www.psychology.emory.edu/cognition/barsalou/index.html).

**References**

Anderson, J. R. (1983). *The architecture of cognition.* Cambridge, MA: Harvard University Press.

Barsalou, L. W. (1987). The instability of graded structure: Implications for the nature of concepts. In U. Neisser (Ed.), *Concepts and conceptual development: Ecological and intellectual factors in categorization* (pp. 101–140). Cambridge, UK: Cambridge University Press.

Barsalou, L. W. (1989). Intraconcept similarity and its implications for interconcept similarity. In S. Vosniadou & A. Ortony (Eds.), *Similarity and analogical reasoning* (pp. 76–121). Cambridge, UK: Cambridge University Press.

Barsalou, L. W. (1992). Frames, concepts, and conceptual fields. In E. Kittay & A. Lehrer (Eds.), Frames, fields, and contrasts: New essays in semantic and lexical organization. Hillsdale, NJ: Lawrence Erlbaum Associates.

Barsalou, L. W. (1993). Flexibility, structure, and linguistic vagary in concepts: Manifestations of a compositional system of perceptual symbols. In A. C. Collins, S. E. Gathercole, & M. A. Conway (Eds.), *Theories of memory* (pp. 29–101). London: Lawrence Erlbaum Associates.

Barsalou, L. W. (1999). Perceptual symbol systems. *Behavioral and Brain Sciences, 22,* 577–660.

Barsalou, L. W. (2003a). Abstraction in perceptual symbol systems. *Philosophical Transactions of the Royal Society of London: Biological Sciences, 358,* 1177–1187.

Barsalou, L. W. (2003b). Situated simulation in the human conceptual system. *Language and Cognitive Processes, 18,* 513–562.

Barsalou, L. W. (2005a). Abstraction as dynamic interpretation in perceptual symbol systems. In L. Gershkoff-Stowe & D. Rakison (Eds.), *Building object categories* (pp. 389–431). Carnegie Symposium Series. Mahwah, NJ: Erlbaum.

Barsalou, L. W. (2005b). Continuity of the conceptual system across species. *Trends in Cognitive Sciences, 9,* 309–311.

Barsalou, L. W. (2008). Grounded cognition. *Annual Review of Psychology, 59,* 617–645.

Barsalou, L. W., Breazeal, C., & Smith, L. B. (2007). Language as coordinated noncognition. *Cognitive Processing, 8,* 79–91.

Barsalou, L. W., & Hale, C. R. (1993). Components of conceptual representation: From feature lists to recursive frames. In I. Van Mechelen, J. Hampton, R. Michalski, & P. Theuns (Eds.), Categories and concepts: *Theoretical views and inductive data analysis* (pp. 97–144). San Diego, CA: Academic Press.

Barsalou, L. W., Niedenthal, P. M., Barbey, A., & Ruppert, J. (2003). Social embodiment. In B. Ross (Ed.), *The Psychology of Learning and Motivation*, Vol. 43 (pp. 43–92). San Diego, CA: Academic Press.

Barsalou, L. W., Pecher, D., Zeelenberg, R., Simmons, W. K., & Hamann, S. B. (2005). Multimodal simulation in conceptual processing. In W. Ahn, R. Goldstone, B. Love, A. Markman, & P. Wolff (Eds.), *Categorization inside and outside the lab: Essays in honor of Douglas L. Medin* (pp. 249–270). Washington, DC: American Psychological Association.

Barsalou, L. W., Santos, A., Simmons, W. K., & Wilson, C. D. (in press). Language and simulation in conceptual processing. In M. De Vega, A. M. Glenberg, & A. C. Graesser (Eds.). *Symbols, embodiment, and meaning.* Oxford: Oxford University Press.

Barsalou, L. W., Simmons, W. K., Barbey, A. K., & Wilson, C. D. (2003). Grounding conceptual knowledge in modality-specific systems. *Trends in Cognitive Sciences, 7,* 84–91.

Barsalou, L. W., & Wiemer-Hastings, K. (2005). Situating abstract concepts. In D. Pecher and R. Zwaan (Eds.), *Grounding cognition: The role of perception and action in memory, language, and thought* (pp. 129–163). New York: Cambridge University Press.

Caramazza, A., & Shelton, J. R. (1998). Domain-specific knowledge systems in the brain: The animate-inanimate distinction. *Journal of Cognitive Neuroscience, 10,* 1–34.

Charniak, E., & McDermott, D. (1985). *Introduction to artificial intelligence.* Reading, MA: Addison-Wesley.

Cree, G.S,. & McRae, K. (2003). Analyzing the factors underlying the structure and computation of the meaning of chipmunk, cherry, chisel, cheese, and cello (and many other such concrete nouns). *Journal of Experimental Psychology: General, 132,* 163–201.

Damasio, A. R. (1989). Time-locked multiregional retroactivation: A systems-level proposal for the neural substrates of recall and recognition. *Cognition, 33,* 25–62.

Donald, M. (1993). Precis of "Origins of the modern mind: Three stages in the evolution of culture and cognition." *Behavioral and Brain Sciences, 16,* 739–791.

Epicurus (1987). Sensation, imagination, and memory. In A. A. Long & D. N. Sedley (1987), *The Hellenistic philosophers*, Vol. 1. New York. Cambridge University Press. (Original work written in 341–270 BC)

Farah, M. J., & McClelland, J. L. (1991). A computational model of semantic memory impairment: Modality specificity and emergent category specificity. *Journal of Experimental Psychology: General, 120,* 339–357.

Fodor, J. A. (1975). *The language of thought.* Cambridge, MA: Harvard University Press.

Gil-da-Costa, R., Braun, A., Lopes, M., Hauser, M. D., Carson, R. E., Herscovitch, P., & Martin, A. (2004). Toward an evolutionary perspective on conceptual representation: Species-specific calls activate visual and affective processing systems. *Proceedings of the National Academy of Sciences, 101,* 17516–17521.

Glaser, W. R. (1992). Picture naming. *Cognition, 42,* 61–105.

Goldberg, R. F., Perfetti, C. A., & Schneider, W. (2006). Perceptual knowledge retrieval activates sensory brain regions. *Journal of Neuroscience, 26,* 4917–4921.

Kan, I. P., Barsalou, L. W., Solomon, K. O., Minor, J. K., & Thompson-Schill, S. L. (2003). Role of mental imagery in a property verification task: fMRI evidence for perceptual representations of conceptual knowledge. *Cognitive Neuropsychology, 20,* 525–540.

Kant, E. (1965). *The critique of pure reason* (N. K. Smith, Trans). New York: St. Martin's Press. (Original work published in 1787).

Kellenbach, M. L., Brett, M., & Patterson, K. (2001). Large, colorful, or noisy? Attribute- and modal activations during retrieval of perceptual attribute knowledge. *Cognitive, Affective, and Behavioral Neuroscience, 1,* 207–221.

Marques, J. F. (2006). Specialization and semantic organization: Evidence for multiple semantics linked to sensory modalities. *Memory & Cognition, 34,* 60–67.

Martin, A. (2001). Functional neuroimaging of semantic memory. In R. Cabeza & A. Kingstone (Eds.), *Handbook of functional neuroimaging of cognition* (pp. 153–186). Cambridge, MA: MIT Press.

Martin, A. (2007). The representation of object concepts in the brain. *Annual Review of Psychology, 58,* 25–45.

McRae, K., de Sa, V. R., & Seidenberg, M. S. (1997). On the nature and scope of featural representations of word meaning. *Journal of Experimental Psychology: General, 126,* 99–130.

Morrison, J. B., & Tversky, B. (1997). Body schemas. In M. G. Shafto & P. Langley (Eds.), *Proceedings of Cognitive Science Society* (pp. 525–529). Mahwah, NJ: Erlbaum.

Niedenthal, P. M., Barsalou, L. W., Winkielman, P., Krauth-Gruber, S., & Ric, F. (2005). Embodiment in attitudes, social perception, and emotion. *Personality and Social Psychology Review, 9,* 184–211.

Newell, A. (1990). *Unified theories of cognition.* Cambridge, MA: Harvard University Press.

O'Reilly, R. C., & Munakata, Y. (2000). *Computational explorations in cognitive neuroscience: Understanding the mind by simulating the brain.* Cambridge, MA: MIT Press.

Paivio, A. (1971). *Imagery and verbal processes.* New York: Holt, Rinehart, & Winston.

Paivio, A. (1986). *Mental representations: A dual coding approach.* New York: Oxford University Press.

Pecher, D., Zeelenberg, R., & Barsalou, L. W. (2003). Verifying properties from different modalities for concepts produces switching costs. *Psychological Science, 14,* 119–124.

Pecher, D., Zeelenberg, R., & Barsalou, L. W. (2004). Sensorimotor simulations underlie conceptual representations: Modality-specific effects of prior activation. *Psychonomic Bulletin & Review, 11,* 164–167.

Pollack, J. (1990). Recursive distributed representations. *Artificial Intelligence, 46,* 77–105.

Prinz, J. J. (2002). *Furnishing the mind: Concepts and their perceptual basis.* Cambridge, MA: MIT Press.

Prinz, J. J., & Barsalou, L. W. (2000). Steering a course for embodied representation. In E. Dietrich & A. Markman (Eds.), *Cognitive dynamics: Conceptual change in humans and machines* (51–77). Cambridge, MA: MIT Press.

Pulvermüller, F. (1999). Words in the brain's language. *Behavioral and Brain Sciences, 22,* 253–336.

Pylyshyn, Z. W. (1973). What the mind's eye tells the mind's brain: A critique of mental imagery. *Psychological Bulletin, 80,* 1–24.

Reid, T. (1969). *Essays on the intellectual powers of man.* Cambridge, MA: MIT Press. (Original work published in 1785).

Rumelhart, D. E., McClelland, J. L., & the PDP Research Group (Eds.) (1986). *Parallel distributed processing. Explorations in the microstructure of cognition, Vol. 1: Foundations.* Cambridge, MA: MIT Press.

Sabsevitz, D. S., Medler, D. A., Seidenberg, M., & Binder, J. R. (2005). Modulation of the semantic system by word imageability. *NeuroImage, 27,* 188–200.

Schwanenflugel, P. J. (1991). Why are abstract concepts hard to understand? In P. J. Schwanenflugel (Ed.), *The psychology of word meaning* (pp. 223–250). Mahwah, NJ: Erlbaum.

Schyns, P. G., Goldstone, R. L., & Thibaut, J. P. (1998). The development of features in object concepts. *Behavioral and Brain Sciences, 21,* 1–54.

Searle, J. R. (1980). Minds, brains, and programs. *Behavioral and Brain Sciences, 3,* 417–424.

Simmons, W. K., & Barsalou, L. W. (2003). The similarity-in-topography principle: Reconciling theories of conceptual deficits. *Cognitive Neuropsychology, 20,* 451–486.

Simmons, W. K., Martin, A., & Barsalou, L. W. (2005). Pictures of appetizing foods activate gustatory cortices for taste and reward. *Cerebral Cortex, 15,* 1602–1608.

Simmons, W. K., Ramjee, V., Beauchamp, M. S., McRae, K., Martin, A., & W. Barsalou, L. W. (2007). Common neural substrates for perceiving and knowing about color and action. *Neuropsychologia, 45,* 2802–2810.

Smith, L. B. (2005). Cognition as a dynamic system: Principles from embodiment. *Developmental Review, 25,* 278–298.

Smith, L., & Gasser, M. (2005). The development of embodied cognition: Six lessons from babies. *Artificial Life, 11,* 13–29.

Smith, E. E., Osherson, D. N., Rips, L. J., & Keane, M. (1988). Combining prototypes: A selective modification model. *Cognitive Science, 12,* 485–528.

Smolensky, P. (1990). Tensor product variable binding and the representation of symbolic structures in connectionist systems. *Artificial Intelligence, 46,* 159–216.

Solomon, K. O. (1997). *The spontaneous use of perceptual representations during conceptual processing.* Doctoral dissertation. University of Chicago, Chicago, IL.

Solomon, K. O., & Barsalou, L. W. (2001). Representing properties locally. *Cognitive Psychology, 43,* 129–169.

Solomon, K. O., & Barsalou, L. W. (2004). Perceptual simulation in property verification. *Memory & Cognition, 32,* 244–259.

Thelen, E. (2000). Grounded in the world: Developmental origins of the embodied mind. *Infancy, 1,* 3–30.

Thompson-Schill, S. L. (2003), Neuroimaging studies of semantic memory: Inferring "how" from "where." *Neurosychologia, 41,* 280–292.

van Gelder, T. (1990). Compositionality: A connectionist variation on a classical theme. *Cognitive Science, 14,* 355–384.

Vermeulen, N., Niedenthal, P. M., & Luminet, O. (in press). Switching between sensory and affective systems incurs processing costs. *Cognitive Science.*

Wiemer-Hastings, K., Krug, J., & Xu, X. (2001). Imagery, context availability, contextual constraint, and abstractness. *Proceedings of the 23rd Annual Conference of the Cognitive Science Society,* 1134–1139. Mahwah, NJ: Erlbaum.

Wilson, C. D., Simmons, W. K., Martin, A., & Barsalou, L. W. (in preparation). Simulating properties of abstract concepts.

Wu, L. L., & Barsalou, L. W. (submitted). Occlusion affects conceptual combination.

Yeh, W., & Barsalou, L. W. (2006). The situated nature of concepts. *American Journal of Psychology, 119,* 349–384.

## 2 Toward the Integration of Bodily States, Language, and Action

Arthur M. Glenberg

This chapter develops an account of human cognition and language centered on three ideas. First, cognition is for action: Only organisms that can orchestrate action have nervous systems, and the basic function of a nervous system is to guide action. The second idea is that of neural exploitation (Gallese & Lakoff, 2005). Namely, as brains evolve, additional functions exploit the operation of neural systems already in place. Importantly, language seems to be such a system in that language comprehension involves the simulation of action calling upon neural systems otherwise used for perception, action, and emotional processing. Third, the simulations invoked by language make use of forward models (e.g., Grush, 2004) that are predominately used in the control of action. Consequently, both short-term (e.g., fatigue, practice, emotional states) and long-term (e.g., development, learning, neural insults) changes in action systems are predicted to affect language comprehension.

COGNITION IS FOR ACTION

### What Brains Are For

"What are brains for?" The answer to that question would seem to be obvious: "Brains are for thinking!" But consider some of the exquisite work that the brain does that one would not ordinarily classify as thinking. The brain controls and coordinates eye and neck muscles that allow us to track an annoying housefly, not to mention the tremendous amount of work done

This work was supported by NSF grant BCS-0315434 and Institute of Education Sciences grant R305H030266 to Arthur Glenberg. Any opinions, findings, and conclusions or recommendations expressed in this material are those of the author and do not necessarily reflect the views of the funding agencies.

by the visual areas of the brain in locating and identifying the fly. The brain coordinates that tracking activity with reaching out with the hand and arm to swat the fly. And finally, the brain simultaneously controls and coordinates virtually every muscle in the body so that the path we walk will intersect the fly's trajectory while reaching with the arm and tracking with the eyes. It is a good bet that the brain coordinates the control of movement much more frequently (and successfully) than thinking. Thus, the answer to the question, "What are brains for?" might well be, "Brains are for action!"

The biologist Rudolfo Llinas puts it this way: "The nervous system is only necessary for multi-cellular creatures . . . that can orchestrate and express active movement" (Llinas, 2001, p. 15). A particularly fascinating illustration of this fact is the life cycle of the sea squirt, a tunicate member of the phylum Chordata (animals with spinal chords, including humans). The sea squirt begins life as an egg and then has a short existence (a few hours to a few days) as a tadpole-like creature with a primitive spinal chord, a brain, a light-sensitive organ, and the ability to express active movement. The sea squirt moves about until it finds a suitable attachment site, such as a rock. After attaching, the sea squirt never leaves – that is, it never again expresses active movement. The fascinating part of the story is that almost as soon as the sea squirt stops moving, it begins to ingest its brain. No action, no need for a brain.

## Action, Evolution of Cognition, and Meaning

Imagine a chipmunk emerging from a hole in the ground to survey the environment. Upon seeing a threat, such as a snake, an effective action for the chipmunk is to dive back into its hole. If the chipmunk attempted to fly away instead, it would be consumed by the snake and not make much of a contribution to the gene pool. In contrast, suppose that it was a robin that sees the snake. Effective action for the robin is to fly away, whereas if it attempted to dive into a hole, it would be dead. And finally, effective action for a human who cannot fly or dive into a hole may be to flick away the snake with a long stick. Although cognition surely evolved from the bird to the chipmunk to the human, in all cases when the cognitive system is determining effective action it must take into account the body morphology of the actor. Thus, it is likely that there has been co-evolution of cognition and the body; that is, the evolution of one is constrained by the evolution of the other.

In addition to contributing to effective action, suppose also that cognition is what makes meaning, or sense, out of the world. Is there any way in which action and meaning can be connected? Glenberg (1997) proposed that the meaning of a situation to an individual (human or nonhuman animal) consists of the set of actions the individual can undertake in that situation. The set of actions is determined by the goal-directed *mesh of affordances.* The notion of an *affordance* was introduced by Gibson (e.g., Gibson, 1979). The term captures an interaction between body morphology and the physical environment. That is, what can be done with a physical object, such as a chair, depends on the body of the animal interacting with it. For an adult human, a kitchen chair affords sitting, standing upon, or even lifting to flick away a snake with one of the chair's legs. For a toddler, the chair affords sitting and standing upon as well as hiding under in a game of hide and seek. However, the chair does not afford lifting for the toddler because the toddler is not strong enough to lift it. Because the affordances of the chair differ for the adult and the child, the claim is that the meaning of the chair also differs.

*Mesh* refers to the process by which affordances are combined to accomplish goals. The mesh process must respect both body and physics. Thus, an adult can mesh the affordances of a kitchen chair (e.g., it can be held and extended) and a solid surface (e.g., it can be stood upon) to accomplish the goal of flicking a snake off a porch. However, it is more difficult to imagine how the adult could mesh the affordances of a chair and the surface of a swimming pool to accomplish the goal of flicking a snake out of the pool.

## The Indexical Hypothesis

This action-based account of meaning seems to be far from our everyday sense of meaning, that is, the sort of meaning conveyed by language. In fact, the data (to be reviewed shortly) point to a strong connection, and the Indexical Hypothesis (IH) was developed by Glenberg and Robertson (1999, 2000) to provide a theoretical description of that connection. The IH postulates that three processes – indexing, derivation of affordances, and meshing as directed by grammar – are used to convert words and sentences into embodied, action-based meaning. That is, we go from the words to a consideration of the actions implied by the sentence; if we can create a smooth and coherent (i.e., doable) simulation, then we can understand the sentence.

Consider how a person might understand a sentence such as, "Art flicked the snake off the porch using the chair." The indexing process maps words (e.g., "Art") and phrases (e.g., "the chair") to objects in the environment or to perceptual symbols (Barsalou, 1999). Perceptual symbols are much like images in that they reflect the perceptual processes used to perceive the object. Thus, on reading the sentence, one indexes "Art" to a male human and "the chair" to perhaps a kitchen chair. Next, one derives affordances from the indexed objects or perceptual symbols. Note that the affordances cannot be derived directly from the words because words do not have affordances in the usual sense. Instead, it is the objects that words designate that have the affordances and are a major source of meaning.

Finally, grammatical knowledge of several sorts is used to mesh or combine the affordances into a coherent simulation. For example, the syntax of, "Art flicked the snake off the porch using the chair," indicates that Art did the flicking, not the snake. In addition, knowledge of the meaning of the syntactic construction sets the goal for the mesh process, that is, what the meshing must accomplish. For example, the first part of the sentence (up to "using") is in the form of the caused motion verb-argument construction (Goldberg, 1995). Goldberg proposes that this syntactic construction conveys the meaning that the subject ("Art") causes the motion of the object ("the snake") to a location ("off the porch"). Kaschak and Glenberg (2000) demonstrated that English speakers are sensitive to these sorts of constructional meanings and that speakers use the meaning of the constructions to help determine the meaning of the individual words within the construction. Other sorts of grammatical knowledge (e.g., the meaning of temporal adverbs such as "while" and "after") direct the temporal course of the meshing process (De Vega, Robertson, Glenberg, Kaschak, & Rinck, 2004).

The IH proposes that a sentence is understood to the extent that the meshing process results in a coherent – that is, doable – simulation of action. However, consider what would happen if you index "chair" to your favorite bean-bag chair. Bean-bag chairs do not afford (easy) lifting, let alone the flicking away of snakes. In this case, you might consider the sentence to be nonsense or the speaker to be misinformed. The point is that the same words in the same sentence might be deemed perfectly sensible or nonsense depending on how those words are indexed, the affordances derived, and whether or not those affordances can be meshed as directed by syntax.

NEURAL EXPLOITATION

The arguments advanced above provide a functional argument for the relation between language and meaning. Gallese and Lakoff (2005) develop another line of reasoning based on the idea of neural exploitation. Given that evolution tends to be conservative, and given that brains evolved to control action, we might suppose that other systems (for example, language) are built on a base of action. Thus, we expect to find that neural systems that evolved to control action, and systems that feed into the control of action such as perception and emotion systems, will also be used during language comprehension. What follows is a brief review of the neuroscientific, developmental, and behavioral work consistent with the idea of neural exploitation by language of action, perception, and emotional systems.

### The Neuroscience of Language and Action

Neuroscience has provided multiple demonstrations of the overlap between areas of the brain contributing to language and those contributing to action (particularly useful reviews are provided by Pulvermüller, 2005, and Rizzolatti & Craighero, 2004). What happens in our brains when we hear words such as "pick," "kick," and "lick?" Of course, there is activation in the left temporal lobe (e.g., Wernicke's area) traditionally associated with language perception. Somewhat surprisingly, there is also activation in the frontal area (e.g., Broca's region) normally thought of as contributing to speech production (e.g., Fadiga et al., 2002). However, the big surprise concerns activation in areas of the brain associated with motor activity. For example, Hauk et al. (2004) used functional magnetic resonance imagery (fMRI) to record brain activity while people listened to verbs. When listening to verbs referring to leg actions, regions of the motor cortex that control the leg were particularly active; when listening to verbs referring to hand actions, regions of the motor cortex that control the hand were particularly active; and so on. Similarly, Tettamanti et al. (2005) tracked areas of activation while people listened to sentences using verbs requiring mouth actions (e.g., "I eat an apple"), hand actions (e.g., "I grasp the knife"), and leg actions (e.g., "I kick the ball"). As predicted by the embodiment position, these sentences selectively activated areas of the brain associated with mouth, hand, and leg actions, respectively.

The fMRI findings can be interpreted in several ways. The data could indicate that understanding these verbs requires activity in motor areas of the brain, or the results might simply reflect a habit of envisioning action after hearing action verbs. The balance of the research points strongly to the first interpretation. For example, Pulvermüller et al. (2003) demonstrated that activity in the motor areas occurs very soon (e.g., 20 ms) after the word produces peak activation in areas of the brain traditionally associated with language. The speed of activation would appear to rule out a conscious or optional process. Pulvermüller (2005) activated motor areas using transcranial magnetic stimulation (TMS). When left-hemisphere leg motor areas were activated, people were quick to identify leg-related words, and when left-hemisphere arm motor areas were activated, people were quick to identify arm-related words. Finally, Buccino, Riggio, Melli, Binkofski, Gallese, & Rizzolatti (2005) reported related findings for whole sentences. That is, when people listened to sentences describing leg (or arm) movements while TMS was applied to leg (or arm) motor centers, there was differential modulation of electrical activity recorded in the legs (or arms). Thus, there are strong connections between language and action that can be found in the brain and that extend out to the periphery of the body. The time course of the effect is too quick, and the causal pathways demonstrated by TMS too convincing, to believe that the link between language and action is optional.

Another finding from the neuroscience literature helps to cement the relation between language and action. Rizzolatti and Arbib (1998) reviewed data on the mirror neuron system and the relation between that system and language. Mirror neurons were first discovered in an area of monkey prefrontal cortex (F5). The mirror neurons in this area respond when the animal takes a particular action, such as ripping a sheet of paper. The same neurons will respond when the animal observes another monkey or a human performing the same action. In fact, these neurons will also respond when the animal simply hears paper being ripped (Kohler et al., 2002). The mirror neuron system has been associated with the ability to recognize the intent of a conspecific's actions – for example, you understand the intent of another person's gesture because the mirror neurons firing are those that would fire when you take action with the same intent. Hence, the system is thought to be particularly important for empathy and social interaction (Gallese et al., 2004).

The story becomes more interesting for the connection between language and action because area F5 in the monkey brain is a homolog of Broca's area (which is involved in speech production) in the human brain. Once this correspondence was noted, research demonstrated that the human Broca's area also contains neurons with mirror-like properties (Fadiga et al., 1995), and that parts of Broca's area control not just the speech articulators but also the hand. From these various correspondences, Rizzolatti and Arbib (1998) suggest that oral language developed from the ability to recognize the communicative intent of actions and gestures. That is, Broca's area evolved into a language area because of its prior usefulness in gestural communication.

The tremendous overlap between neural structures contributing to language and hand/arm movement may help to explain the prevalence of hand gestures in language (McNeill, 1992). Gestures while speaking are nearly universal. Even congenitally blind people speaking to blind listeners gesture (Iverson & Golden-Meadow, 2001), so gesture is unlikely to be something learned or consciously planned for the benefit of the listener. Nonetheless, gestures do enhance communication (e.g., Valenzeno et al., 2003; Kelly et al., 1999). With two assumptions, it becomes clear why gestures are so prevalent while speaking. The first assumption is that much of meaning is based on action, that is, what a sentence means to a listener consists of how that sentence describes, suggests, or modulates actions. The second assumption is that meaning can only be determined by using the motor system. Thus, sentences convey meanings that have action at their core, and many of our humanly important actions involve the hand (e.g., giving, eating, threatening, appeasing). Broca's area controls both the speech articulators (e.g., lips, tongue) and the hand. Thus, there can be nearly simultaneous activation of the speech apparatus and the hand in the service of the same message.

These speculations are consistent with the results of an amazing series of studies conducted by Gentilucci. Gentilucci, Benuzzi, Gangitano, and Grimaldi (2001) who presented participants with large or small objects that they were to grasp while opening their mouths. Lip aperture and velocity was greater when grasping a large object than a small one. When asked to pronounce a syllable printed on the objects, power levels of the pronounced syllable were greater when grasping the larger object. Apparently, commands sent to the hand and arm are also sent to the speech apparatus, as the adjacency of hand and speech neurons in Broca's area would suggest. But are these also mirror neurons that would respond similarly when the actions are observed rather than made? Gentilucci, Bernardis, Crisi, and Volta (2006) studied the F2 formant during the pronunciation of a syllable presented as a printed word, a heard word, a gesture of the word (waving "hello" for the syllable, "ciao"), and the combination of heard word and gesture. Across these conditions, the frequency of F2 increased, indicating a greater tongue protrusion. Furthermore, when these presentation modalities followed repetitive TMS (rTMS) designed to reduce the processing efficiency of Broca's area, the enhanced F2 frequency due to the gesture was eliminated.

## Developmental Support for the Language and Action Connection

Several recent reports in the language acquisition literature provide confirmation of the relation between language and action. One particularly interesting set of studies was reported by Smith (2005), who documented the causal relations among action, naming, and categorization in children between 24 and 35 months old. In one experiment, children were given a graspable toy shaped roughly like an asymmetric barbell, that is, there were bumps on both ends but one bump was larger. The children were told that the object was a "wug." Half the children were taught to hold the wug using both hands, with one hand on each bump, and to play with it by rotating the wrists. Note that this activity treats the wug in a symmetrical manner. The other children were

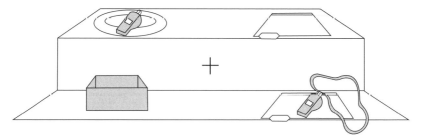

Figure 2.1. Illustration of one environment used in Chambers et al. (2004). Reprinted from *Journal of Experimental Psychology: Learning, Memory, and Cognition*, Vol. 30, Chambers, C. G., Tanenhaus, M. K., and Magnuson, J. S. Actions and affordances in syntactic ambiguity resolution (pp. 687–696), 2004. Used with permission.

taught to hold the wug by using one hand to grasp the smaller bump and to wave the wug about. This activity treats the wug in an asymmetrical manner. Following these activities, children were shown other objects that were either more symmetrical than the original or less symmetrical, and the children were asked which were wugs. Children who acted on the original wug in a symmetrical manner were more likely to classify symmetric variations as wugs than the children who acted on the original in an asymmetric manner, and the reverse was found for the asymmetric variations. In other words, how the children interacted with the original wug helped to determine what other objects would be called the same name.

## Behavioral Support for the Connection between Language and Action

Behavioral work with adults has also produced strong evidence for the interaction of action and language across multiple levels of language processing: grammatical, basic word meaning, and the meanings of sentences about concrete and abstract situations, as well as the interpretation of extended dialog (Noice & Noice, 2006; Ochs et al. 1996; Roth, 1999).

Chambers et al. (2004) used the concept of affordances to show the relation between action and grammatical parsing. In their experiments, participants were faced with real situations, such as that illustrated in Figure 2.1, and they heard instructions regarding how to move the objects. One instruction was, "Put the whistle on the folder in the box." Note that there are two whistles in the situation. Thus, clear communication must use some sort of language (or gesture) to discriminate between the two whistles, and that is exactly the function of the phrase, "on the folder." Which whistle should be moved? The whistle that is "on the folder." In another condition, people held a hook and used it to move objects. In this condition, even though both whistles were physically present, there was only one whistle that afforded moving, namely, the one with the lanyard that can be grabbed with the hook. Thus, when holding the hook, there is really only one whistle to consider, and the phrase "on the folder" is redundant at best (indicating which whistle to move, but we already know that it is the one with the lanyard) or easily misinterpreted at worst. That is, when holding the hook and listening to the sentence, "Put the whistle on the folder . . . ," people could reasonably interpret "on the folder" as a phrase indicating where the (afforded) whistle might be moved. In fact, when holding the hook, people tended to look at the empty folder (as if they were preparing to move the whistle there) much more frequently than when they were not holding the hook. The point is that the affordances of the situation determined how people parsed the phrase, "on the folder." With the "no-hook" affordances, the phrase was parsed as a reduced relative clause indicating which whistle to move; with the "hook" affordances, the phrase was parsed as a prepositional phrase describing where the whistle was to be moved.

Borghi et al. (2004) also used the concept of affordances to demonstrate that the basic meaning of a word taps action. In one of their experiments, participants read a sentence that mentioned an object such as, "There is a car in front of you." The participant then pressed the middle button of a vertically oriented three-button panel. Pressing this button revealed a target word, such as "roof," "wheel," or "road." At that point, the participant was to determine if the target was a part of the object named in the sentence ("roof" or "wheel") or not ("road"). Note that interacting with the roof of a car normally requires action directed upward, whereas interacting with the wheel of a car normally requires action directed downward. Suppose that these different affordances are part of the basic meanings of "car," "roof," and "wheel." That is, suppose that just thinking of the meaning of a word such as "roof" prepares one to act upward. In this case, participants required to move upward to the top response button to indicate "yes" should respond faster to a target such as "roof" than participants required to move downward to indicate "yes." In contrast, for a target word such as "wheel," those participants required to move downward should respond faster. This is exactly what Borghi et al. (2004) found. Apparently, when we think about the meaning of a word, at least part of that meaning is in terms of how to act on the object named by the word.

Glenberg and Kaschak (2002) used a similar methodology to determine the contribution of action to the interpretation of whole sentences. The task was to judge if a sentence was sensible (e.g., "Courtney handed you the notebook," or "You handed Courtney the notebook") or nonsense (e.g., "You drank the house to Joe"). The sensible judgment was made by moving to a button requiring movement away from the body in one condition or toward the body in the other condition. As with the "Courtney" sentences, half of the sensible sentences described action toward the reader and half away. If sentence understanding requires a determination of direction using action systems, then readers literally moving a hand toward the body to make the "sensible" judgment should respond more quickly to sentences describing action toward the body than to sentences describing action away. The opposite should be found for those readers required to respond "sensible" by a moving a hand away from the body. This interaction was found, thus demonstrating a contribution of action to sentence comprehension.

The data described so far involve language about concrete objects and activities. But language can also be used to describe abstract feelings, events, transitions, and so on. At first glance, it would appear that action could not possibly contribute to understanding language of this sort, but the data indicate otherwise. One such illustration comes from Glenberg and Kaschak (2002). In addition to sentences describing the transfer of concrete objects, some described the transfer of information from one person to another, such as, "Liz told you the story," or "You told Liz the story." The same interaction of transfer direction and literal response direction was found, implying a contribution of mechanisms of action to language understanding of at least some abstract situations.

More impressive are the data from Matlock (2004). Her participants first read descriptions of terrains – for example, of a desert described as smooth and flat or rocky and hilly. Matlock then timed the participants' reading of target sentences such as, "A fence runs through it." These sentences describe "fictive" motion (Talmy, 1996), that is, nothing mentioned in the sentence is literally moving. Nonetheless, Matlock observed that people took sub-stantially longer to read target sentences describing fictive motion through complex terrains than through simple terrains. That is, people seemed to be simulating movement through the terrain as they cognitively followed the fence.

Counterfactual language, such as, "If the jeweler had been a good friend of mine, he would have shown me the imperial diamond," is very abstract because the events described (e.g., showing the imperial diamond) did not happen, will not happen, and are not even planned. Nonetheless, De Vega (in press) deduced evidence that these sorts of events are understood through an embodied motor simulation.

## Language and Perceptual Systems

Kaschak et al. (2005) had participants listen to and judge the sensibility of sentences conveying motion in specific directions, such as toward an observer (e.g., "The car approached you") or away (e.g., "The squirrel scurried away"). Simultaneously, the participant looked at a spiral spinning so as to convey visual motion toward or away. Kaschak et al. found that sensibility judgments were slowed by the visual stimulus conveying motion in the same direction as implied by the sentence. Apparently, the same visual processing system required for perceiving the spiral motion was also required for understanding the sentence. Because that system was engaged, sentence understanding was slowed (see Tettamanti et al., 2005, for neural imaging data demonstrating the activation of visual processing areas in understanding language about actions).

Pecher, Zeelenberg, and Barsalou (2003) noted that it takes time to switch attention from one perceptual system (e.g., vision) to another (e.g., audition). If language understanding makes use of the same systems, then one might find a switching cost in the language task, too. In their experiment, participants determined if an object had a particular property (e.g., is a blender loud). Preceding this judgment was another judgment involving the same perceptual dimension (e.g., do leaves rustle) or a different dimension (e.g., are leaves green). Pecher et al. found a small but significant increase in the time needed to make the judgment when the perceptual dimension changed, consistent with the claim that perceptual systems are used in language tasks.

## Language and Emotional Systems

The case can also be made that language is opportunistic in regard to emotion. These data will be reviewed in a later section.

## Language and Neural Exploitation: Summary

The data from neuroscientific, developmental, and behavioral work are clear: language is not an encapsulated system. Instead, language partakes of neural systems that arose for other reasons, namely, control of action, perception (which is for the control of action), and emotion (which may also function primarily to control action, see Frijda, 2005). Thus, the case for neural exploitation is strong. What follows is a theoretical description of the integration between language and action.

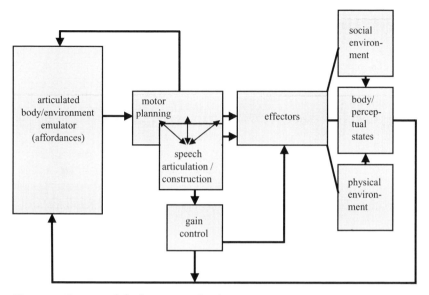

Figure 2.2. Framework for language and action.

A COGNITIVE SYSTEM FOR ACTION

## Overview

The IH can be combined with Gallese and Lakoff's (2005) idea of neural exploitation and the organizing principle that brains are for action. Begin with the proposition that the basic function of the cognitive system is to guide action using a variety of constraints such as those that arise from the body, the environment, and learning (see Figure 2.2). The sketch developed here is intended to demonstrate how language comprehension can arise from a system designed to control action and incorporating those constraints.

## Forward Models and Motor Control

How are various sources of constraints to be combined? In fact, this is the same problem continuously faced by the action system. Consider how even a simple action such as getting up to turn on a light switch requires combining constraints to produce coordination. Raising from the chair requires a consideration of muscle strengths, means of support, and center of gravity. Walking to the wall requires planning to avoid obstacles while reaching with the arm and forming the correct grip with the hand. These actions are controlled (rather than ballistic), but sensory information is sometimes too slow to provide useful feedback for control. One solution for control is the *forward model* (e.g., Grush, 2004; Wolpert & Kawato, 1998). In a forward model, motor commands are sent both to the effector systems and the model. The model computes the expected result of the motor commands and uses this result (along with sensory feedback) to adjust actions midstream.

Grush (2004) discusses several types of forward models. The one of greatest relevance here is the articulated body/environment emulator, a model that uses information about how the body is articulated, muscle masses, and dynamics, as well as objects in the environment (see Figure 2.2) to predict the effect of action. Although the emulator's primary function is the control of action, consonant with the notion of neural exploitation, it can also serve several other functions such as planning, imagery (Grush, 2004), and, as discussed here, language.

The content of the emulator consists of the affordances of the current situation, or as Grush puts it, "The emulator represents objects and the environment *as things engaged with* in certain ways as opposed to how they are considered apart from their role in the organism's environmental engagements" (p. 393, emphasis in original). Because affordances determine how action will change a situation, they are predictions (e.g., Gorniak, 2005) about the effects of action, and acting on an affordance is thus attempting to accomplish the goal of changing the environment in a particular way. Consequently, one can also characterize the content of the emulator as the system's current goals.

The content of the emulator continuously activates motor plans that control the effectors. (The translation of affordances into motor plans is often referred to as a *backward model*.) These motor plans are also fed back to the emulator, and the emulator uses these plans to predict the outcome of the movements, thus acting as a forward model. Because the emulator can change more quickly than the literal body (e.g., there is no need to move literal body masses), predictions derived from the emulator can be made quickly, and thus the model can be used to guide movements in the process of being performed.

The emulator must be updated by sensory information derived from the body (e.g., proprioception) and the environment to keep it attuned to reality. As discussed by Grush (2004), a Kalman filter is used in the updating to weight feedback from sensory systems (gain control in Figure 2.2). In noisy environments, sensory feedback should be less strongly weighted than in those environments in which the feedback is trustworthy.

Forward models of this sort are used to account for a growing literature in action control. Importantly, Grush (2004) also discusses how such models can account for motor imagery and visual imagery, and can contribute to perception (see also Wilson & Knoblich, 2005). For example, in imagery tasks, motor commands are sent to the emulator and the gain control inhibits the operation of the effector systems as well as reducing the degree to which the Kalman filter updates the emulator on the basis of literal bodily states. Thus, the emulator produces a prediction consisting of changes in the articulated body/environment emulator without a corresponding change in the environment.

## Language and Action

The IH proposes that language is comprehended using affordances. Here, those affordances are identified with the operation of the emulator. That is, it is supposed that language has exploited the forward model designed to integrate affordances and coordinate action to integrate ideas and coordinate action and speech.

In Figure 2.2, motor planning and speech articulation are depicted as overlapping systems. This symbolic overlap is meant to capture three ideas. First, there is literal overlap in the neural structures. Broca's area, which has traditionally been thought to control the speech articulators, is now known to also control hand action (Fadiga et al., 1995). Second, word learning (discussed later) is envisioned as a process of associating plans for speech articulation with other motor plans contributing to word meaning. For example, the meaning of the word *bottle* comes from the association of plans for articulating "bottle" with plans (within a particular context) for holding, lifting, and drinking. The multiple associations between speech articulation and motor plans are represented in the figure by the three arrows in the speech articulation area of the diagram. Note that these are double-headed arrows. Thus, motor plans such as those for picking up a bottle will also induce the pronunciation of the word (cf. Gentilucci et al., 2001). Third, the ability to conceptualize using language is based on exactly the same mechanism as used in the forward model of action control. That is, speech articulation planning controls the articulators, activates other motor plans (e.g., for arm movement), and these other motor plans are used to update the emulator. In this way, producing speech changes our own conceptualizations.

At times, we wish to talk without taking overt action other than speech articulation. Thus, language must be able to inhibit the output of effectors. In line with the principle of neural exploitation, it is proposed that language has access to the gain control needed for the operation of the Kalman filter and the modulation of effector systems. That is, language can reduce the extent to which the motor plans influence overt behavior. In the case of language, there is some direct evidence for this inhibition. Buccino et al. (2005) measured muscle evoked potentials (MEP) from the hand and leg while people listened to sentences about hand and leg actions. Upon listening to sentences describing hand actions, the MEPs measured from the hand were decreased relative to listening to sentences about leg actions, and the reverse was found for MEPs measured from the leg.

The indirect effect (through motor planning) of language on conceptualization has several interesting implications. For example, consider the temporal relation between language and gesture. Although the two are tightly linked, gestures most often appear before the associated words are spoken (McNeill, 1992). The reason for this is evident from Figure 2.2. Conceptualization (the emulator) has a direct effect on motor planning, and hence gestures can quickly reflect conceptualization. In contrast, before words can be articulated, the same conceptualization must first activate motor planning, which in turn activates plans for speech articulation, which only then can control the effectors for speech.

## Language Learning

### Mirror System and Word Learning

While not explicitly illustrated, mirror neuron systems play several critical roles in the system depicted in Figure 2.2. One role is the basic function of mirror systems in action recognition and anticipation. Thus, in watching a conspecific take action, the observer's motor system is activated to the extent that the observer can take the same action (cf. Calvo-Merino, Glaser, Grezes, Passignham, & Haggard, 2005). These mirror neurons are presumed to affect motor planning in Figure 2.2; hence, watching a conspecific will update the emulator and produce a new conceptualization of the state of the world.

Second, the action recognition mirror system, as well as the echo-mirror system, are essential for language learning. Parents almost always call attention to objects and actions when naming them for babies (Masur, 1997). The infant's action recognition mirror system will update the infant's conceptualization in exactly the correct way to the extent that the infant can perform the same action as the adult. At the same time, the infant's echo-mirror system activates articulatory gestures corresponding to the spoken words. Note that both sets of activation are likely to be in Broca's area. Thus, the stage is set for learning the meaning of the spoken words by connecting the motor plans activated by recognizing the parent's actions and the articulatory gestures needed to produce speech.

### Learning Abstract Syntactic Constructions

Of course, language is more complex than the utterance of single words. The framework in Figure 2.2 must also accommodate the production and comprehension of longer sequences, and importantly, sequences structured by syntax. How might abstract knowledge of the sort thought to underlie syntax arise from an action system? What follows is a developmental account that is consistent with at least some data (e.g., Tomasello, 2000). Imagine a situation in which an infant is holding a cup and the parent says, "Give me the cup." When the child does nothing, the parent repeats the sentence and takes the cup, thereby extending the infant's arm. With repetition, the child associates "give me..." with the arm motion of reaching out. In terms of Figure 2.2, on hearing "give me..." the echo-mirror system activates planning for the speech articulators and those plans are associated with the plans for extending the arm. Thus, the meaning of "give me..." becomes reaching out with the hand and releasing the object. Because this action-based meaning will be appropriate for a variety of objects (cups, bottles, spoons, toys), "give me..." becomes an abstract construction whose meaning corresponds to reaching out with the hand and giving up whatever might be in the hand.

The construction can be generalized further by varying the recipient of the transferred object. Suppose that the infant hears her father say, "Give Mama the cup." The recipient's name is used to guide attention to the recipient, thus ensuring that affordances of the recipient influence the emulator. Those affordances are used by motor planning to guide the reaching out to the named recipient. What prevents the giving action from being executed immediately on hearing "give"? The delay might be due to immaturity of the system. Another possibility is that the infant learns to delay the overt action of reaching out by learning to set the gain control. Thus, the giving action is activated on hearing "give" but the overt execution of the action is inhibited by gain control. When the recipient is named ("me" or "Mama") and those affordances also come into play, the action plan is more strongly activated and the action of reaching out is executed.

This action-based meaning of "give" can also ground more abstract transfer, such as giving ideas or compliments. In fact, the behavioral data seem to point to just such an account. As described previously, requiring a movement toward the body (to indicate that a sentence is sensible) interferes with judging sentences such as, "You told Liz the story" (Glenberg & Kaschak, 2002). Apparently, the meaning of the sentence is related to arm action away from the body (as if the meaning of "tell" were based on the meaning of "give"), and requiring motor activity in an incompatible direction interferes with comprehension.

## Constraints on Emulation

### Affordances

The emulator is the conceptualization of the current situation in terms of actions that can be taken, that is, a set of affordances. The affordances arise from the operation of perceptual systems sensitive to body morphology and physiology. For example, when a dangerous situation arises, body morphology limits options to running away or fighting but excludes the possibility of literally flying away. Because bodies are in constant flux due to physiological processes such as fatigue, hunger, and emotions, affordances will also change even with a relatively constant environment. Consider again a dangerous situation that arises as one is about to sit down to a meal. The perceived danger literally changes body physiology, which in turn changes the affordances. Thus, the food on the plate no longer affords eating. Instead, the situation now affords using the table as a buffer between the body and the danger, or perhaps throwing the food. More prosaically, consider a plate of food on your desk next to your computer. The situation appears to afford both work and eating. But as hunger grows, the environment-body system may no longer afford work. Instead, given the new (very hungry) body, the only affordances contributing to conceptualization and action are those related to eating.

Finally, as illustrated in Figure 2.2, once an action is generated, that action will itself change the body and possibly the environment and the social situation. Thus, taking one action changes the constraints for selecting the next action, and, in the process, creates a dynamic system (e.g., Van Orden, Holden, & Turvey, 2005).

### Learning

The arrows in Figure 2.2 represent learned relations. Thus, as noted previously, the relations between speech articulation and motor plans are learned. In addition, the relation between motor plans and the control of effectors is learned, as is the relation between motor plans and how the emulator should be updated (the operation of the forward model).

Adaptability of the forward model is required for tool use. That is, motor operations using a tool (e.g., stepping on a gas pedal) can have dramatically different effects than the same operation without the tool. Monkeys show some flexibility in learning the mapping between motor plan and change in the environment (e.g., Ferrari, Rozzi, & Fogassi, 2005), and humans seem to excel at this. Schwartz and Holton (2000) demonstrated a dramatic effect of learning different mappings between motor activity and emulator updating. In their experiment, participants mentally rotated three-dimensional shapes. The speed and accuracy of rotation was improved by simultaneously rotating the hand as if producing the desired rotation in the object. Perhaps more interestingly, Schwartz and Holton (2000) had the participants pull a string attached to a spool so that the spool would rotate the object. In one condition, the string was wound to produce a clockwise rotation upon pulling, and in another condition, the string produced a counterclockwise rotation. After observing the effect of the pulling action, participants were blindfolded and asked to mentally rotate the object while pulling the string. The same pulling action facilitated clockwise but not counterclockwise rotations in one condition, and had the opposite effect in the other condition.

## Mechanistic Action Selection

The system illustrated in Figure 2.2 is intended to act autonomously without a need for an ego, homunculus, or cognitive controller. The system takes into account bodily states and needs such as hunger. As the body changes, and hence its ability to interact with the world changes, the affordances used by the emulator are updated. Similarly, changes in the social situation will change the affordances in several ways. First, other people may change the body through inducing emotions. These emotions produce changes in the body that change affordances. Second, the actions of others, including conversation, will update the emulator because (as discussed previously) language is understood in terms of simulated action. Finally, learning processes (including long-term cultural learning) will promote some affordances above others. The end result is that the combination of body states, social states, interpretation of the situation provided by language, and possibilities promoted by learning will reduce the number of possible actions to one or a small handful. If a handful, then the language-motor planning-emulator loop cycles, thereby creating changes in the emulator until a single action, the one most consistent with the situation (as structured by the body, the environment, and learning) remains. Performing this action will change the environment, the body, and the social situation, as well as inducing new learning, all of which update the emulator and promote a new action.

### TESTS OF THE FRAMEWORK

The framework makes predictions in a variety of domains including perception, action, and development. Here three areas of research testing predictions regarding temporary states and language comprehension are highlighted. Note on the right of Figure 2.2 that changes in the environment, body, and social situation update the emulator affordances. Because those affordances are the ones most readily available for language understanding, temporary changes in the environment or the body should affect the speed of language comprehension processes. This general prediction is tested in three areas: spatial location of objects, effector fatigue, and emotional state.

## Changing Spatial Location of Objects

If an apple is located on the left, then the way to interact with it (e.g., reaching to the left) is different from interactions with it when it is on the right (e.g., reaching to the right). Thus, egocentric spatial location, although temporary, affects affordances. If language comprehension makes use of the same affordances that control action, then these temporary affordances should also affect language comprehension. To test this prediction, Glenberg, Becker, Klötzer, Kolanko, Müller, and Rinck (in preparation) asked participants to judge whether sentences were about ordinary objects (e.g., "The apple has a stem") or unusual objects (e.g., "The apple has an antenna"). Participants responded by moving the hand from a central key (pressed to view the sentence) to a key on either the left or the right. In addition, the ordinary objects themselves were located on the left or the right of the response keyboard.

Supposedly, affordances of these objects structure the emulator. If understanding a sentence about such an object (e.g., an apple on the left) uses these affordances, then reading a sentence such as, "The apple has a stem," should prepare one to act toward the left. Consequently, if the sensible-sentence response key is also on the left, responding should be faster than if the sensible-sentence response key is on the right. Such an interaction in response times between the location of the object referred to in the sentence and the location of the response key is referred to as an action/sentence compatibility effect, or ACE. We observed an ACE both when the sentences described action, such as, "Pick up the apple by the stem," and when the sentence did not refer to action, such as, "The apple has a stem." Thus, affordances are used in language comprehension whether or not the language specifically describes action.

An alternative account of the ACE is that it reflects spatial effects, not affordances. For example, Simon (1990) has demonstrated interference when an irrelevant spatial location (e.g., the location of the apple) conflicts with the location of the correct response. We were able to rule out this alternative in two ways. First, the ACE was not found when participants kept their hands on the left and right response keys; the effect was only found when the participant had to move their hands to the keys. Thus, spatial location of the response was not sufficient to generate an ACE. Second, the ACE was not found if the type of movement to make the response did not conflict with the putative affordances. In one experiment, participants grasped a joystick and moved it (by turning the wrist) to indicate the response. The wrist turn is quite different from the movement of the whole arm toward the object in preparation for interacting with the object. When participants used the joystick for responding, there was nary a hint of an ACE.

## Changing Effector State

The relation between a motor plan and its effect on the emulator must remain flexible. For example, the same motor plan will have different effects on the environment depending on effector fatigue, and hence changes to the emulator must reflect variables such as fatigue. If this reasoning is correct, and if language comprehension makes use of the same emulator, then fatiguing effectors should have an impact on language comprehension. In one set of experiments (Glenberg, Cattaneo, & Sato, in preparation) participants moved 600 beans, one at a time, either away from the body or toward the body. The goal was to differentially fatigue the action control systems and thereby re-program the emulator. For example, as the arm movements away from the body become literally fatigued, the emulator needs to be reprogrammed to predict a slowing of action. Will this change to the emulator differentially affect comprehension of language about action away from the body? In fact, after moving beans away from the body, people were slower to understand sentences such as "You gave Art the pen" and "You told Liz the story" that are understood by simulating action away from the body. In contrast, after moving beans toward the body, people were slower to understand sentences such as "Art gave the pen to you" and "Liz told you the story."

## Changing Emotional State

Havas, Glenberg, & Rinck (2007) report an effect of emotion on the ease of language comprehension. They induced emotions using the Strack et al. (1988) procedure: Participants were asked to hold a pen using only their teeth (inducing a smile and a pleasant emotional state) or lips (inducing a frown or pout and a negative emotional state). Concurrently, participants read sentences describing pleasant situations (e.g., "Your lover chases you play-fully around the bedroom") or unpleasant situations (e.g., "Your supervisor frowns as he hands you the sealed envelope"). The pleasant sentences were read more quickly when the participant was smiling than when frowning, and sentences describing negative situations were read more quickly when frowning than when smiling. Thus, temporary emotional states affect the process of language comprehension in ways specific to the emotion and the content of the sentence.

The framework in Figure 2.2 provides a way of understanding this effect. Through facial feedback, the pen manipulation generates an emotional state. That state has a literal effect on the body (e.g., changing heart rate), which in turn changes the affordances of the situation used by the emulator. For example, when the pen manipulation produces a happy bodily state, one is more likely to perceive affordances of one's lover that support activities such as playful chasing. In contrast, when the pen produces an unhappy state, one is more likely to perceive affordances of one's lover that support argumentation. Thus, congruence between the content of the sentence and the emotional state increases the probability that the affordances needed to simulate the sentence are readily available.

DISCUSSION

The goal of this chapter is to take seriously the claim that brains are for action. If this is the case, then it should be possible to show how other cognitive activities, such as language, can be closely related to action. This was done in three ways. First, a review of the literature indicated surprisingly strong relations between language and action in terms of neuroscientific, developmental, and behavioral research. Second, how a theoretical account developed for action, the Grush emulator, can be extended to language was demonstrated. In so doing, the account was used to explain empirical regularities, such as the temporal relation between language and gesture. Third, new predictions were derived from this account, and data confirming three of those predictions were briefly discussed. The remainder of this discussion focuses on the relation between this account and two others, further predictions, and a discussion of a practical implication.

## Relation to Barsalou and Prinz

This section discusses the relation between the framework in Figure 2.2 and two related proposals. Barsalou (1999) has proposed an account of cognition that is closely related to language activities but is not explicitly concerned with action. Prinz et al. have proposed an account of action that is not explicitly related to language.

Barsalou's (1999) proposal is that perceptual symbol systems underlie cognition. A perceptual symbol is composed of multimodal neural activity extracted from the perception of objects and actions. With repetition, perceptual symbols incorporate more information and come to take part in simulations, and these simulations correspond to knowledge. Barsalou discusses how such a system can become a fully functional conceptual system that supports categorization, propositional reasoning, productivity, and abstract concepts. The framework illustrated in Figure 2.2 is not meant as an alternative to perceptual symbol theory. Instead, Figure 2.2 can be viewed as a specification of those components of perceptual symbols that are related to action. Furthermore, Figure 2.2 identifies the simulation process with the use of forward models of motor control.

The framework in Figure 2.2 also captures some of the essential points of the ideomotor theory as developed by Prinz and colleagues (e.g., Hommel, Müsseler, Aschersleben, & Prinz, 2001). According to Prinz, there are three principles regarding the organization of action. The first is ideomotor mapping, namely, that there are learned associations between actions and their effects and between desired effects and the required actions. These two types of learned associations are represented by the arrow from motor planning to the emulator (the association between action and their effects) and the arrow between the emulator and the motor planning (the association between desired effects produced by acting on affordances and motor processes). The second principle is common coding, "a common representational domain for perception and action, with shared resources for perceiving events and planning actions." Affordances are just such a common representational domain. That is, affordances are derived from perceptual process and control action. The third principle is that the common code has a distal referent, rather than, say, coding in terms of muscle control. Affordances are also consistent with this third principle.

### Further Tests of the Proposal

Because so much is known about the motor system, linking language and action produces a rich source of predictions. Here are three currently untested predictions regarding localization, plasticity, and neuropsychology.

#### Mirror System Localization

The sketch in Figure 2.2 associates language function and the mirror neuron system for action recognition. The signature of this system is that the same neurons become activated when an animal literally takes action or when the animal watches another perform the same action. Thus, Figure 2.2 makes the prediction that the same neural tissue will be active when a person hears about an action as when that action is literally observed.

### Plasticity Induced by Practice

Classen, Liepert, Wise, Hallett, and Cohen (1998) used TMS of the motor cortex to induce a directional thumb movement. Participants then practiced thumb movements in a different direction. After practice, TMS evoked movement in the practiced direction. The authors suggest that practice induced a transient change in the cortical network representing the thumb. The framework in Figure 2.2 suggests that such practice would extend to language comprehension. For example, imagine that a participant practices arm movements associated with the transfer of objects away from the body. If this sort of practice updates motor planning and the emulator, then the practice should also selectively facilitate the comprehension of sentences about the transfer of objects to another (cf. Glenberg & Kaschak, 2002). Note that this prediction is the opposite of the prediction tested in Glenberg, Cattaneo, and Sato (in preparation). In that work we fatigued a particular action system and noted that this slowed comprehension of just those sentences requiring that action system for simulation.

### Movement Disorders and Language

Fiorio, Tinazzi, and Aglioti (2006) studied patients with focal hand dystonia (writer's cramp) performing mental rotation. The patients were asked to mentally rotate pictures of hands and feet. If mental rotation uses neural systems for action and the system for hand action is disordered, then one should find a selective impairment in the mental rotation of hands relative to feet. In fact, this is exactly what they found. The framework in Figure 2.2 suggests that these patients may also show a selective impairment in language about the hand. However, this prediction cannot be made with much confidence. If the patient has been living with the disorder for some time, then the patient may well have discovered other routes to the same linguistic understanding.

## Application to Education

Application of scientific theories to the development of technology provides a way of testing theories outside of the laboratory. For example, confidence in physical theory is justifiably increased by the fact that physicists can get a rocket to Mars, and confidence in biological theory is increased by the successes of medicine. Confidence in a psychological theory should increase when it can be demonstrated that the theory has success in an applied domain such as in educational practice. Toward that end, how a framework such as that in Figure 2.2 might be used to design a program of reading instruction has been investigated.

According to the proposal presented earlier, oral language learning progresses when the articulations corresponding to words become associated with motor programs corresponding to meanings. When learning to read, the child must associate the visual letters with the motor programs, or less directly, with the speech articulations that are themselves associated with the motor programs. However, unlike the situation with oral language, the components of the association are rarely made explicit during reading. That is, when the child is learning to read, the objects and actions being read about are usually not perceptually available. Even when the child succeeds in pronouncing a word from the printed letters, that pronunciation is often far from the fluid pronunciation of speech (and it is that fluid pronunciation that is associated with the motor programs). In this case, the connection between written language and meaning is only tenuous.

This analysis suggests that reading comprehension can be improved by tying it more closely to activity, and Glenberg, Gutierrez, Levin, Japuntich, and Kaschak (2004) devised just such a reading program. Children in the first and second grades read short texts about activities in particular locations, such as on a farm or in a house. In front of the children was a set of toys representing the location (e.g., the farm toys consisted of a toy barn, tractor, animals, and so on). In the physical manipulation condition, as the children read the story, they were prompted to act out the meaning of critical sentences using the toys. In the reread condition, children were prompted to reread the critical sentences. The physical manipulation condition resulted in memory and comprehension almost two standard deviations greater than in the reread condition. Furthermore, after children had practice with physical manipulation, they were able to imagine the manipulation of the toys, and this imagined manipulation produced similar benefits compared to silent rereading.

These findings are consistent with observations made by Montessori (1967):

"One of the greatest mistakes of our day is to think of movement by itself, as something apart from the higher functions . . . Mental development must be connected with movement and be dependent on it. It is vital that educational theory and practice should become informed by this idea...Watching a child makes it obvious that the development of his mind comes about through his movements...Mind and movement are parts of the same entity." (pp. 141–142)

## References

Barsalou, L. W. (1999). Perceptual symbol systems. *Behavioral and Brain Sciences, 22,* 577–660.

Borghi, A. M., Glenberg, A. M., & Kaschak, M. P. (2004). Putting words in perspective. *Memory & Cognition, 32,* 863–873.

Buccino, G., Riggio, L., Melli, G., Binkofski, F., Gallese, V., & Rizzolatti, G. (2005). Listening to action-related sentences modulates the activity of the motor system: A combined TMS and behavioral study. *Cognitive Brain Research,* Aug 2005.

Calvo-Merino, B., Glaser, D. E., Grezes, J., Passingham, R. E., & Haggard, P. (2005) Action observation and acquired motor skills: An FMRI study with expert dancers. *Cerebral Cortex, 15,* 1243–1249.

Chambers, C. G., Tanenhaus, M. K., & Magnuson, J. S. (2004). Actions and affordances in syntactic ambiguity resolution. *Journal of Experimental Psychology: Learning, Memory, and Cognition, 30,* 687–696.

Classen, J., Liepert, J., Wise, S. P., Hallett, M., & Cohen, L. G. (1998). Rapid plasticity of human cortical movement representation induced by practice. *Journal of Neurophysiology, 79,* 1117–1123.

De Vega, M. (in press). Levels of embodied meaning. From pointing to counterfactuals. In M. de Vega, A. M. Glenberg, & A. C. Graesser (Eds.), *Symbols, Embodiment, and Meaning.* Oxford: Oxford University Press.

De Vega, M., Robertson, D. A., Glenberg, A. M., Kaschak, M. P., & Rinck, M. (2004). On doing two things at once: Temporal constraints on actions in language comprehension. *Memory and Cognition, 32,* 1033–1043.

Fadiga, L., Craighero, L., Buccino, G., & Rizzolatti, G. (2002). Speech listening specifically modulates the excitability of tongue muscles: a TMS study. *European Journal of Neuroscience, 15,* 399–402.

Fadiga, L., Fogassi, L., Pavesi, G., & Rizzolatti, G. (1995). Motor facilitation during action observation: A magnetic stimulation study. *Journal of Neurophysiology, 73,* 2608–2611.

Ferrari, P. F., Rozzi, S., & Fogassi, L. (2005). Mirror neurons responding to observation of actions made with tools in monkey ventral premotor cortex. *Journal of Cognitive Neuroscience, 17,* 212–226.

Fiorio, M., Tinazzi, M., & Aglioti, S. M. (2006). Selective impairment of hand mental rotation in patients with focal hand dystonia. *Brain, 129,* 47–54.

Frijda N. (2005). Emotions and action. In A. S. R. Manstead, N. Frijda, & A. Fischer (Eds.), *Feelings and emotions: The Amsterdam symposium.* Cambridge, UK: Cambridge University Press.

Gallese, V., Keysers, C., & Rizzolatti, G. (2004). A unifying view of the basis of social cognition. *Trends in Cognitive Sciences, 8,* 396–403.

Gallese, V., & Lakoff, G. (2005). The brain's concepts: The role of the sensory-motor system in conceptual knowledge. *Cognitive Neuropsychology, 22,* 455–479.

Gentilucci, M., Benuzzi, F., Gangitano, M., & Grimaldi, S. (2001). Grasp with hand and mouth: A kinematic study on healthy subjects. *Journal of Neurophysiology, 86*, 1685–1699.

Gentilucci, M., Bernardis, P., Crisi, G., & Volta, R. D. (2006). Repetitive transcranial magnetic stimulation of Broca's area affects verbal responses to gesture observation. *Journal of Cognitive Neuroscience, 18*, 1059–1074.

Gibson, J. J. (1979). *The ecological approach to visual perception.* New York: Houghton Mifflin.

Glenberg, A. M. (1997). What memory is for. *Behavioral and Brain Sciences, 20*, 1–55.

Glenberg, A. M., Becker, R., Klötzer, S., Kolanko, L., Müller, S., & Rinck, M. (in preparation). Episodic affordances contribute to language comprehension.

Glenberg, A. M., Cattaneo, L., & Sato, M. (in preparation). Grounding abstract language in action? Beans!

Glenberg, A. M., Gutierrez, T., Levin, J. R., Japuntich, S., & Kaschak, M. P. (2004). Activity and imagined activity can enhance young children's reading comprehension. *Journal of Educational Psychology, 96*, 424–436.

Glenberg, A. M., & Kaschak, M. P. (2002). Grounding language in action. *Psychonomic Bulletin & Review, 9*, 558–565.

Glenberg, A. M., & Robertson, D. A. (1999). Indexical understanding of instructions. *Discourse Processes, 28*, 1–26.

Glenberg, A. M., & Robertson, D. A. (2000). Symbol grounding and meaning: A comparison of high-dimensional and embodied theories of meaning. *Journal of Memory and Language, 43*, 379–401.

Goldberg, A. E. (1995). *Constructions: A construction grammar approach to argument structure.* Chicago: University of Chicago Press.

Gorniak, P. (2005). The affordance-based concept. Unpublished doctoral dissertation, Massachusetts Institute of Technology, Cambridge, MA.

Grush, R. (2004). The emulation theory of representation: Motor control, imagery, and perception. *Behavioral and Brain Sciences, 27*, 377–442.

Hauk, O., Johnsrude, I., & Pulvermüller, F. (2004). Somatotopic representation of action words in human motor and premotor cortex. *Neuron, 41*(2), 301–307.

Havas, D. A., Glenberg, A. M., & Rinck, M. (2007). Emotion simulation during language comprehension. *Psychonomic Bulletin & Review, 14*, 436–441.

Hommel, B., Muesseler, J., Aschersleben, G., & Prinz, W. (2001). The theory of event coding (TEC): A framework for perception and action planning. *Behavioral and Brain Sciences, 24*, 849–878.

Iverson, J. M., & Goldin-Meadow, S. (2001). The resilience of gesture in talk: gesture in blind speakers and listeners. *Developmental Science, 4*, 416–422.

Kaschak, M. P., & Glenberg, A. M. (2000). Constructing meaning: The role of affordances and grammatical constructions in sentence comprehension. *Journal of Memory and Language, 43*, 508–529.

Kaschak, M. P., Madden, C. J., Therriault, D. J., Yaxley, R. H., Aveyard, M., Blanchard, A., & Zwaan, R. A. (2005). Perception of motion affects language processing. *Cognition, 94*(3), B79–B89.

Kelly, S. D., Barr, D. J., Church, R. B., & Lynch, K. (1999). Offering a hand to pragmatic understanding: The role of speech and gesture in comprehension and memory. *Journal of Memory and Language, 40*, 577–592.

Kohler, E., Keysers, C., Umiltà, M. A., Fogassi, L., Gallese, V., & Rizzolatti, G. (2002). Hearing sounds, understanding actions: Action representation in mirror neurons. *Science, 297*, 846–848.

Llinas, R. (2001). *The i of the vortex.* Cambridge, MA: MIT Press.

Matlock, T. (2004). Fictive motion as cognitive simulation. *Memory & Cognition, 32*, 1389–1400.

McNeill, D. (1992). *Hand and mind: What gestures reveal about thought.* Chicago: University of Chicago Press.

Masur, E. F. (1997). Maternal labeling of novel and familiar objects: Implications for children's development of lexical constraints. *Journal of Child Language, 24*, 427–439.

Montessori, M. (1967). *The absorbent mind.* Translated from the Italian by Claude A. Claremount. New York: Holt, Rinehart, & Winston.

Noice, T., & Noice, H. (2006). What studies of actors and acting can tell us about memory and cognitive functioning. *Current Directions in Psychological Science, 15*, 14–18.

Ochs, E., Gonzales, P., & Jacoby, S. (1996). "When I come down I'm in the domain state": Grammar and graphic representation in the interpretive activity of physicists. In E. A. Schegloff & S. A. Thompson (Eds.), *Interaction and grammar* (pp. 328–369). Cambridge, UK: Cambridge University Press.

Pecher, D., Zeelenberg, R., & Barsalou, L. W. (2003). Verifying different-modality properties for concepts produces switching costs. *Psychological Science, 14*, 119–125.

Pulvermüller, F. (2005). Brain mechanisms linking language and action. *Nature Reviews Neuroscience, 6*(7), 576–582.

Pulvermüller, F., Shtyrov, Y., & Ilmoniemi, R. J. (2003). Spatio-temporal patterns of neural language processing: An MEG study using minimum-norm current estimates. *Neuroimage, 20*, 1020–1025.

Rizzolatti, G., & Arbib, M. A. (1998). Language within our grasp. *Trends in Neuroscience, 21*, 188–194.

Rizzolatti, G., & Craighero, L. (2004). The mirror-neuron system. *Annual Review of Neuroscience, 27*, 169–192.

Roth, W.-M. (1999). Discourse and agency in school science laboratories. *Discourse Processes, 28*, 27–60.

Schwartz, D. L., & Holton, D. L. (2000). Tool use and the effect of action on the imagination. *Journal of Experimental Psychology: Learning, Memory, and Cognition, 26*, 1655–1665.

Simon, J. R. (1990). The effects of an irrelevant directional cue on human information processing. In R. W. Proctor & T. G. Reeve (Eds.), *Stimulus-response compatibility: An integrated perspective* (pp. 31–86). Amsterdam: North-Holland.

Smith, L. B. (2005). Action alters shape categories. *Cognitive Science, 29*, 665–679.

Strack, F., Martin, L. L., & Stepper, S. (1988). Inhibiting and facilitating condition of facial expressions: A non-obtrusive test of the facial feedback hypothesis. *Journal of Personality and Social Psychology, 54*, 768–777.

Talmy, L. (1996). Fictive motion in language and "ception." In P. Bloom, M. A. Peterson, L. Nadel, & M. F. Garrett (Eds.), *Language and space* (pp. 211–276). Cambridge, MA: MIT Press.

Tettamanti, M., Buccino, G., Saccuman, M. C., Gallese, V., Danna, M., Scifo, P. Fazio, F., Rizzolatti, G., Cappa, S. F., & Perani, D. (2005). Listening to action-related sentences activates fronto-parietal motor circuits. *Journal of Cognitive Neuroscience, 17*, 273–281.

Tomasello, M. (2000). Do young children have adult syntactic competence? *Cognition, 74*, 209–253.

Valenzeno, L., Alibali, M. W., & Klatzky, R. (2003). Teachers' gestures facilitate students' learning: A lesson in symmetry. *Contemporary Educational Psychology, 28*(2): 187–204.

Van Orden, G. C., Holden, J G., & Turvey, M. T. (2005). Human cognition and 1/f scaling. *Journal of Experimental Psychology: General, 134*, 117–123.

Wilson, M., & Knoblich, G. (2005). The case for motor involvement in perceiving conspecifics. *Psychological Bulletin, 131*, 460–473.

Wolpert, D. M., & Kawato, M. (1998). Multiple paired forward and inverse models for motor control. *Neural Networks, 11*, 1317–1329.

# 3     Brain Embodiment of Category-Specific Semantic Memory Circuits

## Friedemann Pulvermüller

At present, abstract symbolic and embodied theories of semantic and conceptual processing compete for the minds of cognitive scientists. Are concepts built in interaction with the world, from perceptual information? Or are they inborn and only in a very distant relationship with the "reality," which contacts the thinking organs (if at all) only via long axons and unreliable sensory organs? Can an abstract thought be built from sensory experience – or would there rather be need for other ingredients to construct abstraction? These are questions that heated the debate in ancient Greece – (cf. Plato's and Aristotle's positions) – and are being warmed up in contemporary cognitive and brain science. Can we add anything new? We have a vast number of nice brain pictures to show – pictures that indicate brain parts active when people think, speak, listen, and understand. But a colored picture is not always easily converted into a thousand words, let alone a new insight. Here, the embodiment question will be addressed on the basis of new evidence from cognitive neuroscience in the hope that the brain pictures, especially the dynamic ones, might speak to the issues – or more modestly, might make a significant contribution to the cognitive debate.

## EMBODIED ACTION-PERCEPTION NETWORKS FOR STORING SEMANTIC INFORMATION: THE CASE OF CATEGORY-SPECIFICITY

Where is word meaning represented and processed in the human brain? This question has been discussed controversially since 19th-century neurologists postulated a "concept center" in the brain that was thought to store the meanings of words (Lichtheim, 1885). Today, the cortical loci proposed for a center uniquely devoted to semantic processing range from the inferior frontal cortex (Bookheimer, 2002; Posner & Pavese, 1998) to the anterior, inferior, superior, or posterior left temporal cortex (Hickok & Poeppel, 2004; Patterson & Hodges, 2001; Price, 2000; Scott & Johnsrude, 2003). Others have proposed that the entire left fronto-temporal cortex is a region equally devoted to semantics (Tyler & Moss, 2001), or that the parahippocampal gyrus (Tyler et al., 2004) or the occipital cortex (Skrandies, 1999) are particularly relevant. As there is hardly any area in the left language-dominant hemisphere for which there is no statement that it should house the semantic binding center, these views are difficult to reconcile with each other (see Pulvermüller, 1999). Is there a way to resolve this unfortunate diversity of opinions?

A way out might be pointed by approaches to category-specific seman-tic processes (Daniele, Giustolisi, Silveri, Colosimo, & Gainotti, 1994; Humphreys & Forde, 2001; Warrington & McCarthy, 1983; Warrington & Shallice, 1984). The idea here is that different types of concepts, and different types of word meaning, draw upon different parts of the brain. Hearing the word "crocodile" frequently together with certain visual perceptions may lead to a strengthening of connections between the activated visual and language-related neurons. Specific form and color detectors in the primary cortex and further neurons responding to more complex features of the perceived gestalt higher in the inferior temporal stream of visual object processing will become active together with neurons in the perisylvian language areas that process the word form. These neurons would bind into distributed networks now implementing word forms together with aspects of their referential seman-tics. In contrast, the learning of an action word, such as "ambulate," critically involves linking an action type to a word form. In many cases, action words are learned in infancy when the child performs an action and the caretaker uses a sentence including an action word describing the action (Tomasello & Kruger, 1992). As the brain circuits for controlling actions are in motor, premotor, and prefrontal cortex, it is clear that, in this case, correlated acti-vation should bind perisylvian language networks to fronto-central circuits processing actions.

The cell assembly model and other theories of perception and action-related category-specificity predict differential distribution of the neu-ron populations organizing action- and object-related words and simi-lar differences can be postulated for other semantic categories (Figure 3.1; Pulvermüller, 1996, 1999). Many nouns refer to visually perceivable objects and are therefore characterized by strong semantic links to visual informa-tion, whereas most verbs are action verbs and link semantically to action knowledge. Like action verbs, nouns that refer to tools are usually also rated by subjects to be semantically linked to actions, and a large number of ani-mal names are rated to be primarily related to visual information (Preissl, Pulvermüller, Lutzenberger, & Birbaumer, 1995; Pulvermüller, Lutzenberger,

action word             visually-related word

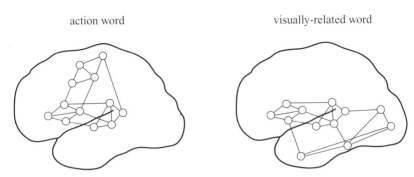

Figure 3.1. A brain-based model of category-specific processing of words with different semantics. Words semantically related to actions may be cortically processed by distributed neuron ensembles linking together word forms and action programs. Words referring to objects that are perceived through the visual modality may be processed by neuron sets distributed over language areas and the visual system (Pulvermüller, 1996).

& Preissl, 1999; Pulvermüller, Mohr, & Schleichert, 1999). A range of neuroimaging studies using electroencephalography (EEG), positron emission tomography (PET), functional magnetic resonance imaging (fMRI), and magnetoencephalography (MEG) techniques found evidence for category-specific activation in the human brain for the processing of action- and visually-related words and concepts (e.g., Cappa, Perani, Schnur, Tettamanti, & Fazio, 1998; Chao, Haxby, & Martin, 1999; Kiefer, 2001; Preissl et al., 1995; Pulvermüller, Lutzenberger, & Preissl, 1999; Pulvermüller, Mohr, & Schleichert, 1999). The results were largely consistent with the model of semantic category-specificity. The processing of action-related words, be they action verbs, tool names, or other lexical items with clear semantic relationship to actions of the speaker's own body, tended to activate the fronto-central cortex, including inferior frontal or premotor areas, more strongly than words without strong semantic action links. The same was found for temporo-occipital areas involved in motion perception. On the other hand, words with visual semantics tended to activate the visual and inferior temporal cortex or temporal pole more strongly than action-related words. This differential activation was interpreted as evidence for semantic category-specificity in the human brain (Martin & Chao, 2001; Pulvermüller, 1999).

## SOME PROBLEMS WITH SEMANTIC CATEGORY-SPECIFICITY

Indeed, the results from metabolic and neurophysiological imaging demonstrate the activation of neuronal assemblies with different cortical distributions in the processing of action- and visually-related words and concepts.

However, it has been asked whether the reason for the differential activation observed would necessarily be semantic or conceptual in nature. Could there be alternative explanations?

Although the broad majority of the imaging studies of category-specificity support the idea that semantic factors are crucial, there is work that could not provide converging evidence (Devlin et al., 2002; Tyler, Russell, Fadili, & Moss, 2001). These studies used particularly well-matched stimuli, so that word length, frequency, and other psycholinguistic factors could not account for any possible differences in brain activation. Therefore, these authors argued that these factors might account for differences between "semantic" categories reported previously. Although some earlier studies reporting semantic category differences performed meticulous stimulus matching for a range of psycholinguistic factors, word length and frequency included (Kiefer, 2001; Preissl et al., 1995; Pulvermüller, Lutzenberger, & Preissl, 1999; Pulvermüller, Mohr, & Schleichert, 1999), the majority of studies did not control for these factors. As pointed out previously (Bird, Lambon-Ralph, Patterson, & Hodges, 2000), nouns tend to have more highly imageable meaning than verbs, whereas verbs tend to have higher word frequency. Any difference in brain activation, and also any differential vulnerability to cortical lesion, could thus be explained as an imageability-frequency dissociation, rather than in terms of semantic categories. Similarly, animals tend to be more similar to each other than tools from a visual and also conceptual point of view, and it has therefore been argued that perceptual and conceptual structure could contribute to the explanation of category dissociations (Humphreys & Riddoch, 1987; Rogers et al., 2004; Tyler, Moss, Durrant-Peatfield, & Levy, 2000). On these grounds, at least some evidence for category-specificity has therefore been criticized as being not fully convincing.

What makes things worse is that predictions on where category-specific activation should occur in the brain have not always been very precise. Whereas rough estimates, such as the prediction that action semantics should involve frontal areas and visual semantics temporo-occipital ones, could be provided and actually confirmed, the more precise localization was sometimes surprising and not a priori predictable. For example, semantic information related to the processing of color and motion information semantically linked to words and pictures was reported to occur at about 2 cm anterior to the areas known to respond maximally to color or motion, respectively (Martin, Haxby, Lalonde, Wiggs, & Ungerleider, 1995). It would be desirable to have evidence for category-specific semantic activation at precisely the locus a brain-based action-perception theory of semantic processing would predict. Such a perspective is opened by looking at subtypes of action words.

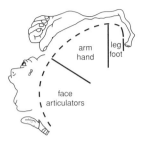

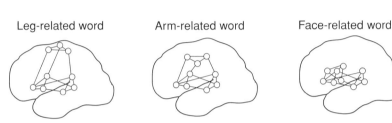

Figure 3.2. Semantic somatotopy model of action word processing: Distributed neuronal assemblies bind information about word forms and the actions they refer to semantically. Because action words can relate to different parts of the body (examples: *lick, pick, kick*), the cortical distributions of their perception-action networks differ between each other (Pulvermüller, 2001). The inset shows the somatotopy of the primary motor cortex as revealed by Penfield and colleagues (Penfield & Boldrey, 1937).

## CORTICAL EMBODIMENT OF SEMANTICS: THE CASE OF ACTION WORDS

Action words are defined by abstract semantic links between language elements and information about actions. These words refer to actions, and the neurons that process the word forms are likely interwoven with neurons controlling actions. The motor cortex is organized in a somatotopic fashion, with the mouth and articulators represented close to the sylvian fissure, the arms and hand at dorsolateral sites, and the foot and leg projected to the vertex and interhemispheric sulcus (Figure 3.2; Penfield & Rasmussen, 1950). Additional somatotopic maps exist in the fronto-central cortex (He, Dum, & Strick, 1993), among which a prominent one lies in the premotor cortex in the lateral precentral gyrus and resembles the map in the primary motor cortex (Matelli, Camarda, Glickstein, & Rizzolatti, 1986; Rizzolatti & Luppino, 2001). As many action words are preferably used to refer to movements of the face or articulators, arm or hand, or leg or foot, the distributed neuronal ensembles would therefore include semantic neurons in perisylvian (face words), lateral (arm words), or dorsal (leg words) motor and premotor cortex (Pulvermüller,

1999). This is the essence of the somatotopy-of-action-word model, which implies differently distributed networks for the English words *lick, pick*, and *kick* (Figure 3.2). The model allows for general predictions on action-word-related cortical activity within the limits of the well-known inter-individual variation of cortical maps, most notably as a result of practice-related reorganization (Elbert, Pantev, Wienbruch, Rockstroh, & Taub, 1995), and is open to further elaboration taking into account additional mapping rules, for example, the topography of coordinated actions in a body-centered workspace suggested by recent work (Graziano, Taylor, & Moore, 2002).

Crucial predictions of the semantic somatotopy model is that perception of spoken or written action words should activate cortical areas involved in action control and execution in a category-specific somatotopic fashion, depending on the semantics of the action words. As the cortical areas of action control and execution can be defined experimentally, one could in principle use such action localizer experiments to predict exactly where semantic activation should occur for different aspects of action-related meaning.

In functional imaging experiments, elementary repetitive movements of single body parts activate the motor and premotor cortex. For example, Hauk et al. reported fMRI data showing that tongue, finger, and foot movements lead to the somatotopic activation pattern (Hauk, Johnsrude, & Pulvermüller, 2004). When the same subjects were instructed to silently read action words related to the face, arm, and leg that were otherwise matched for important psycholinguistic variables (such as word frequency, length, and imageability), a similar pattern of activation emerged along the motor strip (Hauk et al., 2004). Consistent with earlier findings, all words equally activated areas in the temporal cortex and also in the inferior frontal cortex (Pulvermüller, Shtyrov, & Ilmoniemi, 2003; Wilson, Saygin, Sereno, & Iacoboni, 2004; Zatorre, Evans, Meyer, & Gjedde, 1992). The additional category-specific somatotopic activation in response to face-, arm-, and leg-related words seen in the motor system was close to and overlapped with the motor and premotor representations for specific body part movements obtained in the motor localizer tasks. These results indicate that specific action representations are activated in action word understanding. The fact that the locus of semantic activation could be predicted by a theory of perception-action networks provides strong evidence for this theory in particular and for the embodiment of aspects of semantics in action mechanisms in general.

A similar experiment was carried out with action words embedded into spoken sentences. In this case, subjects heard action descriptions such as, "The boy kicked the ball" or "The man wrote the letter," while their brain metabolism was monitored (Tettamanti et al., 2005). Specific premotor areas reflecting the differential involvement of body part information in the semantic analysis of the language input were again found active. Taken together, these fMRI results indicate that somatotopic activation of motor circuits reflects aspects of word and sentence meaning, and that such activation can be elicited by spoken and by written language.

## SOMATOTOPIC SEMANTIC ACTIVATION: COMPREHENSION OR POST-COMPREHENSION INFERENCE?

Although language-related somatotopic cortical activation could be demonstrated, the low temporal resolution of hemodynamic imaging makes it impossible to decide between two interpretations of this finding: One possibility is that the activation of specific action-related networks directly reflects action word recognition and comprehension, as the somatotopy-of-action-word model would suggest. An alternative possibility has been pointed out by Glenberg and Kaschak in the context of behavioral work on embodiment (Glenberg & Kaschak, 2002). It is possible that thoughts about actions actually follow the comprehension process and behavioral, but also brain-physiological, effects relate to such "post-understanding inference." Inferences would be triggered by the comprehension of a word or sentence but would not necessarily reflect processes intrinsically linked to language comprehension. Importantly, earlier fMRI research has shown that observation of action related pictures, but also mere voluntary mental imagery of actions, can activate motor and premotor cortex in a somatotopic fashion (Buccino et al., 2001; Jeannerod & Frak, 1999). Therefore, it is important to clarify whether motor system activation to action-related language processing reflects the comprehension process per se or rather a later stage following language comprehension. Apart from mental imagery of actions, possible post-comprehension processes include planning of action execution, recalling an action performed earlier, and reprocessing the meaning of the language stimulus.

How is it possible to separate comprehension processes from subsequent inferences and other mental activities? It is proposed that brain processes reflecting comprehension can be characterized as (1) *immediate*, (2) *automatic*, and (3) *functionally relevant*.

(1) *Immediacy.* Early effects of lexical and semantic processing are known to occur around 100 to 200 ms after critical stimulus information comes in (Pulvermüller & Shtyrov, 2006; Sereno, Rayner & Posner, 1998 #3564; Pulvermüller, 1996). In contrast, late post-lexical

meaning-related processes are reflected by late components of the event-related potential (ERP) and field, which are maximal around 400 ms after word onset (Holcomb & Neville, 1990). If the activation of motor areas is related to semantic processes intrinsically tied to word form access, it should take place within the first 200 ms after stimulus information allows for the unique identification of an incoming word.

(2) *Automaticity.* When seeing or hearing a word, it is hardly possible to avoid understanding its content, and comprehension might even occur without intentionally attending to the stimuli. So brain processes reflecting comprehension might be expected to persist under distraction, when the subjects' attention is directed away from the critical language stimuli.

(3) *Functional relevance.* If action word presentation leads to the specific activation of motor systems relevant to word processing, one may even expect that a change of the functional state of these motor systems leads to a measurable effect on the processing of words semantically related to actions.

However, if somatotopic activation of motor systems did reflect a post-comprehension process, it can be late (substantially greater than 200 ms) and absent under distraction, and function state changes in the motor system would be without effect on word processing.

A series of experiments was conducted to investigate these three issues. To reveal the time course of cortical activation in action word recognition and find out whether specific motor areas are sparked immediately or after some delay, neurophysiological experiments were conducted. Experiments using ERPs looking at the silent reading of face, arm, and leg words showed that category-specific differential activation was present about 200 ms after word onset (Hauk & Pulvermüller, 2004). Consistent with the fMRI results, distributed source localization performed on stimulus-triggered ERPs revealed an inferior frontal source that was strongest for face-related words and a superior central source that was maximal for leg-related items (Hauk & Pulvermüller, 2004). This dissociation in brain activity patterns supports the notion of stimulus-triggered early lexico-semantic processes. To investigate whether motor preparation processes codetermined this effect, experiments were performed in which the same response – a button press with the left index finger – was required for all words. The early activation difference between face- and leg-related words persisted, indicating that lexico-semantic processes rather than post-lexical motor preparations were reflected

(Pulvermüller, Härle, & Hummel, 2000). This speaks in favor of an interpretation of motor activation in terms of comprehension processes.

The earliness of word category-specific semantic activation along the sensorimotor cortex in passive reading tasks might suggest that this feature might be automatic. To further investigate this possibility, subjects were actively distracted while action words were being presented and brain responses were measured (Pulvermüller, Shtyrov, & Ilmoniemi, 2005; Shtyrov, Hauk, & Pulvermüller, 2004). Subjects were instructed to watch a silent video film and ignore the language input while spoken face-, arm- and leg-related action words were presented. Care was taken to exactly control for physical and psycholinguistic features of the word material. For example, the Finnish words *hotki* ("eat") and *potki* ("kick") – which included the same recording of the syllable [*kI*] spliced to the end of each word's first syllable – were compared. In this way, any differential activation elicited by the critical final syllable [*kI*] in the context of [*hot*] or [*pot*] can be uniquely attributed to its lexicosemantic context. MEG results showed that a mismatch negativity (Näätänen, Tervaniemi, Sussman, Paavilainen, & Winkler, 2001) maximal at 100 to 200 ms after onset of the critical syllable was elicited by face/arm and leg word contexts (Figure 3.3). Relatively stronger activation was present in the left inferior frontal cortex for the face/arm-related word, but significantly stronger activation was seen in superior central areas, close to the cortical leg representation, for the leg-related word (Pulvermüller, Shtyrov, & Ilmoniemi, 2005). These MEG results were confirmed with a different method, EEG, using words from different languages, for example, the English word pair *pick* versus *kick* (Shtyrov et al., 2004). It is remarkable that the activation peak of the superior central source followed that of the inferior frontal source with an average delay of only 30 ms, consistent with the spread of activation being mediated by fast-conducting cortico-cortical fibers between the perisylvian and dorsal sensorimotor cortex. This speaks in favor of the automatic activation of motor areas in action word recognition, and therefore further strengthens the view that this activation reflects comprehension. It appears striking that differential activation of body-part representations in sensorimotor cortex to action word subcategories was seen across a range of cognitive paradigms, including lexical decision, attentive silent reading, and oddball paradigm under distraction. This further supports the idea that word-related, rather than task or strategy-dependent, mechanisms are being tapped into.

Even if action word processing sparks the motor system in a specific somatotopic fashion, this still does not necessarily imply that the motor and premotor cortex influence the processing of action words. Different parts of the

Face/arm word        Leg word

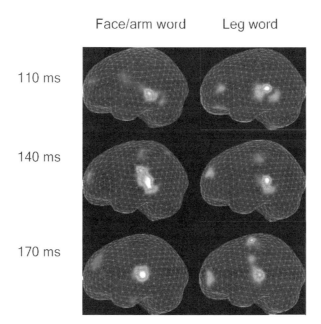

Figure 3.3. Cortical activation (MEG) elicited by face-/arm- (left) and leg-related words (right) at different times after spoken action words could be uniquely recognized. Note the slight upward movement of the inferior central source for the face/arm word and the delayed appearance of the superior central source for the leg word. These activation time courses may reflect the traveling of neuronal activity in distributed neuronal assemblies that represent and process words with different action-related meanings (after Pulvermüller, Shtyrov, & Ilmoniemi, 2005).

motor system were therefore stimulated with weak magnetic pulses while subjects had to process action words in a lexical decision task (Pulvermüller, Hauk, Nikulin, & Ilmoniemi, 2005). To minimize interference between word-related activation of the motor system and response execution processes, lip movements were required while arm- and leg-related words were presented. Sub-threshold transcranial magnetic stimulation (TMS) applied to the arm representation in the left hemisphere, where strong magnetic pulses elicited muscle contractions in the right hand, led to faster processing of arm words relative to leg words, whereas the opposite pattern of faster leg than arm word responses emerged when TMS was applied to the cortical leg area (Pulvermüller, Hauk, Nikulin, & Ilmoniemi, 2005). Processing speed did not differ between stimulus word groups in control conditions in which ineffective "sham" stimulation or TMS to the right hemisphere was applied. This shows a specific influence of activity in the motor system on the processing of action-related words.

Further evidence for specific functional links between the cortical language and action systems comes from TMS-induced motor responses (Fadiga, Craighero, Buccino, & Rizzolatti, 2002). Listening to Italian sentences describing actions performed with the arm or leg differentially modulates the motor responses brought about by magnetic stimulation of the hand and leg motor cortex (Buccino et al., 2005). It appears that effective specific connections of language and action systems can be documented for spoken or written language at the word and sentence levels, and for a variety of languages (English, Italian, German, Finnish) using a variety of neuroscience methods (fMRI, MEG, EEG, TMS).

In summary, these experiments show that the activation of motor systems of the cortex occurs early in action word processing, is automatic to some degree, and has a semantically specific functional influence on the processing of action words. This provides brain-based support for the idea that motor area activation is related to comprehension of the referential semantic meaning of action words. In the wider context of a theory of embodiment of conceptual and semantic processing, the conclusion is that comprehension processes are related to, or embodied in, access to action information. It is noteworthy that neuroscientific evidence was crucial in revealing this (Pulvermüller, 2005). However, it is equally true that behavioral results are consistent with these conclusions and further strengthen the embodiment of language in action-perception mechanisms (Borghi, Glenberg, & Kaschak, 2004; Boulenger, Paulignan, Roy, Jeannerod, & Nazir, 2006; de Vega, Robertson, Glenberg, Kaschak, & Rinck, 2004; Gentilucci, Benuzzi, Bertolani, Daprati, & Gangitano, 2000; Glenberg & Kaschak, 2002).

## THEORETICAL ISSUES: CAN THE MOTOR CORTEX MAP ASPECTS OF SEMANTICS?

One may question the proposal that activity in the motor system can reflect semantic processes for principled theoretical reasons. The idea that there should be a specific center for semantics is still dominating (although there is little agreement between researchers about where the semantics area is situated; see paragraph on one or many semantics centers following). Areas that deal with the trivialities of motor movements, and equally those involved in elementary visual feature processing, are therefore thought by some to be incapable of contributing also to the higher processes one might be inclined to reserve for humans. In this context, it is important to point to the strong evidence that activation in motor systems directly reflects aspects of semantics. Evidence that semantic features of words are reflected in the focal brain activation in different parts of sensorimotor cortex comes from MEG work on action words: There was a significant correlation between local source strengths in inferior arm-/face-related and dorsal leg-related areas of sensorimotor cortex and the semantic ratings of individual words obtained from study participants (Pulvermüller, Shtyrov, & Ilmoniemi, 2005). This means that the subjects' semantic ratings were reflected by local activation strength and leaves little room for interpretations of other than a semantic nature.

Even though the action-related and visually-related features discussed, and the associative learning mechanisms binding them to language materials, may not account for all semantic features of relevant word-related concepts, it appears clear that they reflect critical aspects of word meaning (Pulvermüller, 1999): Crocodiles are defined by certain properties, including form and color features, in the same way as the concepts of walking or ambulating are crucially linked to moving one's legs. Certainly, there is room for derived – including metaphorical – usage. As a big fish might be called the "crocodile of its fish tank" even if it is not green, one may speak of walking on one's hands or a stroll through the mind (thus ignoring the feature of body-part relatedness). One may even tell a story about a crocodile with an artificial heart and kidneys, although it is generally agreed upon (following Frege) that these ingredients are part of the definition of an animal – or, more appropriately, a higher vertebrate (Frege, 1966). That writing is related to the hand may therefore be considered an analytical truth, in the same way as a crocodile is defined as having a heart, and in spite of the fact that it is possible to write in the sand with one's foot. This may simply be considered a modified type of writing, as the post-surgery crocodile is a modified crocodile. An instance of a heartless crocodile and leg-related writing is possible, but probably closer to metaphorical usage of these words than to their regular application. It seems safe to include perceptual properties such as green-ness and action aspects such as hand-relatedness in the set of core semantic and conceptual features. In this context, it must be noted that these core features are not necessarily shared by *all* members of a semantic class (family resemblance argument, see Wittgenstein, 1953; Rosch, 1976; Barsalou, 1982).

A further point has sometimes been mentioned in the context of embodied approaches to semantics, the cell assembly model included. The idea that word-world correlation provides a significant explanation of the acquisition of word meanings has been criticized because it is well known that only a minority of words are actually being learned in the context of reference object perception and action execution (Kintsch, 1974, 1998). However, after action-perception learning of aspects of word meaning has taken place for a sufficiently large set of words, it becomes feasible to learn semantic properties "parasitically" when words occur together in strings, sentences, or texts. A neuroscientific basis for this "parasitic semantic learning" might lie in the overlap of word-related cell assemblies in the perisylvian language areas and the lack of semantic neurons related to action and perception information outside perisylvian space of the networks processing new words with unknown semantic features (Pulvermüller, 2002). In this case, a new word would activate its form-related perisylvian cell assembly, whereas neurons outside perisylvian space processing aspects of the semantic of context words are still active. The correlated activation of the semantic neurons of context words and the form-related perisylvian neurons of the new word may lead to linkage of semantic features to the new word form. This provides a potential basis of second order semantic learning and provides a putative neuroscience explanation for why correlation approaches to word meaning are successful in modeling semantic relationships between words (Kintsch, 2002; Landauer & Dumais, 1997). However, it is important to note that this mechanism can only succeed if a sufficiently large set of semantic features and words is learned through correlation of perception, action, and language-form features in the first place. Otherwise, what Searle called the Chinese room argument, implying that semantic information cannot emerge from correlation patterns between symbols, cannot be overcome (Searle, 1990). Action-perception correlation learning and word-word correlation learning are both indispensable for semantic learning of large vocabularies.

The time course of semantic activation in action word recognition was on a rather short scale. Relevant areas were seen to be active already within 200 ms after critical stimulus information came in (Pulvermüller, Shtyrov, & Ilmoniemi, 2005; Shtyrov et al., 2004). This suggests early semantic activation, as early as the earliest processes reflecting phonological or lexical information access (Hauk, Davis, Ford, Pulvermüller, & Marslen-Wilson, 2006; Obleser, Lahiri, & Eulitz, 2003; Shtyrov, Pihko, & Pulvermüller, 2005). The early neurophysiological reflection of semantic brain processes does not imply that meaning processing is restricted to the first 200 ms after a word can be identified. There is ample evidence for neurophysiological correlates of semantic processes that take place later (Coles & Rugg, 1995). These later processes may follow upon the early semantic access processes and may reflect reinterpretation, which is especially important in circumstances where the context or other factors make comprehension difficult.

ABSTRACTION FROM A BRAIN PERSPECTIVE

Although these results demonstrate that action words activate the cortical system for action processing in a somatotopic fashion and that this somatotopy reflects word meaning, they do not imply that all aspects of the meaning of a word are necessarily reflected in the brain activation pattern that it elicits. It is possible to separate brain correlates of semantic features specifying face-, arm-, and leg-relatedness, or, in the visual domain, of color and form features (Moscoso Del Prado Martin, Hauk, & Pulvermüller, 2006; Pulvermüller & Hauk, 2006; Simmons, Beauchamp, McRae, Martin & Barsalou, 2007). It became even possible to provide brain support for the grounding of words referring to odors in olfactory sensation and evaluation mechanisms in brain areas processing olfactory and emotion-related information (González et al., 2006). However, for other semantic features, the idea that their meaning can be extracted from sensory input, or deduced from output patterns, is more difficult to maintain. Although the question how an embodiment perspective would explain abstraction processes has frequently been addressed (Barsalou, 1999, 2003; Lakoff, 1987), it is still not clear whether all semantic features can – and must – be extracted from input-output patterns.

A brain perspective might help solve aspects of this issue. There are highly abstract concepts for which a deduction from sensory input is difficult to construe. Barsalou grounds the meaning of the word "or" in the alteration of the visual simulations of objects (Barsalou, 1999). However, if this view is correct, one might claim that the disjunction concept would, in fact, be grounded in the alteration mechanism, which would allow the brain to switch on and off alternative representations alternately. Looking at the brain theory literature, it is actually very clear that any brain, even a very primitive nervous system, is equipped with mechanisms for calculating disjunction, conjunction, negation, and other logical operations. This was the content of an early article by McCulloch and Pitts entitled, "A logical calculus of ideas immanent in nervous activity" (McCulloch & Pitts, 1943) and has since inspired much subsequent work (e.g., Kleene, 1956; Schnelle, 1996). Its main points still hold true, although neuron models have significantly improved since the proposal was first made. These authors pointed out that by wiring two neurons onto a third one and by adjusting the activation threshold of number three, conjunction and disjunction can be computed. Negation, identity, and either-or computations would be equally straightforward (requiring slightly more or less neuronal material; Figure 3.4). These examples demonstrate that our brain comes with built-in mechanisms relevant for abstract semantic

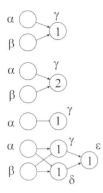

Figure 3.4. Logical circuits immanent to a network of neurons as discussed by McCulloch and Pitts (McCulloch & Pitts, 1943). If two neurons project to a third neuron, the activation threshold of the third neuron will determine whether it acts like a logical element symbolizing "or" (uppermost diagram) or "and" (second from top). Circuits symbolizing "not" and "either-or" can also be implemented. The arrows represent excitatory and *t*-shaped line endings for inhibitory connections. Numbers indicate activation thresholds (after Pulvermüller, 2003).

processing. There is no need to construe the semantics of "and" and "or" and other highly abstract words exclusively from sensory or motor information. It rather appears that the very fact that these mechanisms are built into our brain enables us to abstract away from the sensory input to more and more general concepts.

Such enabling might apply to the computation of actions at different levels of the action description, corresponding to different levels of abstractness. Moving one's arm in such and such a way is a basic action, opening a door could imply exactly the same movement but with characteristic somatosensory and possibly auditory input, and freeing somebody could also be realized by performing the same basic action. To implement the aspects of the action semantics of "open," it is possible to connect disjunction neurons with a range of action control neurons coordinating alternative action sequences that would allow one to open doors, boxes, and other objects. Similarly, to implement action semantics of the word "free," higher order disjunction neurons would be needed that look at a range of different movement programs one could perform in the context of setting somebody or something free. Of course, additional conditions would need to be met, too. For example, the performer would need to assume that someone or something is captured, locked in, or contained in something else. Disjunction neurons looking at different concrete action representations may be located adjacent to motor and premotor sites and would be ideally placed in the prefrontal cortex (Figure 3.5; for discussion, see Pulvermüller, 1999). This hypothesis, that more abstract action-related word meanings are processed in areas adjacent to the motor and premotor cortex, in prefrontal areas, receives strong support from recent imaging work (Binder, Westbury, McKiernan, Possing, & Medler, 2005; Pulvermüller & Hauk, 2006).

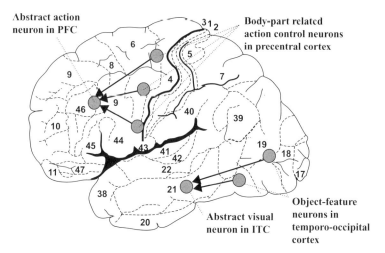

Figure 3.5. A model of modality-specific abstraction processes in the human brain. Abstract words that can refer to a range of actions (e.g., "free") have cell assemblies including neurons that act as disjunction units with input from a range of neurons controlling concrete body-related actions. These abstract action neurons are in the prefrontal cortex. Similar abstract visual semantic neurons performing disjunction computations on visual input are in anterior areas of the inferior temporal "what" stream of visual processing – for example, in the parahippocampal gyrus (for a discussion of experimental evidence, see Pulvermüller & Hauk, 2006).

These hints toward abstraction mechanisms of different types might suffice here to point out some perspectives of a brain-based approach to embodied semantics.

## LANGUAGE PROCESSES IN THE BRAIN: DISTRIBUTED, DISCRETE, OR BOTH?

Similar to most current theories postulating the distributed processing of language and concepts in the mind and brain (Rogers et al., 2004; Seidenberg, Plaut, Petersen, McClelland, & McRae, 1994), the current proposal puts that the cell assemblies processing words are widely distributed. This means that the neuronal ensembles are spread out over different areas of the brain or over different compartments of a neuronal model simulating these brain mechanisms (Braitenberg & Pulvermüller, 1992; Pulvermüller, 1999; Pulvermüller & Preissl, 1991). However, in contrast to most distributed processing accounts, the cell assemblies are conceptualized as functionally coherent networks that respond in a discrete fashion. This implies that the networks representing words, the "word webs," are either active or inactive, and that the full activation of one word's representation is in competition with that of other word-related networks. In this sense, cell assemblies are similar to the localist representations postulated by psycholinguistic theories (Dell, 1986; Page, 2000). Still, as each of the distributed cell assemblies includes neurons processing features related to form or semantics, there can be overlap between cell assemblies representing similar words or concepts. This leads to an interplay of facilitatory and inhibitory mechanisms when word webs become fully active in a sequence. The full activation, or ignition, of a word-related cell assembly can be considered a possible cortical correlate of word recognition – or of the spontaneous pop-up of a word together with its meaning in the mind.

If word webs can become active in a discrete fashion, this does not imply that each ignition is exactly identical to all other full activations of the network. As word webs are linked to each other through the grammar network and also exhibit semantic and form overlap, the context of brain states and other cognitive network activations primes and therefore influences the way in which a given word web ignites. This may provide a mechanism for context-related focusing on semantic features.

A further example is the contextual disambiguation of a semantically ambiguous word. The brain basis of an ambiguous word has been conceptualized as a set of two word webs overlapping in their form-related assembly part (Figure 3.6). In this case, semantic context can disambiguate by priming one of the semantic subassemblies of the two overlapping word representations. The two overlapping cell assemblies would be in both facilitatory (due to form overlap) and inhibitory (due to competition between cell assemblies) interactions. Most likely, the facilitatory effects would precede the inhibitory ones (Pulvermüller, 2003). Discrete representations seem to be helpful for mechanistically implementing semantically ambiguous words, synonyms, and other overlapping representations.

ONE OR MORE SEMANTIC-CONCEPTUAL BINDING SITES?

Although the results on the cortical correlates of semantic word groups cannot be explained if all semantic processes are restricted to one cortical area, they might still be compatible with the general idea of a central semantic binding site. This system would be thought to manage dynamic functional links between multiple cortical areas processing word forms and conceptual-semantic information. The idea of such a central "concept area" or "convergence zone" has a long tradition in the neuroscience of language and seems

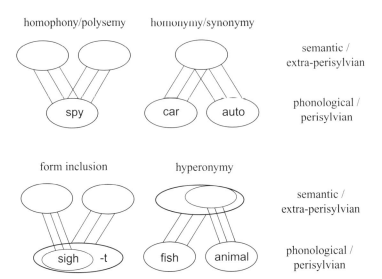

Figure 3.6. Word forms and semantics are proposed to be processed in different parts of the distributed word-related cell assembly. Most semantic information is stored outside the perisylvian language areas, whereas most information related to the phonological word form is in perisylvian space. Words related to each other phonologically or semantically would overlap in their perisylvian or extra-perisylvian sub-assemblies. Relationships between words with the same form but different meanings (homophones and polysemes), with the same meaning but different forms (homonyms and synonyms), with a form-inclusion and a hyperonomy/hyponymie relationship are illustrated (after Pulvermüller, 2003).

to be motivated by the belief that a central locus must exist, at which concepts are related to each other and abstract information is extracted from them. As I have tried to make clear, it may be possible to implement semantic binding by distributed cell assemblies that, as a whole, function as binding networks. In this case, the binding would not be attributable to one specific brain area but rather to a set of areas, those over which the assembly is distributed. Still, there are certainly more peripheral areas – for example, primary motor and sensory cortices – where correlated activation patterns occur in the first place, and areas connecting between these "peripheral" ones, with the major task of linking the correlation patterns together in a most effective manner. These higher or connection areas might naturally be more important for the binding of information from different modalities. Whether or not all these routes for multimodal information linkage necessarily go through the same convergence zone or rather through a range of different areas of association cortex, as neuroanatomical studies might suggest (e.g., Braitenberg & Schüz, 1998; Young, Scannell, Burns, & Blakemore, 1994), remains a matter of future research.

A possible route to answering the question of a center for semantic and conceptual binding is offered by patient studies. Here it is remarkable that patients with semantic dementia usually have a lesion in the temporal pole, and this region was therefore suggested as the areas most important for semantic binding (Patterson & Hodges, 2001). However, the bilateral nature of neural degeneration usually seen in semantic dementia may suggest that one focal lesion is not enough to cause general semantic deficits (Patterson & Hodges, 2001). Multiple semantic binding sites are also supported by the specific semantic deficit in action word processing seen in patients with motor neuron disease (Bak, O'Donovan, Xuereb, Boniface, & Hodges, 2001). More evidence for multiple semantic binding sites came from double dissociations between semantic word categories arising from lesions in right-hemispheric fronto-parietal versus temporo-occipital areas (Neininger & Pulvermüller, 2003), which complement similar observations made earlier for lesions to the left language-dominant hemisphere (Damasio & Tranel, 1993; Daniele et al., 1994). Some of these lesions were so focal that they only affected the motor and premotor cortex, but nevertheless specifically degraded the processing of action words in psychological experiments (Neininger & Pulvermüller, 2001). Dissociations of these types are consistent with the existence of multiple semantic integration systems in both cerebral hemispheres (Pulvermüller & Mohr, 1996).

SUMMARY AND OUTLOOK

Information about actions and perceptions relevant in the explanation of the meaning of referential words appear to be linked to the word forms at the level of the brain. The relevant links may be established by the correlation of neuronal activation in perisylvian word form circuits and semantic circuits in action- and perception-related brain regions. Semantic category differences may be based on the differential involvement of neuronal sets in the inferior-temporal visual cortex, the fronto-central action-related cortex, and other brain parts. Precise predictions on the cortical locus of specific semantic brain processes could be generated for subtypes of action words referring to face-, arm-, and leg-movements, such as *lick*, *pick*, and *kick*. Processing of these words lights up the motor system in a similar way as the respective actions would. Specific activation of the motor systems takes place rapidly during speech and written language processing, is automatic, and makes a functional contribution to word processing. The results provide brain support that language is grounded in, and embodied by, action and perception mechanisms. The rapidity, automaticity, and functional significance of semantically specific sensorimotor processes sparked by word forms argues against an epiphenomenal character and supports the position that "embodied" action-perception circuits contribute to, and are essential for, semantic-conceptual processing. Aspects of abstract semantics can be modeled on the basis of known functional features of neurons, especially their functionality as logical function processors.

The data summarized show that it is fruitful to model the brain basis of meaningful words as distributed cell assemblies binding phonological and semantic information about actions and perceptions at an abstract or cross-modal level. These distributed neuronal ensembles may act as discrete word specific processors including neuron sets in different cortical areas. Different sets may overlap, thereby reflecting shared semantic or phonological features between words, and they may compete for full activation in the perception process. In word recognition, activation of the distributed areas, over which these neuronal assemblies are spread out, is near-simultaneous, thereby binding information from different modalities (e.g., articulatory and acoustic) and linguistic functions (e.g., phonological and semantic). Apart from their role in language, these networks may play a role in conceptual processing.

These proposals and the reviewed neuroscience evidence backing them have important implications for constructing life-like perception-action systems and robots with brain-like control systems (Knoblauch, Markert, & Palm, 2005; Roy, 2005; Shastri, Grannes, Narayana, & Feldman, 2005; Wermter, Weber, Elshaw, Gallese, & Pulvermüller, 2005; Wermter et al., 2004). A major conclusion here is that there are good reasons to link brain-based language models to the body-related motor and perception systems. Such embodied artificial models might succeed for the same reason why the biological originals they copy were successful in evolution. A main point here might be the possibility to process cross-modal information exchange in an extremely rapid manner. A further field of application is clinical practice. The therapy of language defcits caused by stroke and diseases of the brain can be based on neuroscience knowledge and thereby possibly be improved. In this context, it is noteworthy that neuroscience research on language action links has inspired new intensive therapy methods embedding language use more closely into action contexts. The new methods led to surprisingly good therapy outcomes, even in patients with chronic aphasia (Pulvermüller et al. 2001; Maeinzer et al., 2005; Maher et al., 2006).

Still, would not all of the results discussed here be compatible with abstract modular models postulating that aspects of semantics are mapped on different cognitive processors, without a priori prediction on the exact cortical loci where they are located (for discussion, see Caramazza & Mahon, 2003)? It must be admitted that this is certainly the case. However, it is a difference between models that are compatible with a range of brain facts – as any abstract modular theory that does not specify brain correlates necessarily is – and brain-based models that do imply specific loci for, for example, semantic and conceptual brain processes. The advance that has been achieved is in this dimension. Some semantic brain activations in the brain can now be understood and explained on the basis of neuroscientific knowledge. Rather than looking at brain activation pictures, seeing the activations, and therefore stipulating that meaning is sitting here or there, we can now come up with precise a priori predictions and a neuroscientifically grounded explanation attempt. This brings us closer to an answer to the "why" question: Why is conceptual-semantic brain activation occurring here and not there? Even if these explanation attempts are preliminary, they may propel cognitive neuroscience from a science describing phenomena to an explanatory science grounding findings, also about concepts and thought, in the laws of nature.

ACKNOWLEDGEMENTS

This work was supported by the Medical Research Council (UK) and by the European Community under the "Information Society Technologies" and the "New and Emerging Science and Technology" programmes (EU IST-2001–35282, EU NEST-Nestcom, MRC U1055.04.003.00001.01, MRC U1055.04.003.00003.01).

**References**

Bak, T. H., O'Donovan, D. G., Xuereb, J. H., Boniface, S., & Hodges, J. R. (2001). Selective impairment of verb processing associated with pathological changes in Brodmann areas 44 and 45 in the Motor Neurone Disease-Dementia-Aphasia syndrome. *Brain, 124*, 103–120.

Barsalou, L. W. (1999). Perceptual symbol systems. *Behavioral & Brain Sciences, 22*(4), 577–609; discussion, 610–560.

Barsalou, L. W. (2003). Abstraction in perceptual symbol systems. *Philosophical Transactions of the Royal Society of London Series B-Biological Sciences, 358*(1435), 1177–1187.

Binder, J. R., Westbury, C. F., McKiernan, K. A., Possing, E. T., & Medler, D. A. (2005). Distinct brain systems for processing concrete and abstract concepts. *Journal of Cognitive Neuroscience, 17*(6), 905–917.

Bird, H., Lambon-Ralph, M. A., Patterson, K., & Hodges, J. R. (2000). The rise and fall of frequency and imageability: Noun and verb production in semantic dementia. *Brain and Language, 73*(1), 17–49.

Bookheimer, S. (2002). Functional MRI of language: New approaches to understanding the cortical organization of semantic processing. *Annual Review of Neuroscience, 25*, 151–188.

Borghi, A. M., Glenberg, A. M., & Kaschak, M. P. (2004). Putting words in perspective. *Memory & Cognition, 32*(6), 863–873.

Boulenger, V., Roy, A. C., Paulignan, Y., Deprez, V., Jeannerod, M., & Nazir, T. A. (2006). Cross-talk between language processes and overt motor behavior in the first 200 msec of processing. *Journal of Cognitive Neuroscience, 18*(10), 1607–1615.

Braitenberg, V., & Pulvermüller, F. (1992). Entwurf einer neurologischen Theorie der Sprache. *Naturwissenschaften, 79*, 103–117.

Braitenberg, V., & Schüz, A. (1998). *Cortex: statistics and geometry of neuronal connectivity* (2 ed.). Berlin: Springer.

Buccino, G., Binkofski, F., Fink, G. R., Fadiga, L., Fogassi, L., Gallese, V., Seitz, R. J., Zilles, K., Rizzolatti, G., & Freund, H. J. (2001). Action observation activates premotor and parietal areas in a somatotopic manner: an fMRI study. *European Journal of Neuroscience, 13*(2), 400–404.

Buccino, G., Riggio, L., Melli, G., Binkofski, F., Gallese, V., & Rizzolatti, G. (2005). Listening to action-related sentences modulates the activity of the motor system: a combined TMS and behavioral study. *Cognitive Brain Research, 24*(3), 355–363.

Cappa, S. F., Perani, D., Schnur, T., Tettamanti, M., & Fazio, F. (1998). The effects of semantic category and knowledge type on lexical-semantic access: a PET study. *Neuroimage, 8*(4), 350–359.

Caramazza, A., & Mahon, B. Z. (2003). The organization of conceptual knowledge: The evidence from category-specific semantic deficits. *Trends in Cognitive Science, 7*(8), 354–361.

Chao, L. L., Haxby, J. V., & Martin, A. (1999). Attribute-based neural substrates in temporal cortex for perceiving and knowing about objects. *Nature Neuroscience, 2*(10), 913–919.

Coles, M. G. H., & Rugg, M. D. (1995). Event-related brain potentials. In M. D. Rugg & M. G. H. Coles (Eds.), *Electrophysiology of mind. Event-related brain potentials and cognition* (pp. 1–26). Oxford: Oxford University Press.

Damasio, A. R., & Tranel, D. (1993). Nouns and verbs are retrieved with differently distributed neural systems. *Proceedings of the National Academy of Sciences, USA, 90*, 4957–4960.

Daniele, A., Giustolisi, L., Silveri, M. C., Colosimo, C., & Gainotti, G. (1994). Evidence for a possible neuroanatomical basis for lexical processing of nouns and verbs. *Neuropsychologia, 32*, 1325–1341.

de Vega, M., Robertson, D. A., Glenberg, A. M., Kaschak, M. P., & Rinck, M. (2004). On doing two things at once: Temporal constraints on actions in language comprehension. *Memory & Cognition, 32*(7), 1033–1043.

Dell, G. S. (1986). A spreading-activation theory of retrieval in sentence production. *Psychological Review, 93*, 283–321.

Devlin, J. T., Russell, R. P., Davis, M. H., Price, C. J., Moss, H. E., Fadili, M. J., & Tyler, L. K. (2002). Is there an anatomical basis for category-specificity? Semantic memory studies in PET and fMRI. *Neuropsychologia, 40*(1), 54–75.

Elbert, T., Pantev, C., Wienbruch, C., Rockstroh, B., & Taub, E. (1995). Increased cortical representation of the fingers of the left hand in string players. *Science, 270*(5234), 305–307.

Fadiga, L., Craighero, L., Buccino, G., & Rizzolatti, G. (2002). Speech listening specifically modulates the excitability of tongue muscles: A TMS study. *European Journal of Neuroscience, 15*(2), 399–402.

Frege, G. (1966). Der Gedanke. In G. Patzig (Ed.), *Logische Untersuchungen* (pp. 30–53). Göttingen: Huber. (First published 1918–1920).

Gentilucci, M., Benuzzi, F., Bertolani, L., Daprati, E., & Gangitano, M. (2000). Language and motor control. *Experimental Brain Research, 133*(4), 468–490.

Glenberg, A. M., & Kaschak, M. P. (2002). Grounding language in action. *Psychonomic Bulletin & Review, 9*(3), 558–565.

González, J., Barros-Loscertales, A., Pulvermüller, F., Meseguer, V., Sanjuán, A., Belloch, V., & Ávila, C. (2006). Reading cinnamon activates olfactory brain regions. *Neuroimage, 32*(2), 906–912.

Graziano, M. S., Taylor, C. S., & Moore, T. (2002). Complex movements evoked by microstimulation of precentral cortex. *Neuron, 34*(5), 841–851.

Hauk, O., Davis, M. H., Ford, M., Pulvermüller, F., & Marslen-Wilson, W. D. (2006). The time course of visual word recognition as revealed by linear regression analysis of ERP data. *Neuroimage, 30*(4), 1383–1400.

Hauk, O., Johnsrude, I., & Pulvermüller, F. (2004). Somatotopic representation of action words in the motor and premotor cortex. *Neuron, 41*, 301–307.

Hauk, O., & Pulvermüller, F. (2004). Neurophysiological distinction of action words in the fronto-central cortex. *Human Brain Mapping, 21*(3), 191–201.

He, S. Q., Dum, R. P., & Strick, P. L. (1993). Topographic organization of corticospinal projections from the frontal lobe: Motor areas on the lateral surface of the hemisphere. *Journal of Neuroscience, 13*(3), 952–980.

Hickok, G., & Poeppel, D. (2004). Dorsal and ventral streams: A framework for understanding aspects of the functional anatomy of language. *Cognition, 92*(1–2), 67–99.

Holcomb, P. J., & Neville, H. J. (1990). Auditory and visual semantic priming in lexical decision: A comparision using event-related brain potentials. *Language and Cognitive Processes, 5*, 281–312.

Humphreys, G. W., & Forde, E. M. (2001). Hierarchies, similarity, and interactivity in object recognition: "Category-specific" neuropsychological deficits. *Behavioral and Brain Sciences, 24*(3), 453–509.

Humphreys, G. W., & Riddoch, M. J. (1987). On telling your fruit from your vegetables – a consideration of category-specific deficits after brain-damage. *Trends in Neurosciences, 10*, 145–148.

Jeannerod, M., & Frak, V. (1999). Mental imaging of motor activity in humans. *Current Opinion in Neurobiology, 9*(6), 735–739.

Kiefer, M. (2001). Perceptual and semantic sources of category-specific effects: Event-related potentials during picture and word categorization. *Memory & Cognition, 29*, 100–116.

Kintsch, W. (1974). *The representation of meaning in memory*. Hillsdale, NJ: Erlbaum.

Kintsch, W. (1998). *Comprehension: A paradigm for cognition*. New York: Cambridge University Press.

Kintsch, W. (2002). The potential of latent semantic analysis for machine grading of clinical case summaries. *Journal of Biomedical Informatics, 35*(1), 3–7.

Kleene, S. C. (1956). Representation of events in nerve nets and finite automata. In C. E. Shannon & J. McCarthy (Eds.), *Automata studies* (pp. 3–41). Princeton, NJ: Princeton University Press.

Knoblauch, A., Markert, H., & Palm, G. (2005). An associative cortical model of language understanding and action planning. In J. Mira & J. R. Alvarez (Eds.), *International work-conference on the interplay between natural and artificial computation 2005* (Vol. 3562, pp. 405–414). Berlin: Springer.

Lakoff, G. (1987). *Women, fire, and dangerous things. What categories reveal about the mind*. Chicago: University of Chicago Press.

Landauer, T. K., & Dumais, S. T. (1997). A solution to Plato's problem: the Latent Semantic Analysis theory of acquisition, induction, and representation of knowledge. *Psychological Review, 104*, 211–240.

Lichtheim, L. (1885). On aphasia. *Brain, 7*, 433–484.

Maher, L. M., Kendall, D., Swearengin, J. A., Rodriguez, A., Leon, S. A., Pingel, K., Holland, A., & Rothi, L. J. (2006). A pilot study of use-dependent learning in the context of Constraint Induced Language Therapy. *Journal of the International Neuropsychological Society, 12*(6), 843–852.

Martin, A., & Chao, L. L. (2001). Semantic memory and the brain: structure and processes. *Current Oppinion in Neurobiology, 11*(2), 194–201.

Martin, A., Haxby, J. V., Lalonde, F. M., Wiggs, C. L., & Ungerleider, L. G. (1995). Discrete cortical regions associated with knowledge of color and knowledge of action. *Science, 270*, 102–105.

Matelli, M., Camarda, R., Glickstein, M., & Rizzolatti, G. (1986). Afferent and efferent projections of the inferior area 6 in the macaque monkey. *Journal of Comparative Neurology, 251*(3), 281–298.

McCulloch, W. S., & Pitts, W. H. (1943). A logical calculus of ideas immanent in nervous activity. *Bulletin of Mathematical Biophysics, 5*, 115–133.

Meinzer, M., Djundja, D., Barthel, G., Elbert, T., & Rockstroh, B. (2005). Long-term stability of improved language functions in chronic aphasia after constraint-induced aphasia therapy. *Stroke, 36*(7), 1462–1466.

Moscoso Del Prado Martin, F., Hauk, O., & Pulvermüller, F. (2006). Category specificity in the processing of color-related and form-related words: An ERP study. *Neuroimage, 29*(1), 29–37.

Näätänen, R., Tervaniemi, M., Sussman, E., Paavilainen, P., & Winkler, I. (2001). 'Primitive intelligence' in the auditory cortex. *Trends in Neurosciences, 24*(5), 283–288.

Neininger, B., & Pulvermüller, F. (2001). The right hemisphere's role in action word processing: a double case study. *Neurocase, 7*(4), 303–317.

Neininger, B., & Pulvermüller, F. (2003). Word-category specific deficits after lesions in the right hemisphere. *Neuropsychologia, 41*(1), 53–70.

Obleser, J., Lahiri, A., & Eulitz, C. (2003). Auditory-evoked magnetic field codes place of articulation in timing and topography around 100 milliseconds post syllable onset. *Neuroimage, 20*(3), 1839–1847.

Page, M. (2000). Connectionist modelling in psychology: a localist manifesto. *Behavioral & Brain Sciences, 23*(4), 443–467; discussion, 467–512.

Patterson, K., & Hodges, J. R. (2001). Semantic dementia. In R. F. Thompson & J. L. McClelland (Eds.), *International encyclopaedia of the social and behavioural sciences*.

*Behavioral and cognitive neuroscience section* (pp. 3401–3405). New York: Pergamon Press.

Penfield, W., & Boldrey, E. (1937). Somatic sensory and motor representation in the cerebral cortex as studied by electrical stimulation. *Brain, 60,* 389–443.

Penfield, W., & Rasmussen, T. (1950). *The cerebral cortex of man.* New York: Macmillan.

Posner, M. I., & Pavese, A. (1998). Anatomy of word and sentence meaning. *Proceedings of the National Academy of Sciences, USA, 95,* 899–905.

Preissl, H., Pulvermüller, F., Lutzenberger, W., & Birbaumer, N. (1995). Evoked potentials distinguish nouns from verbs. *Neuroscience Letters, 197,* 81–83.

Price, C. J. (2000). The anatomy of language: contributions from functional neuroimaging. *Journal of Anatomy, 197 Pt 3,* 335–359.

Pulvermüller, F. (1996). Hebb's concept of cell assemblies and the psychophysiology of word processing. *Psychophysiology, 33,* 317–333.

Pulvermüller, F. (1999). Words in the brain's language. *Behavioral & Brain Sciences, 22,* 253–336.

Pulvermüller, F. (2001). Brain reflections of words and their meaning. *Trends in Cognitive Sciences, 5*(12), 517–524.

Pulvermüller, F. (2002). A brain perspective on language mechanisms: From discrete neuronal ensembles to serial order. *Progress in Neurobiology, 67,* 85–111.

Pulvermüller, F. (2003). *The neuroscience of language.* Cambridge, UK: Cambridge University Press.

Pulvermüller, F. (2005). Brain mechanisms linking language and action. *Nature Reviews Neuroscience, 6*(7), 576–582.

Pulvermüller, F., Härle, M., & Hummel, F. (2000). Neurophysiological distinction of verb categories. *Neuroreport, 11*(12), 2789–2793.

Pulvermüller, F., & Hauk, O. (2006). Category-specific processing of color and form words in left fronto-temporal cortex. *Cerebral Cortex, 16*(8), 1193–1201.

Pulvermüller, F., Hauk, O., Nikulin, V. V., & Ilmoniemi, R. J. (2005). Functional links between motor and language systems. *European Journal of Neuroscience, 21*(3), 793–797.

Pulvermüller, F., Lutzenberger, W., & Preissl, H. (1999). Nouns and verbs in the intact brain: evidence from event-related potentials and high-frequency cortical responses. *Cerebral Cortex, 9,* 498–508.

Pulvermüller, F., & Mohr, B. (1996). The concept of transcortical cell assemblies: a key to the understanding of cortical lateralization and interhemispheric interaction. *Neuroscience and Biobehavioral Reviews, 20,* 557–566.

Pulvermüller, F., Mohr, B., & Schleichert, H. (1999). Semantic or lexico-syntactic factors: What determines word-class specific activity in the human brain? *Neuroscience Letters, 275,* 81–84.

Pulvermüller, F., Neininger, B., Elbert, T., Mohr, B., Rockstroh, B., Koebbel, P., & Taub, E. (2001). Constraint-induced therapy of chronic aphasia following stroke. *Stroke, 32*(7), 1621–1626.

Pulvermüller, F., & Preissl, H. (1991). A cell assembly model of language. *Network: Computation in Neural Systems, 2,* 455–468.

Pulvermüller, F., & Shtyrov, Y. (2006). Language outside the focus of attention: The mismatch negativity as a tool for studying higher cognitive processes. *Progress in Neurobiology, 79*(1), 49–71.

Pulvermüller, F., Shtyrov, Y., & Ilmoniemi, R. J. (2003). Spatio-temporal patterns of neural language processing: An MEG study using Minimum-Norm Current Estimates. *Neuroimage, 20*, 1020–1025.

Pulvermüller, F., Shtyrov, Y., & Ilmoniemi, R. J. (2005). Brain signatures of meaning access in action word recognition. *Journal of Cognitive Neuroscience, 17*(6), 884–892.

Rizzolatti, G., & Luppino, G. (2001). The cortical motor system. *Neuron, 31*(6), 889–901.

Rogers, T. T., Lambon Ralph, M. A., Garrard, P., Bozeat, S., McClelland, J. L., Hodges, J. R., & Patterson, K. (2004). Structure and deterioration of semantic memory: A neuropsychological and computational investigation. *Psychology Review, 111*(1), 205–235.

Roy, D. (2005). Grounding words in perception and action: Computational insights. *Trends in Cognitive Science, 9*(8), 389–396.

Schnelle, H. (1996). Approaches to computational brain theories of language – a review of recent proposals. *Theoretical Linguistics, 22*, 49–104.

Scott, S. K., & Johnsrude, I. S. (2003). The neuroanatomical and functional organization of speech perception. *Trends in Neurosciences, 26*(2), 100–107.

Searle, J. R. (1990). Minds, brains, and programs. *Behavioral & Brain Sciences, 3*(3), 417–457.

Sereno, S. C., Rayner, K., & Posner, M. I. (1998). Establishing a time line for word recognition: evidence from eye movements and event-related potentials. *NeuroReport, 13*, 2195–2200.

Seidenberg, M. S., Plaut, D. C., Petersen, A. S., McClelland, J. L., & McRae, K. (1994). Nonword pronunciation and models of word recognition. *Journal of Experimental Psychology: Human Perception and Performance, 20*(6), 1177–1196.

Shastri, L., Grannes, D., Narayana, S., & Feldman, J. (2005). A connectionist encoding of parameterized schemas and reactive plans. In G. K. Kraetzschmar & G. Palm (Eds.), *Hybrid information processing in adaptive autonomous vehicles.* Berlin: Springer.

Shtyrov, Y., Hauk, O., & Pulvermüller, F. (2004). Distributed neuronal networks for encoding category-specific semantic information: The mismatch negativity to action words. *European Journal of Neuroscience, 19*(4), 1083–1092.

Shtyrov, Y., Pihko, E., & Pulvermüller, F. (2005). Determinants of dominance: Is language laterality explained by physical or linguistic features of speech? *Neuroimage, 27*(1), 37–47.

Simmons, W. K., Ramjee, V., Beauchamp, M. S., McRae, K., Martin, A., & Barsalou, L. W. (2007). A common neural substrate for perceiving and knowing about color. *Neuropsychologia, 45*(12), 2802–2810.

Skrandies, W. (1999). Early effects of semantic meaning on electrical brain activity. *Behavioral & Brain Sciences, 22*, 301.

Tettamanti, M., Buccino, G., Saccuman, M. C., Gallese, V., Danna, M., Scifo, P., Fazio, F., Rizzolatti, G., Cappa, S. F., & Perani, D. (2005). Listening to action-related sentences activates fronto-parietal motor circuits. *Journal of Cognitive Neuroscience, 17*(2), 273–281.

Tomasello, M., & Kruger, A. C. (1992). Joint attention on actions: Acquiring verbs in ostensive and non-ostensive contexts. *Journal of Child Language, 19*, 311–333.

Tyler, L. K., & Moss, H. E. (2001). Towards a distributed account of conceptual knowledge. *Trends in Cognitive Sciences, 5*(6), 244–252.

Tyler, L. K., Moss, H. E., Durrant-Peatfield, M. R., & Levy, J. P. (2000). Conceptual structure and the structure of concepts: A distributed account of category-specific deficits. *Brain & Language, 75*(2), 195–231.

Tyler, L. K., Russell, R., Fadili, J., & Moss, H. E. (2001). The neural representation of nouns and verbs: PET studies. *Brain, 124*(Pt 8), 1619–1634.

Tyler, L. K., Stamatakis, E. A., Bright, P., Acres, K., Abdallah, S., Rodd, J. M., & Moss, H. E. (2004). Processing objects at different levels of specificity. *Journal of Cognitive Neuroscience, 16*(3), 351–362.

Warrington, E. K., & McCarthy, R. A. (1983). Category specific access dysphasia. *Brain, 106*, 859–878.

Warrington, E. K., & Shallice, T. (1984). Category specific semantic impairments. *Brain, 107*, 829–854.

Wermter, S., Weber, C., Elshaw, M., Gallese, V., & Pulvermüller, F. (2005). Neural grounding of robot language in action. In S. Wermter & G. Palm & M. Elshaw (Eds.), *Biomimetic neural learning for intelligent robots* (pp. 162–181). Berlin: Springer.

Wermter, S., Weber, C., Elshaw, M., Panchev, C., Erwin, H., & Pulvermüller, F. (2004). Towards multimodal neural network robot learning. *Robotics and Autonomous Systems, 47*, 171–175.

Wilson, S. M., Saygin, A. P., Sereno, M. I., & Iacoboni, M. (2004). Listening to speech activates motor areas involved in speech production. *Nature Neuroscience, 7*(7), 701–702.

Young, M. P., Scannell, J. W., Burns, G., & Blakemore, C. (1994). Analysis of connectivity: Neural systems in the cerebral cortex. *Review in Neuroscience, 5*, 227–249.

Zatorre, R. J., Evans, A. C., Meyer, E., & Gjedde, A. (1992). Lateralization of phonetic and pitch discrimination in speech processing. *Science, 256*, 846–849.

# 4    What Thoughts Are Made Of

Lera Boroditsky and Jesse Prinz

## INTRODUCTION

What are thoughts made of? Do we think in pictures? In words? In symbols? What is the currency of human cognition and how do the representations that make up thinking come to be in our minds? In this chapter, we explore the rich sources of input that humans receive from perception and language and how combining information from these two input streams can be used to create the amazing complexity and sophistication of the human knowledge system.

Cognitive science is often seen as emerging from the confluence of two research programs: Chomsky's nativist critique of behaviorist learning theories and the rise of artificial intelligence. Together these two tides lead to a seemingly inevitable pair of conclusions: we think in language-like symbols, and the primitive symbols used in thought are innate. If we think in innate language-like symbols, then obviously we do not think in English, or Russian, or Kuuk Thaayorre. Instead, we think in the universal language of thought – Mentalese" (Fodor, 1975). This conclusion has been explicitly defended by some in cognitive science, but more often it is an unarticulated background assumption. For example, in the literature on concepts and categorization, conceptual representations are often described using structured lists of linguistically labeled features, and researchers rarely suggest that the words used in their theories correspond to mental representations that are radically unlike words. Nor do they suppose that these words correspond to lexical items in a natural language (as evidenced by the relative lack of cross-cultural studies in the first few decades of cognitive scientific research on categories).

In recent times, these assumptions have been critically reexamined and two important (and seemingly contradictory) sources of dissent have emerged.

On the one hand, some critics have argued that we do not think in language-like symbols. Instead, we think using stored records of sensory and motor states. Following Barsalou (1999), we will call this the *perceptual symbols systems* hypothesis, or PSS. On the other hand, some critics have been more willing to accept the claim that language-like symbols are important to thought, but opposed to the claim that the symbols in question belong to an innate and hence universal mental language. Instead, they venture that statistical regularities found in natural languages (e.g., English, Russian, Kuuk Thaayorre) play an important role in constructing and constituting thought, and that speakers of different natural languages may in fact think in interestingly different ways. Call this the *natural language statistics* hypothesis, or NLS.

Whereas these two approaches appear to pull in opposite directions (one away from languaform representations and one toward them), what they share is a focus on representations being constructed from the inputs, from the patterns an individual observes in the course of their experience in the world (e.g, what they see, what they hear).

In this chapter, we discuss the contribution that both of these approaches make to our understanding of how humans construct knowledge, and propose an integration of the two. We will not review the extensive empirical evidence for PSS because that has been done by other authors in this volume (or see Barsalou et al., 2003). Instead, we will discuss what we take to be the major hurdle facing PSS: the problem of abstract ideas. Then we will discuss resources available for coping with this problem and argue that one major resource that has been underexploited by defenders of PSS is language. We describe ways in which language learning may interact with perceptual symbols and influence cognitive processes. We conclude by drawing some morals about why both perceptual symbols and natural languages are important ingredients in the construction of mature human thought.

## PERCEPTUAL SYMBOLS AND THEIR LIMITATIONS

The central idea behind the perceptual symbols systems hypothesis is that the representations (or neural activations) that arise in dedicated input systems during sensation and motor action can be stored and used "offline." When these stored representations are used in thinking, the brain regenerates a pattern of activation similar to the one that occurred during the perceptual episode. For example, when we access the idea of a duck, the brain enters an activation state that is like the state we would be in if we were perceiving a duck.

Philosophers in the empiricist tradition have been defending something like PSS for centuries. For example, Locke (1979) argued against innate knowledge by suggesting that all human concepts can be built simply out of stored copies of experienced perceptual states. Even if humans come equipped with some innate representations, it is clear that a great many representations are learned. This means that we need an account of how concepts can be acquired by means of perception. On the PSS view, perceptual states are simply stored for later use. On an amodal symbol systems view (such as Mentalese), perceptual states can also be stored, but there is an extra step in which an abstract symbol is generated that corresponds to some set of perceptual states. This symbol then (and not the perceptual representations that underlie it) is the representation that is used in thinking. That is, on both views perceptual representations exist in the mind, but on the amodal symbols view, an extra layer of representation (an amodal symbol) is created and used in thinking. The question is, are perceptual representations necessary for conceptual processing, and are they sufficient? And the same for amodal symbols: are they necessary, and are they sufficient?

Are perceptual representations necessary in conceptual processing? Consider for example what we know about ducks. A typical list of duck features that make up a duck representation on an amodal symbols view might include things like ducks have feet, and feathers, and a bill, and can swim, and so on. This sort of feature list is on first pass appealing as a form of representation because a limited set of features can be used to create many different representations. A feature like "feet" can also be used in other representations of things that have feet, like humans, pigs, dogs, bathtubs, and so on. Also, the feature list just seems intuitively sensible. Ducks do have feet, and a bill, and can swim, and so on.

But consider such feature lists a bit more closely. Imagine that you do not already know what ducks are and are told that ducks have feet, and a bill, and feathers, and can swim. How would you know that the feet on a duck were not like the feet inside your shoes, or the feet on a pig or a dog or a bathtub? If you do not already know what duck feet look like, simply knowing that ducks have feet would leave open infinite possibilities. Surely ducks do not just have feet, they have *duck* feet. Further, how would you know where on a duck the feet go? And how many feet? Beyond knowing that ducks have duck feet, you also need to know that they are in number appropriate for a duck and attached like on a duck. And clearly ducks do not just have feathers, they have *duck* feathers – relatively small and smooth and in a particular duck feather shape, attached like on a duck. And when ducks swim, they do not just swim, they swim like ducks swim. They do not do the backstroke, for example. What seemed like a sensible list of features turns out to be vacuous unless one already knows what ducks are like. Every feature in the list must be grounded in perceptual information that an individual already has about ducks, or else it would be useless.

We store a great deal of perceptual information about ducks that is not captured in a typical feature list. We know that duck feet are webbed and that those feet come out of the bottom of a duck, not out of its head. We know the shape of a duck's bill, and we would not mistake a duck bill for a toucan bill or dollar bill. We know that ducks waddle when they walk, that they are larger than doughnuts, and that their eyes are glossy. If we encountered a duck that was even slightly deformed, we would probably notice the defect. Eyes placed too low, feet too far apart, feathers too sharp – any of these things could be detected. The perceptual information that we store includes shapes (the distinctive curve of a duck's bill) that we would find very difficult to describe.

The perceptual details specific to duck feet and feathers and manners of motion are not simply extra information, they are the essential content of our knowledge that allows us to distinguish a duck from a Las Vegas showgirl, for example, who also likely has feet and feathers and can swim. Without the right perceptual grounding, feature lists are insufficient to account for even simple aspects of human cognition. Of course, the perceptual information we store may be blurry, incomplete, and inaccurate in various ways, but such as it is, this information is necessary for normal human cognition (such as distinguishing ducks from showgirls).

The argument so far is that perceptual symbol systems are necessary for basic human cognition, and that amodal symbols are insufficient. The next question is whether amodal symbols are necessary to supplement perceptual symbols, or whether perceptual symbols by themselves are sufficient to account for human conceptual ability.

The most persistent and obvious objection to PSS is that it cannot handle abstract concepts. By definition, abstract concepts are ones whose category instances are not unified by a shared appearance. According to PSS, human conceptual knowledge is built from stored perceptual states. This may work well for concrete observable physical entities (e.g., ducks and showgirls) that can easily be perceptually experienced. But what about things that we can never see or touch? How do we come to represent and reason about abstract domains like time, justice, or ideas? How do we think about kinship, morality, or politics? Our internal mental lives go far beyond those things observable through physical experience: we invent sophisticated notions of number and time, we theorize about atoms and invisible forces, and we worry about love, justice, ideas, goals, and principles. How is it possible for the simple building blocks of perception and action to give rise to our ability to reason about domains like mathematics, time, or ideas? The ability to invent and reason about such abstract domains is arguably the very hallmark of human sophistication, so any theory of mental representation worth its salt should have a way of explaining how such abstract notions are acquired and represented.

One strategy for accommodating abstract concepts in a PSS framework is to appeal to metaphor, the idea that abstract domains are understood through analogical extensions from more experience-based domains (e.g., Boroditsky, 2000; Gibbs, 1994; Lakoff & Johnson, 1980). One of the better-studied examples of such analogical extension is of spatial representations being reused for structuring the more abstract aspects of time. Spatial representations of time abound in our culture – in graphs, time-lines, clocks, sundials, hourglasses, and calendars. In language, time is also heavily related to space, with spatial terms often used to describe the order and duration of events (Clark, 1973; Lakoff & Johnson, 1980; Traugott, 1978). For example, in English, we might move a meeting *forward*, push a deadline *back*, attend a *long* concert, or go on a *short* break. Further, people make consistent spatial gestures when talking about time (e.g., Casasanto & Lozano, 2006; Núñez & Sweetser, 2006), with English speakers gesturing to the left when speaking about the past and to the right when speaking about the future.

People also appear to spontaneously invoke spatial representations when processing temporal language (e.g., Boroditsky, 2000; Boroditsky & Ramscar, 2002), such that priming different spatial perspectives will change the way people interpret and process statements about time. People's understanding of time appears so intimately dependent on space that when people engage in real-life spatial activities, such as making an air journey or waiting in a lunch line, they also unwittingly (and dramatically) change their thinking about time (Boroditsky & Ramscar, 2002). Even simple temporal judgments are affected by spatial information (e.g., Casasanto & Boroditsky, 2008). Finally, cultures that rely on different spatial representations also end up with different representations of time. For example, the Kuuk Thaayorre, who think about space in terms of absolute cardinal directions like North, South, East, and West, also lay out time in absolute space – from East to West, unlike English speakers who tend to lay out time from left to right (Boroditsky & Gaby, 2006).

Of course, there are many other abstract notions to account for beyond time. Some of these have also been linked to spatial representations. For example, people appear to understand kinship concepts spatially; when talking about kin, speakers spontaneously use their hands to draw kinship trees in space (Enfield, 2005). Many other abstract domains have also been shown to elicit consistent spatial gestures, (e.g., up for rising prices, down for falling grades, and so on) (Casasanto & Lozano, 2006). Further, thinking about abstract notions like wealth or honor produces interference for motor actions that are inconsistent with the spatial schemas (e.g., processing a word like "wealthy" makes people slower to make a simple hand movement downward, and processing a word like "poor" makes it harder to make a simple hand movement upward) (Casasanto & Lozano, in press).

A second strategy for accommodating abstract notions in a PSS framework is to appeal to scenarios or scripts (see Shank & Abelson, 1977). For example, the concept of democracy is very hard to visualize because democracies do not look alike. But we certainly know how to act democratically. For example, if asked to settle a problem democratically, we would know to vote. The instructions for doing this can be understood as a script or family of scripts telling us how to behave. Shank and Abelson thought of scripts as language-like, but they can equally well be implemented by sensory and motor representations of the corresponding behaviors. The democracy script may include representations of hand-raising and other means of casting votes.

A third strategy for accommodating abstract concepts in a PSS framework is to appeal to emotional responses. Consider morality: The range of things we call morally bad have little in common perceptually (stealing, cheating, hitting, and so on), so there cannot be a single image of badness. But all of these things are united by the family of emotions they cause in us. Empirical studies suggest that moral concepts indeed have an emotional basis (Haidt, 2001; Prinz, 2007). For example, hypnotically inducing negative emotions can increase a person's intuition about how wrong something is, even in cases where a described behavior is quite benign (Wheatley & Haidt, 2005). Inducing positive emotions can shift intuitions from a deontological moral framework (with rules like: thou shalt not kill) to a consequentialist one (with rules such as: save as many as you can). Valdesolo and DeSteno (2006) found that people were three times more likely to offer consequentialist responses in moral dilemmas after watching a comedy sketch.

There is also evidence that when emotions are diminished, people are unable to grasp moral concepts in the normal way. Psychopaths suffer from flattened affect, and they fail to draw the distinction between moral and conventional rules (Blair, 1995), suggesting that the comprehension of moral rules as such is a matter of emotional responding. There is also considerable research exploring the specific emotions underlying morality. Rozin et al. (1999) have shown that crimes against persons elicit anger, crimes against community elicit contempt, and crimes against nature (or "divinity" in nonsecular societies) elicit disgust. Prinz has shown that when you perpetrate a crime against a person, the modal response is guilt, but if you perform an unnatural act (e.g., violate a sexual more), the response is shame. This suggests that there is not one single moral emotion but many, and these arise in a predictable, context-sensitive way. This fits in perfectly with PSS. On that approach, concepts have "variable embodiment" (Barsalou, 1999). Concepts are temporary constructions in working memory that can vary in their form from context to context. In the view we are suggesting, the concepts of right and wrong are constituted by a variety of emotions of praise and blame. On any given occasion, if a person judges that something is wrong, they activate one or another of these emotions.

All three of these strategies (conceptual metaphors, scripts, and emotional responses) show some promise in advancing our understanding of the representation of abstract ideas within a PSS framework. Of course, much research remains to be done to understand to what extent perceptual information underlies abstract ideas. Whereas perceptual information may go a long way, there may also be some important limitations. Here we outline four limitations that strike us as particularly pressing, and then offer a potential solution.

First, some concepts are associated with a very large number of perceptual features, spanning multiple perceptual modalities. In principle, multiple perceptual features can be bound together without difficulty, but in some cases the binding may become difficult. For example, consider some super-ordinate level concepts, such as vehicle. Many vehicles have shared perceptual features (such as wheels or windows), but some are perceptual outliers (a toboggan or hang glider). To keep track of the fact that these belong in the same category as cars, trucks, and boats may be difficult when we are restricted to perceptual features alone.

Second, some concepts may be perceptually grounded in representations that are either structurally complex or temporally protracted, and when that is the case, there will be a considerable processing cost. Consider the concept of democracy, which we suggested may involve behavioral scripts. It is implausible that the entire script (or family of scripts) runs through the mind every time one thinks about democracy. That would place an exorbitant burden on working memory.

Third, perceptual symbols may also be less than ideal for certain types of reasoning processes, especially formal inference. Human reasoning tends to rely on heuristics and biases, and some of these are easy to accommodate within the PSS framework (such as representativeness or availability). But people can also learn to reason in accordance with rules. We can acquire skills for reasoning in accordance with logic, for example. We can also reason in domains that make heavy use of symbolic tools, such as mathematics. In math, we can reason about numbers that would be impossible to keep track of perceptually.

A fourth limitation of perceptual symbols is that they are poorly suited for communication. Rich multisensory representations are cumbersome to communicate, and even if we use multisensory perceptual representations internally, these representations must often be converted to language to communicate with others.

These four limitations concern some of the more sophisticated aspects of human cognition: reasoning in terms of broad categories, reasoning about complex systems or abstract entities, and the ability to communicate complex messages across individuals. Whereas perceptual symbols may get us a lot of the way to complex cognition, there may be domains where perceptual processing alone falls short. Fortunately, humans are not limited to perceptual input produced by the physical world. In addition to the rich perceptual and motor resources we share with other animals, humans also receive a tremendous amount of information through language. In the next section, we turn to the role that language plays in shaping and constructing knowledge.

Integrating language into a PSS view of cognition is not difficult. Of course, words in a public language are also perceived (either through hearing spoken language, seeing signed or written language, or through the tactile channel such as Braille). This means that a stored record of a perceived word or phrase can be treated as a perceptual symbol, or a stored linguistic experience. Whereas the views that thoughts are made of images versus words are often seen as being in opposition, what they share is a focus on the rich sources of information available in the different input channels in human experience. There is a growing body of evidence that people extract and make use of statistical regularities in language. Linguistic perceptual symbols may be very special, in that they may change the character of thought and extend our cognitive abilities beyond those of creatures that lack language.

## THE ROLE OF NATURAL LANGUAGE STATISTICS

In addition to perceptual and motor experience, people also receive a tremendous amount of information through language. Linguistic input carries highly structured information and comprises many types of statistical regularities. Many of these regularities or patterns of interrelations between sounds, words, and more complex linguistic structures exist only in language, and do not always correspond to the inherent structure of the world. To what extent is people's knowledge constructed out of the patterns of interrelations of elements within the linguistic system?

For example, what role do interrelations between words in a language play in the construction of human knowledge? How much information is extractable simply out of the interrelations of symbols? And do people actually extract and use such information?

The argument in this part goes as follows:

1. There is a wealth of information that is extractable out of the internal sets of relations even between entirely ungrounded symbols. Computational models such as Latent Semantic Analysis (LSA) and Hyperspace Analogue to Language (HAL), as well as statistical translation engines (such as the one implemented by Google), capitalize on such information to solve a large array of problems.

2. Humans are also capable of extracting the types of statistical patterns of co-occurrence that these computational models rely on, even when the sets of interrelations are between ungrounded symbols (e.g., novel words with no given referents).

3. When the symbols are grounded (e.g., when the novel words refer to physical objects), people still rely on the patterns of interrelations between the symbols to inform their representations of the physical objects to which the symbols refer. This is true both for patterns of linguistic interrelations learned in the laboratory as well as those that exist in natural languages. When patterns of interrelations between words differ across languages, people's representations of those words' referents also differ accordingly.

4. Finally, the patterns of interrelations in language can serve a pivotal role in building representations of abstract entities for which direct perceptual grounding is scant or unavailable. Patterns of linguistic correspondence (such as in conventional metaphor) can guide analogical inference and structure building for abstract domains, such that the perceptually based knowledge for more concrete domains can be reused and extended to help reason about abstract entities.

Much information can be extracted just from interrelations of ungrounded symbols. One striking demonstration of how far one can get simply by observing the patterns of interrelations between words (without any knowledge of the physical world) are contextual co-occurrence models such as LSA and HAL (e.g., LSA: Landauer & Dumais, 1997; Landauer, Foltz, & Laham, 1998; HAL: Burgess & Lund, 1997). For example, the LSA model is able to extract enough regularity out of the patterns of contextual co-occurrences between words in a large corpus to pass a multiple-choice TOEFL test (Landauer & Dumais, 1997). Such co-occurrence data has also been used to predict an impressive range of semantic priming effects (Lund, Burgess, & Atchley, 1995) and provide powerful cues to the syntactic categories of words (e.g., Redington, Chater, & Finch, 1998; Burgess & Lund, 1997).

The basic intuition behind such models is that words that occur in similar contexts (that play similar roles in the network of interrelations) will be similar in meaning. If two words occur in identical contexts, then those two words are interchangeable or synonyms. Extending this logic, the more different the patterns of contextual occurrence between two words, the more different they are likely to be in meaning. Models like LSA work simply by measuring the patterns of contextual co-occurrence between words in a large corpus. LSA gets no perceptual information and has no motor effectors – all of its information comes only from the set of interrelations of ungrounded symbols.

Similar principles can be used to find similarities in structure across complex systems of symbols. For example, the ABSURDIST model (Goldstone, Feng, & Rogosky, 2005) is able to find appropriate translations between two nonidentical systems by considering only the structure of the similarity relations among the elements within each system, without any external grounding for the elements themselves. Large-scale probabilistic approaches to machine translation based on the same principles (e.g., the Google translation tool: http://www.google.com/translate) have also yielded impressive results.

Of course, just because some information is in principle extractable, as demonstrated by computer simulations, does not mean that humans are necessarily capable of or inclined to extract it. Do people in fact extract this type of information about the interrelations of words in language?

One striking demonstration of how much information is extractable out of language alone comes from the study of color knowledge in people who are congenitally blind (Shepard & Cooper, 1992). Shepard and Cooper asked people to rate the similarity of colors to one another – for example, how similar violet is to red, or orange to gold, or green to yellow, and so on. When people with normal color vision are asked to do this, their set of color similarity ratings is best captured by a color circle where adjacent colors on the wheel are those that are most similar to one another (e.g., yellow is next to gold, violet is next to purple), and colors that are seen as very dissimilar are on opposite sides of the circle (e.g., green is opposite red). But what if the same questions were posed to people who have never perceptually experienced color, people who are congenitally blind? Whereas the shape of the color space that emerges from the similarity ratings of the congenitally blind is very different in overall shape, what is striking is how many short-distance relationships are preserved. For example, purple is rated as most similar to violet, yellow as most similar to gold, orange to red, and so on. This information about colors is obviously only available through language to people who are congenitally blind. It is remarkable how much information is extracted out of the patterns in language in the absence of any supporting perceptual information.

Many other studies have revealed the exquisite sensitivity that humans have for extracting a complex statistical structure out of linguistic input (e.g., Saffran, Aslin & Newport, 1996; Gomez & Gerkin, 1999; Saffran, 2002). For example, adults and even very young infants can use sound co-occurrence patterns in speech to do things like discover word boundaries and abstract grammatical patterns. Importantly for the purpose of this chapter, people's understanding of linguistic content (i.e., word and utterance meaning) is also affected by patterns of word co-occurrence (Boroditsky & Ramscar, 2003).

For example, Boroditsky and Ramscar (2003) exposed people to a stream composed entirely of novel words. In this stream of novel words, all critical words occurred equally often with each other, but the patterns of contextual occurrence differed. Some words occurred in the same contexts, and some did not. For example, the words *fap* and *zun* never co-occurred with one another, but each occurred frequently with the word *rec*. Another set of words like *kif* and *dut* would never co-occur with *rec*, but would instead co-occur with *niz*, and so on. The subjects were told they were spying on an alien mobile-phone conversation and were asked to learn as much about the meanings of the alien words as they could. When asked to rate the meaning similarity of pairs of novel words, subjects rated those words that occurred in the same contexts (e.g., *fap* and *zun* in this example) as being more similar in meaning.

It appears that humans (much like the simple mechanisms underlying co-occurrence models of semantics such as LSA) do pick up on contextual co-occurrences of novel words, and that they allow this statistical information to inform their judgments about the words' meanings. Of course, participants in this study had no other information about the words' meanings except the patterns of contextual co-occurrence. A further question is whether people would allow co-occurrence statistics in language to inform their similarity judgments about more contentful representations. For example, can co-occurrence relationships between words affect people's representations of those words' referents?

To investigate this question, Boroditsky and Ramscar (2003) taught people nonce names for a set of novel objects. After learning the objects' names, participants then witnessed an "alien conversation" about those objects. In the conversation, the names of the objects co-occurred with context words in the same way as described above. Later, subjects rated the similarity of the objects themselves (using their pictures). The results showed that the co-occurrence properties of the objects' names influenced people's perceptions of similarity of the objects themselves. Pictures of objects whose nonce names occurred in the same nonce linguistic contexts were judged to be more similar to one another than pictures of objects whose names did not share linguistic contexts. It appears that people not only extract patterns of co-occurrence from the linguistic stream and use the patterns of co-occurrence to inform judgments about the meanings of words, they also allow this information from the linguistic stream to influence their judgments about the words' referents (in this case, judgments about the similarity of pictures of objects).

These results suggest that there may be an interesting bidirectional relationship between linguistic co-occurrence and representation. Objects whose names occur in the same linguistic contexts come to be perceived as being more similar. Of course, as objects become more similar, it is more likely that they will be talked about in ever more similar contextual collocations, which might serve in turn to further strengthen the similarities between the objects themselves, and so on. In this way, it appears that co-occurrence statistics may offer people a cognitive mechanism that allows them to sharpen and refine their underlying conceptual representations over time.

A further question to ask is whether people's ability and willingness to learn and use patterns of interrelations between words extends beyond small-scale laboratory demonstrations. The co-occurrence patterns in natural language are far more complex than those introduced in the lab, and must be computed over thousands of word types and many millions of word tokens. Do people naturally extract patterns of interrelations from the giant sea of information they are exposed to in the course of normal language use?

The fact that patterns of interrelations between words differ across languages provides a nice natural test-bed for this question. If people allow patterns of interrelations between words to influence their mental representations of the words' referents, then when patterns of interrelations between words differ across languages, people's representations of those words' referents should also differ.

One natural language example of this idea can be found in the domain of grammatical gender. In languages like Spanish and French, all nouns are divided into either the masculine or feminine grammatical gender. Nouns that are grammatically masculine will co-occur with the same masculine articles, pronouns, adjective endings, and so on, that are used to talk about biological males. Nouns that are grammatically feminine will co-occur with the grammatical markers used for talking about biological females. Conveniently for our purposes, grammatical gender assignments of nouns differ across languages. For example, the word for the sun is grammatically feminine in German but grammatically masculine in Spanish. This allows us to ask whether the relations words bear to each other within a linguistic system (in this case by belonging to the same grammatical category and by virtue of that sharing patterns of contextual co-occurrence) have an influence on how users of that linguistic system conceive of the words' referents. Do German speakers think of the sun as being more like a biological female than do Spanish speakers?

It turns out that such patterns of interrelations between words do influence people's representations of objects in the world. When an object's or entity's name is grammatically masculine in a language, speakers of that language will describe that object using more masculine adjectives, will rate the object as being more similar to biological males, will rate the objects as having more masculine properties, will be more likely to personify the object or entity with a masculine voice or body, and so on (e.g., Boroditsky, Schmidt, & Phillips, 2003; Sera et al., 1994; Jacobson, 1959).

Similar findings have been obtained with other types of relations between words. For example, objects whose names share morphological roots in Dutch but not English will be rated to be more similar by Dutch speakers. For example, in Dutch the words for sink (*wasbak*) and garbage can (*vuilnisbak*) share the root of *-bak*, and as a result have phonological similarity. In English, the names for these objects do not have this type of relationship. Correspondingly, Dutch speakers judge pictures of sinks and garbage cans to be more similar to one another than do English speakers (Baayen & Boroditsky, 2004).

Cross-linguistic differences have been found even in very basic perceptual domains like color. For example, English and Russian color terms divide the color spectrum differently. Unlike English, Russian makes an obligatory distinction between lighter blues (*goluboy*) and darker blues (*siniy*), and this linguistic difference leads to differences in color discrimination (Winawer et al., 2007). Russian speakers are faster to discriminate two colors if they fall into different linguistic categories in Russian (one *siniy* and the other *goluboy*) than if they are from the same linguistic category (both *siniy* or both *goluboy*). English speakers tested on the same stimuli show no such differences across the *goluboy-siniy* border.

In sum, there's a growing body of evidence that people extract complex statistical regularities out of language, and further that they incorporate these extracted patterns into their knowledge representations. Further, there is evidence that patterns of interrelations within language can help us construct new representations by encouraging analogical or metaphorical extensions between knowledge domains that share linguistic descriptions (see discussion of abstract concepts). For example, talking about time using spatial terms encourages people to reuse spatial representations for the purpose of thinking about time. Using spatial representations for thinking about time may allow us to build representations of time that go beyond our physical experience. For example, we often talk about time as if it were a physical path (e.g., we are approaching the holidays, we are getting close to the deadline, we are coming up on New Years'). Once the metaphor is in place and time is conceived of as a path, new possibilities open up for thinking about time that go beyond our normal experience – for example, a physical path you can travel in any direction you want and at whatever speed you want. Extending this idea to time gives us the notion of time travel, not something we have any personal physical experience with. In this way, abstract (or maybe even physically impossible) notions like time travel can be built out of concrete representations by creating and extending metaphors between domains of knowledge.

Further, there is evidence that language plays a constructive role in this process, directing which representations in our spatial knowledge will be reused for thinking about time. Whereas it may be universal that spatial representations are used for time, languages and cultures differ in terms of how time is laid out in space. For example, Núñez & Sweetser (2006) observed that the Aymara talk about the future as being behind them and the past as being ahead of them, and gesture accordingly. English and Mandarin differ in terms of how often they talk and think about time vertically, with Mandarin speakers being much more likely to use vertical metaphors for time than do English speakers (e.g., Boroditsky, 2001).

Of course, language can play this constructive role in knowledge building not just in building abstract domains, but also in expanding our knowledge of the physical world well beyond what we experience in our own lifetimes. Once a number of experienced perceptual states are stored, those representations can be used in new combinations to conjure up distant lands we have yet to visit, or times long ago we have no chance to experience. This conjuring is often done for us through language, by using words in new combinations to create new combinations of perceptual states.

Whereas ungrounded linguistic symbols alone have clear limitations (see our previous discussion of ducks and showgirls), when combined with some stored perceptual information linguistic symbols can be used to greatly expand our knowledge. Even in mundane domains, combining a bit of perceptual information with the combinatorial power of language can be extremely useful. For example, imagine you have perceptual information stored about grapefruits and other citrus fruits but you have never seen or heard of a pomelo. If you are told that pomelos are citrus fruits similar to grapefruits but larger and sweeter and with a thicker rind, you can easily reuse the perceptual information you have stored about other citrus fruits to form a pretty good representation of pomelos without ever having had experience with one. Given this linguistic description and the perceptual information you have stored about other citrus fruits, you would probably be able to iden-tify a pomelo at a fruit stand, and can make some good predictions about how pomelos might behave, look, taste, sound, smell, feel in the hand, and so on.

It is possible that much of our mental representation of the physical world is in fact constituted not out of direct experience but out of reused perceptual representations, with the reuse guided by what we hear in language. This allows us to build knowledge not just out of what we ourselves experience in the physical world, or what we ourselves can conjure up out of our own experiences, but also out of representations others lead us to create, conjured up through language.

SUMMARY

Neither perceptual information alone, nor the sets of correspondences between elements in language alone, are likely to be able to amount to the sophistication, scale, and flexibility of the human conceptual system. Luck-ily, humans receive heaping helpings of both of these types of information. Combining information from these two input streams, as well as extracting the wealth of information that exists in the correspondences across input streams, can help overcome the shortcomings of relying on any single infor-mation stream and can reveal information not available in any one stream. The possibilities for building representations improve drastically when both external grounding information and sets of system-internal interrelations are allowed to play a role.

The findings reviewed in this chapter begin to tell a story about the acqui-sition of knowledge that is simultaneously grounded in perceptual experience and enmeshed within a linguistic system. Conceptual knowledge does not appear to be removed from its perceptual origins, nor from its linguistic ori-gins. It seems that human knowledge is built largely from experience, from the inputs, from observed statistical regularities in the physical world and in language. Appreciating the richness of the information humans receive as input both from these two sources should help us turn what had seemed to be unsolvable mysteries about the origins of knowledge into tractable puzzles.

## References

Baayen, R. H., & Boroditsky, L. (2004). Effects of lexical structure on picture comparison. Edmonton, Canada, Conference: Conceptual Structure, Discourse & language, October 8, 2004.

Barsalou, L. W. (1999). Perceptual symbol systems. *Behavioral and Brain Sciences, 22,* 577–609.

Barsalou, L. W., Simmons, W. K., Barbey, A., & Wilson, C. D. (2003). Grounding conceptual knowledge in modality-specific systems. *Trends in Cognitive Sciences, 7,* 84–91.

Blair, R. (1995). A cognitive developmental approach to morality: Investigating the psychopath. *Cognition, 57,* 1–29.

Boroditsky, L. (2000). Metaphoric structuring: Understanding time through spatial metaphors. *Cognition, 75*(1), 1–28.

Boroditsky, L. (2001). Does language shape thought? English and Mandarin speakers' conceptions of time. *Cognitive Psychology, 43*(1), 1–22.

Boroditsky, L., & Gaby, A. (2006). East of Tuesday: Representing time in absolute space. In the *Proceedings of the 28th Annual Meeting of the Cognitive Science Society*, Vancouver, Canada.

Boroditsky, L., & Ramscar, M. (2002). The roles of body and mind in abstract thought. *Psychological Science, 13*(2), 185–188.

Boroditsky, L., & Ramscar, M. (2003). Guilt by association: Gleaning meaning from contextual co-occurrence. *Proceedings of the 25th Annual Meeting of the Cognitive Science Society*, Boston, MA.

Boroditsky, L., Schmidt, L. A., & Phillips, W. (2003). Sex, syntax and semantics. In D. Gentner & S. Goldin-Meadow (Eds.), *Language in mind: Advances in the study of language and thought* (pp. 61–78). Cambridge, MA: MIT Press.

Burgess, C., & Lund, K. (1997). Modeling parsing constraints with high-dimensional context space. *Language & Cognitive Processes, 12,* 177–210.

Casasanto, D., & Boroditsky, L. (2008). Time in the mind: Using space to think about time. *Cognition.*

Casasanto, D., & Lozano, S. (2006). Metaphor in the mind and hands. *Proceedings of 28th Annual Conference of the Cognitive Science Society*. Vancouver, Canada. 142–147.

Casasanto, D., & Lozano, S. (in press). Meaning and motor action. *Proceedings of 29th Annual Conference of the Cognitive Science Society*. Nashville, TN.

Clark, H. H. (1973). Space, time, semantics, and the child. In T. E. Moore, *Cognitive development and the acquisition of language*. New York: Academic Press.

Enfield, N. J. (2005). The body as a cognitive artifact in kinship representations. Hand gesture diagrams by speakers of Lao. *Current Anthropology, 46,* 51–81.

Fodor, J. (1975). *The language of thought*. Cambridge, MA: Harvard University Press.

Gibbs, R. J. (1994). *The poetics of mind: Figurative thought, language, and understanding*. New York: Cambridge University Press.

Goldstone, R. L., Feng, Y., & Rogosky, B. (2005). Connecting to the world and each other. In D. Pecher & R. Zwaan (Eds.), *Grounding cognition: The role of perception and action in memory, language, and thinking* (pp. 292–314). Cambridge, UK: Cambridge University Press.

Gomez, R. L., & Gerken, L. A. (1999). Artificial grammar learning by one-year-olds leads to specific and abstract knowledge. *Cognition, 70*, 109–135.

Haidt, J. (2001). The emotional dog and its rational tail: A social intuitionist approach to moral judgment. *Psychological Review, 108, 4*, 814–834.

Jacobson, R. (1959). On linguistic aspects of translation. In R. A. Brower (Ed.), *On translation* (pp. 232–239). Cambridge, MA: Harvard University Press.

Lakoff, G., & Johnson, M. (1980). *Metaphors we live by*. Chicago: University of Chicago Press.

Landauer, T. K., & Dumais, S. T. (1997). A solution to Plato's problem: The latent semantic analysis theory of acquisition, induction, and representation of knowledge. *Psychological Review, 104*, 211–240.

Landauer, T. K., Foltz, P. W., & Laham, D. (1998). An introduction to latent semantic analysis. *Discourse Processes, 25*, 259–284.

Locke, J. (1979). An essay concerning human understanding. P. H. Nidditch (Ed.). Oxford: Oxford University Press. (Originally published 1690).

Lund, K., Burgess, C., & Atchley, R. A. (1995). Semantic and associative priming in high-dimensional semantic space. *Proceedings of the Seventeenth Annual Conference of the Cognitive Science Society* (pp. 660–665). Pittsburgh, PA: Erlbaum.

Núñez, R. E., & Sweeter, E. (2006). With the future behind them: Convergent evidence from Aymara language and gesture in the crosslinguistic comparison of spatial construals of time, *Cognitive Science, 30*(3), 401–450.

Prinz, J. J. (2007). *The emotional construction of morals*. Oxford: Oxford University Press.

Redington, M., Chater, N., & Finch, S. (1998). Distributional information: A powerful cue for acquiring syntactic categories, *Cognitive Science, 22*(4), 425–469.

Rozin, P., Lowery, L., Imada, S., & Haidt, J. (1999). The CAD triad hypothesis: A mapping between three moral emotions (contempt, anger, disgust) and three moral codes (community, autonomy, divinity). *Journal of Personality and Social Psychology, 76*, 574–586.

Saffran, J. R. (2002). Constraints on statistical language learning. *Journal of Memory & Language, 47*, 172–196.

Saffran, J. R., Aslin, R. N., & Newport, E. L. (1996). Statistical learning by 8-month old infants. *Science, 274*, 1926–1928.

Sera, M. D., Berge, C., & del Castillo, J. (1994). Grammatical and conceptual forces in the attribution of gender by English and Spanish speakers. *Cognitive Development, 9*(3), 261–292.

Shepard, R. N., & Cooper, L. A. (1992). Representation of colors in the blind, color–blind, and normally sighted. *Psychological Science, 3*(2), 97–104.

Shank, R. C., & Abelson, R. (1977). *Scripts, plans, goals and understanding*. Hillsdale, NJ: Elbarum.

Traugott, E. C. (1978). On the expression of spatiotemporal relations in language. In J. H. Greenberg (Ed.), *Universals of human language, Vol. 3: Word structure* (pp. 369–400). Stanford, CA: Stanford University Press.

Valdesolo, P., & DeSteno, D. (2006). Manipulations of emotional context shape moral judgment. *Psychological Science, 17*(6), 476–477.

Wheatley, T., & Haidt, J. (2005). Hypnotic disgust makes moral judgments more severe. *Psychological Science, 16*(10), 780–784.

Winawer, J., Witthoft, N., Frank, M., Wu, L., Wade, A., & Boroditsky, L. (2007). Russian blues reveal effects of language on color discrimination. PNAS published April 30, 2007, 10.1073/pnas.0701644104.

# PART TWO

# EMBODIMENT OF SOCIAL COGNITION
# AND RELATIONSHIPS

# 5    Grounding Social Cognition

*Synchronization, Coordination, and Co-Regulation*

Gün R. Semin and John T. Cacioppo

The tabula of human nature was never rasa.

W. D. Hamilton

## INTRODUCTION

Understanding the social in *social cognition* has presented a number of challenges that have been with us from the very beginnings of "modern" psychology (cf. Semin, 1986). The first challenge is to come to terms with what the "social" means. As Gallese noted recently: "The hard problem in 'social cognition' is to understand how the epistemic gulf separating single individuals can be overcome" (Gallese, 2006, p. 16). The foundations of *Völkerpsychologie* in the 1850s (Lazarus, 1861; Lazarus & Steinhal, 1860; Wedewer, 1860; Waitz, 1859) constituted an attempt to overcome the then prevailing individual-centered psychology in German psychology by introducing a social level of analysis. The emerging modern social psychology in the early 20th century grappled with this problem, fluctuating between notions of "group mind" and "instinct," with Durkheim, LeBon, Ross, Tarde, and Wundt arguing in different voices for collective representations, group mind, collective mind, collective consciousness, or *Völkerpsychologie*. Of these various influences, the prevailing view that emerged was driven by Allport's vision of a social psychology that was individual-centered and regarded as a subdiscipline of psychology (Allport, 1924; cf. Post, 1980; Graumann, 1984, inter alia). This has very much remained the dominant view of mainstream social cognition and is underlined with reference to the biological finitude of the individual.

The second challenge is to be found in the traditional perspective in social psychology that social cognition is best understood in terms of an individual's internal mental representations, with the "social" in social cognition referring to the external stimulus being a person, dyad, group, collective, or social event. Characteristically, traditional models of information processing are symbolic, and knowledge is represented in an amodal fashion, namely, dissociated from any sensory and motor bases. Consequently, a translation must take place between the symbolic representational system and the experienced event, with high-level symbolic processes driving cognition – a view that is modeled upon fundamental concepts and principles from computer science (e.g., Fodor, 1975; Newell & Simon, 1972; Marr, 1982; Vera & Simon, 1993). The treatment of social cognition as equivalent to the information processing of social stimuli is compatible with this traditional perspective.

A third challenge is presented by a representational or symbolic perspective on social cognition that does not take into account the fact that cognition did not evolve as an end in itself but rather to foster adaptive action. The result is the relative neglect of the dynamic and adaptive functions of social cognition (cf. Smith & Semin, 2004). Recent developments in cognitive sciences (e.g., A. Clark, 1997; Clancey, 1993, 1997; Kirshner & Whitson, 1997; Barsalou, 1999; Yeh & Barsalou, 2000), neuroscience (e.g., Adolphs, 2006; Amodio & Firth, 2006; Rizzolatti & Craighero, 2004; Firth & Firth, 2006; Gallese, 2006; Sommerville & Decety, 2006), and primate cognition (e.g., Barrett & Henzi, 2005) have introduced different ways of looking at social cognition and have contributed to the social cognition model advanced in this chapter (see Semin & Cacioppo, 2007, in preparation).

As detailed elsewhere in this book (e.g., Barsalou, this volume; Glenberg, this volume), our representations of the social world are fundamentally connected with the actions that our bodies perform. An adaptive and dynamic view suggests that a model of social cognition should address the constraints and capacities provided by the perceptuomotor apparatus and the complex and continuously changing demands of the social environment in which social cognition evolved. We argue here that neural systems evolved that were tuned to particular embodiments and environments. In this view, social cognition is best understood as grounded in (rather than abstracted from) perceptuomotor processes and intertwined with a wealth of interpersonal interaction and specialized for a distinctive class of stimuli. In the course of our lives, we are exposed to a vast range of stimuli: cars, buildings, household objects, books, and, of course, other humans and an array of other life forms. Other human beings and their bodily movements constitute a distinctive class of stimuli, because the movements of other human beings can be mapped onto our own bodies.

The interindividual mapping of observed movements to the observer's mirror neuron system leads to the final challenge, namely, social cognition is not driven entirely by inner processes and representations but relies on resources that are distributed across neural, bodily, and environmental features (e.g., Hutchins, 1995; Kirsch, 1995; Brooks, 1999; Agre, 1997) with the social and physical environment supporting social action and interaction (Smith & Semin, 2004). That is, two or more individuals are capable of joint work to perform a feat that supersedes their individual capabilities, and co-cogitate and co-regulate to achieve this joint feat.

In this chapter, we advance a model of social cognition that is driven by the above considerations and their implications. We argue that social cognition is embodied; consists of affective, cognitive, behavioral, and neurophysiological processes whose organization and function within brains and bodies are promoted by an analysis across brains and bodies; and is manifested in synchronization, coordination, and co-regulation of behaviors.

The aim is to supplement individualistic accounts in embodiment research with a social framework that promotes the rigorous study of processes ranging from joint perception to joint action as well as temporally distributed regularities. To this end we present a *social cognition model* (SC model), which conceptualizes social cognition as an emergent product of jointly recruited and time-locked processes rather than individual ones. Contrary to Floyd Allport's individualistic perspective, such an analysis takes the dyad as the smallest possible unit of analysis. Moreover, the model provides an embodied grounding of social cognition by anchoring these jointly recruited processes at the sensory motor level and constrained by the types of "tasks" (e.g., dancing, playing tennis, a resource conflict, a dialogue).

In the first part, we put forward the outline of our SC model (cf. Semin & Cacioppo, 2008, in press). There is considerable empirical evidence from diverse research traditions, ranging from neurophysiology to social, developmental, and ecological psychology that speak to different parts of the model. The relevant literatures are often nonintersecting and, as such, provide only preliminary evidence for the proposed model. Representative studies from this literature are reviewed in the second part in relation to the SC model. In the final section, we shall draw further conceptual and research implications of the model.

## THE SOCIAL COGNITION (SC) MODEL

Two important functions of social cognition are the adaptive regulation of the behavior of another person (e.g., issuing instructions to another person) and adaptive co-regulation (e.g., the regulation of social interaction). For action to be efficient and adaptive, it must be closely tuned to the relevant social

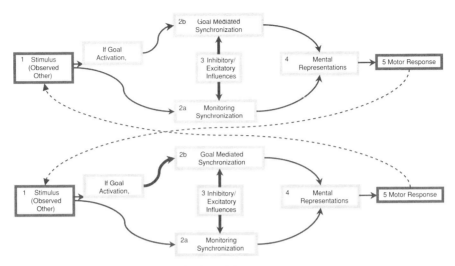

Figure 5.1. The Social Cognition (SC) model.

environment. Adaptive social action is the emergent outcome of a dynamic process of moment-by-moment interaction between conspecifics. To adapt to a continuously changing environment, the organism must have a finely tuned mechanism in place that is responsive to the multifaceted and dynamic features of the physical and social environment. Whereas these features may apply generally to cognition and its functions, the unique feature of social cognition is that it is distributed across brains in a distinctive manner.

Understanding how a state of correspondence between two agents is established and the mechanisms that contribute to achieving a state of correspondence is critical to the examination of the socially distributed nature of social cognition. However, a full conceptualization of social cognition entails more, including the processes by which regulation of others' behavior and the co-regulation of social interactions are achieved. This is precisely what the SC model depicted in Figure 5.1 is designed to capture.

- *The observation of the action of another person serves as a stimulus whose effects depend upon its goal-relevance.*

This is the starting point (1) in Figure 5.1. Aside from activating a goal, any action – irrespective of whether it is significant or not –activates an implicit monitoring processes that we refer to as:

- *Monitoring Synchronization*

The multimodal neurophysiological sensorimotor processes involved in the execution of any real (or imagined) action give rise to synchronization of neurophysiological sensorimotor processes in the observer of human action (2a in Figure 5.1). The process of synchronization is time-locked to the observed stimulus. Specifically, we define *synchronization* as jointly and simultaneously recruited sensory motor processes that are evident in a neurophysiological mirroring of the producer by the perceiver.[1] These synchronization processes enable organisms to continuously monitor and adaptively respond to their social environment by means of discrete, recurrent and short-lived temporal intervals (Andrews & Coppola, 1999; Andrews & Purves, 2005; vanRullen & Koch, 2003). That is, these recurrent processes maintain the sensitivity of the organism to changes in the environment, serve a mutual monitoring function, and facilitate dynamic adaptation.

Aside from their monitoring function, these processes link two or more human agents, thereby putting them on a similar footing. It is jointly recruited processes with overlapping "identities" that facilitate understanding (co-cogitation) and adaptive co-action (co-regulation) between two or more individuals. In other words, such mechanisms facilitate reaching a state of correspondence between the individuals. What counts for the one member may not initially have counted for the other, but through interaction these two become synchronized to approach being on the same page – that is, for what counts for one individual also counts for the other. Such synchronization can occur without the presence of explicit intent or goals (see Figure 5.1).

- *Monkey See, Monkey Do?*

If synchronization alone were to lead to complete equivalence between the sensorimotor processes of a producer and a perceiver, then there would be confusion between producer and perceiver, self, and other (e.g., Adolphs & Spezio, 2007). Moreover, complete identity could lead to a never-ending loop of continuously performing the very same actions. Therefore,

---

[1]  Notational Clarification: The literature in this field is replete with diverse terms to represent processes that are induced in co-action, may these be jointly recruited neural processes (e.g., mirroring, resonance) or behavior (e.g. mimicking, imitation, empathy). In this chapter, *synchronization* refers to the time-locked co-activation of neural processes that in the case of the monitoring pathway manifests as mirroring but in the case of the goal-directed pathway may manifest as complementarity. Jointly executed matching behaviors, if not driven by any explicit goal, is referred to as *entrainment* when they represent periodic behaviors. Coordination of co-actions takes numerous forms, as further specified in the last section of the main part of this chapter.

synchronization promotes partial, not full, correspondence between producer and perceiver (see 2a, Figure 5.1).

The complexity of the social environment and the adaptiveness required of social cognition is not only to continuously monitor but also to selectively respond to significant features of a dynamic social environment by setting goals for action. It is important to address how adaptive action is induced in response to "significant" stimuli. Visualize a table tennis game in which your partner makes a backhand smash. Whereas monitoring that action is critical, it will not win you the game. You must take effective complementary actions. Thus, if the stimulus is goal-relevant, then higher-level cognitive processes are recruited that entail goal-mediated synchronization of neurophysiological activations whose specific form need not mirror the actions that are observed. Whereas the monitoring process is critical, adaptive action is not merely a product of monitoring processes. We therefore propose that the identification of significant stimuli recruits goal-driven higher-level decision processes that can run in addition to continuous monitoring processes (see 2b, Figure 5.1).

The higher-order goal-mediated synchronization and adaptive action (2b) depicted in Figure 5.1 are separable functionally from the monitoring synchronization (2a) depicted in Figure 5.1. One reason for this functional distinction is that the processes depicted in (2a) are thought to be automatic, whereas those depicted in (2b) involve automatic and controlled processes. In terms of the table tennis example, this means that the backhand smash of the opponent is monitored – a process that is achieved by the nonconscious synchronization of neurophysiological activations corresponding to that motor movement. Synchronization as a continuous monitoring process serves a predictive function by detecting changes in the environment. Yet, the table tennis player must make a decision about how to counter the backhand and defend themselves. This decision to counter the backhand leads to the requisite neurophysiological activation for the execution of the countermove rather than simply the mirror image of the observed action. Although specific aspects of goal-mediated synchronization can be automated, the act as a whole is not.

- *Synchronization and higher-level processes are dissociated but jointly shape the mental representation of the stimulus and are both subject to inhibitory and excitatory influences (3, Figure 5.1) before they shape these mental representations (4, Figure 5.1) that is then translated to action in the form of a motor response.*

Both goal-mediated synchronization processes and monitoring synchronization recruit neurophysiological activity and jointly contribute to the shape of the representations that are translated into motor action (4, Figure 5.1). In the absence of goal-mediated synchronization, the neurophysiological activation from monitoring synchronization shapes the representation. However, this does not necessarily mean the automatic execution of the observed action because other factors can contribute to the representation. Moreover, both excitatory and inhibitory factors can modulate the contributions of the processes (2a) and (2b) depicted in Figure 5.1 to the representation. For instance, inhibitory processes can contribute to blocking continuous automatic reproduction of what is observed (e.g., Baldissera, Cavallari, Craighero, & Fadiga, 2001).

• *The structural features of the environment or task will contribute to the type of co-regulation processes that will emerge.*

The type of task environment requiring two or more persons that can be socially shaped (e.g., dancing, playing tennis, conversation) or by the physical characteristics of a joint task (e.g., carrying a large and heavy object) presents distinctive affordances that shape the co-regulation of the social interaction.

• *The behavior of one individual becomes the stimulus for the other when the individuals are actively interacting, with each iteratively producing co-action effects. Consequently, synchronization and adaptive co-regulation of behaviors are detectible when the unit of analysis is at the social rather than the individual level.*

This yields the emergent social cognition as represented in Figure 5.1 with direct loops from (5) to (1), namely, where the behavior of a member of the dyad provides information pickup for the other member in an iterative process.

In the following section, we shall examine the proposed model in the light of the existing empirical evidence. In referring to the empirical evidence, we shall also contrast the SC model with different models that have been developed for specific phases (e.g., synchronization, entrainment, task driven joint action) of the general model we have outlined.

THE SC MODEL: THE EVIDENCE

The evidence for the SC model comes from research at neural, emotional, and behavioral levels. The empirical evidence adduced here in terms of the SC model comes in three sections. The first has to do with synchronization processes advanced in the model. These are neurophysiological studies highlighting synchronization in the face of action observation as well as the observation of emotions. The second section is empirical evidence pertaining to goal-driven processes exclusively. The final section is about behavioral processes displaying entrainment, "mimicry," and coordination.

## Synchronization of Action

The neural basis of synchronization processes can be understood based on neurophysiological evidence with human and nonhuman primates. This evidence suggests that intentional action, and the perception of such action, has a shared neural notation. This line of research gained momentum with the discovery of mirror neurons in area F5 of the monkey premotor cortex (e.g., di Pellegrino, Fadiga, Fogassi, Gallese, & Rizzolatti, 1992; Gallese, Fadiga, Fogassi, & Rizzolatti, 1996; Rizzolatti, Fadiga, Gallese, Fogassi, 1996). Rizzolatti et al. (1996) demonstrated the existence of a particular class of visuomotor neurons (in the F5 area of the macaque monkey premotor cortex) that discharge when the monkey engages in a particular action (e.g., grasping a peanut) and when it observes another monkey engaging in the same action (for a review, see Rizzolatti & Craighero, 2004).

A subset of these neurons – termed '*mirror neurons*' – also become active even when the final part of the action (e.g., grasping the peanut) is hidden (Umiltà, Kohler, Gallese, Fogassi, Fadiga, Keysers, & Rizzolatti, 2001). Critically, in the hidden condition the monkey must "know" that an object (peanut) is behind the occluder and must observe the experimenter's hand going behind the occluder without seeing the completion of the action. More recently, Keysers and his colleagues (Keysers, Kohler, Umiltà, Nanetti, Fogassi, & Gallese, 2003) have reported that specific populations of neurons (audiovisual mirror neurons) in the ventral premotor cortex of the monkey discharge not only when a monkey performs a specific action but also when it sees or hears another monkey perform the same action. These neurons therefore represent actions independently of whether these actions are performed, heard, or seen. Converging evidence about the adaptive nature of the mirror neuron system comes from Kohler, Keysers, Umiltà, Fogassi, Gallese, and Rizzolatti (2002), where monkeys were trained to rip a piece of paper. It was shown that once trained, the mirror neurons involved in the execution of this action were recruited in response to only the sound of ripping. These studies suggest that single neurons in the premotor cortex synchronize not only to the actions that the other is executing but also that the action along with the "goal" is represented and inferred across different modalities. The correlation between mirror neuron activation in partially observed or merely heard conditions corresponds largely to the pattern of neurons recruited in the full performance of the actions, which result in a sound (peanut crack-ing) or complete action (grasping food). These studies suggest that single neurons in the premotor cortex synchronize not only to the actions that the other is executing but also that the action "goal" is represented and inferred in different modalities.

There are specific features of the neurophysiological evidence on syn-chronization processes for action. First of all, it is correlational. Second, it is based on the observation and execution of single, discrete behaviors. Third, the behaviors that serve as stimuli are either transitive (e.g., cracking a peanut) or intransitive (i.e., mouth movements such as lip smacking, biting, licking; Ferrari, Gallese, Rizzolatti, & Fogassi, 2003; Ferrari, Maiolini, Addessi, Fogassi, Visalberghi, 2005). Finally, this research underlines the multimodal (e.g., visual, auditory) quality of synchronization processes.

Whereas the evidence noted above is from nonhuman primates, there is also an emerging body of evidence indicating the neural substrates of general action in humans, supporting the notion that a system of neurons synchro-nize to observed actions. The human premotor cortex, which is involved in voluntary movements of the body, is organized somatotopically. Using func-tional magnetic resonance imaging (fMRI), Buccino, Binkofski, Fink, Fadiga, Fogassi, Gallese, Seitz, Zilles, Rizzolatti, and Freund (2001) localized areas of the brain that were active during the observation of movement by another individual. They found that regions of the premotor cortex were activated when individuals observed the actions of another and, more specifically, that the areas activated in the premotor cortex corresponded to the regions that would be active were the individual to have executed the observed actions. The findings of Buccino et al. (2001) are in accord with the hypothesis that there is a brain circuit that extracts and neurologically represents the motor commands of another individual's observed actions – the so-called "direct matching hypothesis." The type of "mirroring" noted by Buccino et al. (2001) does not require voluntary control.

Evidence from other researchers indicates that imitative reactions are faster than simple visual reaction times, and that people's awareness of their own imitative reactions occurs significantly later than their imitative reactions. Indeed, there is considerable cumulative evidence revealing that observing movements of the finger, hand, arm, mouth, or foot leads to the activation of motor-related areas of the cortex (e.g., Grafton, Arbib, Fadiga, & Rizzolatti, 1996; Iacoboni et al., 1999; Manthey, Shubotz, & von Cramon, 2003; Stevens, Fonlupt, Shiffrar, & Decety, 2000). These findings hold in the case of move-ments that are biologically possible and not for impossible movements, as for instance an arm passing through a leg (Stevens et al., 2000).

Recent research has also revealed that listening to speech sounds activates premotor areas in the brain overlapping with areas that are responsible for the production of speech (Wilson, Saygin, Sereno, & Iacoboni, 2004). These research findings provide evidence for the existence of a shared neural notation and suggest a mechanism by which neural "parity" (e.g., Liberman & Mattingly, 1985; Liberman & Whalen, 2000) between a producer and receiver is achieved in an automatic manner.

### Synchronization of Emotion

Whereas the evidence for synchronization processes emerging from movement or motor action has been in the forefront of neurophysiological research, the evidence for synchronization with emotional behavior is accumulating rapidly. Increasingly, the research on emotions suggests that afferent feedback generated by elementary motor entrainment with behavior expressive of emotions produces a matching emotional experience (e.g., Hatfield, Cacioppo, & Rapson, 1994; Dimberg, Thunberg, & Elmehed, 2000). Studies using functional neuroimaging techniques have shown that observing facial expressions of disgust and feelings of disgust activated very similar sites in the anterior insula and anterior cingulate cortex (e.g., Wicker, Keysers, Plailly, Royet, Gallese, & Rizzolatti, 2003) and are involved in inducing empathy (e.g., Decety, 2005; Jabbi, Swart, & Keysers, 2007). Indeed, single neuron recording experiments with humans show that the observation of pain and its experience activate the same neurons (Hutchison, Davis, Lozano, Tasker, & Dostrovsky, 1999). The argument developed by a number of authors (e.g., Adolphs, 2006; Carr, Iacoboni, Dubeau, Mazziotta, & Lenzi, 2003; Decety & Grèzes, 2006) is akin to an insight offered by Lipps in the beginning of the 20th century when he advanced the concept of *Einfühlung*. "In the perception and comprehension of certain sensory objects, namely those which we represent afterwards as the body of another individual (or generally as the sensory appearance of such) is immediately grasped by us ... This grasp happens immediately and simultaneously with the perception, and that does not mean that we see it or apprehend it by means of the senses, We cannot do that, since anger, friendliness, or sadness cannot be perceived through the senses. We can only experience this kind of thing ourselves" (Lipps, 1903, p. 713, translation G. Jahoda, 2005). The emerging picture in the current research literature suggests that synchronization in the case of emotions activates the processes in the central nervous system underlying the experience or feeling of the somatic state of the other, which does not necessarily reach sufficient strength to be consciously accessible. The cumulating evidence suggests that synchronization observed for action is also applicable to emotion (cf. Adolphs, 2003, 2006). Indeed, research using electromyography (EMG) techniques has shown that observers' facial expressions synchronize within a time window of 500 msec, even with subliminally presented facial expressions of emotion (e.g., Dimberg et al., 2000).

Further evidence along these lines is provided by Carr, Iacoboni, Dubeau, Mazziotta, and Lenzi (2003). Using fMRI, Carr and colleagues (2003) found that the brain regions important for action representation and imitation, such as the superior temporal sulcus (STS), are related to activation in the insula and amygdala – regions in the limbic lobe that are involved in emotions. Indeed, recent research suggests that the observation of another person's emotional state recruits structures like the insula (Jackson, Meltzoff, & Decety, 2005; Singer, Seymour, O'Doherty, Kaube, Dolan, & Firth, 2004), a part of the cortex that is also involved in the representation of our own somatic states. Additionally, there is evidence of an association of the insula with the conscious experience of one's own bodily state (Critchley, Wiens, Rotshtein, Oehman, & Dolan, 2004). Indeed, observations of emotional states (e.g., a fearful body) not only induce increased activity in brain areas related to emotional processes but also areas that are responsible for the representation of action, suggesting that the synchronization process goes beyond establishing symmetry in experience but puts the organism in a state of readiness for action (e.g., De Gelder, Snyder, Greve, Gerard, & Hadijkhani, 2004).

Before closing this section, we should note that synchronization does not suggest complete equivalence or identity between producer and receiver but correspondence or "parity." Thus, in the research on mirror neurons with monkeys observing and performing an action, approximately 20% of the neurons in the F5 are overlapping (Gallese et al., 1996). Similarly in behavioral research, which we shall review in the next section, it is very specific behaviors out of a range of behaviors that synchronize. Moreover, Baldissera et al. (2001) examined whether the observation of action involves not only cortical motor areas but also low-level motor structures that resonate the observed actions as if they were performed by the observer. They had participants observe hand opening and closure and measured H-reflex size (to examine spinal cord excitability) evoked in the flexor and extensor muscles. The findings reveal that observing participants H-reflex for flexors increased for hand opening and decreased for hand closing. The reverse was noted for extensors. These results suggest that there is an inhibitory mechanism in the spinal cord that stops the execution of the observed hand action. Thus, it is important to qualify that synchronization does not produce identity between producer and perceiver but parity or correspondence. Obviously, the result of synchronization would be the equivalence between a producer's and perceiver's actions and emotions rather than a partial overlap. As Adolphs and Spezio (2007) have suggested, this would lead to complete confusion between producer and perceiver repeatedly performing the same actions all the time.

The converging research evidence we have selectively reviewed suggests that the architecture of the human perceptual and neural system is specifically designed for the recognition of movements of conspecifics in a privileged way Indeed, if mapping human beings and their bodily movements does constitute a special or distinctive case, then it should be somewhat species-specific. Buccino, Lui, Canessa, Patteri, Lagravinese, Benuzzi, Porro, and Rizzolatti (2004) examined human observers who were exposed to mouth movements performed by humans, monkeys, and dogs. The movements were either transitive (e.g., biting a piece of food) or intransitive (e.g., barking, silent speech, lip smacking). Interestingly, where the observation of biting reactions recruited the mirror circuit, intransitive mouth actions gave rise to the activation of different cortical foci as a function of the observed species, showing that actions within the motor repertoire of the human subjects were mapped on their motor system, whereas nonhuman movements were mapped as a function of their visual properties.

The body of research reviewed here underlines the fact that the perception of bodily movements constitutes a distinctive class of stimuli. These findings speak to species-specific mapping process and underline the view that synchronization leads to the formation of a type of sensory neural representation that has an entirely different ontological status than knowledge about the world in general. One can therefore regard synchronization as a foundation of communication and the embodied building block of social cognition.

The central question that can be raised here is about the function of synchronization processes. This question also invites an evaluation of theoretical accounts that have been advanced to come to terms with the explosively accumulating and increasingly sophisticated data on mirroring processes.

## Functional Utility of Synchronization

There are a variety of accounts addressing the meaning and function of the findings reviewed previously (e.g., Firth & Firth, 2006; Grèzes & Decety, 2001; Decety & Grèzes, 2006; Iacoboni, 2005; Jeannerod, 1999; Goldman, 2002, 2005; Keysers & Gazzola, 2006). For space reasons, we shall deal with only one prominent account, namely, the one advanced by Gallese. Central to Gallese's conceptualization is the notion of "shared manifold" (e.g., Gallese, 2001, 2003, 2005), namely, a shared meaningful interpersonal space (e.g., Gallese, 2001). "Shared manifold" is regarded by Gallese as grounding the understanding of action or emotion. The shared manifold is achieved in a process in which the perception of an action or emotion induces a motor "simulation." This embodied simulation process is direct, automatic, and escapes conscious access, and leads the observer to achieve a neural coupling with an agent, thereby reconstituting the other's emotion or intentional action and creating a shared bodily state. In Gallese's view, this "experienced state" constitutes the basis of mutual or direct understanding. "By means of embodied simulation, we do not just 'see' an action, an emotion, or a sensation. Side by side with the sensory description of the observed social stimuli, internal representations of the body states associated with these actions, emotions, and sensations are evoked in the observer, 'as if' he/she would be doing a similar action or experiencing a similar emotion or sensation" (Gallese, 2006, p. 6). The neural correlate of such an embodied simulation mechanism is to be found in mirror neuron systems and – as the quote implies – the shared neural state of the bodies of the agent and observer follow the same functional rules in which the other becomes another "self." Mutual understanding in this view is nonpropositional. The shared bodily state achieved through embodied simulation is at a basic level of understanding and does not entail declarative representation. Most importantly, in this view the function of mutual understanding is not merely modeling agents, their actions and emotions, but also the successful prediction of upcoming events.

Admittedly, social cognition does not consist of merely passive experiences of observing another perform an action or express a particular affective state. Moreover, social cognition does not consist of internal or intra-individual processes alone, even if these processes constitute a genuinely social state, as in the case of a "shared manifold" to which Gallese refers. Social cognition consists of dynamic, unfolding processes that take place between two or more agents who are engaged in action and reaction, and the shape of this interaction takes a multitude of forms ranging from a wide range of different nonverbal to verbal exchanges. What does the embodied simulation model represent in the context of a broader conception of social cognition, namely, as distributed processes taking place between two or more individuals? In the context of the SC model advanced here, the embodied simulation processes to which Gallese refers correspond to what we refer to as monitoring *synchronization*. What is at issue here is not the simulation process but the interpretation of the function and the reach of the account advanced by Gallese. There is convergence in terms of the jointly and simultaneously recruited sensory motor processes that give partial access between producer and perceiver at a neural level and are predictive of the other's actions or states. However, in the case of the SC model, we regard synchronization as a monitoring mechanism, which is paralleled by goal-mediated complementary neurophysiological processes that jointly contribute to "mutual understanding" in context, which also involves mental representations that result in co-cogitation and co-regulation of action.

Gallese's model of social cognition is informed by a research paradigm in which the agent is a passive observer contemplating the "essence of existence" rather than an agent in interaction with another agent involved in a continuously unfolding dynamic monitoring process of co-regulation. That is, the unit of analysis is the individual. The function of synchronization in this co-regulation process is to put both agents on the same sensorimotor page and serve the anticipation of what is to follow next. However, monitoring alone does not shape unfolding interaction.

While in agreement with Gallese's account of the simulation process inducing a "shared bodily state," which we refer to here as synchronization, the proposed SC model has a broader framework that consequently situates "embodied simulation" mechanisms within a different functional context. Whereas understanding how two or more agents achieve "being on the same somatic state-page" is important in identifying mechanisms by which the epistemic gulf separating single individuals is bridged at a biological level, it does not address or incorporate the general process of what social cognition covers and the multitude of bridging layers that exist at a behavioral and linguistic level (Semin, 2007).

Moreover, the SC model specifies the interaction between goal-driven synchronization and monitoring synchronization, namely, processes that shape ideomotor representations and contribute to the formation and subsequent impact of motor responses.

## Goal Mediated Synchronization

There is substantial research literature on how explicitly provided goals drive co-regulation of behavior in dyads. A considerable amount of the research speaking to this issue relies on a experimental paradigm involving an explicit imitation instruction of touching a body part or an object on the child's left or right side with a left or right hand movement (e.g., Swanson & Benton, 1955; Wapner & Cirillo, 1968). Thus, the experimental conditions induce an explicit motor response goal that is further specified by the body part or object that defines the motor responses' designation (for an overview, see Wohlschläger,

Gattis, & Bekkering, 2003). This research has a bearing on the SC model we advance here because it constitutes an instance of behavior that is driven by externally set goals. In that context, we make the assumption that under certain circumstances the behavior shown subsequent to the observed action is a reflection of the neurophysiological activation that has been induced by the observed action.

Two features of the research in this field are relevant for the examination of what it means when a model and a participant perform the very same movement. These two features are the goal of the movement (i.e., the object or body part to be touched) and the hand movement (i.e. right or left hand movement). The research reveals that if there is a goal to the executed movement – for instance, two adjacent dots are stuck on a table and the model covers one of the dots with a hand movement – then the child (average age 4.4 years) always covers the correct dot. However, if the model executed a contralateral hand movement to cover the dot, then the child uses an ipsilateral hand movement (Bekkering, Wohlschlager, & Gattis, 2000, Experiment 3; Schofield, 1976). If the goal (dot) is removed and the same hand movements are executed, then the child performs the same movement. Ipsilateral movements produce ipsilateral performance, and contralateral model movements lead to the production of contralateral hand movements.

Thus, in terms of the SC model one finds that the presence of a goal (instructionally provided significant stimulus, e.g., a dot) inhibits the production of the very same behavior under these experimental conditions. Obviously, the important caveat in the context of "imitation" experiments is that participants receive explicit instructions to "imitate" the model. Consequently, reproduction of the same movement in such conditions is not automatically driven but explicitly instructed. Interestingly, the same hand movements ensue when a "higher" goal (dot) is not present. Here, we make the assumption that participants synchronize to the behavior that they automatically simulate when they observe the behavior and that they subsequently reproduce this previously simulated behavior, at least when there are no external cues (e.g., dots) that provide significant alternative, higher-order goals.

## CO-REGULATION OF BEHAVIOR: ENTRAINMENT, MIMICRY, AND COORDINATION

The SC model we have advanced configures the steps from perception to production, incorporating its expression in joint action. In this section, we review evidence on the co-regulation of behavior (see 5, Figure 5.1), which is a dynamic and emergent process. To this end, we distinguish between three qualitatively different forms of co-action as instances of co-regulation. The first is *entrainment* and is exemplified by periodic co-action and occurs in cycles. This can be illustrated with the example of rhythmic clapping. The second form is when co-action is nonperiodic, as in the case of *mimicry*. The third case is exemplified in situations that involve a number of people who have to interface each others' actions in the course of performing a complex task (e.g., open-heart surgery, playing tennis). This is the functional effect of co-action, namely, *coordination*, which entails the execution of complementary actions in the pursuit of accomplishing the task (e.g., successful surgery, winning the game). These different forms of the co-regulation of behavior can obviously all occur simultaneously and to different degrees. In the following, we present the distinctive features of each of these three forms and the related research.

### Entrainment

We refer to *entrainment* as the alignment of behaviors or rhythms during social interaction, borrowing the term from earlier work (e.g., Condon & Ogston, 1966, 1967).[2] The earliest reference to entrainment is by McDougall (1908), who noted that spectators assume the postural manner of athletes they were observing. It is a multimodal form of co-action (verbal, affective, movement) and refers to a state between two persons that results when the cyclical behavioral movements of one person influence the cyclical movements of another person and they oscillate in rhythm. A typical example of entrainment is provided in the spontaneous transition of an applauding audience from disordered clapping to entrained clapping (Neda, Ravasz, Brechet, Vicsek, & Barabasi, 2000) and then back again to disordered clapping only for entrained clapping to reemerge again a little later. This remarkable phenomenon is evidenced despite considerable individual differences in clapping tempos. It would appear that the transition to entrained clapping enhances noise intensity and requires less effort, whereby each clapper affects the other both locally and globally. Entrained behavior occurs rhythmically, and one way of capturing their regularities is to model its cycles, periods, frequencies, and amplitudes. Depending on the particular behavior and interaction in question, behavioral cycles of entrainment in interpersonal behavior can range from milliseconds to hours. Entrainment is not specific to human social behavior alone (cf. Strogatz, 2003), and its investigation can focus on

---

[2]  Subsequently used as synchrony specifically referring to the judged "gestaltlike harmoniousness or meshing of interpersonal behaviors" (Bernieri et al., 1988).

the degree to which behavioral cycles of a couple are in phase or not (e.g., early developmental work by Brazelton, Koslowski, & Main, 1974; Bullowa, 1975; Davis, 1982; Rosenfeld, 1981; Stern, 1974).

Recent work from an ecological perspective has revitalized research on entrainment. This approach has treated interaction as the unit of analysis with the objective of modeling the temporal organization of the movements of two (or more) people. This research often relies on instructionally induced periodic co-action (but not always, e.g., Shockley et al., 2007), thus supplying a goal (2b, Figure 5.1) and revealing the systematic temporal dynamics of behavior (5, Figure 5.1). However, the processes by which two agents pick up information from each other and how this information shapes the different phases of movements do not present any specific theoretical interest from this perspective. This approach is equally mute about the processes that contribute to the temporal co-organization of these movements (cf. Marsh et al., 2006). From an ecological perspective, the suggestion is that movement is "lawfully" constrained by other people's movements (Marsh et al., 2006) and best modeled in terms of coupled oscillator theory without any recourse to any jointly recruited intrapersonal processes, may these be neural or psychological.

For instance, Shockley and his colleagues (2003; Shockley, Baker, Richardson, & Fowler, 2007) examined whether conversation fosters interpersonal postural entrainment (postural sway) and revealed that convergent speaking patterns mediate interpersonal postural entrainment (see also Condon & Ogston, 1966; Kendon, 1970; LaFrance, 1982). Postural sway is not the only behavior that entrains outside of conscious access but also speech rate (Street, 1984). Similarly, pausing frequency (Cappella & Planalp, 1981) has been shown to entrain. Entrainment has also been shown to hold for gestural (see Furuyama, Hayashi, & Mishima, 2005) movements of interacting individuals without the individuals intending to entrain. Spontaneous entrainment occurs when interactants have full visual access to each other (i.e., joint attention, cf. Sebanz et al., 2006), but the previous studies suggest that visual information is not the only medium recruited by participants to entrain.

The ecological perspective on this research draws on human movement science and coupled oscillator theory to explain periodically recurring regularities in the movements of two persons (for an overview, see Marsh et al., 2006) by focusing exclusively on behavioral data. Their argument is that an embodied approach to uncovering perception-action systems resulting in entrainment must rely on the examination of dynamic properties of actual behavior taking place between individuals rather than mentalistic, representational constructs. Whereas modeling the temporal organization of movement provides an insight into the regularities, their cycles, the break-down of regularities, and relies on very sophisticated technology to record joint movements, it makes no attempt to understand the neural and psy-chological forces driving such behavior. Consequently, specific phenomena such as the affective and motivational precursors – as well as consequences of entrainment, the contribution of entrainment, and coordination to socially distributed knowledge and more complex multimodal processes such as con-versation and dialogue – do not currently seem to feature as relevant phenom-ena in this approach. Thus, while convergent with the perspective adopted in the SC model, that the object of social cognition is an emergent interaction unit – an outcome of joint action – this approach differs in that the primary focus is the analysis of behavior.

*Mimicry*
Interest in nonperiodic co-action seems to have gone in ebbs and tides since the 1960s (e.g., Bernieri, 1988; Bernieri, Reznick, & Rosenthal, 1988; Bernieri, Davis, Rosenthal, & Knee, 1994; Condon & Ogston, 1966, 1967; Kendon, 1970; Tickle-Degnen & Rosenthal, 1987; Bavelas, Black, Chovil, Lemery, & Mullett, 1988; Bavelas, Black, Lemery, & Mullett, 1986). Notably, this early research uses "social interaction" as the unit of analysis rather than the individual (e.g., Scheflen, 1982). Among these, a line of research is to be found running under the labels of *mirroring* or *mimicry* (e.g., Bavelas, Black, Lemery, & Mullett, 1986; Dabbs, 1969; O'Toole & Dubin, 1968), namely, a focus on an individual's imitation or mimicking of the limb movements performed by another. This focus was reintroduced in the 1990s (e.g., Chartrand & Bargh, 1999; Hatfield et al., 1994; van Baaren, Maddux, Chartrand, de Bouter, & van Knippenberg, 2003). For instance, Chartrand and Bargh (1999) had a trained experimenter rubbing her nose or shaking her foot while interacting with a participant. Their results revealed that when the experimenter rubbed her nose, then participants were more likely to do so as well rather than shake their foot, and in the experimental condition when the experimenter shook her foot, then the likelihood of participants shaking their foot was higher than rubbing their nose.

   Earlier research by Bavelas and her colleagues (e.g., Bavelas, Black, Chovil, Lemery, & Mullett, 1988; Bavelas, Black, Lemery, & Mullett, 1986) examined what they also refer to as "motor mimicry," defined as behavior by an observer that is appropriate to the situation of another (e.g., wincing at the other's injury or ducking when the other does). They argue that the function of such motor mimicking is primarily communicative (Bavelas et al., 1988). They created a situation with a victim of an apparently painful injury and controlled the amount of eye contact that the victim had with a participant observing the victim. They were able to reveal that motor mimicry displayed by the observing participant was significantly shaped by the visual availability of the victim, suggesting that mimicry may serve a communicative function.

The research evidence to date suggests that mimicry occurs outside of conscious awareness and without any intent to mimic or imitate. Numerous studies have investigated the diverse moderating conditions and consequences of "mimicry" such as self-monitoring (Cheng & Chartrand, 2003) and type of self-construal (van Baaren, Maddux, Chartrand, de Bouter, & van Knippenberg, 2003; van Baaren, Horgan, Chartrand, & Dijkmans, 2004). One of the interesting consequences of mimicry or entrainment is that it leads to an increased liking of an interaction partner (Chartrand & Jefferis, 2003; Dijksterhuis & Bargh, 2001). Indeed, there appears to be reliable evidence for the relationship between liking and the entrainment or mimicry of different types of movements (Bernieri & Rosenthal, 1991; Chartrand & Bargh, 1999; Julien, Brault, Chartrand, & Begin, 2000; LaFrance, 1982; LaFrance & Broadbent, 1976; Lakin & Chartrand, 2003).

Currently, mimicry research, which has the individual as the unit of analysis, relies on a priming account. The assumption is that "perceiving an action activates the mental representation of this action, which in turn leads to the performance of the action" (Dijksterhuis & Bargh, 2001, p. 8). Indeed, this account of entrainment shows no theoretical interest in the temporally distributed regularities in joint movement – a central focus in ecological work – nor does it show an interest in jointly recruited mediating processes as advanced by the SC model. Indeed, the so-called "perception-action expressway" (Dijksterhuis & Bargh, 2001) has an uncomplicated approach to explaining how an individual's behavior affects the behavior of another individual. Thus, in this view the temporal dynamics of interpersonal entrainment do not feature. There is no distinction between coordination and entrainment, though the data on which the mimicry research relies consists of the frequency with which a target displays the same behavior as a confederate.

## Coordination

*Coordination* of behavior can take a great variety of manifest forms, ranging from a dialogue, talking and walking, a soccer game, the performance of open-heart surgery, two people moving a very heavy object, to implementing a war strategy. Four features of coordination stand out. One is that the participants in a joint action must be on the same page regarding the "task" at hand, namely, share a "common ground" and engage in joint action abiding by the rules pertinent to the "task" (dialogue, tennis, surgery, pushing a large object, and so on) that are quintessential to grounding the task. The second feature is that joint action is an open system (whatever the task) and can lead to the same result (goal or end state) despite differences in the initial conditions. In other words, coordination is not a determinate path but is characterized by equifinality. Third, coordination can take place over behavioral cycles that can vary from milliseconds to hours or longer. The temporal nature of these cycles is a function of the type of "task" that is being performed. This can be illustrated with any type of social interaction that consists of situated linguistic or behavioral exchanges, such as a dialogue or a tennis game. Finally, coordination in social interaction is multimodal (e.g., verbal, motor movement).

### Co-regulation of Behavior

Entrainment, mimicry, and coordination are simultaneously occurring processes during social interaction. For instance, consider a dialogue. Any dialogue features a variety of instances of multimodal coordination, entrainment, and mimicry. A dialogue can simultaneously manifest coordination, as in the case of turn-taking in a conversation (e.g., Sachs, Schegloff, & Jefferson, 1974) or introducing a new topic, at a syntactic level (e.g., syntactic priming; Bock, 1986, 1989; Bock & Loebell, 1990), or an affective level (e.g., mood contagion, Neumann & Strack, 2000). Simultaneously, it is possible to see cyclically occurring instances of affective facial expressions (e.g., Dimberg et al., 2000) and breathing movements (e.g., Furuyama, Hayashi, & Mishima, 2005). Coordination and entrainment can converge when joint behavior is goal-driven (e.g., playing tennis versus choral singing), be consciously accessible, or escape conscious access (two people moving a heavy object versus emotional contagion), or a combination of both.

In presenting the SC model, we argued that the goal of joint action along with the type of task environment (social or physical features of the task) contributes to the shape and nature of cognition and joint action. The nature of coordination, mimicry, and entrainment in co-regulation will obviously vary depending on whether two people are attempting to move a heavy stone, a large table, an abstract idea, or a concrete business plan. Of course, there is a well-established tradition on how language is used to coordinate joint action and establish what is termed "common ground" (H. Clark, 1996). A significant portion of this work has relied on the transmission of "representations" in interpersonal communication (cf. Krauss & Chiu, 1998; Krauss & Fussell, 1996). A recurrent theme in this field is what one may be referred to as "coordination in communication," namely, the different ways in which "representational correspondence" can be established in joint action by, for instance, "audience design" (e.g., Krauss & Fussell, 1996), "referential communication" (Clark & Brennan, 1991; Fussell & Krauss, 1989a, 1989b), and "grounding" (e.g., Clark, 1996; Keysar, 1997).

In contrast, the approaches to co-action (e.g., Sebanz et al., 2006; Marsh et al., 2006) do not speak to how the different pathways activated by significant goals and synchronization processes contribute to the shape of entrainment and coordination. The SC model specifies these conditions. In the absence of goal activation that recruits coordination (e.g., playing table tennis), synchronization processes (subject to inhibitory and excitatory influences) contribute to the shape of the cognitive, co-native, and affective mental representations that configure the motor responses of the perceiver. Arguably, this is what is noted in the mimicry research. This is argued to be the result of a semistochastic transduction process leading to some nonperiodic co-action.

Obviously, there are numerous naturally occurring instances where the behavioral goals of co-actors are explicitly prescribed, as in the case of gospel singing and dancing, inter alia. These are instances where behavior entrainment (entrainment of motor responses) is likely to occur when goal-mediated neurophysiological activation is synchronized with the stimulus as a function of appropriate relevance and significance. A consequence of entrainment involving such fusion of action is the emergence of considerable identity overlap resulting in the reduction of psychological distance, increased proximity, and heightened rapport between co-actors, as the early and recent research on mimicry has demonstrated. These are situations where the boundaries between self and other are reduced or on extreme occasions nearly dissolve, such as in religious rituals.

CONCLUSION

The cognitive revolution led by psychologists, anthropologists, and linguists in the 1950s was a response to the claim by behaviorists that mental processes did not fall under the purview of science (e.g., Chomsky, 1959). Mental representations and processes were rendered testable through the use of mathematical and computer models that specified stimulus inputs, information processing operations that acted on and transformed these inputs to produce and change representational structures, and information processing operations that led to observable responses. Accordingly, the dominant metaphor for the mind became the solitary computer – a device with massive information processing capacities in which knowledge is represented in an amodal fashion, divorced from the building blocks of behaviorism – sensory and motor bases.

The past decade has seen a sea change in theory and research on embodied cognition, as evidenced by the other contributions to this volume. Humans are also a fundamentally social species. Human cognitive capacities not only evolved as a means of increasing the adaptive possibilities between stimuli and responses but do so through adaptive dyadic and collective action. Accordingly, we have argued that to fully understand social cognition, one must extend the levels of analysis beyond the study of the solitary individual. This suggested expansion of focus has a metaphorical counterpart in computer science, where the notion of the solitary computer now seems antiquated. Computers today are massively interconnected devices with capacities that extend far beyond the resident hardware and software of any single computer. For instance, the rapid evolution of the Internet has led to possibilities and capacities that could not have been envisioned a few decades ago. The hominid brain and telereceptors (e.g., eyes, ears) have provided wireless broadband interconnectivity among conspecifics for millions of years. Just as computers have capacities and processes that are transduced through but extend far beyond the hardware of a single computer, the human brain has evolved to promote cognitive, social, and cultural capacities and processes that are transduced through but that extend far beyond a solitary brain (Cacioppo & Hawkley, 2005). By extending the level of analysis of social cognition beyond the study of solitary individuals, these capacities and the mechanisms responsible for them can be more completely discerned (see also chapters by Smith and Schubert et al., this volume).

Indeed, our environment consists of a boundless array of variegated sources of stimulation ranging from diverse inanimate artifacts to the cosmos of nature. Within this boundless diversity, human beings and their bodily movements constitute a distinctive class of stimuli (e.g., Buccino et al., 2004). The architecture of the human perceptual and neural system is specifically designed for the recognition of species-specific movements in a privileged way, thereby establishing a type of knowledge that has an entirely different ontological status than knowledge about the world in general (Semin, 2007). The SC model we advanced in this chapter builds upon the work on embodied cognition to argue that cognition is social – in the sense that it is the consequence of interactions among individuals – because neurophysiological mechanisms exist that facilitate achieving some common or symmetrical base between individuals. Consequently, the model relies on an analytic unit that is different from the traditional Western focus – evident in the writings of Plato and Aristotle – of the isolated, thinking individual. The individual is also a prominent unit for practical methodological reasons. Such an analytic incision offers itself readily given the biological finitude of the individual. However, it does not necessarily lend itself as readily for conceptualizing what it means to be a "social species" and the analysis of social cognition in general. Consequently, a complete understanding of social cognition may require an analytic unit that includes coupled individuals and jointly recruited processes. We hope this is one of the contributions of the SC model to the emerging embodiment literature.

## References

Adolphs, R., & Spezio, M. (2007). The neural basis of affective and social behavior. In J. T. Cacioppo, L. G. Tassinary, & G. G. Berntson (Eds.), *Handbook of psychophysiology* (3ed ed.) (pp. 540–554). New York: Cambridge University Press.

Adolphs, R. (2003). Cognitive neuroscience of human social behaviour. *Nature Reviews Neuroscience, 4,* 165–178.

Adolphs, R. (2006). How do we know the minds of others? Domain specificity, simulation, and enactive social cognition. *Brain Research, 1079,* 25–35.

Agre, P. E. (1997). *Computation and human experience.* New York: Cambridge University Press.

Allport, F. H. (1924). *Social psychology.* Boston: Houghton Mifflin.

Amodio, D. M., & Firth, C. D. (2006). Meeting of minds: The medial frontal cortex and social cognition. *Nature Reviews Neuroscience, 7,* 268–277.

Andrews, T. J., & Coppola, D. M. (1999). Idiosyncratic characteristics of saccadic eye movements when viewing different visual environments. *Vision Research, 39,* 2947–2953.

Andrews, J. T., & Purves, D. (2005). The wagon-wheel illusion in continuous light. *Trends in Cognitive Sciences, 9,* 261–263.

Baldissera, F., Cavallari, P., Craighero, L., & Fadiga, L. (2001). Modulation of spinal excitability during observation of hand actions in humans. *European Journal of Neuroscience, 13,* 190–194.

Barrett, L., & Henzi, P. (2005). The social nature of primate cognition. *Proceedings of the Royal Society: Biological Sciences, 272,* 1865–1875.

Barsalou, L. W. (1999). Perceptual symbol systems. *Behavioral & Brain Sciences, 22,* 577–660.

Bavelas, J. B., Black, A., Chovil, N., Lemery, C. R., & Mullett, L. (1988). Form and function in motor mimicry: Topographic evidence that the primary function is communicative. *Human Communication Research, 14,* 275–299.

Bavelas, J. B., Black, A., Lemery, C. R., & Mullett, L. (1986). I show how you feel: Motor mimicry as a communicative act. *Journal of Personality and Social Psychology, 50,* 322–329.

Bekkering H., Wohlschlager A., & Gattis M. (2000). Imitation of gestures in children is goal-directed. *Quarterly Journal of Experimental Psychology, A53,* 153–164.

Bernieri, F., & Rosenthal, R. (1991). Interpersonal coordination, behavior matching, and interpersonal synchrony. In R. Feldman & B. Rime (Eds.), *Fundamentals of nonverbal behavior* (pp. 401–433). Cambridge, UK: Cambridge University Press.

Bernieri, F. J. (1988). Coordinated movement and rapport in teacher student interactions. *Journal of Nonverbal Behavior, 12,* 120–138.

Bernieri, F. J., Davis, J. M., Rosenthal, R., & Knee, C. R. (1994). Interactional synchrony and rapport: Measuring synchrony in displays devoid of sound and facial affect. *Personality and Social Psychology Bulletin, 20,* 303–311.

Bernieri, F. J., Reznick, J. S., & Rosenthal, R. (1988). Synchrony, pseudosynchrony, and dissynchrony: Measuring the entrainment process in mother infant interactions. *Journal of Personality and Social Psychology, 54,* 243–253.

Bock, L. J. (1986). Syntactic priming in language production. *Cognitive Psychology, 18,* 355–387.

Bock, L. J. (1989). Close class immanence in sentence production. *Cognition, 31,* 163 189.

Bock, L. J., & Loeblell, H. (1990). Framing sentences. *Cognition, 35,* 1–39.

Brazelton, T. B., Koslowski, B., & Main, M. (1974). Origins of reciprocity: The early mother-infant interaction. In M. Lewis & L. Rosenblaum (Eds.), *The effect of the infant on its caregiver* (pp. 49–76). New York: Wiley.

Brooks, R. (1999). *Cambrian intelligence.* Cambridge, MA: MIT Press.

Buccino, G., Binkofski, F., Fink, G. R., Fadiga, L., Fogassi, L., Gallese, V., Seitz, R. J., Zilles, K., Rizzolatti, G., & Freund, H. J. (2001). Action observation activates premotor and parietal areas in a somatotopic manner: An fMRI study. *European Journal of Neuroscience, 13,* 400–404.

Buccino, G., Lui, F., Canessa, N., Patteri, I., Lagravinese, G., Benuzzi, F., Porro, C. A., & Rizzolatti, G. (2004). Neural circuits involved in the recognition of actions performed by nonconspecifics: An fMRI study. *Journal of Cognitive Neuroscience, 16,* 114–126.

Bullowa, M. (1975). When infant and adult communicate, how do they synchronize their behavior? In A. Kendon, R. M. Harris, & M. R. Keys (Eds.), *Organization of behavior in face-to-face interaction* (pp. 95–127). The Hague, Netherlands: Mouton.

Cacioppo, J. T., & Hawkley, L. C. (2005). People thinking about people: The vicious cycle of being a social outcast in one's own mind. In K. D. Williams, J. P. Forgas, and W. von Hippel (Eds.), *The social outcast: Ostracism, social exclusion, rejection, and bullying* (pp. 91–108). New York: Psychology Press.

Cappella, J., & Planalp, S. (1981). Talk and silence sequences in informal conversations. III. Interspeaker influence. *Human Communication Research, 7,* 117–132.

Carr, L., Iacoboni, M., Dubeau, M.-C., Mazziotta, J. C., & Lenzi, G. L. (2003). Neural mechanisms of empathy in humans: A relay from neural systems for imitation to limbic areas. *Proceedings of the National Academy of Sciences of the United States of America, 100,* 5497–5502.

Chartrand, T. L., & Bargh, J. A. (1999). The Chameleon effect: The perception-behavior link and social interaction. *Journal of Personality and Social Psychology, 76,* 893–910.

Chartrand, T. L., & Jefferis, V. E. (2003). Consequences of automatic goal pursuit and the case of nonconscious mimicry. In J. P. Forgas (Ed.), *Social judgments: Implicit and explicit processes* (pp. 290–305). New York: Cambridge University Press.

Cheng, C. M., & Chartrand, T. L. (2003). Self-monitoring without awareness: Using mimicry as a nonconscious affiliation strategy. *Journal of Personality and Social Psychology, 85,* 1170–1179.

Chomsky, N. (1959). A Review of B. F. Skinner's verbal behavior. *Language* 35(1), 26–58.

Clancey, W. J. (1993). Situated action: A neuropsychological interpretation. Response to Vera and Simon. *Cognitive Science, 17,* 87–116.

Clancey, W. J. (1997*). Situated cognition: On human knowledge and computer representations.* New York: Cambridge University Press.

Clark, A. (1997). *Being there.* Cambridge, MA: MIT Press.

Clark, H. H. (1996). *Using language.* New York: Cambridge University Press.

Clark, H. H., & Brennan, S. E. (1991). Grounding in communication. In L. Resnick, J. Levine, & S. Teasley (Eds.), *Perspectives on socially shared cognition.* Washington, DC: American Psychological Association.

Condon, W. S., & Ogston, W. D. (1966). Sound film analysis of normal and pathological behavior patterns. *Journal of Nervous and Mental Diseases, 143,* 338–457.

Condon, W. S., & Ogston, W. D. (1967). A segmentation of behavior. *Journal of Psychiatric Research, 5,* 221–235.

Critchley, H. D., Wiens, S., Rotshtein, P., Oehman, A., & Dolan, R. J. (2004). Neural systems supporting interoceptive awareness. *Nature Neuroscience, 7,* 189–195.

Dabbs, J. M. (1969). Similarity of gestures and interpersonal influence [Summary]. *Proceedings of the 77th Annual Convention of the American Psychological Association, 4,* 337–338.

Davis, M. (1982). *Interaction Rhythms: Periodicity in Communicative Behavior.* New York: Human Sciences Press.

De Gelder, B., Snyder, J., Greve, D., Gerard, G., & Hadijkhani, N. (2004). Fear fosters flight: A mechanism for fear contagion when perceiving emotion expressed by a whole body. *Proceedings of the National Academy of Sciences of the United States of America, 47,* 16701–16706.

Decety, L. (2005). Perspective taking as the royal avenue to empathy. In: B. F. Malle & S. D. Hodges (Eds.), *Other minds: How humans bridge the divide between self and other* (pp. 135–149). New York: Guilford Publications.

Decety, J., & Grèzes, J. (2006). Multiple perspectives on the psychological and neural bases of understanding other people's behavior. *Brain Research, 1079,* 4–14.

di Pellegrino, G., Fadiga, L., Fogassi, L., Gallese, V., & Rizzolatti, G. (1992). Understanding motor events: A neurophysiological study. *Experimental Brain Research, 91,* 176–180.

Dijksterhuis, A., & Bargh, J. A. (2001). The perception-behavior expressway: Automatic effects of social perception on social behavior. *Advances in Experimental Social Psychology, 33,* 1–40.

Dimberg, U., Thunberg, M., & Elmehed, K. (2000). Unconscious facial reactions to emotional facial expressions. *Psychological Science, 11,* 86–89.

Ferrari, P. F., Gallese, V., Rizzolatti, G., & Fogassi, L. (2003). Mirror neurons responding to the observation of ingestive and communicative mouth actions in the monkey ventral premotor cortex. *European Journal of Neuroscience, 17,* 1703–1714.

Ferrari, P. F., Maiolini, C., Addessi, E., Fogassi, L., & Visalberghi, E. (2005). The observation and hearing of eating actions activates motor programs related to eating in macaque monkeys. *Behavior & Brain Research, 161,* 95–101.

Firth, C. D., & Firth, U. (2006). How we predict what other people are going to do. *Brain Research, 1079,* 36–46.

Fodor, J. A. (1975). *The language of thought.* Cambridge, MA: Harvard University Press.

Furuyama, N., Hayashi, K., & Mishima, H. (2005). Interpersonal coordination among articulations, gesticulations, and breathing movements: A case of articulation of /a/ and flexion of the wrist. In H. Heft & K. L. Marsh (Eds.), *Studies in perception and action* (pp. 45–48). Mahwah, NJ: Erlbaum.

Fussell, S. R., & Krauss, R. M. (1989a). The effects of intended audience on message production and comprehension: Reference in a common ground framework. *Journal of Experimental Social Psychology, 19,* 509–525.

Fussell, S. R., & Krauss, R. M. (1989b). Understanding friends and strangers: The effects of audience design on message comprehension. *European Journal of Social Psychology, 19*, 509–526.

Gallese, V. (2001). The "shared manifold" hypothesis: From mirror neurons to empathy. *Journal of Consciousness Studies, 8*(5–7), 33–50.

Gallese, V. (2003). The manifold nature of interpersonal relations: The quest for a common mechanism. *Philosophical Transactions of the Royal Society London, Series B Biological Sciences, 358*, 517–528.

Gallese, V. (2005). Embodied simulation: From neurons to phenomenal experience. *Phenomena of Cognitive Science, 4*, 23–48.

Gallese V. (2006). Intentional attunement: A neurophysiological perspective on social cognition and its disruption in autism. *Brain Research, 1079*, 15–24.

Gallese, V., Fadiga, L., Fogassi, L., & Rizzolatti, G. (1996). Action recognition in the premotor cortex. *Brain, 119*, 593–609.

Goldman, A. I. (2002). Simulation theory and mental concepts. In J. Dokic & J. Proust (Eds), *Simulation and knowledge of action* (pp. 1–19). Amsterdam: John Benjamins Publishing Company.

Goldman, A. I. (2005). Imitation, mind reading, and simulation. In S. Hurley & N. Chater (Eds.), *Perspective on imitation, from neuroscience to social science, Vol. 2* (pp. 79–93). Cambridge, MA: MIT Press.

Grafton, S. T., Arbib, M. A., Fadiga, L., & Rizzolatti, G. (1996). Localization of grasp representations in humans by PET. 2. Observation compared with imagination. *Experimental Brain Research, 112*, 103–111.

Graumann, C. (1984). The individualization of the social and the desocialization of the individual: Floyd H. Allport's contribution to the history of social psychology. *Archiv für die Geschichte der Psychologie, Historische Reihe*, No. 10. Heidelberg: Institute of Psychology.

Grèzes, J., & Decety, J. (2001). Functional anatomy of execution, mental simulation, observation, and verb generation of actions: A meta-analysis. *Human Brain Mapping, 12*, 1–19.

Hatfield, E., Cacioppo, J. T., & Rapson, R. L. (1994). *Emotion contagion.* Cambridge, UK: Cambridge University Press.

Hutchins, E. (1995). *Cognition in the wild.* Cambridge, MA: MIT Press.

Hutchison, W. D., Davis, K. D., Lozano, A. M., Tasker, R. R., & Dostrovsky, J. O. (1999). Pain-related neurons in the human cingulate cortex. *Nature-Neuroscience, 2*, 403–405.

Iacoboni, M. (2005). Neural mechanisms of imitation. *Current Opinion in Neurobiology, 15*, 632–637.

Iacoboni, M., Woods, R. P., Brass, M., Bekkering, H., Mazziotta, J. C., & Rizzolatti, G. (1999). Cortical mechanisms of human imitation. *Science, 286*, 2526–2528.

Jabbi, M., Swart, M., Keysers, C. (2007). Empathy for positive and negative emotions in the gustatory cortex. *Neuroimage, 34*, 1744–1753.

Jackson, P. L., Meltzoff, A. N., & Decety, J. (2005). How do we perceive the pain of others: A window into the neural processes involved in empathy. *Neuroimage, 24*, 771–779.

Jeannerod, M. (1999). The 25th Bartlett Lecture. To act or not to act: Perspectives on the representation of actions. *Quarterly Journal of Experimental Psychology: Human Experimental Psychology, 52*, 1–29A.

Julien, D., Brault, M., Chartrand, E., & Begin, J. (2000). Immediacy behaviours and synchrony in satisfied and dissatisfied couples. *Canadian Journal of Behavioural Science, 32*, 84–90.

Kendon, A. (1970). Movement coordination in social interaction: Some examples described. *Acta Psychologica, 32*, 100–125.

Keysar, B. (1997). Unconfounding common ground. *Discourse-Processes, 24*, 253–270.

Keysers, C., & Gazzola, V. (2006). Towards a unifying neural theory of social cognition. *Progress in Brain Research*, xxxx.

Keysers, C., Kohler, E., Umiltà, M. A., Nanetti, L., Fogassi, L. & Gallese, V. (2003). Audiovisual mirror neurons and action recognition. *Experimental Brain Research, 153*, 628–636.

Kirsch, D. (1995). The intelligent use of space. *Artificial Intelligence, 73*, 31–68.

Kirshner, D., & Whitson, J. A. (1997). *Situated cognition: Social, semiotic, and psychological perspectives*. Mahwah, NJ: Lawrence Erlbaum Assoc.

Kohler, E., Keysers, C., Umiltà, M. A., Fogassi, L., Gallese, V., Rizzolatti, G. (2002). Hearing sounds, understanding actions: Action representation in mirror neurons. *Science, 297*, 846–848.

Krauss, R. M., & Fussell, S. R. (1996). Social psychological models of interpersonal communication. In E. T. Higgins & A. W. Kruglanski (Eds.), *Social psychology: Handbook of basic principles* (pp. 655–701). New York: Guilford.

Krauss, R. M., & Chiu, C. (1998). Language and social behavior. In D. T. Gilbert, S. T. Fiske, & G. Lindzey (Eds.), *Handbook of social psychology* (4th ed., Vol. 2) (pp. 41–88). New York: McGraw-Hill.

LaFrance, M. (1982). Posture mirroring and rapport. In M. Davis (Ed.), *Interaction rhythms: Periodicity in communicative behavior* (pp. ). New York: Human Sciences Press.

LaFrance, M., & Broadbent, M. (1976). Group rapport: Posture sharing as a nonverbal indicator. *Group and Organization Studies, 1*, 328–333.

Lakin, J. L., & Chartrand, T. L. (2003). Using nonconscious behavioral mimicry to create affiliation and rapport. *Psychological Science, 14*, 334–339.

Lazarus, M. (1861). Über das Verhältnis des Einzelnen zur Gesamtheit. *Zeitschrift für Völkerpsychologie und Sprachwissenschaft, 2*, 393–453.

Lazarus, M., & Steinhal, H. (1860). Einleitende Gedanken über Völkerpsychologie als Einladung zu für Völkerpsychologie und Sprachwissenschaft. *Zeitschrift für Völkerpsychologie und Sprachwissenschaft, 1*, 1–73.

Liberman, A. M., & Mattingly, I. G. (1985). The motor theory of speech perception revised. *Cognition, 21*, 1–36.

Liberman, A. M., & Whalen, D. H. (2000). On the relation of speech to language. *Trends in Cognitive Sciences, 4*, 187–196.

Lipps, T. (1903). Einfühlung, innere Nachahmung, und Organempfindungen. *Archiv für die gesamte Psychologiue, 2*, 185–204.

Manthey, S., Schubotz, R. L., & von Cramon, D. Y. (2003). Premotor cortex in observing erroneous action: An fMRI study. *Cognitive Brain Research, 15*, 296–307.

Marsh, K. L., Richardson, M. J., Baron, R. M., & Schmidt, R. C. (2006). Contrasting approaches to perceiving and acting with others. *Ecological Psychology, 18*, 1–38

McDougal, W. (1908). *An introduction to social psychology*. London: Methuen.

Neda, Z., Ravasz, E., Brecht, Y., Vicsek, T., & Barabasi, A. L. (2000). The sound of many hands clapping: Tumultuous applause can transform itself into waves of synchronized clapping. *Nature, 403*, 849–850.

Neumann, R., & Strack, F. (2000). "Mood contagion": The automatic transfer of mood between persons. *Journal of Personality and Social Psychology, 79*, 211–223.

Newell, A., & Simon, H. (1972). *Human problem solving.* Englewood Cliffs, NJ: Prentice-Hall.

O'Toole, R., & Dubin, R. (1968). Baby feeding and body sway: An experiment in George Herbert Mead's taking the role of the other. *Journal of Personality & Social Psychology, 10*, 59–65.

Post, D. L. (1980). Floyd H. Allport and the launching of modern social psychology. *Journal for the History of the Behavioral Sciences, 16*, 369–376.

Rizzolatti, G., & Craighero, L. (2004). The mirror-neuron system. *Annual Review of Neuroscience, 27*, 169–192.

Rizzolatti, G., Fadiga, L., Gallese, V., & Fogassi, L. (1996). Premotor cortex and the recognition of motor actions. *Cognitive Brain Research, 3*, 131–141.

Rosenfeld, H. M. (1981). Whither interactional synchrony? In K. Bloom (Ed.), *Prospective issues in infancy research* (pp. 71–97). Hillsdale, NJ: Erlbaum.

Sachs, H. A., Schegloff, E. A., & Jefferson, G. (1974). A Simplest systematics for the organization of turn-taking for conversation. *Language, 50*, 696–735.

Scheflen, A. E. (1982). Comments on the significance of interaction rhythms. In M. Davis (Ed.), *Interaction rhythms: Periodicity in communicative behavior* (pp. 13–22). New York: Human Sciences Press.

Schofield, W. N. (1976). Do children find movements which cross the body midline difficult? *Quarterly Journal of Experimental Psychology, 28*, 571–582.

Sebanz, N., Bekkering, H., & Knoblich, G. (2006). Joint action: Bodies and minds moving together. *Trends in Cognitive Sciences, 10*, 70–76.

Semin, G. R. (1986). The individual, the social and the social individual. *British Journal of Social Psychology, 25*, 177–180.

Semin, G. R. (2007). Grounding communication: Synchrony. In A. Kruglanski & E. T. Higgins (Eds.), *Social psychology: Handbook of basic principles* (2nd edition) (pp. 630–649). New York: Guilford Publications.

Semin, G. R., & Cacioppo, J. T. (2007). From representation to co-regulation. In J. A. Pineda (Ed.), *Mirror neuron systems: The role of mirroring processes in social cognition.* Totowa, NJ: Humana Press.

Semin, G. R., & Cacioppo, J. T. (in prep). Social cognition: A model. (In prep).

Shockley, K., Santana, M. V., & Fowler, C. A. (2003). Mutual interpersonal postural constraints are involved in cooperative conversation. *Journal of Experimental Psychology: Human Perception and Performance, 29*, 326–332.

Shockley, K., Baker, A. A., Richardson, M. J., & Fowler, C. A. (2007). Articulatory constraints on interpersonal postural coordination. *Journal of Experimental Psychology: Human Perception and Performance, 33*, 201–208.

Singer, T., Seymour, B., O'Doherty, J., Kaube, H., Dolan, R. J., & Frith, C. F. (2004). Empathy for pain involves the affective but not the sensory components of pain. *Science, 303*, 1157–1162.

Smith, E. R., & Semin, G. R. (2004). Socially situated cognition: Cognition in its social context. *Advances in Experimental Social Psychology, 36*, 53–117.

Sommerville, J. A., & Decety, J. (2006). Weaving the fabric of social interaction: Articulating developmental psychology and cognitive neuroscience in the domain of motor cognition. *Psychonomic Bulletin and Review, 13,* 179–200.

Stern, D. N. (1974). Mother and infant at play. In M. Lewis & L. Rosenblaum (Eds.), *The effect of the infant on its caregiver* (pp. 187–213). New York: Wiley.

Stevens, J. A., Fonlupt, P., Shiffrar, M., & Decety, J. (2000). New aspects of motion perception: Selective neural encoding of apparent human movements. *NeuroReport, 11,* 109–115.

Street, R. L., Jr. (1984). Speech convergence and speech evaluation in fact-finding interviews. *Human Communication Research, 11,* 139–169.

Strogatz, S. (2003). *SYNC: Rhythms of nature, rhythms of ourselves.* London: Allen Lane: Penguin

Swanson, R., & Benton, A. L. (1955). Some aspects of the genetic development of right-left discrimination. *Child Development, 26,* 123–133.

Tickle-Degnen, L., & Rosenthal, R. (1987). Group rapport and nonverbal behavior. *Review of Personality and Social Psychology, 9,* 113–136.

Umiltà, M. A., Kohler, E., Gallese, V., Fogassi, L., Fadiga, L., Keysers, C., & Rizzolatti, G. (2001). "I know what you are doing": A neurophysiological study. *Neuron, 32,* 91–101.

van Baaren, R. B., Maddux, W. W., Chartrand, T. L., de Bouter, C., & van Knippenberg, A. (2003). It takes two to mimic: Behavioral consequences of self-construals. *Journal of Personality And Social Psychology, 84,* 1093–1102.

VanRullen, R., & Koch, C. (2003). Is perception discrete or continuous? *Trends in Cognitive Sciences, 7,* 207–213.

Vera, A., & Simon, H. A. (1993). Situated action: A symbolic interpretation. *Cognitive Science, 17,* 7–48.

Waitz, T. (1859). In Gerland, G. Psychologische Anthropologie. *Zeitschrift für Völkerpsychologie und Sprachwissenschaft, 1,* 387–412.

Wapner, S., & Cirillo, L. (1968). Imitation of a model's hand movements: Age changes in transposition of left-right relations. *Child Development, 39,* 887–894.

Wedewer, H. (1860). Über die Wichtigkeit und Bedeutung der Sprache. *Zeitschrift für Völkerpsychologie und Sprachwissenschaft, 1,* 180.

Wicker, B., Keysers, C., Plailly, J., Royet, J.-P., Gallese, V., & Rizzolatti, G. (2003). Both of us disgusted in my insula: The common neural basis of seeing and feeling disgust. *Neuron, 40,* 655–664.

Wilson, S. M., Saygin, A. P., Sereno, M. I., & Iacoboni, M. (2004). Listening to speech activates motor areas involved in speech production. *Nature Neuroscience, 7,* 701–702.

Wohlschläger, A., Gattis, M., & Bekkering, H. (2003). Action generation and action perception in imitation: An instance of the ideomotor principle. *Philosophical Transactions of the Royal Society of London, Series B, 358,* 501–515.

Yeh, W., & Barsalou, L. W. (2000). The situated nature of concepts (unpublished), Department of Psychology, Emory University, Atlanta, GA.

# 6    An Embodied Account of Self-Other "Overlap" and Its Effects

Eliot R. Smith

The bonds that connect each person to important others, whether individuals (e.g., friends, romantic partners, close kin) or social groups (teams, workgroups, national or religious groups) are a core conceptual focus of the field of social psychology. Historically, research on personal relationships and research on in-group ties have proceeded as two largely independent streams. Recently, theorists and researchers have recognized the strong conceptual parallels between these issues and have moved to take advantage of them (Sedikides & Brewer, 2001; Smith, Murphy, & Coats, 1999; Smith & Henry, 1996).

In both areas, two phenomena are of central importance. One is the influence of a personal relationship or significant group membership on people's thoughts and feelings about themselves – an effect of the other person or group on the self. For example, when a social group membership becomes salient, people tend to see themselves in terms of the typical or stereotypical characteristics of the group rather than in terms of their unique personal identities, a process known as *depersonalization* (Turner et al., 1987). Conversely, the second phenomenon is the influence of the self on thoughts and feelings about the other person or group. For example, people tend to project their own individual characteristics (e.g., their attitudes and preferences) onto other group members, assuming that those others are similar to themselves (Robbins & Krueger, 2005). The positive esteem that people

Preparation of this chapter and the research reported here were supported by NSF Grants BCS-0091807 and BCS-0527249. The author is grateful to Frederica Conrey, Elise P. Hall, Thomas Schubert, Charles Seger, Beate Seibt, and Gün Semin for assistance and suggestions. Author address: Department of Psychological and Brain Sciences, Indiana University, 1101 E. Tenth St., Bloomington, IN 47405-7007, or esmith4@indiana.edu.

typically feel for other in-group members is also largely due to projection onto the group of people's generally positive feelings about themselves (Otten & Wentura, 2001).

Conceptual analyses of these processes in the areas of both personal relationships and group memberships have made heavy use of the metaphor of "overlap" between self and other. In a seminal paper, Aron et al. (1991, p. 242) wrote that "much of our cognition about the other in a close relationship is cognition in which the other is treated as self or confused with self – the underlying reason being a self/other merging or . . . 'including others in the self.'" Aron and colleagues (1991) demonstrated three distinct effects of this self-other overlap. People's allocation of valued resources between the self and a close other becomes neutral or balanced, rather than displaying the typical bias favoring the self, because the close other is in effect a part of the self. Typical differences in perspective between actors and observers are also diminished because in observing a close other, we mentally take on that person's perspective as an actor. Finally, the other's characteristics, such as personality traits, become confused with our own; it is easy for us to report ways in which we resemble the close other and difficult to report ways in which we differ. Research has applied the same idea of "overlap" to understand the relation between the self and in-group, obtaining similar results (e.g., Smith & Henry, 1996).

Despite the prominence in the literature of discussions of the metaphoric "overlap" between self and other, theoretical analyses of its nature have been limited and incomplete. The original paper by Aron et al. (1991, p. 243) suggested only that "the precise nature of what it means to have included other into self, in terms of cognitive structure, is probably multifold. For example, cognitive representations of self and other might contain common elements or might occupy overlapping regions of a cognitive matrix, and access to them might follow similar pathways." Smith, Coats, and Walling (1999) proposed an elaboration and specification of this suggestion in a connectionist model of the mental representation of self and other, and demonstrated how their model might account for the types of results found in empirical studies of self-other overlap. Their model is restricted to the cognitive aspects of overlap, such as representations of self and other in terms of similar or overlapping traits and other characteristics.

Thus, existing theoretical analyses of self-other overlap have assumed that the overlap is cognitive in nature, having to do with shared aspects of mental representations of self, close others, or groups – and have ignored the embodied aspects of self-other overlap. Recent conceptual and empirical work in my laboratory has begun to remedy this lack. This line of theory and research is important because plentiful evidence demonstrates the impact of embodiment on many aspects of cognition, emotion, and behavior (reviewed in several chapters in this volume). However, the great majority of that evidence pertains to embodiment effects on aspects of individual functioning, such as language comprehension. Indeed, the embodied perspective itself may be seen as implying that the individual self, bounded by the skin, has a special status. But this emphasis omits the social dimension of our relationships and group memberships, which define our lives as social beings and provide the context in which our adaptive behavior unfolds. Thus, exploration of the role of embodiment in constructing our relationships with other persons and groups seems important and timely. This chapter describes two distinct lines of research that explore how bodily interactions can cause us to extend our representations of ourselves to include, or overlap with, other individuals or social groups.

## EMBODIED CUES AND RELATIONAL MODELS

The general framework for our thinking is the Relational Models Theory of Fiske (2004). This theory is reviewed by Schubert, Waldzus, and Seibt (this volume) and we need not repeat that discussion here. In overview, Fiske holds that there are four basic types of social relationship, of which one (communal sharing, or CS) corresponds to what has been described as "self-other overlap" in the social psychological literature. This is the type of relationship found between close kin and friends, and also among members of a social group when shared group identity is salient (Turner et al., 1987). In a CS relationship, people focus on what they have in common (rather than on their unique individual attributes), freely share resources, and work toward shared goals.

Fiske also discusses the ways in which different types of relationships are embodied. CS relationships have as embodied cues touch and physical proximity, shared physical appearance (clothing or bodily marks such as tattoos), shared (synchronized) movements, and shared substances (such as shared food). Importantly, embodied cues such as these both express the nature of a relationship and encourage or bias people in the direction of such a relationship (Schubert et al., this volume). A clear test of the second part of this idea can come from studies that manipulate embodied cues such as synchrony and touch, and measure their effects – the types of studies to be described in this chapter. Data that shows only a correlation between a relationship type and an embodied cue would be ambiguous on this point.

## INTERPERSONAL SYNCHRONY AND SELF-OTHER OVERLAP

According to Fiske's (2004) Relational Models Theory, synchronized movement is one cue to a communal sharing relationship. Recent research in several disciplines has explored the mechanisms and effects of behavioral synchrony or imitation (e.g., Hurley & Chater, 2005). Interpersonal synchrony of movements is a key part of our social interactions almost from birth (Meltzoff & Decety, 2003). In fact, autism, a condition associated with severe social decrements, has been linked to impairments in the ability to imitate the movements of other people (Williams, Whiten, Suddendorf, & Perrett, 2001). One important line of research has focused on mirror neurons, which form part of a brain system that appears to be functional both in perception and action. Evidence and different lines of theory suggest that such brain systems play a role in understanding others' actions, by mapping them onto one's own motor planning system; coordinating joint action with others; self-identification; and perceptual prediction (e.g., Wilson & Knoblich, 2005; Gallese et al., 2004).

In parallel to the studies considering these and other similar cognitive functions, another body of literature has examined broader effects of the overlap between mental representations of one's own and others' movements, such as effects on affective experiences, on the representation of the self, or on relationships with others. This research, mostly within social psychology, documents the impact of interpersonal mimicry on these types of broader outcomes. Mimicry includes such everyday examples as adopting similar bodily postures or facial expressions with a conversational partner. Mimicry is distinct from synchrony because it involves two people making similar movements but not in a time-locked fashion. Mimicry produces increased liking (Chartrand & Bargh, 1999), increased susceptibility to social influence (Bailenson & Yee, 2005), and increases in positive, prosocial behavior toward the mimicker (van Baaren et al., 2003). In addition, plentiful correlational evidence attests that people who like each other more also show more interpersonal coordination in their behavior (e.g., Bernieri & Rosenthal, 1991). However, this work in social psychology has yet to make much contact with theories (e.g., regarding mirror neuron systems) from other subdisciplines. In an ongoing program of research, we are investigating the consequences of interpersonal synchrony and mimicry. We believe that the existing findings of increased interpersonal liking and increased social influence can be parsimoniously explained by a single mechanism: shared movements act as a cue to a CS relationship, creating overlap between self and other.

Fiske (2004) postulated that synchrony is a cue to CS, citing several anthropological examples of this association. He did not elaborate an argument for precisely why this particular cue, movement synchrony, should indicate that the other is part of the self, but there is a clear and plausible conceptual rationale. Cross-modal synchrony (vision matching muscle movements) is a key mechanism that an infant can use to determine where his or her body begins and ends: If I wave my hand, and I see a hand waving in synchrony, that must be my hand. Such cross-modal synchrony helps us determine the boundary between the self and the outside world (Knoblich & Flach, 2003). In fact, numerous researchers, beginning with Gallup (1970), have taken self-recognition in a mirror as an indicator of self-awareness in infants and nonhuman primates. Mirror self-recognition must be based on perceiving the synchrony of one's own movements with those of the face in the mirror (because young children or chimpanzees cannot know what they look like physically). For these reasons, witnessing an entity behaving in accordance with one's motor commands defines that entity as part of the self.

Importantly, whereas cross-modal synchrony is a powerful means of discriminating between the controllable self and other elements in the environment, it can lead to the inclusion of more than just the individual in the self. If the infant sees that mother smiles when I smile or winces when I feel pain, then it is natural for the infant to think that mother is, in some very real way, a part of me. This line of reasoning suggests that interpersonal synchrony is a basic, automatic cue that the other person is part of the psychological self.

This argument implies that time-locked synchrony and looser (not time-locked) mimicry involve somewhat separate, though related, psychological mechanisms that link the self to the other. Interpersonal synchrony should strongly activate brain systems that function in both perception and action because the person's own motor movements as well as the perception of the other's movements will simultaneously activate those systems. It has been suggested that this especially high level of activation mediates the perception that what is perceived is part of the self (Knoblich & Flach, 2003). Mimicry (as opposed to synchrony) is looser, involving generally similar behaviors performed by two people in only loose temporal relationship, such as the many ways people tend to adopt each others' facial expressions and coordinate bodily movements when in conversation.

Both synchrony and mimicry should be cues that the other person is linked to the self, and should therefore lead to greater liking and persuasiveness of the mimicker (as demonstrated by Chartrand & Bargh, 1999; Bailenson & Yee, 2005). After all, if the other person is me, then I like him because I like myself, and I assume that his views about things are correct because they are my own views. However, synchrony and mimicry also differ in important ways. The effect of synchrony may be more automatic and less a matter of conscious awareness, so it may affect systematically different types of dependent variables than mimicry. Synchrony may drive affective feelings and unreflective perceptions that the other is similar to the self, whereas mimicry may relate more to considered judgments (e.g., How much do I like this person? How much do I accept his arguments?). These speculations demand further research contrasting exact interpersonal synchrony with the looser, more conversational mimicry manipulations whose effects have been investigated within social psychology (e.g., Chartrand & Bargh, 1999).

Work in our laboratory is using virtual reality technology to investigate the impact of interpersonal synchrony and mimicry on representations of self and other. In these studies, participants are seated in front of a computer monitor with a representation of the head of a male avatar ("John") facing them. For participants in the *synchrony* condition, the monitor becomes a virtual mirror, and John's head movements synchronize perfectly with their own as they complete experimental tasks and questionnaires. This is accomplished by attaching a motion sensor to the participant's head (on the headband of a pair of headphones), and using the sensor's output to control the computer-animated movements of John's head. For participants in the *mimicry* condition, the computer-generated head duplicates the participant's movements with a 4-sec time lag. We arbitrarily chose this lag to match that used in the study by Bailenson and Yee (2005). Finally, for participants in the *control* condition, the avatar's head movements are yoked to a previous participant's movements, so they do not synchronize with the participant's own movements.

Although this research is ongoing, results to date ($N = 86$) suggest that interpersonal synchrony (but not delayed mimicry) does result in extension of the self to include the other. Explicit ratings of similarity and liking for John show no significant effects. However, self-ratings and ratings of John on various dimensions are positively correlated in the synchrony condition – significantly more positively than in the mimicry condition. For example, in the synchrony condition, participants' self-ratings and ratings of John on political liberalism versus conservatism are positively correlated, whereas the correlation in the mimicry condition is nonsignificantly negative (with the control condition in between). The data are shown in Figure 6.1. The difference between the synchrony and mimicry slopes is statistically reliable. The same pattern is found for ratings of self and John on the question of how much value is placed on public service; again, the slope difference is reliable.

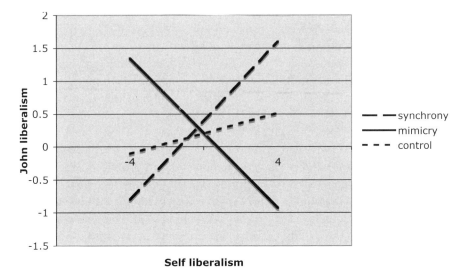

Figure 6.1. Regression slopes relating ratings of John's liberalism versus conservatism to participants' own liberalism versus conservatism, each on a scale from –4 to +4, by experimental condition.

In all cases, the control condition shows no significant correlation between ratings of self and of John.

This research is ongoing but tentatively supports three conclusions. First, synchrony does appear to be a cue for self-other overlap (or a CS relationship), indicated by the positive correlation between the ratings participants give to themselves and the synchronizing other. Second, the effect seems to be at least somewhat automatic and nonconscious, in that it appears on an indirect measure of self-other similarity (the correlation between independent ratings of self and other) but does not occur on explicit measures of similarity or liking. This argues, in the language of Schubert et al. (this volume), that the effect is not deliberative or inferential.

Finally, mimicry (i.e., mirroring of movements with a 4-sec time lag) does not produce the same results as synchrony; if anything, its effect is the opposite. Note that our result does not contradict the finding of Bailenson and Yee (2005) that mimicry with a 4-sec delay produced increased openness to social influence from the avatar, a dependent measure that is quite different from ours. Our results support the idea that, as discussed previously, synchrony and mimicry differ in important ways. Our argument that exact synchrony is a cue that the other is part of oneself does not apply to looser mimicry, so we believe that the processes in the two situations are at least somewhat different. In particular, the 4-sec delay was sufficient so that no participants in Bailenson and Yee's (2005) study noticed that the avatar's movements were similar to their own, although exact synchrony with zero lag is very obvious and noticeable. This difference in conscious awareness may have large effects on the ways people respond to the other person. At the very least, it seems that the research literature has been overly hasty in assuming that time-locked synchrony and looser mimicry engage the same underlying psychological processes.

## INTERPERSONAL TOUCH AND SELF-OTHER OVERLAP

Fiske's (2004) Relational Models Theory suggests that touch as well as synchrony is an embodied cue to self-other overlap. Supporting this idea, existing research in social psychology has demonstrated that even casual, incidental, interpersonal touch, as when a library clerk brushes a patron's hand when returning a library card, leads to greater liking for the librarian and for the environment (Fisher et al., 1976). These researchers' theory (p. 417) was simply the idea that "a momentary touch between interacting strangers would be experienced as a mildly pleasant stimulus, and that it would arouse positive affect." This affect was expected to become "attached" to the toucher only by affective generalization, not in any direct way. Similarly, in a more recent study, Kurzban (2001) offered the idea that touch may "act as a social signal of closeness of relationship," presumably as a result of cultural learning. Additional research supporting the idea that touch increases helping and other types of positive behavior toward the toucher is reviewed by Schubert et al. (this volume). Notably, the effects of touch appear not to be mediated by conscious or deliberative inferences, for they occur even when the person is unaware of having been touched (Guéguen, 2002).

Based on Fiske's theory that touch (like synchrony) is a cue to a CS relationship, it is possible to make an additional, more far-reaching prediction. Feelings about not only the individual toucher, but also about the toucher's social group, should be made more positive by touch. This prediction is based on the idea that group memberships (like close individual others) are incorporated in the self (Wright et al., 1997). If being touched by another person causes me to extend my self to include that person, then my self is also extended to include the person's group memberships, even those groups of which I may not be personally a part. Thus, increased positive feelings should extend not only to the toucher but also his fraternity brothers or those who share his racial or ethnic identity, and so on. Supporting this hypothesis, much research on intergroup contact (Pettigrew & Tropp, 2006) shows that interpersonal contact and especially friendship (i.e., a CS relationship) with an individual member of an out-group leads to generalized positive feelings about the out-group, presumably through inclusion of the other and their group membership in the self.

Therefore, we sought to determine whether touch by an out-group member could actually improve people's attitudes toward that out-group – that is, reduce prejudice against the group. In our first study (Seger & Smith, 2007), the experimenter, a female African-American, briefly and casually touched some Caucasian participants as she seated them at the computer and gave them task instructions. Other participants were treated identically but with no physical touch. The participants' tasks on the computer then included making evaluations of themselves, the experimenter as an individual, and African-Americans as a group. Findings show that touch significantly improved evaluations of African-Americans on an implicit measure based on response times (an evaluative priming measure). However, no effect was found on two explicit self-report measures of liking for the group. A second study replicated and extended this result, with an Asian-American as well as a different African-American experimenter. Touch made participants' implicit attitudes toward the experimenter's particular racial group more positive, and this effect was stronger for participants who did not recall having been touched. As with the results of the synchrony study described previously, this pattern suggests that the effect of touch on the attitude is not deliberative and inferential, but reflects a more automatic type of processing.

The chapter by Clore and Schnall (this volume) raises an interesting conceptual question about the effects of touch (or synchrony), a question that also has potential practical ramifications. The question is, would touch create more positive feelings about the toucher and their group even if the toucher was disliked as an individual? Our experimenters were attractive and pleasant, so the question did not arise in our studies, but it is relevant to real-life contact between members of hostile groups and the reduction of prejudice. There are two different perspectives on this question. One stems from the meta-analysis by Pettigrew and Tropp (2006), which shows that in virtually all cases, personal contact with an out-group member reduces prejudice. This finding makes it plausible that, in many cases, even contact with a mildly disliked out-group member has positive effects. This would be understandable if contact produces self-other overlap (and hence overlap between the self and the other's group) regardless of one's liking for the other – within reasonable limits. A second perspective is that taken by Clore and Schnall (this volume) in their suggestion that embodied cues must agree with the person's consciously held beliefs to have a real impact. By analogy with the research results described in their chapter, they might predict that touch by a person who is perceived as pleasant, likable, and so on, would lead to self-other overlap and other positive consequences. In contrast, touch by a person who is rude, dislikable, and so on, would have no effect or even produce greater disliking.

This is obviously an empirical question, and one that has practical implications regarding the efficacy of intergroup contact as a means of reducing prejudice. There is one aspect of Clore and Schnall's (this volume) thinking that makes us somewhat optimistic. Say the toucher (like most human beings) has a mixture of positive and negative qualities. Touch is a cue to a positive CS relationship with that person. Clore and Schnall (this volume) suggest that embodied cues and the resulting feelings can provide "evidence" for, increase confidence in, and increase the weight given to beliefs that are congruent with the feelings. Based on this idea, touch might make the perceiver's thoughts about positive aspects of the toucher more accessible and more impactful in judgments and future behaviors while making negative aspects less accessible. As a result, the effects of touch would overall be positive. Again, this intriguing idea demands further research.

## CONCLUSIONS

The rapidly expanding literature on embodiment (e.g., Barsalou, Niedenthal, Barbey, & Ruppert, 2003) has focused mainly on embodiment effects on intra-individual cognitive representation and processing, including tangentially social aspects such as perception of others' actions. But embodied cues such as interpersonal synchrony and touch may also be key in our social functioning. They may link us to close relationship partners or to fellow group members, facilitating and enabling the social relationships that make up such an important part of our life. Lindblom (2006) argues that the principle of embodiment means the body serves as both a "social resonance mechanism" that helps us understand and relate to others, and as a "representational device" that grounds processes of cognition and of social interaction. In this perspective, bodily actions do not simply express internal states, such as one's relationships to others, but actually constitute those states, as part and parcel of them. The idea has vast implications, which are only beginning to be studied, regarding our relationships to significant others in our lives and our group memberships.

**References**

Aron, A., Aron, E. N., Tudor, M., & Nelson, G. (1991). Close relationships as including other in the self. *Journal of Personality and Social Psychology, 60,* 241–253.

Bailenson, J. N., & Yee, N. (2005). Digital chameleons: Automatic assimilation of nonverbal gestures in immersive virtual environments. *Psychological Science, 16*(10), 814–819.

Barsalou, L. W., Niedenthal, P. M., Barbey, A. K., & Ruppert, J. A. (2003). Social embodiment. In B. H. Ross (Ed.), *Psychology of learning and motivation*. New York: Academic Press.

Bernieri, F. J., & Rosenthal, R. (1991). Interpersonal coordination: Behavior matching and interactional synchrony. In R. S. Feldman & B. Rime (Eds.), *Fundamentals of nonverbal behavior* (pp. 401–432). Cambridge, UK: Cambridge University Press.

Chartrand, T. L., & Bargh, J. A. (1999). The chameleon effect: The perception-behavior link and social interaction. *Journal of personality and social psychology, 76*(6), 893–910.

Fisher, J. D., Rytting, M., & Heslin, R. (1976). Hands touching hands: Affective and evaluative effects of an interpersonal touch. *Sociometry, 39*, 416–421.

Fiske, A. P. (2004). Four modes of constituting relationships: Consubstantial assimilation; space, magnitude, time, and force; concrete procedures; abstract symbolism. In N. Haslam (Ed.), *Relational models theory: A contemporary overview* (pp. 61–146). Mahwah, NJ: Lawrence Erlbaum Associates.

Gallese, V., Keysers, C., & Rizzolatti, G. (2004). A unifying view of the basis of social cognition. *Trends in Cognitive Sciences, 8*, 396–403.

Gallup, G. G. (1970). Chimpanzees: Self-recognition. *Science, 167*, 86–87.

Guéguen, N. (2002). Touch, awareness of touch, and compliance with a request. *Perceptual and Motor Skills, 95*, 355–360.

Hurley, S., & Chater, N. (Eds.) (2005). *Perspectives on imitation: From neuroscience to social science*, Vol. 2. Cambridge, MA: MIT Press.

Knoblich, G., & Flach, R. (2003). Action identity: Evidence from self-recognition, prediction, and coordination. *Consciousness & Cognition, 12*, 620–632.

Kurzban, R. (2001). The social psychophysics of cooperation: Nonverbal communication in a public goods game. *Journal of Nonverbal Behavior, 25*, 241–259.

Lindblom, J. (2006). Embodied action as a 'helping hand' in social interaction. *Proceedings of the 28th Annual Conference of the Cognitive Science Society* (pp. 477–482). Accessed July 26, 2006 from http://www.cogsci.rpi.edu/CSJarchive/proceedings/2006/docs/p477.pdf.

Meltzoff, A. N., & Decety, J. (2003). What imitation tells us about social cognition: A rapprochement between developmental psychology and cognitive neuroscience. *Philosophical Transactions: Biological Sciences, 358*(1431), 491–500.

Otten, S., & Wentura, D. (2001). Self-anchoring and in-group favoritism: An individual profiles analysis. *Journal of Experimental Social Psychology, 37*, 525–532.

Pettigrew, T. F., & Tropp, L. R. (2006). A meta-analytic test of intergroup contact theory. *Journal of Personality and Social Psychology, 90*, 751–783.

Robbins, J. M., & Krueger, J. I. (2005). Social projection to ingroups and outgroups: A review and meta-analysis. *Personality and Social Psychology Review, 9*(1), 32–47.

Sedikides, C., & Brewer, M. B. (2001). *Individual self, relational self, collective self.* New York: Psychology Press.

Seger, C. R., & Smith, E. R. (2007). Interpersonal touch by an outgroup member reduces implicit prejudice. Unpublished, Indiana University, Bloomington.

Smith, E. R., Coats, S., & Walling, D. (1999). Overlapping mental representations of self, in-group, and partner: Further response time evidence and a connectionist model. *Personality and Social Psychology Bulletin, 25*(7), 873–882.

Smith, E. R., & Henry, S. (1996). An in-group becomes part of the self: Response time evidence. *Personality and Social Psychology Bulletin, 22*, 635–642.

Smith, E. R., Murphy, J., & Coats, S. (1999). Attachment to groups: Theory and measurement. *Journal of Personality and Social Psychology, 77*, 94–110.

Turner, J. C., Hogg, M. A., Oakes, P. J., Reicher, S. D., & Wetherell, M. S. (1987). *Rediscovering the social group: A self-categorization theory.* Oxford: Blackwell.

Van Baaren, R. B., Maddux, W. W., Chartrand, T. L., De Bouter, C., & van Knippenberg, A. (2003). It takes two to mimic: Behavioral consequences of self-construals. *Journal of Personality and Social Psychology, 84*, 1093–1102.

Williams, J. H. G., Whiten, A., Suddendorf, T., & Perrett, D. I. (2001). Imitation, mirror neurons and autism. *Neuroscience & Biobehavioral Reviews, 25*(4), 287–295.

Wilson, M., & Knoblich, G. (2005). The case for motor involvement in perceiving conspecifics. *Psychological bulletin, 131*(3), 460–473.

Wright, S. C., Aron, A., McLaughlin-Volpe, T., & Ropp, S. A. (1997). The extended contact effect: Knowledge of cross-group friendships and prejudice. *Journal of Personality and Social Psychology, 73*, 73–90.

# 7 The Embodiment of Power and Communalism in Space and Bodily Contact

## Thomas W. Schubert, Sven Waldzus, and Beate Seibt

Imagine you visit a village on some remote island, with a culture with which you are not familiar. On this island, you discover a number of strange behaviors of which you try to make sense. For instance, some of the islanders rub their noses with each other as a greeting. You also learn that others eat potions "using combinations of ingredients such as rocks from the tallest mountain-peaks and epiphytes growing atop the highest trees" (Fiske, 2004, p. 95). How would you interpret these behaviors? Perhaps you would guess those with nose-to-nose contact are generally close to each other, and those eating the potions made of high things enjoy or attain high status. What you have figured out then are perhaps the two most basic and important dimensions of social relations: community relations and power relations (Mead, 1934).

What is the basis of such a judgment that relates unknown behaviors to social relations? In this chapter, we will approach this question from the standpoint of Relational Models Theory (RMT) developed by Fiske (1992; Fiske & Haslam, 2005). This theory identifies community and power as two of the basic relational models humans use to structure and coordinate their social interactions. In a nutshell, when people have a community relation or *communal sharing* (CS), they focus on what they have in common. Thus, resources are seen as common in a CS relation and shared according to needs. Such a relation is typically found between mothers and their children in all cultures and among members of a group when this shared group identity is salient. It is also commonly found among members of a family clan in many cultures. A power relation or *authority ranking* (AR) means people structure their interaction according to ordered differences.[1] These relations

---

[1] The term *power* usually refers to both a coercive form of control over another person's positive and negative reinforcements (Heckhausen, 1989) and other forms of asymmetric influence

are very common in the workplace and in all institutions. They are also common between fathers and their children and men and women in many cultures.

Because in a given relation the focus can be either on the commonalities or on status differences, the relational model can change over time. The applied relational model also depends on categorization processes, e.g., whether an individual categorizes somebody else as an in-group or an out-group member. Two other models, which are likely to be younger in phylogenetic terms and are learned later in ontogenetic terms, are *equality matching*, a model that underlies basic exchanges of goods or "tit-for-tat" types of relations, and *market pricing*, a model that underlies exchanges of goods using values assigned to them. In this chapter, we will concentrate on CS and AR.

According to RMT (Fiske, 2004), most of the many ways in which community relations are established, communicated, and confirmed share a common representational basis or schema: Those who touch noses with each other might also dance in sync at the evening feast and have the same tattoos on their faces. Furthermore, their huts might stand close together, and they might wear similar clothes. One could say their community relation is *embodied* in these behaviors and artifacts. RMT contends that these and most other embodiments of CS index the schema that the bodies of those in the relation share a common substance (which could be real, imagined, or implied). Fiske (2004) terms this underlying schema *consubstantial assimilation*. Thus, bodily contact, joint eating, and assimilation of outer appearance, by virtue of their connectedness to the sharing of a common substance, indicate the presence of a CS relation. The importance of this practice for close relations (e.g., kinship) has been noted already by early theorists (Durkheim, 1893) and remains a central topic in anthropology (Sobal, 2000).

Similarly, there are abundant ways of establishing, communicating, and confirming authority ranking relations. In addition to eating highness potions, the more powerful might sit on larger chairs, wear bigger hats, and live in larger huts. As for CS relations, RMT argues that these and most other behavioral and artifactual embodiments of AR relations share a common schematic basis, namely, they refer to order in space, especially on the vertical dimension. The more authority one has, the bigger, the taller, and the

that are rather based on authority, expertise, or legal hierarchical structures (e.g., Raven & French, 1959; Turner, 2005). Although many of the findings discussed in this chapter might be relevant for the first meaning of power, we are concentrating more on the second because it actually entails a superiors' pastoral responsibility for subordinates and, thus, is more strongly associated to the cooperative character of relational models in general.

higher.[2] Thus, the medium of cultural conformation and communication of AR is order in space.

Why is it the case that humans think of CS as sharing essences, and of AR as order in space? It seems the answer has to do with the ways in which the human body interacts with other human bodies and the environment. For instance, babies literally share a substance from their mothers' bodies when being breastfed, which helps establish a CS relation between mother and child. However, sharing essence in such close mother-child interactions has to be understood in a wider sense, including proximity and bodily contact. For instance, human babies seek warmth and comfort through close bodily contact, similar to other primate babies (Harlow, 1958). From these experiences, the association of sharing bodily substances with CS relations might develop. Similarly, we interact with our bodies in an environment where gravity is a permanent unidirectional force pulling our bodies along the vertical dimension. Thus, being higher in space is associated with overcoming ubiquitous influence, and being lower is associated with submitting. This unidirectional force makes the vertical dimension distinct from other spatial dimensions and, thus, might be one basis for the embodiment of clearly asymmetric AR relations. It is also true that tall and strong persons are in general more able to force their will upon short and weak persons than vice versa. Children learn this, often painfully, and adults experience this as well. Again, it is easy to see this leads to an association of size and power. Apart from such a learning through individual experience, RMT assumes that the proclivity to interpret consubstantial assimilation as CS and spatial order as AR could also be passed on as a genetic predisposition due to the survival value of quickly understanding social systems. According to RMT, this proclivity facilitates the passing on of collective forms of those representations from generation to generation within cultures through communication, socialization, and tradition (Fiske, 2004).

In sum, we assume the existence of universal cognitive schemata for the representation of social relations among humans. In particular, we claim the schema for CS relations contains behavioral manifestations of consubstantial assimilation, and the schema for AR relations contains behavioral

---

[2]   In addition, Fiske provides substantial anthropological evidence that force, coming earlier in time, and being in front are further modal dimensions in which power is embodied. We do not discuss these here further because there is not yet much evidence from experimental psychological studies for each of these, and because we suspect that coming earlier in time and being in front depend on additional context cues to gain their meaning as embodiments of power. Therefore, a thorough discussion of these would be beyond the scope of the present chapter.

manifestations of vertical order in space. These schemata prepare us to create and understand behaviors and artifacts that embody the two relational models, and thereby to establish, communicate, and confirm social relations – and to understand what people on a strange island – or anywhere in the world – do.

## THE MENTAL REPRESENTATION OF RELATIONAL MODELS: COGNITIVE EMBODIMENT

Assuming schemata for CS and AR rely on consubstantial assimilation and order in space has an interesting implication: It suggests that our mental representation of CS and AR includes modal information about behaviors and spatial relations. Fiske (2004) explicitly argued that perceptual information about space (AR) and the body (CS) is part of mental representations, or in other words, CS and AR are *cognitively embodied* in these modalities. Interestingly, this fits recent theorizing in cognitive psychology. The idea that conceptual knowledge can consist of perceptual information has recently received a lot of attention in research on perception and memory (Clark, 1996; Glenberg, 1997; Smith & Semin, 2004), and comprehensive theories are available that allow the modeling of such perceptually based knowledge. One prominent account is Barsalou's (1999) perceptual symbol systems theory. Barsalou argued that conceptual knowledge consists of abstracted and generalized perceptual experiences, so-called *perceptual symbols*. Importantly, perceptual symbols keep the modal character of the perception that led to the symbols' formation because thinking with perceptual symbols involves the activation of the same sensorimotor areas that were involved in the acquisition of these perceptual symbols. Thus, perceptual symbols are not amodal but still tied to the modality in which they were formed. Thinking that uses perceptual symbols involves the construction of mental simulations (Barsalou, 1999). Thus, the previous sensorimotor experience is partly reenacted, but the simulations will be partial and sketchy and adapted to the active context (i.e., situated). These assumptions are at odds with amodal theories of mental representation both in general psychology and in social cognition (cf. Niedenthal, Barsalou, Winkielman, Kraut-Gruber, & Ric, 2005).

The assumption that concept representations consist of schematic representations of perceptual content offers a way to model how the schematic knowledge about CS and AR is represented mentally. Such an integration of Barsalou's (1999) and Fiske's (2004) theories suggests that CS and AR are mentally represented as highly schematized perceptual symbols. For CS, perceptual content about bodily contact and bodily sharing of substances is schematized into a perceptual symbol of *shared essences* (consubstantial assimilation). For AR, perceptual content of orders in space along the dimensions of size, height, and vertical position is schematized into a perceptual symbol for asymmetric *order in space*. These symbols are then used to run simulations that allow the understanding of unfamiliar behavioral and artifactual embodiments and, indeed, also the creation of new ones. When one thinks about CS relations, the perceptual symbol of shared essences will be activated. This leads to simulations using sensorimotor experiences of sharing substances, imitation, or bodily contact (variants of consubstantial assimilation) to construct the relation. When one thinks about AR, sensorimotor experience of order in space will become active. Depending on other activated information, this can be about size, height, vertical position, or a mix of those. These simulations then represent the power relation. Of course, the concrete contents of these simulations will depend on personal learning history and the fit to the situation.

The implications of this hypothesis can be understood by contrasting it from one alternative: the possibility that social relations are inferred through propositional reasoning. Back on the island, when you perceive one hut as much larger than the other, you could categorize the hut as large and then, on the basis of knowledge about the world, form the proposition that the hut belongs to a powerful person because you know large huts often belong to powerful persons. However, the perceptual symbol hypothesis suggests, because size is part of the power schema, that the size of the hut has an immediate influence on your perception of its owner's power. Thus, we would expect that the perception of a large hut naturally goes along with thinking of the owner as powerful. Of course, inferences could still come into play, especially when you want to correct your impression of the owner on the basis of additional information, e.g., that he has only inherited it from his father but is in fact not powerful in the community. In the following, we will further develop the integration of Barsalou's and Fiske's theories by first deriving criteria that can be used to distinguish between these two possibilities. We will then report first evidence suggesting that both CS and AR are represented as perceptual symbols.

## TESTING FOR COGNITIVE EMBODIMENT

How is it possible to show that a social relation or a concept in general is mentally represented in modal form? We propose there are at least four types of empirical evidence that can demonstrate cognitive embodiment. A first type shows there is a correlation between human behavior and a state or process, or in other words, there is *behavioral* or *artifactual evidence* for embodiment. For example, the observation that happy people tend to smile and smiling people are usually happy (Ekman & Friesen, 1971) is evidence for behavioral embodiment of happiness as smiling. This type of evidence is often so obvious that it is not studied empirically. Furthermore, some forms of embodiment do not involve overt behavior, so no evidence for embodiment on the behavioral level can be collected.

The other three types of evidence measure the outcome of cognitive processes to infer the nature of the representations involved in them. Evidence for an embodied process thus means the process involves modal representations. The second type shows modal information has an influence on the assumed cognitive process and its direct outcomes, especially judgments and feelings. Thus, the difference from the first type is that not only behavior itself but inputs for and outcomes of cognition are the focus of the investigation (although behavior will of course mostly be used as an index of the cognitive process). Because the type of evidence targeted here involves showing that modal information biases the cognitive processes, we will refer to this type of evidence as *bias evidence.*

When we speak of an embodiment effect, we assume there is an effect of the modal information on the cognitive process because the cognitive process uses representations in these modalities. However, bias and behavioral evidence are not sufficient to demonstrate such an embodiment because they could still be explained by inferential processes. Modal information could be categorized in a higher mental process, become the basis of a propositional representation, and then be used to form a judgment. This process could lead to bias evidence. Thus, a third type of evidence is necessary to show that such a biasing influence is not mediated by inferential processes, and the influence happens in an automatic fashion. We will call this type of evidence *automaticity evidence.* Automaticity evidence often measures performance (e.g., speed or accuracy) in the cognitive process that is hypothesized to be embodied, whereas modal information is presented simultaneously. The assumption is if the candidate modality is involved in the conceptual representation of the target concept or in generating a response, then any sensory input in this modality should influence the performance. Experiments testing for automaticity preclude influence of inferences on the performance measure, for instance, through inducing mental load, time constraints, or hindering the correct categorization. Thus, the ruling out of inferential processes that could explain a bias finding is a crucial feature of automaticity evidence. In addition, explicit measures can test whether conscious inferences took place. Finding automatic effects without effects on explicit measures is particularly good evidence against a high level inference (for instance, see the chapter by Smith, this volume).

Finally, a fourth type of evidence shows that the use of the modal representation is necessary and important for the assumed process and not an epiphenomenon. We will call this type *mediational evidence.* Finding mediational evidence implies showing that the modal representations are not only able to influence a cognitive process but also indeed mediate this process. Evidence for mediation of cognition through embodied representations is still rare. Some examples from outside the field of social relations are provided by Niedenthal et al. (2001) and Wilson and Knoblich (2005).

This typology can be used to sort the evidence, but it does not suggest one type of evidence is inherently better than another. Instead, the types of evidence are complementary. Behavioral/artifactual evidence and bias evidence are better suited to demonstrate the phenomenon in question and to demonstrate its importance in a given domain. On the other hand, automaticity and mediational evidence show more information about the process and are able to rule out alternative explanations. A further type of evidence not discussed in this chapter is provided by brain-imaging techniques (see the chapters by Barsalou and Pulvermüller, this volume).

## EVIDENCE FOR COGNITIVE EMBODIMENT OF COMMUNAL SHARING

Equipped with this framework for empirical tests of cognitive embodiment, what is now the evidence that the relational models CS and AR are, in fact, embodied as shared essences and order in space? We will first discuss the evidence for CS, ordered by the different variants of consubstantial assimilation that Fiske (2004) discusses: physical proximity, bodily contact, imitation, and sharing of food.

### Physical Proximity

Intergroup research on the well-known contact hypothesis (Allport, 1954) has accumulated an impressive amount of evidence demonstrating that physical proximity improves attitudes towards members of outgroups (Dovidio, Gaertner, & Kawakami, 2003; Pettigrew & Tropp, 2000). Among others, identification with a common in-group including those out-group members, interpersonal friendship, and affect bonds, all typical instantiations of a CS relation, have been shown to be important mediators of this effect (Gaertner, Dovidio, & Bachman, 1996; Tropp & Pettigrew, 2005).

The behavioral embodiment of CS in physical proximity is shown more directly in social psychological work that used proximity behavior as an index for the need to affiliate: Wisman and Koole (2003) showed that increasing the need for affiliation through a manipulation making death salient led to a wish to sit within a group instead of sitting alone (see also Pleban & Tesser, 1981; Schachter, 1959; Shah, Brazy, & Higgins, 2004; Tice, 1992). Similarly, the artifactual embodiment of closeness has been used to construct measures of social distance: Aron, Aron, and Smollan (1992) developed a scale consisting of overlapping circles representing the self and another person. They demonstrated that the perception of oneself as overlapping with another person was a valid indicator of social distance. This measure can also be used to measure the identification with groups (Schubert & Otten, 2002; Tropp & Wright, 2001).

## Bodily Contact

Regarding bodily contact, there is ample evidence that touching influences helping behavior, which can be seen as a marker of CS relations (Cialdini, Brown, Lewis, Luce, & et al., 1997). Briefly touching the arm or shoulder for one or two seconds, in comparison to not touching, increased compliance with a variety of requests for help, such as to fill out a questionnaire (Hornik, 1987), to sign a petition (Willis & Hamm, 1980), to return a forgotten dime (Brockner, Pressman, Cabitt, & Moran, 1982), or to give away a dime (Kleinke, 1977). Awareness of the touch does not influence the compliance (Guéguen, 2002). Furthermore, touching waitresses receive larger tips (Cruscoe & Wetzel, 1984; Stephen & Zweigenhaft, 1986).

All of these findings are primarily reflecting behavioral evidence of embodiment. In a series of recent studies, we have started to collect bias and automaticity evidence for the embodiment of CS as bodily contact. The type of CS relation we were interested in was strong identification with a social group. In a first study (Seibt et al., in preparation), we were interested in whether experiencing bodily contact with a fellow in-group member would induce feelings of identification with the in-group. As in the studies just cited, we manipulated bodily contact by having an experimenter touch half of the participants on the shoulder for one second while handing over a questionnaire. Both the experimenter and the participants were students, and the questionnaire assessed identification with the student in-group using a pictorial overlap scale (Schubert & Otten, 2002). As expected, we found that touched participants indicated a significantly higher overlap, i.e. a higher identification with their student in-group. (There were no effects on participants' mood.) Furthermore, touch might even have an influence on the evaluation of persons who do not belong to the own in-group (see Smith, this volume).

Although participants did not indicate any awareness of a possible influence by touch, conscious inferences could still have mediated this effect. In a further series of studies, we also collected automaticity evidence ruling out such an interpretation (Schubert, Seibt, Waldzus, & Schmidt, in preparation). With this set of studies, we investigated whether individuals have an automatic tendency to reciprocate bodily contact by members of their in-group (i.e., those with whom they have a CS type relation) but not by members of an out-group. The studies followed the typical paradigm for such an automaticity study by activating information in the modality suspected to be involved and assessing the reaction time for a judgment of the investigated concept. The activated information consisted in these studies in fact of two different modalities at the same time, visual and motor information. We showed participants pictures of persons who were either standing in a normal posture or standing and extending their right hand, as if inviting a handshake (see Figure 7.1; this was the visual information). The shown persons belonged either to the in-group of the participant or to a clearly visible out-group; the participants' task was to categorize the persons according to their in-group/out-group membership. To answer, they were required to use a regularly sized but special keyboard with only three keys left (one in the middle and one on each side), which implemented the motor component. It was placed lengthwise between the participant and the screen. A person was categorized as an in-group member either by pressing the key near the screen, moving the hand forward, or by pressing the key near the body, moving the hand backward. (Participants had to press the middle key to start each trial.) Thus, the task tested whether participants would be influenced in their hand movements by the outstretched hand of the person on the screen, depending on that person's category. If an in-group categorization is embodied in bodily contact, the corresponding movement should be facilitated when bodily contact is offered. We tested this hypothesis in two studies using gender and age as categorization dimensions. We found in both studies the hypothesized pattern: Reaction times were influenced by the targets' hand postures for in-group targets but not for out-group targets. Specifically, for in-group targets we found that forward movements were facilitated when the in-group person offered a handshake, compared to no offered handshake, and the backward movements were impeded by an offered handshake, compared to no offered handshake. When an out-group member offered a handshake, this had no effect on the participants' reactions. Only in the in-group, bodily

Figure 7.1. Offered bodily contact influences latencies of in-group membership judgments.

contact is automatically reciprocated. Notably, the gender effect found in the gender study did not replicate in the age study, showing it was really the activated categorization driving the effect.[3] These findings represent initial

---

[3] The described effects are not equivalent to approach-avoidance effects as described by Vaes, Paladino, Castelli, Leyens, and Giovanazzi (2003) or Castelli, Zogmaister, Smith, and Arcuri (2004), who originally developed the keyboard we used in this study. We found no simple approach-avoidance effect (i.e., a faster approach response to in-group and a faster avoidance response to out-group members), and when scores for the bodily contact effect and the approach-avoidance effect were computed, they did not correlate. Our interpretation is that the approach-avoidance effect primarily reflects antipathy against the out-group, whereas the effect of reciprocating bodily contact primarily reflects a CS relation to the in-group.

automaticity evidence for the embodiment of CS as bodily contact. We can rule out conscious inferential processes as an alternative explanation for two reasons: First, the reaction times were far less then one second, making it unlikely that the participants drew inferences and reacted on their basis. Second, questioning of the participants after the study did not reveal any insight into our hypothesis that the offered handshake of an in-group person would influence their own reactions.

## Imitation

An extensive literature shows there is a pervasive tendency to imitate others who are perceived or whose stereotype is activated (Chartrand & Bargh, 1999; Dijksterhuis & Bargh, 2001). Meanwhile, there is also evidence that categorization borders moderate this tendency. Automaticity evidence comes from studies reported by Schubert and Häfner (2003) and Spears, Gordijn, Dijksterhuis, and Stapel (2004). They showed that the automatic enactment of activated group stereotypes found in various studies (e.g., Bargh, Chen, & Burrows, 1996; Dijksterhuis & van Knippenberg, 1998) can be impeded by depicting these groups clearly as out-groups. Thus, behavior of out-groups (i.e., groups with whom the participant does not have a CS relation) is not imitated. This is automaticity evidence because the participants did not intend consciously to imitate or not imitate. Further evidence is available for the mimicry of single individuals: Van Baaren, Maddux, Chartrand, de Bouter & van Knippenberg (2003) found individuals primed with words such as *together, group,* and *cooperate* were more likely to mimic another person unconsciously than individuals in a control condition. Priming with words such as *unique, alone,* and *individual* led to less mimicry. Although van Baaren et al. interpret these primes as activating an interdependent versus an independent self-concept, we think it is also possible to understand these primes as activating versus not activating a CS relation. Furthermore, van Baaren, Holland, Steenaert, and van Knippenberg (2003) demonstrated that being mimicked without being aware of it led to similar consequences as being touched: mimicking waitresses receive larger tips. This can be interpreted as a form of helping behavior typical of CS relations (because it is unreciprocated). Van Baaren, Holland, Kawakami, and van Knippenberg (2004) found being mimicked leads to an increase in various types of helping behavior, replicating the effects of bodily contact with a different CS manipulation. Furthermore, Ashton-James, van Baaren, Chartrand, Decety, and Karremans (2007) showed that mimicked individuals seated themselves closer to a stranger than persons who were not mimicked, which shows that imitation and physical proximity, two of the assumed indicators of CS, are related. Finally, they found that being mimicked led to a feeling of closeness to other people in general (i.e., a stronger tendency to feel like in a CS relation). All these results, except those of the tipping study, can be considered automaticity findings because they largely rule out conscious inferences.

## Food Sharing

Miller, Rozin, and Fiske (1998) investigated if seeing people exchange food has an influence on the impression of their relation. They showed their participants a five minute videotape of a couple eating in a restaurant. In a brief sequence, the two persons either handed each other salt and pepper or shared food with or without feeding. The findings confirmed that sharing of food is associated with personal – as opposed to professional – relationships, and feeding is associated with a sexual/romantic relationship, i.e., types of a CS relation.

In sum, there is ample evidence for behavioral and artifactual embodiment of CS as the sharing of essences. In addition, there is now also initial evidence for a biasing influence of imitation and bodily contact on feelings of identification, and even initial evidence that bodily contact automatically biases judgments about CS relations. However, no evidence has been reported so far that CS cognitions are indeed mediated by or rely on perceptual content related to sharing of essences.

### EVIDENCE FOR COGNITIVE EMBODIMENT OF AUTHORITY RANKING

As outlined previously, Fiske argued that AR conformation involves a comparison of vertical positions or sizes. Because most of the available evidence confounds size and height, we first report on these two combined and then report evidence for the embodiment of AR in vertical position.

## Size and Height

Behavioral embodiment of AR in size would mean people adjust their apparent size to the power they have. Hall, Coats, and Smith LeBeau (2005) confirmed this in their recent meta-analysis of studies testing the relation between nonverbal behavior and impressions of power and dominance. They found postural openness (i.e., gestures making the appearance larger, such as arms and legs akimbo) is one of the very few behaviors that is correlated with actual power and dominance, along with facial expressiveness (Keltner, Gruenfeld, & Anderson, 2003). Similarly, there is evidence that people adjust their signature size to their chronic status, both in Western societies and in Iran (Aiken & Zweigenhaft, 1978; Zweigenhaft, 1970).

However, there is also ample evidence for biasing effects of size and height on the perception of power. Perceived size can vary both because of the tallness (and width) and because of the posture of a person. Evidence suggests both sources of size variance influence impressions of power. Boyson, Pryer, and Butler (1999) asked participants to rate a couple depicted on a picture; the woman's figure was manipulated to be considerably shorter, slightly shorter, or slightly taller than the man's figure. The woman was rated as more dominant than the man when she was pictured as taller. Tiedens and Fragale (2003) manipulated a confederate's behavior to be either expanded or constricted, and found higher ratings of dominance for the expanded confederate and predominantly complementary (instead of mimicking) behavior from the participants who interacted with the confederate (see also Montepare, 1995). Interestingly, the reverse – that is, an influence of power on size judgments – is also true: The successful presidential candidate of the 1988 Canadian election was judged taller after than before the election, whereas the reverse was true for the losers (cf. Dannemaier & Thumin, 1964; Judge & Cable, 2004). Thus, the perception of power and that of size and height mutually bias each other.

However, one question remaining is to what extent these effects are mediated by inferences of the type, "I know tall persons are often dominant, so I assume this is the case here as well," or whether size has an immediate impact on the dominance rating because dominance is mentally represented as size. To test this latter hypothesis and rule out conscious inferences, we conducted a study using a reaction time paradigm and manipulating font size instead of body size (Schubert & Waldzus, 2005). Pairs of group labels (e.g., *teacher* and *student*) were presented to the participants. The pairs were constructed in such a way that one group was clearly more powerful than the other. One half of the participants had to judge as quickly as possible which of the two groups was the powerful group by pressing the assigned response key; the other half had to judge which was the powerless group. One of the two presented group labels was always written in large font size (42 points), the other one in small font (12 point, Figure 7.2). Each pair was presented twice, with reversed font size in the second presentation. Both response latencies and errors in judgment were analyzed as a function of whether the powerful or the powerless group was written in the larger font size. If larger size is associated with larger power, it should be easier to judge the group as more powerful when its label is written in a larger font than when it is written in

Figure 7.2. Varying font size influences power judgments.

a smaller font; the reverse was expected for powerless groups. We found the expected pattern. When the task was to find the powerful group, more errors were made when the powerful target groups were written in small letters than when they were written in large letters. The opposite was true when the task was to find the powerless group. Here, more errors were made when the powerless target groups were written in large letters than when they were written in small letters, resulting in a significant task by font size interaction effect. Though not significant, a similar pattern was found for the reaction times: When the task was to find the powerful group, responses were slower when the powerful target groups were written in smaller letters than when they were written in larger letters; when the task was to find the powerless group, there was no difference between the response latencies.

In a further study using a similar paradigm (Schubert, Waldzus, & Giessner, in press), we presented not pairs of groups but single group labels in either small or big font size. Participants had to judge whether the group was typically powerful or powerless. Replicating the previous findings, both reaction times and error data showed that large font size, compared to small font size, facilitated "powerful" answers (shorter reaction times, less errors) but impeded "powerless" answers (longer reaction times, more errors). We interpret these reaction time findings as showing an automatic, unintended influence of modal information about size on thinking about power, and thus indicative of a cognitive embodiment of power as size.

## Vertical Position

Vertical position or elevation can be thought of as a surrogate or illusion of height. Anthropological evidence confirms elevation in space is used to constitute and communicate relative rank. Power can be embodied as elevation in architecture (Garvin & Riesenberg, 1952; Keating, 2000) and furniture

(Hewes, 1955), or the elevation can be expressed through spatial metaphors in language (Schwartz, 1981). Individuals can either benefit from association with high artifacts (e.g., sitting in a tall building) but also by being actually elevated themselves (e.g., sitting on the top floor in a tall building). Bias evidence is also available: Spiegel and Machotka (1974) collected ratings of men depicted in line drawings. One of the men stood on an elevated surface. The higher figure was rated as more superordinate, important, and haughty than the lower figure. Similar evidence was presented by Schwartz, Tesser, and Powell (1982). Their subjects were asked to identify the "socially dominant" person in 64 drawings of dyads. The persons in the dyads varied on a number of dimensions, such as sitting versus standing, horizontal differences, and elevation in space. Elevation emerged as the strongest influence on the dominance ratings; elevated figures (standing on pedestals) were more likely judged as the dominant person.

In another series of studies, Giessner and Schubert (2007) collected similar evidence using a more unobtrusive manipulation of vertical location. Specifically, we asked participants to form judgments about a business manager who had several subordinates. In addition to a picture and biographical information about the manager, a typical organization graph visualized that he was on top and had five subordinates. Between participants, we varied the length of the vertical line between manager and subordinates. Importantly, this length is not officially codified information in organization charts, and should be meaningless. Nevertheless, in three independent samples we found the length of the line had a significant effect on participants' judgments of the manager's power and authority. A longer line increased perceived power. Importantly, when questioned afterwards, participants were not aware of taking the length of the line into account, suggesting that the embodiment effect probably occurred automatically.

Another study in this series fulfills the criteria of automaticity evidence even better. Again, participants judged the power of a leader after reading information about him. However, between the impression formation and the judgment, an additional task was inserted that involved either the processing of large vertical or small vertical spatial differences, or the processing of large horizontal or small horizontal differences. We reasoned that the impression of the manager's power should be distorted by the processing of vertical, but not horizontal, differences. This was indeed the case: Processing large vertical differences led people to attribute more power to the manager, whereas processing small vertical differences led to the attribution of less power to the manager. Processing large versus small horizontal differences did not affect the power judgments. In this study, no inference about the manager's power was possible from the height information processed as it was completely irrelevant to the impression formation task.

Further studies also show automaticity evidence for the cognitive embodiment of AR as differences in vertical position (Schubert, 2005). Using essentially the same interference paradigm as in the study on size previously described, group labels were presented on a screen and the layout of the presentation included spatial information about elevation: In one study, pairs of groups were presented, and one group label was located above the other group label. In this study, participants had to identify the more powerful group (or, in another condition, the powerless group) as quickly as possible by pressing a key. In another study, single group labels were presented either at the top or at the bottom of the screen, and the participants' task was to judge whether the presented group was typically powerful or powerless. The findings confirmed that the vertical positions on the screen significantly influenced the (very short) reaction times. Powerful groups at the top of the screen were more quickly identified as powerful compared to the bottom of the screen. This was true when they were presented alone or together with another group. In contrast, powerless groups at the bottom of the screen were more quickly identified as powerless compared to the top of the screen, again both when presented alone or together with another group. Thus, modal information about vertical position automatically biases our perception of power: we can more easily recognize powerful groups when they are on top and powerless groups when they are at the bottom. Further evidence confirmed that this effect is independent of the effect that things on top are also more quickly identified as positive; the task of the participants and thus the salient concept moderate whether the vertical dimension cognitively embodies valence or power. This was most clearly visible for dangerous yet powerful groups. The valence judgment (negative) of those groups was facilitated when they were presented at the bottom, but the power judgment (powerful) was facilitated when they were presented at the top.

In sum, behavioral, artifactual, bias, and automaticity evidence confirms AR is embodied as size, height, and elevation in space. In addition, evidence shows elevation is automatically used as a medium to express authority and power (Giessner & Schubert, 2007). However, there is as yet no mediational evidence.

CONCLUSIONS

In this chapter, we used Barsalou's (1999) symbol systems theory to provide a theoretical framework for the cognitive underpinnings of Fiske's (1992,

2004b) Relational Model Theory. Conceptualizing the cognitive representation of the two basic social relations *communal sharing* and *authority ranking* as perceptual symbols, we were able to integrate a broad range of findings, from behavioral and artifactual correlates of social relations to biased cognitions and evidence on the automatic influence of modal information on cognitive processes.

Notably, there is so far no evidence that mental simulations of modal content mediate the processing of social-relational information, let alone that they mediate social processes. This is a shortcoming that this young line of research shares with the embodiment literature in general. It remains for future research to show the phenomena described here are not just epiphenomena but are also crucial and important for thinking about social processes in the interpersonal or intergroup realm, and thus also for the processes themselves.

The integration we have presented and the findings we see as evidence for it focus primarily on the cognitive aspects, namely, on the idea that relational models are mentally represented as modal information tied to perceptual content. Equipped with this evidence, the communicative aspects emphasized in RMT can now be investigated from a perceptual symbols perspective. Most importantly, we think there is a recursive relation between the cognitive representation of relations and their behavioral and artifactual embodiment. Humans enact the CS and AR perceptual symbols always anew by constructing artifacts and rituals, by using the respective metaphors in language, and by behaving accordingly. Thereby, they provide again stimuli that others (e.g., their children) can schematize, thereby enhancing and modifying the existing perceptual symbols of social relations. Thus, the learning and reification of perceptual symbols of social relations reinforce each other and together lead to their perpetuation.

### Implications of Embodied Relational Models

We hope that our approach also sheds light on further issues that might not be seen as directly related to embodiment at first. For instance, recognizing the embodied nature of social relations may foster a new perspective on the question of cultural universals. In the following, we will try to develop a speculative account of how cultural universals result from the embodiment of social relations. On the one hand, the environment provides us with concrete universal experiences requiring interpretation. Thus, in all cultures, it makes sense to ask who is above me, who is below, who is in front of me, who is behind, who moves with me in the same direction, in the same rhythm, and who does not. On the other hand, just as empirical data ultimately prove or falsify theories in science, our senses are the ultimate source of validation for our thoughts, together with communication and social consensus about what we have seen with our own eyes. Because sensorimotor experiences relate the mind to the empirical world, they deliver constraints distinguishing reality from the world of possibilities. If our thinking about social relations is embodied, it is subject to these empirical constraints. This is the source of universality. In the nature-nurture debate, some argue that our mind is almost infinitely flexible, and cultural anthropology has concentrated on cultural specifics. Acknowledging the construed character of social relations and the overwhelming cultural diversity, claims of universality in social relations (e.g., sexual relations) almost always rely on evolutionary arguments, but these are mostly post-hoc, which weakens their explanatory power. Because the blueprint of our body, our senses, and our physical world is universal, embodiment is a source of more concrete and more plausible claims of universality.

Let us give an example for how universal properties of authority ranking can be explained by embodiment of power in space. Physical ranking in terms of height or size is transitive. If A is higher than B, and B is higher than C, A is higher than C. Theoretically, it is possible to think about a nontransitive power relation: A can have power over B, and B can have power over C, but A does not necessarily have power over C. Instead, C could have power over A. However, such a relation appears to be odd because it violates constraints that are natural in the physical world. As a result, our thinking about power is shaped by our experience with transitive size relations in the physical world. Without embodiment, we would need extra assumptions to account for the transitivity of power. With embodiment, this is not necessary because the rule of transitivity is a natural law applying to all embodiments of power such as size and height.

Another example considers the universal experience of the second principle of thermodynamics and CS. Once two substances are mixed, they will remain mixed (except for long-lasting sedimentation processes that are not perceptually accessible). The separation of mixed substances needs extra effort to work against the tendency toward entropy. This experience is reflected in people's naïve understanding and theories about mixing substances. Because of this knowledge, we can speculate here that people might be inclined to think that single acts of consubstantial assimilation establish enduring CS relations. Furthermore, we would expect undoing CS relations will be considered more difficult than establishing them. To explain this without embodiment would necessitate extra assumptions about the limited, not totally impossible reversibility of CS relations contingent on extra effort. Building on the grounding of CS in thinking about substances, this difficult but possible reversibility follows from our experiences with properties of the physical world.

The body-based plausibility of the assumption that consubstantial assimilation creates communal sharing relations that are difficult to dissolve may also explain why immutability has been identified as one important component of psychological essentialism, that is, of the belief members of a certain group or category share a common essence, making them what they are and not something else (Medin & Ortony, 1989). Essentialism is closely linked to natural kinship, a typical kind of consubstantial assimilation. The idea that both kinship and immutability go together in CS relationships is consistent with the finding that these two form a common dimension of essentialism that has to be distinguished from other dimensions such as discreteness and the assumption that all category members are similar, that is, the inductive potential of the category (Haslam, Rothschild, & Ernst, 2002; Rothbart & Taylor, 1992).

Another important consequence of the constraints implied in embodiment concerns the compatibility of different relational models in real-life relations. RMT assumes that relations in real life are combinations of these different models; however, because they are embodied, the possibility of combinations are limited. For instance, if AR relations are characterized by ordered differences in space and CS is embodied in physical proximity, the possible ways to combine these two are limited and require additional moderators. Future research may identify how such predictable incompatibilities shape human relations (such as incest taboos across authority ranking positions) and which universal or culturally specific patterns are used to eliminate those incompatibilities in domains where they would be dysfunctional.

As a last outlook, we would like to remind the reader that in this chapter we discussed only the embodiment of CS and AR because they are phylogenetically older than other relationship types and their embodiment may be more obvious. In addition, more empirical evidence exists for the embodiment of these two relational models than for that of the other two. However, according to Barsalou's perceptual systems approach, even more abstract concepts (such as those that are the basis of the other two types of relations, equality matching and market pricing) should be embodied. Exploring the embodiments of these two relational models will be challenging because they are constituted by concrete operations (e.g., exchange of placeholders) and by the calculation of ratios by means of an abstract universal but symbolic medium (e.g., money), respectively. One could assume their embodiment may be much more flexible and dependent on historically and culturally varying conventions about symbolical meanings than the embodiment of CS and AR.

AUTHOR NOTE

Thomas Schubert, Free University Amsterdam, The Netherlands. Sven Waldzus, Instituto Superior de Ciências do Trabalho e da Empresa, Lissabon, Portugal. Beate Seibt, University Utrecht, The Netherlands. The preparation of this chapter was supported by a Feodor-Lynen Fellowship awarded by the Humboldt Foundation to Thomas Schubert and by a stipend awarded by the Deutsche Forschungsgemeinschaft to Beate Seibt. We thank Alan Fiske, Steffen Giessner, Nick Haslam, Gün Semin, Eliot Smith, and Fritz Strack for helpful comments on earlier versions, and Haley Smith for her proofreading. Correspondence should be addressed to Thomas Schubert, schubert@igroup.org.

## References

Aiken, L. R., & Zweigenhaft, R. L. (1978). Signature size, sex, and status in Iran. *The Journal of Social Psychology, 106,* 273–274.

Allport, G. W. (1954). *The nature of prejudice.* Reading, MA: Addison-Wesley.

Aron, A., Aron, E. N., & Smollan, D. (1992). Inclusion of Other in the Self scale and the structure of interpersonal closeness. *Journal of Personality and Social Psychology, 63,* 596–612.

Ashton-James, C., Van Baaren, R. V., Chartrand, I. L., Decety, J. & Karremans, J. (2007). Mimicry and me: The impact of mimicry on self-construal. *Social Cognition, 25,* 518–535.

Bargh, J. A., Chen, M., & Burrows, L. (1996). Automaticity of social behavior: Direct effects of trait construct and stereotype activation on action. *Journal of Personality and Social Psychology, 71,* 230–244.

Barsalou, L. W. (1999). Perceptual symbol systems. *Behavioral and Brain Sciences, 22,* 577–609.

Boyson, A. R., Pryor, B., & Butler, J. (1999). Height as power in women. *North American Journal of Psychology, 1,* 109–114.

Brockner, J., Pressman, B., Cabitt, J., & Moran, P. (1982). Nonverbal intimacy, sex, and compliance: A field study. *Journal of Nonverbal Behavior, 6,* 253–258.

Castelli, L., Zogmaister, C., Smith, E. R., & Arcuri, L. (2004). On the automatic evaluation of social exemplars. *Journal of Personality and Social Psychology, 86,* 373–387.

Chartrand, T. L., & Bargh, J. A. (1999). The chameleon effect: The perception-behavior link and social interaction. *Journal of Personality and Social Psychology, 76,* 893–910.

Cialdini, R. B., Brown, S. L., Lewis, B. P., Luce, C., & et al. (1997). Reinterpreting the empathy-altruism relationship: When one into one equals oneness. *Journal of Personality and Social Psychology, 73,* 481–494.

Clark, A. (1996). *Being there. Putting brain, body, and world together again.* Cambridge, MA: The MIT Press.

Cruscoe, A. H., & Wetzel, C. G. (1984). The Midas Touch: The effects of interpersonal touch on restaurant tipping. *Personality and Social Psychology Bulletin, 10,* 512–517.

Dannemaier, W. D., & Thumin, F. J. (1964). Authority status as a factor in perceptual distortion of size. *Journal of Social Psychology, 63,* 361–365.

Dijksterhuis, A., & Bargh, J. A. (2001). The perception-behavior expressway: Automatic effects of social perception on social behavior. In M. P. Zanna (Ed.), *Advances in experimental social psychology, Vol. 33* (pp. 1–40). San Diego, CA: Academic Press.

Dijksterhuis, A., & van Knippenberg, A. (1998). The relation between perception and behavior, or how to win a game of Trivial Pursuit. *Journal of Personality and Social Psychology, 74,* 865–877.

Dovidio, J. F., Gaertner, S. L., & Kawakami, K. (2003). Intergroup contact: The past, present, and the future. *Group Processes & Intergroup Relations, 6,* 5–20.

Durkheim, E. (1893). *De la division du travail social.* Paris: Félix Alcan.

Ekman, P., & Friesen, W. V. (1971). Constants across cultures in the face and emotion. *Journal of Personality and Social Psychology, 17,* 124–129.

Fiske, A. P. (1992). The four elementary forms of sociality: Framework for a unified theory of social relations. *Psychological Review, 99,* 689–723.

Fiske, A. P. (2004). Four modes of constituting relationships: Consubstantial assimilation; space, magnitude, time, and force; concrete procedures; abstract symbolism. In N. Haslam (Ed.), *Relational models theory. A contemporary overview* (pp. 61–146). Mahwah, NJ: Lawrence Erlbaum Associates.

Fiske, A. P., & Haslam, N. (2005). The four basic social bonds: Structures for coordinating interaction. In M. W. Baldwin (Ed.), *Interpersonal cognition* (pp. 267–298). New York: Guilford.

Gaertner, S. L., Dovidio, J. F., & Bachman, B. A. (1996). Revisiting the contact hypothesis: The induction of a common ingroup identity. *International Journal of Intercultural Relations, 20,* 271–290.

Garvin, P. L., & Riesenberg, S. H. (1952). Respect behavior on Panape: An ethnolinguistic study. *American Anthropologist, 54,* 201–220.

Giessner, S., & Schubert, T. W. (2007). High in the hierarchy: How vertical location and judgments of leaders' power are interrelated. *Organizational Behavior and Human Decision Processes, 104,* 30–44.

Glenberg, A. M. (1997). What memory is for. *Behavioral and Brain Sciences, 20,* 1–55.

Guéguen, N. (2002). Touch, awareness of touch, and compliance with a request. *Perceptual and Motor Skills, 95,* 355–360.

Hall, J. A., Coats, E. J., & Smith LeBeau, L. (2005). Nonverbal behavior and the vertical dimension of social relations: A meta-analysis. *Psychological Bulletin, 131,* 898–924.

Harlow, H. F. (1958). The nature of love. *American Psychologist, 13,* 573–685.

Haslam, N., Rothschild, L., & Ernst, D. (2002). Are essentialist beliefs associated with prejudice? *British Journal of Social Psychology, 41,* 87–100.

Heckhausen, H. (1989). *Motivation und Handeln.* Berlin: Springer.

Hewes, G. W. (1955). World distribution of certain postural habits. *American Anthropologist, 57,* 231–244.

Hornik, J. (1987). The effect of touch and gaze upon compliance and interest of interviewees. *Journal of Social Psychology, 127,* 681–683.

Judge, T. A., & Cable, D. M. (2004). The effect of physical height on workplace success and income: Preliminary test of a theoretical model. *Basic and Applied Social Psychology, 89*, 428–441.

Keating, E. (2000). Moments of hierarchy: Constituting social stratification by means of language, food, space and the body in Pohnpei, Micronesia. *American Anthropologist, 102*, 303–320.

Keltner, D., Gruenfeld, D., & Anderson, C. P. (2003). Power, approach, and inhibition. *Psychological Review, 110*, 265–284.

Kleinke, C. (1977). Compliance to requests made by gazing and touching experimenters in field settings. *Journal of Experimental Social Psychology, 13*, 218–223.

Mead, G. H. (1934). *Mind, Self and Society*. Chicago: University of Chicago Press.

Medin, D. L., & Ortony, A. (1989). Psychological essentialism. In S. Vosniadou & A. Ortony (Eds.), *Similarity and analogical reasoning* (pp. 179–195). New York: Cambridge University Press.

Miller, L., Rozin, P., & Fiske, A. P. (1998). Food sharing and feeding another person suggest intimacy; two studies of American college students. *European Journal of Social Psychology, 28*, 423–436.

Montepare, J. M. (1995). The impact of variations in height on young children's impressions of men and women. *Journal of Nonverbal Behavior, 19*, 31–47.

Niedenthal, P., Barsalou, L. W., Winkielman, P., Kraut-Gruber, S., & Ric, F. (2005). Embodiment in attitudes, social perception, and emotion. *Personality and Social Psychology Review, 9*, 184–211.

Niedenthal, P., Brauer, M., Halberstadt, J. B., & Innes-Ker, A. H. (2001). When did her smile drop? Contrast effects in the influence of emotional state on the detection of change in emotional expression. *Cognition and Emotion, 15*, 853–864.

Pettigrew, T. F., & Tropp, L. R. (2000). Does intergroup contact reduce prejudice: Recent meta-analytic findings. In S. Oskamp (Ed.), *Reducing prejudice and discrimination* (pp. 93–114). Mahwah, NJ: Lawrence Erlbaum Associates.

Pleban, R., & Tesser, A. (1981). The effects of relevance and quality of another's performance on interpersonal closeness. *Social Psychology Quarterly, 44*, 278–285.

Raven, B. H., & French, J. R. (1959). Group support, legitimate power, and social influence. *Journal of Personality, 26*, 400–409.

Rothbart, M., & Taylor, M. (1992). Category labels and social reality: Do we view social categories as natural kinds? In K. Fiedler (Ed.), *Language, interaction and social cognition* (pp. 11–36). Thousand Oaks, CA: Sage Publications.

Schachter, S. (1959). *The psychology of affiliation: Experimental studies on the sources of gregariousness*. Stanford, CA: Stanford University Press.

Schubert, T. W. (2005). Your Highness: Vertical positions as perceptual symbols of power. *Journal of Personality and Social Psychology, 89*, 1–21.

Schubert, T. W., & Häfner, M. (2003). Contrast from social stereotypes in automatic behavior. *Journal of Experimental Social Psychology, 39*, 577–584.

Schubert, T. W., & Otten, S. (2002). Overlap of self, ingroup, and outgroup. Pictorial measures of self-categorization. *Self and Identity, 1*, 535–576.

Schubert, T. W., Seibt, B., Waldzus, S., & Schmidt, S. (in prep). Shaking hands: Ingroup members afford bodily contact. Manuscript in preparation.

Schubert, T. W., & Waldzus, S. (2005). Font size influences comparative power judgments. Unpublished dataset.

Schubert, T. W., Waldzus, S., & Giessner, S. R. (in press). Control over the association of power and size. *Social Cognition.*

Schwartz, B. (1981). *Vertical classification: A study in structuralism and the sociology of knowledge.* Chicago: University of Chicago Press.

Schwartz, B., Tesser, A., & Powell, E. (1982). Dominance cues in nonverbal behavior. *Social Psychology Quarterly, 45,* 114–120.

Seibt, B., Schubert, T. W., Strack, F., Hall, E. P., Seger, C. R., & Smith, E. R. (in prep). Embodied contact: Being touched affects social identification and prejudice.

Shah, J., Brazy, P. C., & Higgins, E. T. (2004). Promoting us or preventing them: Regulatory focus and manifestations of intergroup bias. *Personality and Social Psychology Bulletin, 30,* 433–446.

Smith, E. R., & Semin, G. R. (2004). Socially situated cognition: Cognition in its social context. In M. P. Zanna (Ed.), *Advances in experimental social psychology, Vol. 36* (pp. 53–117). San Diego, CA: Elsevier Academic Press.

Sobal, J. (2000). Sociability and meals: Facilitation, commensality, and interaction. In H. L. Leiselman (Ed.), *Dimensions of the meal: The science, culture, business and art of eating* (pp. 119–133). Gaithersburg, MD: Aspen.

Spears, R., Gordijn, E., Dijksterhuis, A., & Stapel, D. A. (2004). Reaction in action: Intergroup contrast in automatic behavior. *Personality and Social Psychology Bulletin, 30,* 606–616.

Spiegel, J., & Machotka, P. (1974). *Messages of the body.* New York: Free Press.

Stephen, R., & Zweigenhaft, R. L. (1986). The effect on tipping of a waitress touching male and female customers. *Journal of Social Psychology, 126,* 141–142.

Tice, D. M. (1992). Self-concept change and self-presentation: The looking-glass self is also a magnifying glass. *Journal of Personality and Social Psychology, 63,* 435–451.

Tiedens, L. Z., & Fragale, A. R. (2003). Power moves: Complementarity in dominant and submissive nonverbal behavior. *Journal of Personality and Social Psychology, 84,* 558–568.

Tropp, L. R., & Pettigrew, T. F. (2005). Differential relationships between intergroup contact and affective and cognitive dimensions of prejudice. *Personality and Social Psychology Bulletin, 31,* 1145–1158.

Tropp, L. R., & Wright, S. C. (2001). Ingroup identification as the inclusion of ingroup in the self. *Personality and Social Psychology Bulletin, 27,* 585–600.

Turner, J. C. (2005). Explaining the nature of power: A three-process theory. *European Journal of Social Psychology, 35,* 1–22.

Vaes, J., Paladino, M. P., Castelli, L., Leyens, J. P., & Giovanazzi, A. (2003). On the behavioral consequences of infrahumanization: The implicit role of uniquely human emotions in intergroup relations. *Journal of Personality and Social Psychology, 85,* 1016–1034.

Van Baaren, R. B., Holland, R. W., Kawakami, K., & van Knippenberg, A. (2004). Mimicry and prosocial behavior. *Psychological Science, 15,* 71–74.

Van Baaren, R. B., Holland, R. W., Steenaert, B., & van Knippenberg, A. (2003). Mimicry for money: Behavioral consequences of imitation. *Journal of Experimental Social Psychology, 39,* 393–398.

Van Baaren, R. B., Maddux, W. W., Chartrand, T. L., De Bouter, C., & van Knippenberg, A. (2003). It takes two to mimic: Behavioral consequences of self-construals. *Journal of Personality and Social Psychology, 84,* 1093–1102.

Willis, F., & Hamm, H. (1980). The use of interpersonal touch in securing compliance. *Journal of Nonverbal Behavior, 5,* 49–55.

Wilson, M., & Knoblich, G. (2005). The case for motor involvement in perceiving conspecifics. *Psychological Bulletin, 131,* 460–473.

Wisman, A., & Koole, S. (2003). Hiding in the crowd: Can mortality salience promote affiliation with others who oppose one's worldview? *Journal of Personality and Social Psychology, 84,* 511–526.

Zweigenhaft, R. L. (1970). Signature size: A key to status awareness. *The Journal of Social Psychology, 81,* 49–54.

# 8 Embodied Persuasion

*Fundamental Processes By Which Bodily Responses Can Impact Attitudes*

Pablo Briñol and Richard E. Petty

This chapter concerns embodiment and people's attitudes. Attitudes commonly refer to the general evaluations people hold regarding various objects, issues, and people (e.g., Petty & Cacioppo, 1981). The link between the attitude concept and bodily responses has a long history, going back to the use of the term *attitude* to refer to the posture of one's body (Galton, 1884) and to expressive motor behaviors (e.g., a scowling face was said to indicate a hostile attitude; Darwin, 1965). Today, we still ask for people's *position* on an issue though the meaning refers to an evaluative rather than a physical orientation.

In this chapter, we review research focused on the impact of a person's own bodily responses on attitudes such as when vertical head movements lead to more favorable attitudes than horizontal (Wells & Petty, 1980). As we describe in this review, a large number of bodily movements have been studied and many effects found. We use the term *embodiment* to refer to the idea that the body contributes to the acquisition, change, and use of attitudes.

We review contemporary social psychological literature with a focus on how the body can influence attitudes. In particular, we will: outline a general framework that articulates the key psychological processes by which one's body can affect attitudes; describe how different bodily postures and movements have been postulated to influence persuasion by each of these fundamental mechanisms; highlight a recently discovered new mechanism called *self-validation* and describe how this mechanism can contribute to understanding bodily influences on evaluation; and outline some remaining issues and directions for future research.

## FUNDAMENTAL PROCESSES OF EMBODIED PERSUASION

Although the ability of bodily movements to influence attitudes seems to be a well-established phenomenon, most research on this topic has not focused on the psychological mechanisms by which this influence occurs. Understanding these processes is essential to predict whether, when, and how attitudes change, as well as to predict whether, when, and how attitudes would result in further behavioral changes. Next, we describe the processes by which any behavior of the recipient can influence attitudes.

Consistent with the Elaboration Likelihood Model (ELM) of persuasion (Petty & Cacioppo, 1981, 1986; Petty, Priester, & Briñol, 2002; Petty & Wegener, 1999), we argue that the psychological processes relevant to attitude change can be organized into a finite set. The ELM specifies several discrete mechanisms of attitude change and holds that these processes operate at different points along an elaboration continuum ranging from little or no thought about the attitude object to complete and extensive thought about the attitude object. A person's bodily movements or responses, like other variables in persuasion settings, can influence attitudes by affecting one or more of these underlying processes: affecting the amount of issue-relevant thinking that occurs; producing a bias to the thoughts that come to mind; affecting structural properties of the thoughts such as thought confidence; serving as persuasive evidence (i.e., arguments); and serving as simple peripheral cues to change. At the low end of the thinking continuum (i.e., when motivation and ability to think are highly constrained), variables are most likely to serve as simple cues. At the high end of the thinking continuum, variables are examined as evidence, bias the ongoing thoughts, or affect thought confidence. When thinking is not constrained to be high or low, variables affect the extent of thinking.

According to the ELM, understanding the process by which bodily responses affect attitudes is important for a number of reasons. For example, when behavior influences attitudes through low thinking processes (e.g., serving as a cue), the attitudes formed are less persistent, resistant to change, and predictive of subsequent behaviors than when the same behavior produces the same amount of change by a high thinking process (e.g., biasing the thoughts generated). Thus, identifying the processes by which bodily movements affect attitudes is informative about the immediate and long-term consequences of persuasion (Petty, Haugtvedt, & Smith, 1995). Next, we review each of the mechanisms by which bodily responses can affect attitudes according to the ELM. After reviewing how the body can affect each process, we explain how any one bodily response can affect attitudes via multiple processes in different situations.

## Bodily Responses Can Serve as Simple Cues

Perhaps the simplest way in which the body can affect attitudes is by serving as a simple cue when the extent of thinking about the attitude object is low. Much prior research has shown that under low thinking conditions, attitudes are influenced by a variety of low effort processes that can emerge from the recipient's own behavior, such as mere association (Cacioppo, Marshall-Goodell, Tassinary, & Petty 1992) or reliance on simple heuristics, such as drawing direct inferences from one's body (e.g., if my heart is beating fast, I must like it; Valins, 1966). When bodily responses serve as simple cues, the impact on attitudes is consistent with the perceived valence of the bodily response.

### Basic Associative Processes

A simple mechanism by which a bodily response can affect attitudes is evaluative conditioning. When an initially unconditioned (neutral) stimulus is encountered along with a conditioning stimulus that is already strongly associated with positive or negative reactions, the initially neutral stimulus can come to elicit positive or negative reactions. Given that contractions of certain muscles are associated with positive or negative affect, they can influence attitudes by serving as conditioning stimuli. In line with this logic, Cacioppo, Priester, and Berntson (1993) observed that neutral Chinese ideographs presented during arm flexion (approach behavior) were subsequently evaluated more favorably than ideographs presented during arm extension (avoidance behavior).

   Consistent with the idea that arm movements can affect attitudes through a relatively low-effort conditioning process, Priester, Cacioppo, and Petty (1996) found that isometric flexion versus extension of upper arm muscles influenced preferences for neutral non-words (which, of course, were not associated with any preexisting meaning or knowledge) more than for neutral, previously known words. Also using a conditioning conceptualization, Tom, Pettersen, Lau, Burton, and Cook (1991) asked participants to move their heads up and down or side to side and found that nodding resulted in the establishment of an increased preference for a previously neutral object (e.g., a pen), whereas shaking the head led to a decline in preference for the neutral pen. According to their interpretation, because head movements are associated with positive reactions, these may have become associated with the neutral product through a low elaboration conditioning process.

In line with Darwin's idea that facial and postural feedback facilitates the emergence of related emotions, research has also found that approach-avoidance behavior directly triggers compatible responses. For example, in one study, Strack, Martin, and Stepper (1988) asked participants either to hold a pen between their teeth (which facilitates a facial expressing similar to smiling) or to hold a pen between their lips (which inhibits smiling) while watching cartoons. Although participants did not recognize the meaning of their facial expression, they judged cartoons to be more humorous in the former than the latter condition (see also Stepper & Strack, 1993; Ito et al., 2006). In another series of studies, Zajonc, Murphy, and Inglehart (1989) asked participants to repeatedly make sounds like the "u" sound of German, which makes a facial expression like disgust. When making this sound, the participants reported less pleasant feelings. Thus, bodily responses influence associated evaluations and affective states (for a review, see Laird & Bresler, 1992).

### Simple Inferences from Bodily Responses

Another simple mechanism by which bodily responses can have an impact on attitudes is via self-perception processes (Bem, 1972). Bem reasoned that just as people assume that the behavior of others and the context in which it occurs provides information about the presumed attitudes of others, so too does a person's own behavior provide information about the person's own attitude (see Olson & Hafer, 1990). Of most relevance here, research shows that physiological responses emanating from the body can lead people to infer that they like or dislike something due to misattribution processes. In particular, if people are feeling pleasant, they will look to the environment for a cause of this feeling and may misattribute the feeling to any plausible object in the environment. The opposite is true for negative feelings – a search is made for plausible negative causes (Petty & Cacioppo, 1983).

As noted earlier, according to the ELM, people should be more likely to rely on simple processes such as inferring an attitude directly from a bodily response when the overall extent of thinking is low. Consistent with this view, in one study, Taylor (1975) asked women to evaluate pictures of men who they believed they would actually meet (high relevance inducing high thinking) or not (low relevance inducing low thinking). Participants received false feedback about their "positive physiological responses" toward some of the men. The false information provided about their body influenced the women's reported attitudes when they were not expecting a meeting with the man in the picture but not when a meeting was anticipated.

In the research by Taylor (1975), the women assumed that their bodily responses were due to their positive reaction to the men. In general, when people experience unexplained arousal, they will seek some explanation, and salient factors in the current situation can be used to explain the bodily reactions. As suggested in the classic study by Schachter and Singer (1962), participants may interpret any ambiguous arousal (e.g., from an injection of epinephrine) as happiness or anger depending on the contextual cues available (e.g., the behavior of a confederate placed in the same room who acts in a happy or angry manner). These and many similar findings suggest that bodily responses (even false feedback) can influence attitudes by triggering simple inferences, and that such an effect is more likely to occur when motivation to think is relatively low (see also Chaiken & Baldwin, 1981).

### Bodily Responses Can Influence the Amount of Thinking

One of the most fundamental things that the body can do to influence attitudes is to affect the amount of thinking a person does. That is, various behaviors can influence attitudes by increasing or decreasing the amount of thinking in which people engage when making a social judgment. According to the ELM, this effect is most likely to occur when the likelihood of thinking is not already constrained to be high or low by other variables, and therefore thinking is free to vary in any direction. Importantly, an attitude formed as a result of effortful information processing will be well articulated and bolstered by supporting information, and as a consequence it should be strong (Petty et al., 1995). If a bodily variable increases thinking, attitudes will be more favorable when the increased thinking leads to favorable thoughts, such as when the arguments in a message are strong. However, increased thinking can lead to less favorable attitudes when the increased thinking produces more negative thoughts, such as when the arguments in a message are weak.

### *Body Postures*

In an early demonstration that body posture can affect susceptibility to a persuasive communication by affecting the extent of thinking, Petty, Wells, Heesacker, Brock, and Cacioppo (1983) asked undergraduate students to try a new headphone to rate its qualities. Some participants were then told to stand while testing the headphone, whereas others were told to lie down. After the participants were in the appropriate body position, participants listened to a persuasive message composed of either strong or weak arguments. Varying the quality of the arguments in a message allows evaluating different mechanisms for the effects of any variable on persuasion (Petty & Cacioppo,

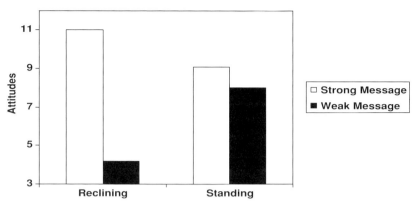

Figure 8.1. Attitudes as a function of argument quality and body position (data from Petty & Cacioppo, 1983).

1986). For example, the standing posture can facilitate the production of negative thoughts (biasing thinking) or produce discomfort that can serve as a simple negative cue (e.g., evaluative conditioning process). Both the biased processing and cue accounts predict a main effect for the posture manipulation regardless of the quality of the arguments. In contrast, if body posture influences persuasion by affecting the amount (rather than the direction) of thinking, an interaction between posture and argument quality should be observed. For example, if a standing posture reduces thinking relative to reclining, then the attitudes of reclining participants should be more polarized in response to the strong and weak arguments than the attitudes of standing participants. This result is because if reclining participants are thinking more about the message, they should better recognize the flaws in the weak arguments and the virtues in the strong ones.

Consistent with the idea that posture can affect thinking, this study showed that reclining participants were differentially persuaded by the strong and weak arguments but standing participants were not (see Figure 8.1). This research is consistent with the idea that the physical posture of the message recipient can affect the extent of message processing and thereby their susceptibility to persuasion. In line with the attitudinal findings and with this interpretation, the interaction between argument quality and posture also was found on a measure of the valenced thoughts that participants generated in response to the proposal.[1]

---

[1] In a series of studies, Caicoppo (1979) found that internal body changes can influence attitudes by affecting the amount of thinking. For example, in one study elevated (versus decreased) heart rate reduced persuasion by increasing counter-argumentation. Although a more definitive

The findings for posture and persuasion are consistent with research conducted in other domains that has shown that various body postures can influence motivation and ability to think. For example, Riskind and Gotay (1982) found that slumped-over, relative to upright, physical posture affected the amount of thinking by reducing the amount of time spent on various tasks. One interesting possibility is that posture may have affected information processing in prior studies by influencing participants' sense of power. That is, wisdom and anecdotal evidence suggest that people in a standing posture are seen as (and may feel) more powerful than people who are seated, slumped over, or lying down. We turn next to a more detailed analysis of the body and power.

### Bodily States Indicating Power

One of the ways in which our bodies are used is to exert power, and people can infer power from different bodily states. For example, research indicates that people who are standing are viewed as more dominant than people who are sitting (Schwartz, Tesser, & Powell, 1982), that big people hit little people (Felson, 2002), and the victor in a fight is typically on top. Indeed, children learn that their taller parents are more powerful and that taller siblings or other taller children are able to coerce them physically (e.g., Argyle, 1988).

In accord with metaphorical evidence that suggest that power equals "up" (Lakoff & Johnson, 1999), recent research has shown that judgments of power are influenced by the vertical position in space in which some target appears and the motor responses implying vertical movement in which a person engages (Schubert, 2005). If people who are standing also feel more powerful than people who are seated or reclining, this may predispose them to feel confident (e.g., Keltner & Haidt, 2003), thereby reducing their motivation to process information compared to individuals in a reclining position (Tiedens & Linton, 2001).[2]

To examine more closely the link between power-related behaviors and confidence, and also to test whether behaviors other than posture can also influence attitude change by affecting the amount of thinking, Briñol, Petty, Valle, Rucker, and Becerra (2007, Experiment 2) randomly assigned

---

support for the view that an elevated heart rate enhances processing in general (and not counter-arguing in particular) would have required including a message that elicits predominantly favorable thoughts, these studies suggest that heart rate acceleration is associated with cognitive effort.

[2] Meier and Robinson (2004) found that a vertical spatial dimension is also associated with valence, such as *good* is "up" and *bad* is "down."

participants to engage in a group of behaviors associated with relatively high or low power. Specifically, students were assigned either to a boss role (high power condition), or to an employee role (low power condition) and were asked to engage in work meeting role-playing. Importantly, the person assigned to play the role of the manager was sitting down in a taller and better-looking chair than the one playing the role of the subordinate. Previous studies have also revealed that merely displaying a single behavior as if possessing power (e.g., a male making a fist; Schubert, 2004) can create differential levels of power.

In the Briñol, Petty, Valle, et al. study, after the behavior-based power induction, the extent to which participants processed information was assessed by varying the quality of the arguments contained within a persuasive message and by measuring the impact of the arguments on attitudes. Participants received a persuasive message consisting of an advertisement for a new mobile phone. As illustrated in Figure 8.2 (top panel), this research found that being placed in a position of high or low power prior to receipt of a message affected attitudes toward it. In particular, behaviors associated with power decreased the impact of an argument quality manipulation on attitudes, consistent with the idea that power can reduce information processing.

## Bodily Responses Can Influence the Direction of Thinking[3]

Our bodies can influence persuasion not only by affecting the amount of thinking but also by affecting the direction of that thinking. Perhaps the most extensively explored idea is that one's bodily responses can shape attitudes by affecting the valence (positive or negative) of the thoughts that come to mind when thinking about an attitude object. According to the ELM, bodily responses can influence attitudes by biasing the valence of one's thoughts when the likelihood of thinking is relatively high. That is, when motivation and ability to think are high, people are engaging in careful thought about a proposal, but that thinking can be biased by a person's own behavior. This is important because, as noted earlier, attitude change is a function of the number and valence of thoughts that come to mind when elaboration is high. Next, we discuss some key variables that have been postulated to affect the valence of thoughts.

---

[3] In this review, we focus on relatively simple overt behaviors that are compatible with either positive or negative thinking. It is important to note that more complex behaviors can also induce attitude change by affecting the thoughts that come to mind, as illustrated by the classic role-playing (Janis & King, 1954) and dissonance paradigms (Festinger, 1957).

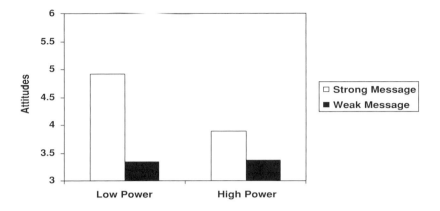

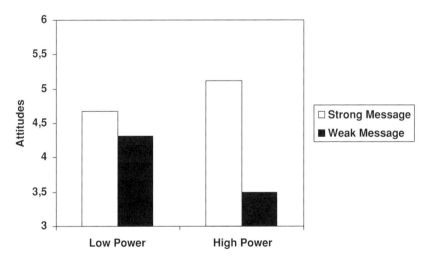

Figure 8.2. Attitudes as a function of argument quality and power, when power is induced before (top panel) or after (bottom panel) information processing (data from Briñol, Petty, Valle, et al., under review).

### Head Movements

In the original research on head nodding and persuasion, Wells and Petty (1980) asked participants to move their heads in an up-and-down (vertical, or nodding "yes") manner, in a side-to-side (horizontal, or shaking "no") manner, or gave no instructions about head movements (control) as they listened to music and an editorial over headphones. The ostensible purpose of this was to conduct a consumer test of whether the headphones would perform adequately during walking, jogging, dancing, and so forth. Following the message, participants provided ratings of the headphones as well as attitudes toward the editorial. The results showed that nodders agreed with the message more than shakers, with the control group falling in between.

Wells and Petty suggested that when nodding, favorable thoughts to the message would be facilitated and unfavorable thoughts would be inhibited, but when shaking, unfavorable thoughts would be facilitated and favorable thoughts would be inhibited. Although this is a plausible account if the message arguments were somewhat ambiguous and the extent of thinking was high, additional mechanisms are possible. Thus, we noted earlier that Tom and colleagues (1991) suggested that head nodding can serve as a simple cue if motivation to think is low. In a subsequent section, we describe research by Briñol and Petty (2003) suggesting that head nodding can also affect confidence in one's thoughts if the likelihood of thinking is high and the message arguments are clearly strong or weak.

In line with the Wells and Petty proposal about behavior biasing thinking, Neumann, Förster, and Strack (2000) argued that overt behavior can directly trigger compatible thoughts that facilitate the encoding and processing of evaluatively congruent information. These compatible thoughts can in turn influence evaluations by affecting how people encode and respond to the information that is received. In one demonstration, Förster and Strack (1996) found that participants who nodded while encoding positive and negative words were more likely to show enhanced recognition of the positive words. In contrast, participants who shook their heads while encoding were better at recognizing the negative words. In another relevant study by Förster (2004), valenced objects were presented moving vertically or horizontally on a screen, thereby inducing either head nodding or head shaking. Nodding led to more favorable evaluations of positively valenced products but did not affect the evaluation of negatively valenced ones. In contrast, head shaking led to more unfavorable evaluations of negatively valenced products but did not affect the evaluations of positive ones.

### Arm Flexion Versus Extension

Different behaviors other than head movements have been postulated to show similar compatibility effects. For example, as noted earlier, because people seek to minimize the distance between themselves and desirable objects (approach behavior), and seek to maximize the distance between themselves and undesirable objects (avoidance behavior), approach and avoidance movements are postulated to be linked to valence (Cacioppo et al., 1993), and thus can be linked to valenced thinking. For example, in an early study by Solarz (1960), participants were required to push cards with words either toward or away from their bodies. In this study, participants were faster at moving words forward (approach) when words were positive rather than negative. When the task was to push the words away (avoidance), they responded faster to negative than positive words. In another relevant study, Chen and Bargh (1999) asked participants to evaluate words on a computer screen as good or bad by either pushing or pulling a lever. Consistent with previous findings, participants were faster at evaluating positive words when pulling the lever toward them but were faster at evaluating negative words when pushing the lever away (see Lang et al., 1990, for a conceptually similar effect using the blink reflex as an avoidance behavior).

Although in most of these studies thoughts were not assessed, they support the idea that certain behaviors can activate thoughts and actions that are compatible with the valence of the behavior, facilitating encoding, categorization, and processing of positive or negative information. In subsequent research, Neumann and Strack (2000) also found that positive words were categorized faster than negative words when participants flexed both arms, whereas negative words were categorized faster than positive words when participants extended their arms (for additional examples, see Förster & Stepper, 2000; Stepper & Strack, 1993).[4] It is important to note that the precise processes underlying the compatibility effects observed in these studies is not completely clear; that is, the compatibility between certain bodily movements with certain valences can be a result of biased processing (as assumed by some authors reviewed in this section) or to simple association processes as reviewed earlier (e.g., Cacioppo et al., 1993). Thus, although it seems clear that some bodily movements are more compatible with some valences than others, the mediation of these effects has not been carefully explored. As we have argued throughout, and has been the case with other types of compatibility phenomenon (e.g., Petty, Wheeler, & Bizer, 2000), designing studies that allow the identification of the underlying psychological processes is essential.

## Bodily Responses Can Influence Thought-Confidence

So far, we have described evidence revealing that the body can influence attitudes by serving as simple cues and by affecting either the amount or

---

[4]   A recent line of research suggests that these motor compatibility effects can occur even when extension and flexion arm movements are performed with only one of the arms, as long as that arm is the dominant one (Cretenet & Dru, 2004).

direction of thinking. Recently, we have proposed and documented another mechanism through which behavior can work that also appears to have considerable integrative potential. Unlike the previous processes, which focus on primary or first-order cognition, this new process emphasizes secondary or metacognition. Primary thoughts are those that occur at a direct level of cognition and involve our initial associations of some object with some attribute. Following a primary thought, people can generate additional thoughts that occur at a second level that involve reflection upon the first level thoughts. *Metacognition* refers to these second-order thoughts, or our thoughts about our thoughts or thought processes (e.g., Petty, Briñol, Tormala & Wegener, 2007). We propose that behavior not only can influence the amount and direction of primary cognition but also what people think about their thoughts.

An essential and much studied dimension of metacognitive thought consists of the degree of confidence people place in their thoughts, ranging from extreme certainty to extreme doubt in the validity of one's thoughts. Thus, two people might have the same thought but one person might have considerably greater confidence in that thought than the other, and the greater confidence in the thought, the greater its impact on judgment. This idea is referred to as the *self-validation hypothesis* (Petty et al., 2002). The key notion is that generating thoughts is not sufficient for them to have an impact on judgments; rather, one must also have confidence in them. We have argued that the body, like any other variable, can influence persuasion by affecting the confidence with which people hold their thoughts (Briñol & Petty, 2003). In fact, the self-validation view argues that the confidence that emerges from behavior can magnify the effect of anything that is currently available in people's minds, including not only their thoughts to a persuasive message but also other cognitions, emotions, goals, and so forth.

### Head Movements

Consider the research on head nodding described earlier that had assumed that nodding one's head in a vertical (versus horizontal) manner produced more positive attitudes either because vertical head nodding biased thinking in a favorable direction (Wells & Petty, 1980) or because head nodding served as a relatively simple affective cue (Tom et al., 1991). The self-validation hypothesis (Petty et al., 2002) suggests another possibility – that just as vertical head movements from others give us confidence in what we are saying, our own vertical head movements could give us confidence in what we are thinking. In a series of studies, Briñol and Petty (2003) found that head movements affected the confidence people had in their thoughts, and thereby had

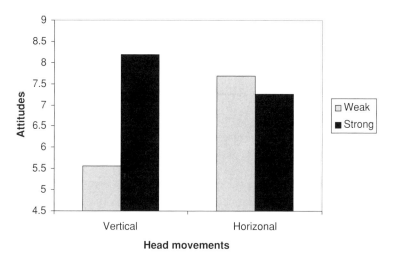

Figure 8.3. Attitudes as a function of head movements and argument quality (data from Briñol & Petty, 2003).

an impact on attitudes. Thus, as illustrated in Figure 8.3, when people listened through headphones to the strong arguments in an editorial advocating that students be required to carry personal identification cards on campus, vertical movements led to more favorable attitudes than when horizontal movements were made as would be expected if vertical movements increased confidence in the favorable thoughts. However, when people listened to weak arguments toward the magnetic cards, vertical movements led to less favorable attitudes than when horizontal movements were made, as would be expected if vertical movements increased confidence in the negative thoughts. Additional analyses indicated that the head movements did not have any impact on the number or valence of thoughts listed but did have an impact on the confidence with which people held their thoughts. Furthermore, this thought confidence mediated the impact of head movements on attitudes.

As noted earlier, the confidence that emerges from the body can be applied to whatever the salient or available mental contents are at the time. Thus, in a subsequent line of research examining self-validation processes in the domain of intergroup attitudes, DeMarree, Briñol and Petty (under review) subliminally primed participants with words related to the black (vs. white) stereotype. Following this induction, participants were instructed to follow a ball moving vertically or horizontally on the screen with their heads. Consistent with the self-validation logic, DeMarree et al. found that the direction of the prime affected participants' felt aggression on an implicit measure as well as their deliberative ratings of closeness to African-Americans in a stereotype-congruent fashion in the head nodding but not the head shaking condition. Thus, as was the case with head nodding affecting confidence in thoughts to a persuasive message, so too did it appear to affect the validity and use of subtly activated mental content. Also consistent with the idea that head nodding validates mental content compared to shaking, the effects of self-generated anchors in an anchor and adjust paradigm (Epley & Gilovich, 2001) and emotional thoughts (Tamir et al., 2004) have been found to be larger when nodding than shaking.

### Dominant Versus Non-Dominant Hand

A relevant question is whether the self-validation effects observed for head nodding could also emerge for different behaviors and in different attitudinal domains. In one exploration of this possibility (Briñol & Petty, 2003, Experiment 4), we asked participants, as part of a presumed graphology study, to think about and write down their best or worst qualities (thought-direction manipulation) using their dominant or non-dominant hand (overt behavior manipulation). Then participants rated the confidence in their thoughts and reported their self-esteem. Because writing with the non-dominant hand is very infrequent and difficult, and whatever is written with the non-dominant may appear "shaky," we expected and found that using the non-dominant hand decreased the confidence with which people held the thoughts they just listed. As a consequence, the effect of the direction of thoughts (positive/negative) on current self-esteem was significantly greater when participants wrote their thoughts with their dominant rather than their non-dominant hand. That is, writing positive thoughts about oneself with the dominant hand increased self-esteem relative to writing positive thoughts with the non-dominant hand, but writing negative thoughts with the dominant hand resulted in the reverse pattern.

Follow-up research has demonstrated that the self-validation effects of handwriting also influence the extent to which people rely on their internal states when making emotional judgments. In particular, in one study (Rucker, Briñol, & Petty, under review) participants were asked to write about instances in the past when they were either happy or sad with either their dominant or their non-dominant hand. The prior emotional experiences written had a greater impact on reported emotions when written with the dominant than the non-dominant hand consistent with the self-validation hypothesis (for a demonstration that a facial expression associated with mental difficulty can impact judgments of perceived fame, see Strack & Neumann, 2000).

### Behavioral Indicators of Power

As a final example of the potential of self-validation to explain some of the mechanisms underlying the influence of behavioral factors on attitudes, consider the research on a recipient's power and persuasion described earlier. Recall that this research found power-related behaviors to be associated with confidence, and that increased confidence from power affected persuasion by reducing elaboration of the message (Briñol, Petty, Valle et al., 2007; see Figure 8.2, top panel). In that research, people were placed in a state of high or low power prior to receiving the message, and the likelihood of thinking was not constrained to be high or low. In this situation power should validate pre-message mental content (i.e., prior attitudes), making the need to process new information less necessary. In contrast, low power individuals should have doubt in their views, leading to more processing. However, under different conditions, power-related behavior should influence attitudes by different mechanisms. For example, when elaboration is very low, people might simply assume they are correct if they are of high power and incorrect if they are of low power with little thinking. On the other hand, when motivation and the ability to think are high and people have already processed the persuasive information, we have found that power behaviors can affect attitudes by influencing confidence in the thoughts recently generated to the message.

More specifically, the self-validation prediction is that when induced to feel powerful following thinking, people should be more confident in their thoughts. This prediction is in line with prior research that suggests a link between power and approach tendencies (e.g., Keltner, Gruenfeld, & Anderson, 2003). In one study testing this idea (Briñol, Petty, Valle et al., 2007; Experiment 3), participants were first led to generate either positive or negative thoughts about a new cell phone by manipulating the quality of the arguments contained in the message. Then participants were assigned either to a boss role in a taller chair (high power condition) or to a subordinate role in a lower chair (low power condition). Relative to powerless individuals, those induced to have power following message processing were expected to have greater confidence in their recently generated thoughts about the cell phone. As shown in Figure 8.2 (bottom panel), this research found that the effect of the direction of the thoughts generated by participants on attitudes was greater when power was high rather than low. Further studies in this line of research demonstrated that thought-confidence mediated the observed effects on persuasion. As in prior self-validation studies, these effects only occurred under high elaboration conditions and only when power followed thought generation.[5]

In a subsequent line of research, we have shown that under high elaboration circumstances, other body postures that do not involve changes in verticality can also affect attitudes by influencing thought confidence. For example, in one study, we (Briñol & Petty, 2007) asked participants to read a message containing either strong or weak arguments while they were sitting down with their back erect and pushing their chest out (confident posture) or slouched forward with their back curved (doubt posture). In line with the self-validation hypothesis, we found that the direction of the thoughts generated in response to the messages only affected attitudes in the relatively high confident posture. Taken together, this group of studies reveals that body actions, such as head nodding, handwriting, postures, and behavioral roles can all influence persuasion by affecting thought-confidence.

## Additional High Elaboration Processes for Bodily Responses

Guided by the ELM, we have described four ways in which behavior can affect attitudes: serving as simple cues, affecting the extent of thinking, affecting the direction of thinking, and affecting confidence in thinking. It is important to note that when people are thinking about an attitude object, people assess the relevance of all the information in the context and that comes to mind to determine the merits of the attitude object under consideration (Petty & Cacioppo, 1986). Thus, when thinking is high, people can examine their own body and behavior as possible arguments for favoring or disfavoring the attitude object. That is, a final role for variables within the ELM is that the body can influence persuasion by serving as an argument itself. This is likely to be the case when behavior itself is potentially informative regarding the merits of the object. For example, a very muscular person might use his or her body shape as a relevant argument to decide whether he or she likes certain professional careers, such as sports or modeling.

It is worth noting that if people believe that their thoughts are somehow being biased or influenced by their bodily actions in some way, and they do not

---

[5]   We conducted another study (Briñol, Petty, Valle, et al., under review; Experiment 5) in which the message was presented either immediately before or after participants engaged in the power induction role-playing manipulation. Replicating our findings described earlier (see Figure 8.2) within the same design, the results of this study revealed that the same power behaviors can have different (and opposite) effects in persuasive settings depending on when the manipulation is introduced.

want this to occur, they can adjust their judgments in a direction opposite to the expected bias (*correction processes*; Wegener & Petty, 1997). For example, if people felt they were slumping in a chair because they were sick, they might expect this to bias their assessment of a movie and therefore correct their judgment in a positive direction when asked how good the movie was. These correction processes have the greatest impact when the amount of thinking is high because it is only in such situations that people have a substantial number of issue-relevant thoughts with the potential to shape attitudes. Furthermore, a high amount of thinking suggests that people care about the issue or object under consideration and thus might be most motivated to be accurate in their assessment. Thus, individual and situational differences in the extent of thinking moderate these potential correction processes.

## Distinguishing Between the Different Processes by Which the Body Affects Attitudes

The processes described in this chapter are dependent upon various contextual factors such as the specific levels of elaboration, the ambiguity of information presented, or the order in which events occur (Petty & Cacioppo, 1986). For example, our studies on power suggest that the same body actions can influence persuasion by different mechanisms (e.g., affecting the amount of thinking or thought confidence) depending on the circumstances (see Figure 8.2).

As just one example of the multiple roles that a variable can play in persuasion depending on the extent of thinking in the situation, consider how a person's incidental emotions – whether induced via facial expressions or some other means – can impact evaluative judgments according to the ELM. First, when thinking is constrained to be low, emotions tend to serve as simple associative cues and produce evaluations consistent with their valence regardless of the merits of the arguments presented (e.g., Petty, Schumann, Richman, & Strathman, 1993). When the likelihood of thinking is not constrained to be high or low by other variables, then emotions can affect the extent of thinking. For example, people may think about messages more when in a sad than a happy state either because sadness signals a problem to be solved (Schwarz, Bless, & Bohner, 1991) or conveys a sense of uncertainty (Tiedens & Linton, 2001). If people think more in a sad than a happy state, then sad individuals will be more persuaded than happy people by a strong message but less persuaded by a weak one. When thinking is high, emotions can bias the ongoing thoughts (Petty et al., 1993). For example, positive consequences seem more likely when people are in a happy than a sad state (DeSteno, Petty, Wegener, & Rucker, 2000). When thinking is high, people also assess their emotions as an argument. For example, people might report liking a poignant drama the more sad it makes them because emotion induction is relevant to the merits of the movie (see Martin, Abend, Sedikides, & Green, 1997; for a review of the multiple mechanisms by which emotions affect attitudes, see Petty et al., 2003).

Research on the self-validation hypothesis has shown that emotion can also affect thought confidence. This possibility follows directly from the finding that emotional states can relate to confidence, with happy people being more certain and confident than sad individuals (Tiedens & Linton, 2001). If emotion influences thought confidence, then people in a happy state should be more reliant on their thoughts than people in a sad state, at least when the extent of thinking is high and emotion follows thought generation. In one study examining this idea, Briñol, Petty, and Barden (2007) had participants read a persuasive message about a new foster care program composed of either strong or weak arguments. The message was presented prior to receiving an emotion manipulation described as a part of a research project for the art school designed to assess participants' dramatic skills. Emotion inductions were accomplished by having participants complete the Velten (1968) technique in which people are required to behave according to a happy or sad script. As predicted by the self-validation perspective (and shown in the bottom panel of Figure 8.4), when participants received a strong message (and thoughts were thus mostly favorable), those who were asked to act as if they were happy following message processing were more persuaded than those asked to act as if they were sad. However, when participants received a weak message on the same topic (and thoughts were mostly unfavorable), the effects of the emotion induction were reversed. Furthermore, the effects of emotion on attitudes was mediated by the confidence people placed in their thoughts, with happy individuals expressing more thought confidence than those who were sad.

Of most importance for the ELM multiple roles idea, the self-validation effects for emotion were confined to situations of high thought, e.g., for individuals high in need for cognition (NC) (Cacioppo & Petty, 1982). In contrast, for people low in NC, emotions had a direct effect on attitudes unmediated by confidence in thoughts. That is, for low NC individuals, behaving in an emotionally positive way following the message acted as a simple cue leading to more positive attitudes when happy than sad, regardless of argument quality (see top panel of Figure 8.4). As noted earlier, this is

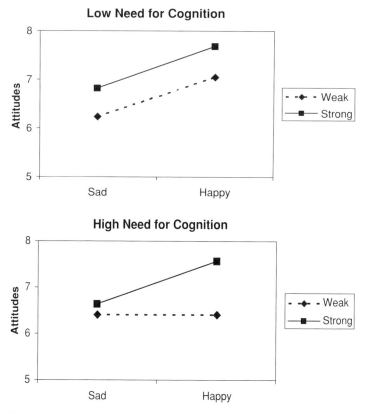

Figure 8.4. Attitudes toward the message as a function of argument quality, emotion, and need for cognition (graphed at ±1 SD; data from Briñol et al., 2007).

consistent with prior research suggesting that low elaboration individuals are more likely to use their emotions as input to an affect heuristic (e.g., Petty et al., 1993).

Also consistent with the idea that emotions can validate cognitions, Stepper and Strack (1993) found that when people recalled behaviors of self-assurance when smiling rather than frowning, they felt more self-assured, but when they recalled behaviors of low self-assurance, they felt less self-assured when smiling than frowning. If smiling enhances confidence in the recalled behaviors compared with frowning, the self-validation hypothesis can explain these results.[6]

---

[6] As one more example of multiple processes, Cacioppo et al. (1993) found that arm flexion was associated with more positive evaluations than arm extension primarily when the target stimuli had no prior meaning. More recently, Centerbar and Clore (2006) found that arm

## Summary and Conclusions

In the present chapter, social psychology's major research findings regarding how one's body affects attitudes and attitudinal processes have been described. These bodily factors have been shown to have an important impact on different aspects (and measures) relevant to attitudes and persuasion. Importantly, the main psychological processes by which bodily responses influence evaluations have been outlined in detail, as well as the antecedents and consequences associated with those mechanisms. Because most of this research was not designed to test these mechanisms, our accounts for many studies are necessarily speculative. However, we hope that future research on embodiment and attitudes will include the necessary conditions and measures to examine the fundamental processes by which previously studied and new behaviors produce their effects.

We conclude by mentioning some remaining issues relevant to embodied persuasion. First, future research might benefit from the exploration of new behaviors other than the ones covered in this review (e.g., a consideration of linguistic behaviors; Lakoff & Johnson, 1999). Second, most of the behaviors used in the experiments described in this review have very clear meanings attached (e.g., nodding is associated with agreement). However, the meaning of those behaviors can vary among individuals and situations. We argue that if the meaning associated with a behavior changes, the effect of that behavior on subsequent attitudes could also change, at least under high elaboration conditions and when attitudes are assessed with explicit measures (e.g., Briñol, Petty, & Tormala, 2006). Third, people not only can differ with respect to the meaning associated with behaviors but also with respect to a wide variety of factors potentially relevant to embodiment. For example, Laird and Bresler (1992) have reported that people differ consistently and reliably in how large an impact a bodily state will have on a variety of cognitive processes relevant to attitude change (see also Briñol & Petty, 2005). Fourth, some of the studies described in this chapter suggest that it might not be necessary to physically

---

flexion (versus extension) only led to more positive evaluations when the stimuli evaluated were already considered positive. Interestingly, arm flexion (versus extension) was associated with less favorable evaluations for previously negative stimuli. If one assumes that participants generated either positive or negative thoughts (in response to the valenced material), then arm flexion (versus extension) could have affected attitudes by influencing the confidence with which those thoughts were held. Taken together, these two lines of research seem to imply that, similar to other behaviors, arm flexion can influence attitude change by serving as a simple cue (when elaboration is low) or by affecting thought confidence (when elaboration is high). See Clore & Schnall (this volume) for a different interpretation.

act for behavior to produce attitude change. Indeed, merely believing that the behavior occurred, reminding one of past behavior, imaging future behavior, or observing the behaviors of others can often produce effects similar to those obtained from actual motor behavior. We argue that future research should explore whether the different means by which the mental representations of behavior are activated (e.g., by performing versus observing the behavior) are consequential for persuasion.

## References

Argyle, M. (1988). *Bodily communication* (2nd ed.) New York: Methuen.

Bem, D. J. (1972). Self-perception theory. In L. Berkowitz (Ed.), *Advances in experimental Social Psychology*, Vol. 6 (pp. 1–62). New York: Academic Press.

Briñol, P., & Petty, R. E. (2003). Overt head movements and persuasion: A self-validation analysis. *Journal of Personality and Social Psychology, 84*, 1123–1139.

Briñol, P., & Petty, R. E. (2005). Individual differences in persuasion. In D. Albarracín, B. T. Johnson, & M. P. Zanna (Eds.), *The handbook of attitudes and attitude change* (pp. 575–616). Hillsdale, NJ: Erlbaum.

Briñol, P., & Petty, R. E. (2007). Embodied persuasion: A self-validation analysis. Unpublished manuscript.

Briñol, P., Petty, R. E., & Barden, J. (2007). Happiness versus sadness as determinant of thought-confidence in persuasion: A self-validation analysis. *Journal of Personality and Social Psychology, 93*, 711–727.

Briñol, P., Petty, R. E., & Tormala, Z. L. (2006). The meaning of ease and its malleability. *Psychological Science, 17*, 200–206.

Briñol, P., Petty, R. E., Valle, C., Rucker, D. D., & Becerra, A. (2007). The effects of message recipients' power before and after persuasion: A self-validation analysis. *Journal of Personality and Social Psychology, 93*, 1040–1053.

Cacioppo, J. T. (1979). The effects of exogenous changes in heart rate on the facilitation of thought and resistance to persuasion. *Journal of Personality and Social Psychology, 37*, 483–496.

Cacioppo, J. T., Marshall-Goodell, B. S., Tassinary, L. G., & Petty, R. E. (1992). Rudimentary determinants of attitudes: Classical conditioning is more effective when prior knowledge about the attitude stimulus is low than high. *Journal of Experimental Social Psychology, 28*, 207–233.

Cacioppo, J. T., & Petty, R. E. (1982). The need for cognition. *Journal of Personality and Social Psychology, 42*, 116–131.

Cacioppo, J. T., Priester, J. R., & Berntson, G. G. (1993). Rudimentary determinants of attitudes. II: Arm flexion and extension have differential effects on attitudes. *Journal of Personality and Social Psychology, 65*, 5–17.

Chaiken, S., & Baldwin, M. W. (1981). Affective-cognitive consistency and the effect of salient behavioral information on the self-perception of attitudes. *Journal of Personality and Social Psychology, 41*, 1–12.

Chen, M., & Bargh, J. A. (1999). An automatic effect of (all) attitudes on behavior: Preconsious approach and avoidance responses to liked and disliked stimuli. *Personality and social Psychology Bulletin, 25*, 215–224.

Cretenet, J., & Dru, V. (2004). The influence of unilateral and bilateral arm flexion versus extension on judgments: An exploratory case of motor congruence. *Emotion, 4*, 282–294.

Darwin, C. (1965). *The expression of emotions in man and animals.* Chicago: University of Chicago Press. (Original work published 1872).

DeMarree, K. G., Briñol, P., & Petty, R. E. (under review). Implicit self-validation: The effects of overt behavior on primed social constructs.

DeSteno, D., Petty, R. E., Wegener, D. T., & Rucker, D. D. (2000). Beyond valence in the perception of likelihood: The role of emotion specificity. *Journal of Personality and Social Psychology, 78*, 397–416.

Epley, N., & Gilovich, T. (2001). Putting adjustment back in the anchoring and adjustment heuristic. Differential processing of self-generated and experimenter-provided anchors. *Psychological Science, 12*, 391–396.

Felson, R. B. (2002). *Violence and gender reexamined.* Washington, DC: American Psychological Association.

Festinger, L. (1957). *A theory of cognitive dissonance.* Evanston, IL: Row, Peterson.

Förster, J. (2004). How body feedback influences consumers' evaluation of products. *Journal of Consumer Psychology, 14*, 416–426.

Förster, J., & Stepper, S. (2000). Compatibility between approach/avoidance simulation and valenced information determines residual attention during the process of encoding. *European Journal of Social Psychology, 30*, 853–871.

Förster, J., & Strack, F. (1996). Influence of overt head movements on memory for valence words: A case of conceptual-motor compatibility. *Journal of Personality and Social Psychology, 71*, 421–430.

Galinsky, A. D., Gruenfeld, D. H., & Magee, J. C. (2003). From power to action. *Journal of Personality and Social Psychology, 85*, 453–466.

Galton, F. (1884). Measurement of character. *Fortnightly Review, 42*, 179–185.

Ito, T. A., Chiao, K. W., Devine, P. G., Lorig, T. S., & Cacioppo, J. T. (2006). The influence of facial feedback on race bias. *Psychological Science, 17*, 256–261.

Janis, I. L., & King, B. T. (1954). The influence of role-playing on opinion change. *Journal of Abnormal and Social Psychology, 49*, 211–218.

Keltner, D., Gruenfeld, D. H., & Anderson, C. (2003). Power, approach and inhibition. *Psychological Review, 110*, 265–284.

Keltner, D., & Haidt, J. (2003). Approaching awe, a moral, spiritual, and aesthetic emotion. *Cognition and Emotion, 17*, 297–314.

Laird, J. D., & Bresler, C. (1992). The process of emotional experience: A self-perception theory. In M. S. Clark (Ed.). *Review of Personality and Social Psychology*, Vol. 13 (pp. 213–234). Newbury Park, CA: Sage.

Lakoff, G., & Johnson, M. (1999). *Philosophy in the flesh: The embodied mind and its challenge to western thought.* New York: Basic Books.

Lang, P. J., Bradley, M. M., & Cuthbert, B. N. (1990). Emotion, attention, and the startle reflex. *Psychological Review, 97*, 377–395.

Meier, B. P., & Robinson, M. D., (2004). Why the sunny side is up: Associations between affect and vertical position. *Psychological Science, 15*, 243–247.

Neumann, R., & Strack, F. (2000). Approach and avoidance: The influence of proprioceptive and exteroceptive cues on encoding of affective information. *Journal of Personality and Social Psychology, 79*, 39–48.

Niedenthal, P. M., Barsalou, L. W., Winkielman, P., Krauth-Gruber, S., & Ric, F. (2005). Embodiment in attitudes, social perception, and emotion. *Personality and Social Psychology Review, 9*, 184–211.

Olson, J. M., & Hafer, C. L. (1990). Self- inference processes: Looking back and ahead. In J. M. Olson, & M. P. Zanna (Eds.). *Self-inference processes: The Ontario symposium*, Vol. 6 (pp. 293–320). Hillsdale. NJ: Erlbaum.

Petty, R. E., Briñol, P., & Tormala, Z. L. (2002). Thought confidence as a determinant of persuasion: The self-validation hypothesis. *Journal of Personality and Social Psychology, 82*, 722–741.

Petty, R. E., Briñol, P., Tormala, Z. L., & Wegener, D. T. (2007). The role of meta-cognition in social judgment. In E. T. Higgins & A. W. Kruglanski, (Eds.) *Social psychology: A handbook of basic principles*, 2nd ed. (pp. 254–284). New York: Guilford Press.

Petty, R. E., & Cacioppo, J. T. (1981). *Attitudes and persuasion: Classic and contemporary approaches*. Dubuque, IA: Wm. C. Brown.

Petty, R. E., & Cacioppo, J. T. (1983). The role of bodily responses in attitude measurement and change. In J. T. Cacioppo & R. E. Petty (Eds.), *Social psychophysiology: A sourcebook* (pp. 51–101). New York: Guilford.

Petty, R. E., & Cacioppo, J. T. (1986). *Communication and persuasion: Central and peripheral routes to attitude change*. New York: Springer-Verlag.

Petty, R. E., Haugtvedt, C., & Smith, S. M. (1995). Elaboration as a determinant of attitude strength: Creating attitudes that are persistent, resistant, and predictive of behavior. In R. E. Petty & J. A. Krosnick (Eds.), *Attitude strength: Antecedents and consequences* (pp. 93–130). Mahwah, NJ: Erlbaum.

Petty, R. E., Priester, J. R., & Briñol, P. (2002). Mass media attitude change: Implications of the Elaboration likelihood model of persuasion. In J. Byant & D. Zillmann (Eds.), *Media effects: Advances in theory and research*, 2nd ed. (pp. 155–199). Hillsdale, NJ: Erlbaum.

Petty, R. E., Schumann, D. W., Richman, S. A., & Strathman, A. J. (1993). Positive mood and persuasion: Different roles for affect under high and low elaboration conditions. *Journal of Personality and Social Psychology, 64*, 5–20.

Petty, R. E., & Wegener, D. T. (1998). Attitude change: Multiple roles for persuasion variables. In D. Gilbert, S. Fiske, & G. Lindzey (Eds.), *The handbook of social psychology*, 4th ed., Vol. 1 (pp. 323–390). New York: McGraw-Hill.

Petty, R. E., & Wegener, D. T. (1999). The Elaboration Likelihood Model: Current status and controversies. In S. Chaiken & Y. Trope (Eds.), *Dual process theories in social psychology* (pp. 41–72). New York: Guilford Press.

Petty, R. E., Wells, G. L., Heesacker, M., Brock, T. C., & Cacioppo, J. T. (1983). The effects of recipient posture on persuasion: A cognitive response analysis *Personality and Social Psychology Bulletin, 9*, 209–222.

Petty, R. E., Wheeler, S. C., & Bizer, G. (2000). Matching effects in persuasion: An elaboration likelihood analysis (pp. 133–162). In G. Maio & J. Olson (Eds.), *Why we evaluate: Functions of attitudes*. Mahwah, NJ: Erlbaum.

Priester, J. M., Cacioppo, J. T., & Petty, R. E. (1996). The influence of motor processes on attitudes toward novel versus familiar semantic stimuli. *Personality and Social Psychology Bulletin, 22*, 442–447.

Riskind, J. H., & Gotay, C. C. (1982). Physical posture: Could it have regulatory or feedback effects on motivation and emotion? *Motivation and Emotion, 6*, 273–298.

Rucker, D. D., Briñol, P., & Petty, R. E. (under review). The role of meta-cognition in relying on one's emotions.

Schachter, S., & Singer, J. E. (1962). Cognitive, social, and physiological determinants of emotional state. *Psychological Review, 69*, 379–399.

Schubert, T. W. (2004). The power in your hand: Gender differences in bodily feedback from making a fist. *Personality and Social Psychology Bulletin, 30*, 757–769.

Schubert, T. W. (2005). Your highness: Vertical positions as perceptual symbols of power. *Journal of Personality and Social Psychology, 89*, 1–21.

Schwartz, B., Tesser, A., & Powell, E. (1982). Dominance cues in nonverbal behavior. *Psychology Quarterly, 45*, 114–120.

Schwarz, N., Bless, H., & Bohner, G. (1991). Mood and persuasion: Affective status influence the processing of persuasive communications. In M. Zanna (Ed.), *Advances in experimental social psychology*, Vol. 24 (pp. 161–197). San Diego, CA: Academia Press.

Solarz, A. K. (1960). Latency of instrumental responses as a function of compatibility with the meaning eliciting verbal signs. *Journal of Experimental Psychology, 59*, 239–245.

Stepper, S., & Strack, F. (1993). Propioceptive determinants of emotional and nonemotional feelings. *Journal of Personality and Social Psychology, 64*, 211–220.

Strack, F., & Neumann, R. (2000). Furrowing the brow may undermine perceived fame: The role of facial feedback in judgments of celebrity. *Personality and social Psychology Bulletin, 26*, 762–768.

Strack, F., Martin, L., & Stepper, S. (1988). Inhibiting and facilitating conditions of the human smile: A nonobtrusive test of the facial feedback hypothesis. *Journal of Personality and Social Psychology, 54*, 768–777.

Tamir, M., Robinson, M. D., Clore, G. L., Martin, L. L., & Whitaker, D. J. (2004). Are we puppets on a string? The contextual meaning of unconscious expressive cues. *Personality and Social Psychology, 30*, 237–249.

Taylor, S. E. (1975). On inferring one's attitude from one's behavior: Some delimiting condition. *Journal of Personality and Social Psychology, 31*, 126–131.

Tiedens, L. Z., & Linton, S. (2001). Judgment under emotional certainty and uncertainty: The effects of specific emotions on information processing. *Journal of Personality and Social Psychology, 81*, 973–988.

Tom, G., Pettersen, P., Lau, T., Burton, T., & Cook, J. (1991). The role of overt head movement in the formation of affect. *Basic and Applied Social Psychology, 12*, 281–289.

Valins, S. (1966). Cognitive effects of false heart-rate feedback. *Journal of Personality and Social Psychology, 4*, 400–408.

Velten, E. (1968). A laboratory task for induction of mood states. *Behavior Research and Therapy, 6*, 473–482.

Wegener, D. T., & Petty, R. E. (1997). The flexible correction model: The role of naive theories of bias in bias correction. In M. P. Zanna (Ed.), *Advances in experimental social psychology*, Vol., 29 (pp. 141–208). San Diego, CA: Academic Press.

Wells, G. L., & Petty, R. E. (1980). The effects of overt head movements on persuasion: Compatibility and incompatibility of responses. *Basic and Applied Social Psychology, 1*, 219–230.

Zajonc, R. B., Murphy, S. T., & Inglehart, M. (1989). Feeling and facial efference: Implications of the vascular theory of emotion. *Psychological Review, 96*, 395–416.

# PART THREE

# EMBODIMENT AND AFFECT

# 9    Affective Coherence

*Affect as Embodied Evidence in Attitude, Advertising, and Art*[1]

Gerald L. Clore[2] and Simone Schnall

Existence precedes and rules essence.

Sartre, J. P. (1943). *Being and Nothingness*

In this chapter, we review behavioral research connecting affective embodiment and evaluative cognition. We argue that affect and belief exist in a dynamic relationship. Evaluative beliefs elicit affective experience, and affective experience provides data for evaluative conception. We propose that such reciprocal relationships exist because emotions are, in part, embodiments of evaluation. That is, emotions exist when the same goodness or badness is represented simultaneously in multiple systems. Indeed, emotion is arguably nothing but the co-occurrence of evaluation in thought, feeling, physiology, expression, and so on. The embodied nature of some of these representations makes evaluative beliefs especially compelling. Thus, in contrast to a mere idea that something may be good or bad in some way, an emotion is an embodied commitment to such a reality.

Our general research program focuses on the idea that embodied affective reactions act as critical information for making judgments, guiding cognitive processing, and selecting events to remember. However, in this chapter we focus on how such embodiment serves to validate or invalidate evaluative beliefs. We also suggest that the impact of an idea in art often depends on its ability to elicit embodied reactions, that is, its ability to move people.

The experience of emotion has two discriminable components – valence and arousal (Barrett, this volume; Russell, 2003). In turn, these components

[1] Support is acknowledged from National Institute of Mental Health grant MH 50074 and National Science Foundation grant BCS 0518835.

[2] Thanks to the Department of Psychology, New York University, for accommodating Gerald Clore as a Visiting Scholar during the Spring of 2006.

are embodied representations of value and importance (Clore & Schnall, 2005). The embodiment is evident not only in the experience of affective feelings but presumably also in the neurochemistry upon which such experiences rest. For example, valence might be marked by dopamine release (Knutson, Adams, Fong, & Hommer, 2001) and arousal by adrenaline production (e.g., Cahill & McGaugh, 1998). If so, such biochemical and experiential events are both parts of an embodied understanding of the world. They represent what people care about, including what people hope for, sacrifice for, and vote for, as well as what they crave, cry over, regret, and are embarrassed by.

Even everyday decisions are made on the basis of anticipated emotion (Baumeister, Vohs, & Tice, 2006). We decide on one course of action rather than another because some portion of relevant affect or emotion is elicited at the prospect of taking that path. Thus, we imagine that we will be pleased at having chosen a particular option. We choose investments that seem likely to yield reward and unlikely to lead to disappointment. We choose partners that seem likely to make us happy and effective, vacations that appear to offer more enjoyment than hassle, and restaurants that we believe will be enjoyable and satisfying. We choose whether to have a medical procedure based on whether we anticipate being glad we did so in the long run. Thus, although thinking may be for acting, action itself is motivated by embodied perceptions and anticipations of the good, the bad, and the important.

## EMBODIED VALIDATION OF BELIEFS

In this section, we examine one cognitive consequence of being moved. We propose that affective reactions function as validation or invalidation of evaluative cognitions. Just as people rely on their sensory experiences of seeing and hearing as evidence about reality, embodied experiences of affect can also be a source of evidence. The difference is that whereas sensory experiences are relevant to *descriptive* beliefs, affective experiences concern *evaluative* beliefs. In both cases, experience generally trumps cognition. Thus, if one believes it to be sunny but opens the door to find rain, the belief about sunshine quickly vanishes. Similarly, if one believes that eating cheesecake is bad but, on seeing a moist piece of cheesecake, experiences the idea of eating cheesecake as good, experience may again trump belief. Interestingly, the compelling experience in the latter case is self-generated rather than sensory.

## Being Moved

The problem of embodiment can be seen as part of a larger mind-body problem and a larger problem of understanding. For example, psychotherapists discern whether clients understand the meanings of the insights they verbalize by noting whether they appear appropriately moved; whether their bodies, manners, and intonations register the implications of what they have said. An observation basic to our goal in this chapter is that just as others' affective expressions inform us about them, our own subjective experiences of affect inform us about ourselves. However, because we ourselves produce our affective reactions, one might reasonably ask why we need to be informed.

Of course, the answer is that like many other psychological processes, emotional appraisals take place largely outside of awareness. Thus in some respects, we are "strangers to ourselves" (Wilson, 2002). As a result, we accept that people can meaningfully ask themselves, "Who am I?" and in other ways seek self-knowledge. Therefore, people may find it useful to be informed by their embodied, affective reactions that they have encountered something good or bad. Indeed, we have argued that many evaluative judgments are made essentially by asking ourselves, "How do I feel about it?" (Schwarz & Clore, 1988).

Decision-making too is apparently largely unconscious. Thus, Wegner (2002) argues that the belief that decisions arise from conscious deliberation is an illusion resulting from the fact that the mind both decides and produces relevant conscious experiences at the same time. A conviction that our conscious deliberations are the source of our decisions is therefore difficult to escape. But however compelling, such subjective experiences may not be the critical factor. Indeed, when making decisions, people often simply ruminate about alternatives until one of them announces itself as the right choice. In this view, the subjective experience of one alternative as particularly desirable is a reflection of having decided unconsciously. Of course, it is still we who decide, but our conscious deliberations may not be where the action is.

Especially for big decisions, we expect to be informed by our affect. When choosing a spouse or buying a house, people expect their decision to be accompanied by embodied evidence. If one is lucky, one might be able to justify one's choice by the experience of having instantly fallen in love with the person, apartment, college, or pair of shoes that one chooses. Such an experience confers great legitimacy on one's decision because we accept that affective feelings are embodied information about what people want, like, and value.

In fact, we rely so much on embodied affect as a source of information that its absence can also be informative. For example, a recent book by model and actress Brooke Shields (2005) described her experience of becoming a mother. As she held her new daughter, whose birth was the realization of a life-long dream, she was devastated to discover that she felt nothing at all. The baby in her arms seemed like an alien object. The absence of feelings of intimacy and nurturance, so basic to motherhood, suggested to her that she was a shallow and worthless person. She even considered suicide. Only after treatment for postpartum depression did the appropriate, embodied experiences arise to validate her more positive beliefs about herself. This process of embodied invalidation and validation of beliefs about the self has been the subject of recent research in our laboratory, as described in the next section.

## THE COGNITIVE COSTS OF AFFECTIVE INVALIDATION

### Affective Certainty

In one series of studies (Tamir, Robinson, & Clore, 2002), we examined the idea that embodied affective reactions could serve as data for people's theories about themselves. As a source of affective cues, we induced a happy or sad mood in individuals who had indicated that they believed themselves to be either high or low in trait positive affect, as measured by an extraversion scale. In each case, we found that whether a person's momentary feelings helped or hurt their cognitive performance depended on whether the feelings supported or conflicted with their beliefs about being a happy or unhappy person.

The mood induction procedure involved listening to happy (Mozart) or melancholy (Mahler) music. Participants then responded as quickly as possible to words (e.g., pain, failure, praise, gifts) by indicating whether a word referred to something desirable or undesirable. Decisions were faster when state and trait affect were both positive or both negative than when they differed. By itself, being happy conferred no advantage, regardless of whether it was trait or state happiness. In fact, individuals viewing themselves as generally unhappy were faster when also unhappy in the moment. The critical factor was then not the affect but its congruence with evaluative beliefs.

Tamir et al. (2002) interpreted their results as demonstrating the benefits of "affective certainty," which allowed participants to devote themselves fully to the task at hand. In contrast, affective uncertainty appeared to have saddled them with a secondary task, which slowed their reactions. This account is compatible with the general idea that affective experience can serve as evidence for affective beliefs.

### Affect-as-Evidence

The "affect-as-evidence" hypothesis (Clore & Gasper, 2000) holds that self-generated experiences of affect might serve as evidence of evaluative beliefs, just as sensory experiences routinely serve as evidence for descriptive beliefs about the world. For people who believe themselves to be happy individuals, feeling happy would provide evidence for that belief. For those who believe themselves to be unhappy persons, feeling unhappy would provide belief confirmation. The Tamir et al. (2002) results suggest that such confirmation leads to faster decisions.

One alternative possible result for these experiments would have been for trait positive and negative affect to have made respondents especially sensitive to similarly valenced feelings (Gray, 1970, 1981). A second possibility would have been for a positive and negative mood to activate positive and negative concepts in memory, leading to faster reactions to similarly valenced stimuli (Bower, 1981; Isen, 1984; Forgas, 1995). Neither of these patterns emerged. Instead, in keeping with the "affective certainty" hypothesis proposed by Tamir et al. (2002), trait-state congruence led to faster processing of all stimuli. According to that hypothesis, when embodied affect does not match affective beliefs about the self, the person is left with an epistemic problem, which may interfere with ongoing processing.

In subsequent research, we examined further the idea that incongruence between affect and cognition has cognitive costs, and that affective reactions that are congruent promote cognitive effectiveness. This research expanded the question by examining memory, rather than reaction time, as a measure of cognitive efficiency, as described in the next section.

## Affective Coherence

"Affective coherence" refers to the compatibility of affective concepts and embodied experiences, and is believed to facilitate ongoing cognitive processing (Centerbar, Schnall, Clore, & Garvin, in press). In contrast, "affective incoherence" (incompatibility between conceptual and embodied affect) should interfere with cognitive efficiency and fluency of processing. The conditions of affective coherence should tend to induce "affective certainty" and show effects similar to those observed by Tamir et al. (2002). Five experiments examined recall of a story about a series of happy and sad events that are recounted by the main character. The story consisted of happy events, such as "getting a bicycle for his birthday," and sad events, such as "the day his dog died." In each experiment, before reading the story participants completed a sentence unscrambling task designed to prime happy or sad concepts. Only the sources of the embodied affective cues differed across experiments. In one experiment, we induced mood by having participants listen to happy or sad music. In other experiments, such affective cues came from having participants contract the facial muscles involved in smiling or frowning. And in yet other experiments, they engaged in approach or avoidance actions by gently pulling up or pushing down on a desktop.

The results were the same in all experiments. When mood, facial expressions, or actions were appropriate to the valence of the primed cognitions, overall memory for the story was superior. When such embodied cues were incompatible with the valence of the primed happy or sad thoughts, memory suffered. Again, as in the reaction time data of Tamir et al. (2002), the effect was general, not specific to positive or negative items of information. Thus, the ability to remember well depends partly on the degree to which one's current embodied affect agrees with one's current evaluative thoughts.

Similar results can be found in the emotion regulation literature. For example, Richards and Gross (2000) showed emotionally evocative film clips and asked some participants to inhibit any emotional expression. They found impaired memory in these individuals, and concluded that affective suppression hurts performance. However, such suppression also involves a mismatch between affective beliefs (about the film) and affective expressions of the same type as those examined above. Hence, the cognitive costs that appear to be due to the suppression of emotion could be due to the incongruence between emotional beliefs and neutral expressions, a possibility that has yet to be examined.

## Enactment

The hypothesis that there are costs to disagreeing with oneself turns out to have wide applicability. Other relevant data come from studies employing the Implicit Association Test (IAT) (Greenwald, McGhee, & Schwartz, 1998). In such studies, people's verbally expressed beliefs about their attitudes (explicit attitudes) can be compared to behaviorally expressed attitudes (enacted attitudes). Evidence of the cost of disagreement between belief-based and enacted attitudes comes from a study of implicit versus explicit measures of erotic orientation (Vargas, 2004).

The study involved exposure to photographs of same and opposite sex individuals and both belief-based and enacted (IAT) measures of how appealing participants found them. Vargas (2004) found that individuals whose explicit and implicit reactions to the pictures disagreed had elevated somatic symptoms and a reduced sense of well-being when compared to those whose concrete behavior (enacted attitudes) agreed with their beliefs about themselves (explicit attitudes). Here again, disagreeing with oneself appears to carry costs.

Compatible results come from other studies assessing explicit and implicit self esteem (Robinson, Vargas, & Crawford, 2003). In these studies, disagreement between reported beliefs about oneself (explicit self esteem) and behavioral reactions to the self on the IAT was associated with being in a worse mood. This was true both in a laboratory assessment and when affect was assessed over time as part of a daily diary study. Even for individuals with low esteem, having their low esteem beliefs confirmed by enactments of low esteem on the IAT left them feeling marginally better than having such beliefs disconfirmed. These experiments suggest that disagreement between believed and enacted attitudes can be costly emotionally as well as cognitively. It should be noted that we do not know to what extent these respondents developed an awareness of the attitudes they were enacting as they responded to the IAT. Therefore, we cannot be sure that the effects depended on the cognitive costs of affective uncertainty. However, people apparently often do experience some IAT conditions as harder than others and see their enactments as attitudinally disclosing. Indeed, Monteith, Voils, and Ashburn-Nardo (2001) used such experiences on the IAT as a guilt induction to promote compensatory responses.

Other supportive data are less exclusively about embodiment, but are nevertheless noteworthy because they show the importance of agreement between general beliefs about oneself and concrete, experiential, or episodic data. As part of a formalized interview, investigators of attachment (e.g., Allen & Land, 1999) often ask adolescents to express their general beliefs about their relationship with their parents. In addition, they ask the adolescent for specific examples that would support their belief. It turns out that being unable to recall concrete instances that would support the adolescents' abstract beliefs about having a good or bad relationship with their mothers or fathers is a powerful predictor of bad life outcomes (drug use, teen pregnancy, truancy). The investigators suggest that problems in everyday coping become magnified when children lack validation in the form of readily recallable experiences for such core beliefs as whether or not their parents love them.

## Summary

The data reviewed in this section concerned the congruence between general beliefs and specific embodiments, enactments, and experiences. They showed that incongruence has negative effects on decision speed, memory performance, and feelings of happiness, as well as on specific life outcomes. Our interpretation emphasized the idea that embodied cues that are incongruent with evaluative cognitions may be experienced as disconfirmation of those cognitions, creating an epistemic load that hinders performance. However, a question that arises is whether there is also evidence for the reverse, that is, is there evidence that cognitions accompanied by congruent embodied cues are more credible or powerful, rather than their incongruence making them less credible or powerful? Evidence comes from two sources. The first is evidence that congruence can influence how compelling or effective information is in a marketing context. The second consists of evidence of attitudinal effects from engaging in affectively coherent approach-avoidance action.

## Affect-Confirmation

Do embodied affective cues that are believed to serve as evidence for evaluative cognitions have any discernable impact on the effectiveness of such cognitions? Experiments by Adaval (2001) induced mood by having participants spend several minutes writing a description of a happy or sad personal experience. Afterward, they considered positive and negative information about various consumer goods and rated the appeal of the various products and their willingness to purchase them. Adaval discovered that when participants experienced affective feelings of the same valence as the positive or negative information they were considering about a product, that information then carried greater weight in the final judgments. She concluded that the embodied affective cues appeared to serve as confirmation or disconfirmation of the information. Her "affect-confirmation" interpretation is thus similar to the related proposals of "affect-as-evidence" (Clore & Gasper, 2000) and "affect certainty" (Tamir et al., 2002). Each of these hypotheses proposes that self-produced, affective reactions can provide evidence for, confirm, or increase confidence in affect-congruent beliefs.

In addition to increasing the confidence that one has in congruent information, what else might follow from the experience of coherence between body and mind? To the extent that body and mind are on the same page, we might expect what is in the mind to be processed with greater fluency. And because processing fluency has been shown to be inherently positive (Winkielman & Cacioppo, 2001), we might expect that mind-body coherence should result in more positive attitudes toward stimuli that are processed fluently. We review evidence on this point next.

## Approach-Avoidance Action and Affect

In a series of experiments, Centerbar and Clore (2006) examined the effects of engaging in arm flexion (as in approach) and arm extension (as in avoidance) while processing liked and disliked stimuli. The idea was that approach should be a motivationally congruent action toward liked objects and avoidance should be a motivationally congruent action toward disliked objects. In addition to validating the attitude toward the object, as shown in Centerbar et al. (in press), congruent actions should promote processing fluency and hence liking.

The experiment consisted of viewing novel stimuli (Chinese ideographs) that had been rated for attractiveness. As each ideograph was shown on a computer screen, a participant either pressed gently down on a tabletop (arm extension) or up from the bottom of the tabletop (arm flexion). Subsequent evaluations of the ideographs showed that when such approach or avoidance action was motivationally congruent with initial liking for a particular ideograph, liking for that ideograph increased. When the action and liking for the object were motivationally incongruent, liking decreased. We infer that engaging in action that was motivationally congruent with the value of a particular ideograph increased the fluency with which that ideograph was processed, and engaging in action that was motivationally incongruent decreased the fluency with which that ideograph was processed. As a result, fluently processed ideographs received a small boost in liking relative to those processed with greater difficulty. These results are therefore consistent with Winkielman and Cacioppo's (2001) finding that processing fluency is affectively positive (for further discussion of perceptual fluency, see Schwarz & Clore, 2007).

Note that we previously cited Adaval's (2001) finding in which embodied validation of product beliefs in a consumer context conferred greater weight on those beliefs in purchase decisions. In view of that finding, should we have expected more disliking (rather than more liking) when the enactment of avoidance confirmed participants' dislike for certain ideographs? The answer is no, because Adaval found that the embodied confirmation of negative product beliefs changed only their weighting and not their value. Hence, we did not expect an enactment of avoidance to make disliked ideographs more negative. Rather, the experience of fluency from affective coherence (both from avoiding disliked ideographs and from approaching liked ideographs) was expected to add a small positive value, making both seem slightly more likable, which is what was found. The obtained effect is analogous to what Higgins (2000) has referred to as "value from fit." It is worth noting that the effect was (and was expected to be) small, so that its impact was apparent only for mildly unappealing ideographs.

## Summary

The similarity of results across repeated studies (Centerbar & Clore, 2006) indicated that there is positive value in affective coherence. Specifically, positive value increased, as indicated by increased liking, when enactments of approach validated pre-existing liking. Importantly, the same increase in liking appeared when enactments of avoidance validated perceptions of lack of appeal. Thus, the increase in value is one of affective coherence, which in this case was the experience of having one's initial liking or disliking confirmed by finding oneself engaging in motivationally congruent actions.

The phenomena under consideration concern the role of embodied and enacted reactions as evidence for evaluative cognitions and beliefs. Whereas sensory data can validate descriptive beliefs, we cannot see, hear, or touch the goodness or badness that is the content of evaluative beliefs. Instead, evidence must be self-generated in the form of our own affective feelings, expressions, and actions. Such embodied reactions do not in turn need verification, as the compelling nature of such reactions make them the data of choice.

The discussion has focused on embodiment as data for cognition rather than on cognition as embodied. Before proceeding, it is important to clarify the implications of these results for the larger idea of embodied cognition. On the one hand, they support the hypothesis that embodiment plays a critical, epistemic role. But on the other, they also show constraints on how we should think about embodiment, the issue to which we turn next.

### IMPLICATIONS FOR EMBODIED COGNITION

An important conclusion of the experiments just reviewed (Centerbar & Clore, 2006) was that, contrary to popular belief, enactment by itself did not affect attitude. The role of enactment was to confirm or disconfirm existing perceptions and cognitions of value. This point is of great relevance for achieving a viable conception of embodied cognition.

Discussions of embodiment and social psychology (e.g., Niedenthal, Barsalou, Winkielman, Krauth-Gruber, & Ric, 2005; Smith & Semin, 2004) invariably begin by citing findings of direct links between action and affect. For example, Smith and Semin (2004, p. 26) state that:

Consistent with the embodiment assumption, recent work in social psychology...underlines the close connections of attitudes to sensori-motor systems and therefore to our bodies. For instance...horizontal or vertical head movements... (Wells & Petty, 1980) and...flexion and extension of the upper arm...influence evaluative judgments (e.g., Cacioppo, Priester, & Berntson, 1993).

Expositions of the simulation view have also highlighted these findings as prime evidence for embodiment (e.g., Niedenthal et al., 2005). In this section, we review evidence suggesting that the inferences we psychologists usually draw from these studies may need reconsidering. First, we examine the impact of approach-avoidance action on attitudes toward Chinese ideographs, revisiting a study described in the previous section.

## Do Actions Cause Attitudes?

The research on the effect of approach-avoidance actions on the liking of ideographs discussed previously (Centerbar & Clore, 2006) was adapted from the often-cited research by Cacioppo et al. (1993). In an elegant series of studies, Cacioppo and colleagues found that engaging in approach (arm flexion) or avoidance (arm extension) created rudimentary attitudes toward novel stimuli (Chinese ideographs). The paper is admirably thorough and careful. Nevertheless, we revisited the issue, and happened onto an interesting discovery, as described previously. When one takes into account differences among the ideographs in how appealing they are, one finds that rather than acting directly, such action interacts with the value of the object being approached or avoided.

Using Cacioppo et al.'s (1993) original ideographs, we found that the effect of approach-avoidance action depended completely on the initial liking of the ideographs. Thus, the increase in liking as a result of the approach action and the decrease in liking from the avoidance action held only for ideographs that were initially liked. For ideographs that were initially disliked, the results were reversed so that approach reduced liking and avoidance created liking. Also, in response to neutral ideographs, approach and avoidance had no effects on liking. Thus, the attitudinal effect does not lie in the actions themselves.

The original results of Cacioppo et al. (1993) appear to have resulted from a sample of ideographs that were more liked than disliked, so that on balance approach had positive and avoidance had negative effects. Our results thus expand on their initial findings and suggest that Heider (1958) may have been correct when he observed that approach-avoidance motions may not have any affective implications out of context. It appears that the attitude effect arises not from approach-avoidance action itself but from the congruence between the liking implied by the action and pre-existing liking. The affective coherence of engaging in actions that validate one's attitude is a positive experience that creates liking, whereas the affective incoherence of engaging in actions that invalidate one's attitude is a negative experience that creates dislike.

The notion that motor action requires context to acquire meaning and have impact is intended to be highly general. The argument is that in our search for compelling examples of embodiment in cognition, we may be insufficiently attentive to the fact that the meaning of actions, like that of other psychologically significant stimuli, is embedded, situated, and emergent (Smith & Semin, 2004). This point is illustrated for expressive action in an additional series of studies.

### Expression and Affect

To examine the effects of expressive action on affect, a series of experiments varied the context in which expressive actions were observed or enacted (Tamir, Robinson, Clore, Martin, & Whitaker, 2004). The findings confirmed the idea that expressive actions can contribute to affective reactions, but in none of the experiments was the influence direct. In each, the direction of the effect depended again on the context in which it appeared.

For example, one set of experiments assessed the affective influence of shaking one's head while processing information, in a manner similar to what Wells and Petty (1980) had done in their classic experiments. Specifically, participants engaged in head shaking as they watched a short film and then indicated their reactions to the characters. One of the films showed an interview with a convict who had murdered a young girl in a psychotic delusion. In the film, the convict argues that he is perfectly fine and should be set free. Head shaking while watching the psychotic killer assert his harmlessness increased the angry feelings of participants and increased their tendencies to see him as responsible for his actions. However, the very same head shaking action produced the reverse effect when the film showed a pregnant young heroin addict explaining her sad situation. Head shaking in that context increased viewers' sympathy rather than their anger. It acted like a form of agreement about the sadness of her plight, rather than as an impetus to blame. The effects of this expressive action were therefore totally contingent on the context, rather than being direct and context-independent. Another study in this series examined the effects of brow tension on decisional confidence. Again, the effects reversed depending on the contextual variable that was manipulated.

In an essay entitled, "Of Men and Mackerels," Dijksterhuis, Bargh, and Miedema (2000) proposed that expressive effects have automatic and invariable effects on affect, judgment, and behavior. They maintained that expressive cues have fixed influences that people can minimize only by exercising conscious control. To assess this claim, Tamir et al. (2004) presented smiles subliminally during a competitive game. Despite the fact that the smiles were presented unconsciously, flashing them during the scoring of participants' performances resulted in positive feelings and beliefs that they had performed well. Conversely, flashing the subliminal smiles during the scoring of their opponents' performance resulted in negative feelings and beliefs on the part of participants that they had not done very well.

The results again indicate that expressions do not have fixed, invariable, effects. Moreover, this result was obtained despite the fact that participants' lack of awareness of the smiles would have prevented them from engaging in the type of cognitive control that had been hypothesized as necessary to counter the obligatory link between expression and affect. Instead, the results show that the affective influences of the smiles depended on the context in which they appeared.

Earlier theorizing by Zajonc and Markus (1984) had suggested a "hard interface" between muscular responses and affect that did not involve cognitive processing. However, our own results were more consistent with proposals by Darwin (1872/1965), who emphasized that expressions amplify emotions. He did not hold that expressions cause emotions, as some have assumed. Thus, we concur with Tamir et al. (2004) in the conclusion that emotions emerge not from the muscles but from the mind.

In summary, the expressive action studies (Tamir et al., 2004) and the approach-avoidance action studies (Centerbar & Clore, 2006) lead to similar conclusions. They expand the important findings of Wells and Petty (1980) and of Cacioppo et al. (1993) to show the sometimes hidden role of context. In both, the same actions had opposite consequences when the mental context was altered. If these results are any guide, we should expect that embodied meaning, no less than lexical meaning, depends on the context in which it appears. The results are consistent with an emphasis on the situated nature of social cognition (Smith & Semin, 2004), whether embodied or not, and they are inconsistent with views that assume that embodied stimuli have direct and unmediated effects (e.g., Dijksterhuis et al., 2000; Zajonc & Markus, 1984).

A similar analysis can be applied to related results, including those from the clever and often cited study by Strack, Martin, and Stepper (1988). In this study, participants held a pencil in their mouths as they viewed cartoons. By varying whether the pencil was held by the lips or the teeth, participants contracted muscles that either facilitated or inhibited a smile. They found that flexing the muscles involved in smiling increased enjoyment of cartoons. The experiment thus showed that expressions can intensify affect but not, as often assumed, that they create affect. That is, they showed that in the context of looking at cartoons, smiling increases enjoyment, not that such muscle action has a direct or context-free impact on affect. The data are not evidence for a hard interface, but they are important evidence that engaging in affect-congruent action can validate or intensify affective meaning.

EVALUATIVE EMBODIMENT IN EVERYDAY LIFE

We have presented evidence of some detrimental effects of incongruent bodily cues and some positive effects of congruent bodily cues. The positive effects included greater impact of verbal information when accompanied by congruent embodiment (Adaval, 2001), and increased liking of visual stimuli when participants engaged in approach during positive stimuli and avoidance during negative stimuli. This effect was believed to result from more fluent processing during preference-congruent action (Centerbar & Clore, 2006).

These experiments involved the promotion of particular evaluative beliefs by manipulating congruent embodiments. Similar attempts at influence are frequently encountered in everyday life. For example, banks have traditionally been large buildings with stone columns and great stone facades that give the impression of solidity and safety. Bankers presumably created such impressive structures in hopes that the physical solidity of massive stone structures would provide compelling, experiential evidence for the abstract idea of financial solidity. Subsequently, when the safety and solidity of banks was generally assumed, the architecture changed accordingly to send a new message. Thus, neighborhood branches of modern banks have eliminated the formality of steps and columns and the coldness of marble and granite to emphasize accessibility, openness, and friendliness. But the process is the same. Architecture is chosen to embody, and hence to validate in the subjective experiences of potential customers, whatever ideas about the bank are promoted in advertising. In this way, they seek (literally) to achieve a concrete representation of a desired brand image.

A technique readily apparent in government buildings and memorials is to use physical elevation to elicit the idea of greatness. Thus, the Lincoln Memorial is an imposing structure atop many stone steps. Lincoln himself is rendered in an enormous, awe-inspiring statue intended to reflect our national beliefs about his greatness. Congress too is housed in an impressive building with many steps to convey the high calling of the legislature. In courtrooms too, judges are elevated physically so that our experiences of their physical elevation might validate beliefs in their elevated judgment. The importance of elevation can perhaps be appreciated by imagining judges rendering their decisions from the depths of a pit instead of from an elevated bench.

Of course, the world of advertising is full of attempts to instill experiences relevant to whatever beliefs advertisers are employed to promote. Advertisers generally try to convey claims and create validating experiences within the same brief ad. Using music, images, and film techniques that have no actual bearing on the product itself, advertisers seek to elicit excitement, feelings of elegance, purity, sensuality, or whatever affect the product message requires. If successful, experiences are generated that are instinctively compelling so that they function as evidence for the belief being promulgated. A potential benefit of this process for product producers is that once the desired beliefs about the product have been validated in this way, it may no longer be necessary for actual experience with the product itself to provide such validation.

## Research

A series of studies has examined such embodied and experiential analogies in the laboratory. One set of experiments examined the experience of lightness and darkness as a universal metaphor for goodness and badness, and whether it might facilitate the processing of evaluative concepts. The experiments involved the presentation on a computer screen of evaluative words in light- or dark-colored fonts (Meier, Robinson, & Clore, 2004). The participants' task was to classify the words as positive or negative as quickly as possible. In many experiments, it was clear that evaluations could be made more rapidly when positive words appeared in a bright font and negative words appeared in a dark font compared to the reverse pattern. Moreover, the rapid stimulus presentations and response times involved suggested that, at least in the context of making evaluations, the facilitation and interference effects were more or less automatic.

A second series of experiments examined a related physical metaphor for evaluation – vertical location (Meier & Robinson, 2004). In these studies, words were evaluated as positive or negative after they were presented either at the top or the bottom of a computer screen. The results showed faster evaluations when positive words appeared at the top and negative words appeared at the bottom than when the words and positions had the reverse pattern. Together, these studies indicate that physical analogies for goodness and badness, in the form of lightness versus darkness and of high versus low elevation, promote fluent processing of affectively congruent cognitions compared to affectively incongruent cognitions.

### EMBODIMENT IN ART

An approach to characterizing emotion, which may be useful in thinking about art, sees emotion as an affective state (Clore & Ortony, 2000). The "affect" part simply means that emotions are about evaluation, but the "state" part implies that emotions involve multiple systems that simultaneously register the same thing. An emotion then emerges when multiple evaluative representations are too similar to keep track of separately and too different to combine. The resulting multidimensional representation is an emotional state. Such emergence occurs only as the information from multiple sources coheres. Something analogous seems to operate in some works of art. Both emotions and artistic forms that trade in emotions involve multiple modes of evaluation. Thus, poets employ connotation, imagery, metaphor, symbol, repetition, and rhythm to create a single experience in readers (Perrine, 1956). With economy of language, the poet seeks multiple, partially redundant ways to represent themes both cognitively and experientially. Through multimodal representations of the same idea at the same time, ineffable but compelling experiences may be created.

One of the things that graphic artists frequently do is to use lightness, darkness, and vertical location (the dimensions examined in the studies described previously) as well as other physical metaphors to instill their conceptualization in people's experiences. The power of artists' ideas often depends on whether their portrayal, depiction, or enactment is effective in eliciting embodied reactions in audiences. We have suggested that doing so may require multiple, partially redundant representations. Of course, each additional elaboration of the theme that is attempted carries with it the risk of inadvertently creating some affective incoherence, which would dissolve the emergent state. In the next section, we turn to Renaissance art for examples of successful attempts to use art to create emotional experiences. In addition, we consider an example in which Leonardo da Vinci also knowingly created incoherence in the service of inducing embodied involvement in viewers of his work.

## PERSPECTIVE IN RENAISSANCE ART

From the 4th to the 14th century or so, the Byzantine style of painting generally involved two-dimensional depictions that lacked any sense of depth. Painters depicted formalized spiritual themes with flat, archetypal figures. They were typically rendered rigidly, symmetrically, without depth or proper proportions, and without expression or individuality.

Beginning with Giotto, figures in later works became more rounded and realistic, and were often engaged in action. They were more likely to be expressive, to look directly at the viewer, and to be painted with shadows and depth. One of the great advances of Italian Renaissance art (1300–1500) was the development of perspective to create a sense of depth.

In contrast to earlier flat representations, Renaissance painters were capable of pulling viewers into the scenes they painted, giving them greater potential to elicit affective reactions appropriate to the themes of adoration and awe they sought to depict. In addition, because perspective involves an infinite vanishing point, it also served as a religious metaphor for the abstract infinity of God. As commented by Kubovy (1986), "Perspective often enabled the Renaissance artist to cast the deeply religious contents of his art in a form that could produce in the viewer spiritual effects that could not have been achieved by any other formal means" (Part XI, p. 4).

The research described previously (Meier et al., 2004; Meier & Robinson, 2004) found a relationship between people's evaluative inclinations and both the lightness of color and the vertical position in which something appears. The development of perspective allowed Renaissance and later Baroque painters to exploit this relationship. The technique is abundantly evident on the walls and ceilings of Italian churches, cathedrals, and museums. Painting in perspective enabled viewers to look up through clouds and the ascending angels to radiant holy figures. The arms and legs and the drape of their garments give the feel of these figures rising upward to grace and light. Surely for believers and pilgrims of the time, even more than for us, they were inspiring. Of course, there were also paintings of the damned, showing them descending into the darkness of the lower depths. The viewer can thus experience the elevation and lightness of the good and the lowering and darkening of the bad, even though both are simply paint applied to flat surfaces. In that context, the power of perspective lay in its ability to create embodied experiences consistent with ideas about the glory and sweetness of the good and the pain and dread of the bad. The embodied affective experiences engendered by this new technique presumably served to validate the evaluative ideas depicted, so that perspective became a powerful tool of persuasion.

One particularly interesting application of the "good-is-up" principle can be seen in Leonardo da Vinci's fresco, "The Last Supper." The work shows ample use of perspective techniques, which da Vinci understood and promulgated in written advice to artists of his day. He said a cardinal principle was that to be convincing, the center of projection where everything converges must be at the viewer's eye. However, Kubovy (1986) points out that in this famous fresco, da Vinci violated his own principle. An analysis of the work shows clearly that the center of projection was not the viewer's eye but a point 15 feet above the viewer. According to Kubovy (1986),

Figure 9.1. Andrea Pozzo, The Glory of S. Ignazio (detail) Church of S. Ignazio, Rome, 1691–1694. *Source:* http://commons.wikimedia.org/wiki/Image:Rome_santignazio_ ceiling_hdr.jpg.

this violation of principle was motivated. To accommodate to the center of projection above them, viewers are forced to adopt an elevated perspective. Being forced to consider the painting from a higher perspective means that viewing it is quite literally an uplifting experience (to learn more, see http://webexhibits.org/arrowintheeye).

In this section, we proposed that art is one domain in which an effort is often made to induce the body to aid the mind in a manner similar to that proposed in the embodiment hypothesis. An emotional cycle presumably characterizes some artistic projects such that an artist's horror at war or a poet's experience of love impels them to create works that elicit related responses both to convey an idea and to validate it. The driving force would seem to be a symbiosis between ideas represented in mind and body. Paintings from the Italian Renaissance were used as examples of attempts to create embodied responses that realized abstract ideas about good, evil, divinity, and infinity.

Figure 9.2. Leonardo da Vinci, The Last Supper (1495–1498). *Source:* http://commons. wikimedia.org/wiki/Image.

## AFFECTIVE ACCOUNTING

This concluding section proposes a particular set of conditions that may underlie the process whereby multiple sources of affect and evaluative meaning converge and become potent. Much of our work looks at how people succeed and fail in emotional bookkeeping (Schwarz & Clore, 1983). For example, in depression one's negative affect becomes unaccountable. With no clear cause in view, the affect becomes promiscuous, attaching itself to anything and everything. The source of any experience may be clear when experienced by itself, but the experience may become less accountable when two causes produce similar experiences at the same time.

This process is evident in the domain of visual experience. In vision, different but highly redundant images are presented by the two eyes. Our eyes move together so that the images that are projected are almost, but not quite, the same. Indeed, they are so similar that visual accounting fails. It is impossible to keep books on which eye is contributing which image. As a result, we see an emergent three-dimensional image rather than separate, flat images from each eye. We see objects in hologram-like reality as both eyes provide parallel but slightly different images of the same thing. Presumably, such emergence reflects the fact that it is computationally simpler to see one object as "out there" rather than keeping track of two highly redundant sensory streams.

A related principle appears to operate when we apprehend more than one type of goodness or badness simultaneously emanating from a single object. According to one theory of emotion (Ortony, Clore, & Collins, 1988), there are three different types of affect – being pleased at outcomes, approving of actions, and the liking of objects or their attributes. These reflect the appraisals of outcome desirability, the praise-blameworthiness of actions, and the appeal of objects. Finally, these appraisals emanate from different sources of evaluation – goals, standards, and tastes. Specific emotions are then elaborations of these three types of good. The important point for the present purpose is that the three types of affect and evaluation are incommensurate. That is, although utility, morality, and beauty (examples of the three sources of value) are all good, it is not possible to add them up in any sensible way. Something that manifests all three is simply experienced as something unaccountably, multidimensionally wonderful. Consider a political leader whose policies are good in a utilitarian sense, who also engages in admirable actions, and who is additionally handsome and well-spoken. Such a figure may command a degree of loyalty that none of these attributes by themselves would have elicited, in part because of the difficulty of keeping straight what aspects of our experience of goodness comes from what source. As a result, the leader may be experienced as transcendentally good.

Through a similar process, people fall in love, not only because their beloved helps in the satisfaction of their goals, but also because they may be seen as excellent or admirable in some way and because they may seem beautiful or handsome. The emergent experience of their goodness becomes, in fact, beyond accounting. Falling in love thus renders some people inarticulate, whereas it inspires others to poetry. Both reactions may flow from the same impossibility of sorting out which aspects of one's fascination with the other are accounted for by which aspects of their goodness.

There are many such emergent experiences that may arise for similar reasons. Thus, the experience of nostalgia may be one in which one experiences oneself in the present remembering something in the past, feeling at once the immediacy of a sweet memory of an event at the same time that one is experiencing the sadness of its distance in time. Similarly, an intimate conversation or romantic encounter may seem important not only because it may be intense, but perhaps also because one constructs from the visual, verbal, and nonverbal feedback from the other a model of their experience at the same time that one entertains one's own view. To the extent that partial redundancy blurs clear accounting, a joint experience may emerge. The process is also seen in an operatic duet or a string quartet. Rather than hearing only music from separate players, a new entity emerges in one's experience that transcends their individual contributions. In the interpersonal situation, such convergence may be experienced as a vital entity that is somehow more than each person's input. Couples often point to such experiences as the moment in which they fell in love. Are such experiences illusions? Perhaps no more so than three-dimensional images are illusions.

Failures of emotional accounting, just like those of visual accounting, allow one to experience multiple facets of the same person, place, or event at the same time. In the emotional case, the different sources of good are incommensurate. They must remain separate but because they emanate from the same entity and are apprehended at the same time, no such separate accounting is possible. As a result, a multifaceted new entity with all of the incommensurate but redundant features is experienced as one emergent reality, the whole of which seems greater than the sum of its parts – which, of course, it is.

## CONCLUSIONS

We started this chapter with Sartre's famous dictum, "Existence precedes and rules essence." Like Sartre, we have argued for a situated view of psychological reality (see also Smith & Semin, 2004). In this view, the meaning of abstract ideas lies ultimately in how they are situated, instantiated, and exemplified. We focused in particular on evaluative ideas and their affective embodiment. We noted that when accompanied by affective reactions, they are made believable and persuasive because such affect indicates one's commitment to the evaluation being entertained. Indeed, because they involve multiple systems, emotions have been viewed (Clore & Gasper, 2000) as commitments to particular realities. For example, once angry, one is no longer entertaining the possibility of injustice; rather, anger is an embodied commitment to the apparent reality of injustice. In related ways, all types of affective embodiments, including feelings, expressions, and actions can serve as evidence that makes persuasive the belief that one has encountered something good or bad.

In this chapter, we made eight basic points, which may be summarized as follows:

1. Embodied and enacted affective reactions can function to validate or invalidate evaluative cognitions. Specifically, the valence component of affect can provide evidence of evaluative ideas and the arousal component provides evidence of their importance. Especially when making big decisions, people expect to be informed by their affect, and the absence of supporting affect may be distressing and lead to unstable decisions.

2. When embodied affective cues do not match current evaluative beliefs, the person may be left with an epistemic problem, which can then interfere with ongoing processing. Consistent with this "affect-as-evidence" view, Tamir et al. (2002) found slower reaction times among individuals whose momentary affective feelings were incongruent with their general affective beliefs about themselves. For example, people who thought of themselves as unhappy individuals performed better when they were sad than when they were happy. Other studies (Centerbar et al., in press) showed poorer memory performance when embodied affect (expressions, feelings, actions) did not match primed happy or sad concepts.

3. Evidence of the generality of these proposals came from research using the IAT. Failures of affective enactments on the IAT to confirm explicit evaluations were shown to result in elevated symptoms and lowered mood. Attachment research (e.g., Allen & Land, 1999) also finds poorer life outcomes among adolescents whose specific, episodic memories fail to support their general evaluative beliefs about their relationships with their parents. Again, affective coherence was important independent of the positive or negative nature of the affect and evaluation involved.

4. We proposed that congruent embodied cues should make congruent cognitions more credible or powerful. In studies of consumer preference (Adaval, 2001) and approach-avoidance motor action (Centerbar & Clore, 2006), congruence between evaluative cognitions and embodied and enacted affective cues made the cognitions potent.

5. The impact of expressions and enactments of affect turn out to depend on the context in which they appear. Despite appropriate cautions by the authors, discussions of embodied cognition invariably cite studies of facial expression (Strack et al., 1988), head nods (Wells & Petty, 1980), and approach-avoidance action (Cacioppo et al., 1993) as evidence of direct and unmediated effects of motor action on affect and attitude. However, research varying the context of these enactments (Centerbar & Clore, 2006; Tamir et al., 2004) has shown that such interpretations are unwarranted. The conclusions are consistent with an emphasis on the situated nature of social cognition (Smith & Semin, 2004) and inconsistent with views that assume that embodied stimuli have direct and unmediated effects (e.g., Dijksterhuis et al., 2000; Zajonc & Markus, 1984).

6. The promotion of evaluative beliefs through congruent embodiments can be seen in public architecture where the evaluative implications of light and dark colors and elevated physical locations are employed in the design of monuments and public buildings. The world of advertising too is full of attempts to instill experiences relevant to the beliefs to be promoted.

Laboratory research was presented showing faster reactions when the evaluative meanings of words were supported by appearing in light or dark fonts (Meier et al., 2004) or by appearing on the top or bottom of a computer screen (Meier & Robinson, 2004).

7. The research presented can be interpreted as evidence of the costs of embodiment and enactment that is incongruent with evaluative beliefs. For evidence of possible benefits of congruent embodiment, we turned to art. We suggested that the power of poems, paintings, and plays often depends on eliciting embodied reactions that are congruent with the ideas being purveyed. The use of perspective in Renaissance and Baroque painting illustrates one way of fostering experiences of elevation and awe when depicting religious scenes. Kubovy (1986) argued that Leonardo da Vinci knowingly created incoherence by making the perspective in his fresco, "The Last Supper," converge above viewers to create visual and hence spiritual elevation.

8. We concluded by noting that artistic and commercial exploitation of these principles ultimately rests on a failure of affective accounting. We have only one window on our affective experiences, making it impossible to keep straight which part of our affective reactions comes from which source (Schwarz & Clore, 1983). One's experience can transcend the individual components when their partial redundancy makes appropriate experiential bookkeeping impossible, as when listening to an operatic duet or a string quartet. We argued that this difficulty contributes to all sorts of profound experiences, including art, religious revelation, political loyalty, and romantic love.

## References

Adaval, R. (2001). Sometimes it just feels right: The differential weighting of affect-consistent and affect-inconsistent information. *Journal of Consumer Research, 28,* 1–17.

Allen, J., & Land, D. (1999). Attachment in adolescence. In J. Cassidy & P. Shaver (Eds.), *Handbook of attachment* (pp. 319–335). New York: Guilford.

Baumeister, R. F., Vohs, K. D., & Tice, D. M. (1996). How emotion helps and hurts decision making. In J. Forgas (Ed.), *Hearts and Minds: Affective influences on social cognition and behaviour*. New York: Psychology Press.

Bower, G. H. (1981). Mood and memory. *American Psychologist, 36,* 129–148.

Cacioppo, J. T., Priester, J. R., & Bernston, G. G. (1993). Rudimentary determination of attitudes. II. Arm flexion and extension have differential effects on attitudes. *Journal of Personality and Social Psychology, 65,* 5–17.

Cahill, L., & McGaugh, J. L. (1998). Mechanisms of emotional arousal and lasting declarative memory. *Trends in Neuroscience, 21,* 294–299.

Centerbar, D., & Clore, G. L. (2006). Do approach-avoidance actions create attitudes? *Psychological Science, 17*, 22–29.

Centerbar, D. B., Schnall, S., Clore, G. L., & Garvin, E. (in press). Affective incoherence: When affective concepts and embodied reactions clash. *Journal of Personality and Social Psychology*.

Clore, G. L., & Gasper, K. (2000). Feeling is believing: Some affective influences on belief. In N. H. Frijda, A. S. R. Manstead, & S. Bem (Eds.), *Emotions and beliefs: How do emotions influence beliefs?* (pp. 10–44). Cambridge, UK: Cambridge University Press.

Clore, G. L., & Ortony, A. (2000). Cognitive in emotion: Never, sometimes, or always? In L. Nadel & R. Lane (Eds.), *The cognitive neuroscience of emotion* (pp. 24–61). New York: Oxford University Press.

Clore, G. L., & Schnall, S. (2005). The influences of affect on attitude. In D. Albarracín, B. T. Johnson, & M. P. Zanna (Eds.), *The handbook of attitudes* (pp. 437–490). Mahwah, NJ: Erlbaum.

Darwin, C. (1965). *The expression of emotion in man and animals.* Chicago: University of Chicago Press. (Original work published 1872).

Dijksterhuis, A., Bargh, J. A., & Miedema, J. (2000). Of men and mackerels: Attention and automatic behavior. In H. Bless & J. P. Forgas (Eds.), *Subjective experience in social cognition and behavior* (pp. 36–51). Philadelphia: Psychology Press.

Forgas, J. P. (1995). Mood and judgment: The affect infusion model. *Psychological Bulletin, 117*, 39–66.

Gray, J. A. (1970). The psychophysiological basis of introversion extraversion. *Behavior Research and Therapy, 8*, 249–266.

Gray, J. A. (1981). A critique of Eysenck's theory of personality. In H. J. Eysenck (Ed.), *A model for personality* (pp. 246–276). Berlin: Springer-Verlag.

Greenwald, A. G., McGhee, D., & Schwartz, J. L. K. (1998). Measuring individual differences in cognition: The Implicit Association Task. *Journal of Personality and Social Psychology, 74*, 1469–1480.

Heider, F. (1958). *The psychology of interpersonal relations.* New York: Wiley.

Higgins, E. T. (2000). Making a good decision: Value from fit. *American Psychologist, 55*, 1217–1230.

Isen, A. (1984). Toward understanding the role of affect in cognition. In R. S. Wyer & T. Srull (Eds.), *Handbook of social cognition* (pp. 179–236). Hillsdale: Erlbaum.

Knutson, B., Adams, C. M., Fong, G. W., & Hommer, D. (2001). Anticipation of increasing monetary reward selectively recruits nucleus accumbens. *Journal of Neuroscience, 21*, 1–5.

Kubovy, M. (1986). *The psychology of perspective and Renaissance art.* New York: Cambridge University Press.

Meier, B. P., & Robinson, M. D. (2004). Why the sunny side is up: Associations between affect and vertical position. *Psychological Science, 15*, 243–247.

Meier, B. P., Robinson, M. D., & Clore, G. L. (2004). Why good guys wear white: Automatic inferences about stimulus valence based on color. *Psychological Science, 15*, 82–87.

Monteith, M. J., Voils, C. I., & Ashburn-Nardo, L. (2001). Taking a look underground: Detecting, interpreting, and reacting to implicit racial biases. *Social Cognition, 19*, 395–417.

Niedenthal, P. M., Barsalou, L. W., Winkielman, P., Krauth-Gruber, S., & Ric, F. (2005). Embodiment in attitudes, social perception, and emotion. *Personality and Social Psychology Review, 9*, 184–211.

Ortony, A., Clore, G. L., & Collins, A. (1988). *The cognitive structure of emotions*. New York: Cambridge University Press (reprinted 1999).

Perrine, L. (1956). *Sound and sense: An introduction to poetry*. New York: Harcourt, Brace.

Richards, J. M., & Gross, J. J. (2000). Emotion regulation and memory: The cognitive costs of keeping one's cool. *Journal of Personality and Social Psychology, 79*, 410–424.

Robinson, M. D., Vargas, P., & Crawford, E. G. (2003). Putting process into personality, appraisal, and emotion: Evaluative processing as a missing link. In J. Musch & C. Klauer (Eds.), *The psychology of evaluation: Affective processes in cognition and emotion* (pp. 275–306). Mahwah, NJ: Erlbaum.

Russell, J. A. (2003). Core affect and the psychological construction of emotion. *Psychological Review, 110*, 145–172.

Schwarz, N., & Clore, G. L. (1983). Mood, misattribution, and judgments of well- being: Informative and directive functions of affective states. *Journal of Personality and Social Psychology, 45*, 513–523.

Schwarz, N., & Clore, G. L. (1988). How do I feel about it? The informative function of mood. In K. Fiedler & J. Forgas (Eds.), *Affect, cognition, and social behavior* (pp. 44–62). Toronto: C. J. Hogrefe.

Schwarz, N., & Clore, G. L. (2007). Feelings and phenomenal experiences. In E. T. Higgins & A. Kruglanski (Eds.), *Social psychology. A handbook of basic principles* 2nd ed. (pp. 385–407). New York: Guilford Press.

Shields, B. (2005). *Down came the rain: My journey through postpartum depression*. New York: Hyperion Books.

Smith, E. R., & Semin, G. R. (2004). Socially situated cognition: Cognition in its social context. *Advances in Experimental Social Psychology, 36*, 53–117.

Strack, F., Martin, L. L., & Stepper, S. (1988). Inhibiting and facilitating conditions of the human smile: A nonobtrusive test of the facial feedback hypothesis. *Journal of Personality and Social Psychology, 54*, 768–777.

Tamir, M., Robinson, M. D., & Clore, G. L. (2002). The epistemic benefits of trait-consistent mood states: An analysis of extraversion and mood. *Journal of Personality and Social Psychology, 83*, 663–677.

Tamir, M., Robinson, M. D., Clore, G. L., Martin, L. L., & Whitaker, D. J. (2004). Are we puppets on a string? The contextual meaning of unconscious expressive cues. *Personality and Social Psychology Bulletin, 30*, 237–249.

Vargas, P. (2004). Implicit and explicit measures of sexual orientation: You may not be as straight as you think you are, and it's making you sick. Paper presented at the meeting of the European Association of Experimental Social Psychology (Conference on Attitudes), Madrid, Spain, June 2004.

Wegner, D. M. (2002). *The illusion of conscious will*. Cambridge, MA: MIT Press.

Wells, G. L., & Petty, R. E. (1980). The effects of overt head movements on persuasion: Compatibility and incompatibility of responses. *Basic and Applied Social Psychology, 1*, 219–230.

Wilson, T. D. (2002). *Strangers to ourselves: Discovering the adaptive unconscious*. Cambridge, MA: Belknap/Harvard Press.

Winkielman, P., & Cacioppo, J. T. (2001). Mind at ease puts a smile on the face: Psychophysiological evidence that processing facilitation leads to positive affect. *Journal of Personality and Social Psychology, 81,* 989–1000.

Zajonc, R. B., & Markus, H. (1984) Affect and cognition: The hard interface. In C. E. Izard, J. Kagan, & R. B. Zajonc (Eds.), *Emotions, Cognition, and Behavior* (pp. 73–102). Cambridge, UK: Cambridge University Press.

# 10    The Embodiment of Emotion

## Lisa Feldman Barrett and Kristen A. Lindquist

In current psychological discourse, it is fashionable to talk about emotions as "embodied" phenomena. At first glance, this idea is not novel. Historically, almost all psychological theories of emotion have proposed that emotional reactions are constituted by the body in some fashion. Some suggest that changes in the body cause changes in the mind; others suggest the opposite, or that the body and mind interact to produce an emotional response. Amid theoretical differences, these theories use the common metaphor that the body and mind are separate and independent forces that can act upon one another in an emotional episode. Current embodiment theories of the mind challenge this assumption by suggesting that the body helps to constitute the mind in shaping an emotional response. This view has novel implications for understanding the structure and content of the conceptual system for emotion, as well as for defining what emotions are and how they are caused.

In the present chapter, we explore a more modern embodiment view of emotion. First, we discuss how the Cartesian "machine metaphor" underlies much theorizing about emotion, as we situate an embodied view of emotion in its historical context. Our historical review is not intended to be comprehensive but rather to illustrate how emotion theories to date have conceptualized the role of the body and mind in emotion. Next, we briefly review new theories of embodied cognition in light of accumulating findings from emotion research, which together suggest some novel hypotheses about how the conceptual system for emotion is constituted and used. Finally, we discuss how an embodied perspective might contribute to a paradigm shift in the scientific study of emotion.

## A BRIEF HISTORY OF THE MIND AND THE BODY IN EMOTION THEORY

### Cartesian Dualism and the Machine Metaphor

According to Bloom (2004), people are born Cartesian dualists, and dualistic thinking – the notion that the body is a biological machine, whereas the mind is something separate and apart – remains firmly entrenched in our everyday reasoning about the world. Most scientists have explicitly abandoned dualist assumptions in their attempts to explain human behavior, but its residue is highly conserved in psychological theories of mind in the form of the *machine metaphor*: the idea that any psychological phenomenon can be understood to function like a machine, with processes that can be separated into definable bits and pieces that have no necessary causal relation to one another but that can interact. The machine metaphor is deeply entrenched in modern scientific thinking about how the mind and the body relate in emotion. A central tenet of emotion theories is that the body and the mind are intrinsically distinct and separate entities that can influence one another during the generation of an emotional response.

### Emotion Theory: A Brief History

Three historically distinct (but often complementary) frameworks that rely on the machine metaphor can be distinguished (see Figure 10.1). One group of models has focused on how the body influences or impacts the mind. In these models, perception of a stimulus causes some change in a bodily state, which is then felt as an emotion. A second approach has focused on the ways in which the mind influences or changes the body. In these models, perception of a stimulus causes some sort of mental state, which in turn causes some bodily change. In fact, the contemporary era of emotion theory began with a debate between William James and Charles Darwin on the causal ordering of the body and the mind in the emergence of an emotional experience. A third approach sees the mind and the body as complementary forces that together generate an emotional response.[1] A common thread running through most

---

[1]  A fourth approach, involving models that deny a role of the mind in constituting emotion (e.g., behaviorist views; LeDoux, 1996; Watson, 1924; Cannon, 1927), where body states and mental representations of emotion are viewed as spuriously related via their shared cause in the brain (see also Bard, 1928; MacLean, 1949, 1993; Panksepp, 1998), and theories that do not give a role to the body in constituting emotion (i.e., some cognitive views; Ortony, Clore, & Collins, 1988; Smith & Ellsworth, 1985) are not included in the present review.

# THE BODY AND MIND IN EMOTION

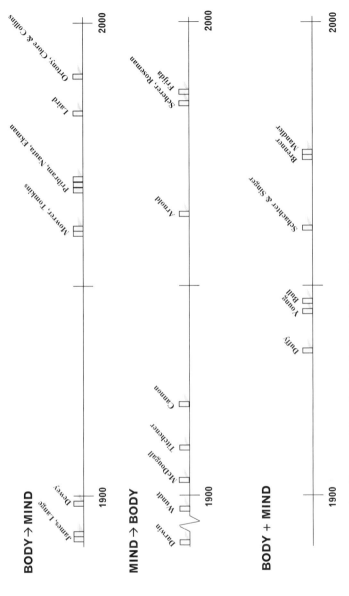

Figure 10.1. A brief history of the role of the body and the mind in emotion.

239

models is the idea that the stimulus situation plays some role in generating an emotional response. In some views, the situation is considered to be the physical elements or objects that trigger a body state (James, 1884, 1894/1994, 1890/1950), whereas in others it is the event that triggers an interpretation (Schachter & Singer, 1962). What these theories have in common is that the situation, like the mind and body, are distinct parts that can be separated from one another in their causal influence without any one losing its character.

To facilitate a discussion of these models, it is necessary to devise a clear and consistent terminology. The term *mental state* is used to stand for the mental representation of a stimulus or stimulus situation that is thought to trigger an emotional response. Several theories assume that some form of mental state sets the stage for other mental or bodily changes that constitute an emotional response. Theories have characterized mental states as "instincts" (e.g., McDougall, 1928), "psychological situations" (e.g., Young, 1943), "attitudes" (e.g., Dewey, 1894), and "motor attitudes" (e.g., Bull, 1945). The phrase *mental representation of emotion* is used to signify a consciously experienced emotion (cf. Barrett et al., 2007). Theories differ greatly in how they describe the mental representation involved in emotion. This mental representation has been characterized as a "state of mind" (Darwin, 1965), a "feeling" (e.g., Bull, 1945), "facial feedback" (Tomkins, 1962, 1963) or simply "an emotion" (e.g., James, 1884). The term *body state* refers to some physical change in the peripheral nervous system or behavior. Theorists have characterized bodily state as "vasomotor changes" (Lange, 1885/1922), "bodily perturbations" (James, 1884), "expressions" (e.g., Darwin, 1965), "organic changes" (e.g., Dewey, 1894), or "energy level" (e.g., Duffy, 1941, 1957). Finally, the term *neural representation* refers to any sort of neural activation that is specified in a theory. For example, a neural representation of a bodily state would involve activations in somatosensory and insular cortices (Craig, 2002, 2003). The neural representations that instantiate emotional responses are often ill-defined in theories of emotion, but most theories assume some sort of neural representation is necessary for an emotional response to occur.

### The Body Influences the Mind in Emotion

The idea that a body state causes a mental representation of emotion played an early, formative role in the history of the emotion theory. The modern version of this idea was first put forth by James (1884, 1890/1950, 1894/1994) and Lange (1885/1922), who famously suggested that experience of emotion results from the normal sensory processing of somatic, visceral, and motor (James) or vascular and motor (Lange) cues from the body that are automatically and reflexively elicited by external stimuli. The James-Lange theory was primarily concerned with explaining mental representations of emotion (e.g., the feeling of being angry). Although James (and by implication, Lange) was criticized for not dealing with emotion states per se (e.g., the state of being angry), it is commonly assumed (beginning with Dewey, 1894) that the emotion state is the change in body state that occurs in response to the stimulus, and that this change is what is perceived as the experience of emotion.

Many early theories of emotion were explicitly designed to reconcile the James-Lange view with the common-sense inspired Darwinian view that mental representations of emotion cause changes in bodily states (e.g., Dewey, 1894; Bull, 1945). One popular attempt can be found in Tomkins' (1962, 1963) theory of emotion. Tomkins scaffolded the James-Lange view (the idea that mental representations of emotion are constituted by efferent feedback from a body state) onto Darwin's idea that there are certain emotional expressions that are preserved by evolution. Replacing Darwin's idea of a "state of mind" with an "affect program," Tompkins argued that these evolutionarily preserved, inborn programs cause a body state (particularly constituted by facial muscle movements), the feedback from which instantiates a mental representation of emotion. This view is largely re-presented in Ekman's (1972) theory of emotion, although Ekman added the idea that human beings (but not other animals) have developed the capacity to modify the link between an affect program and facial muscle movement (i.e., "display rules"). Laird (1984; Duclos, Laird, Schneider, & Sexter, 1989) also fashioned a theory reminiscent of both James' notion that mental representations of emotion stem from sensory information from the body and Tomkin's view that mental representations result from facial muscle feedback. However, Laird added Bem's (1967, 1972) ideas of self-perception, and in doing so seems to interject cognitive processing between body states and mental representations of emotion. Nonetheless, his view is grounded in the idea that facial (Laird, 1984; Duclos et al., 1989) and body (Duclos et al., 1989) muscle movements initiate a mental representation of emotion.

Another example of the Body → Mind approach can be found in Nauta's (1971) idea that efferent information from the body is integrated with sensory processing of the external world to give affective meaning or value to objects in the world. Nauta did not really have a theory of emotion as much as ideas about how the frontal cortex marshals information from the body to guide decision making about objects of value. Nonetheless, his idea is consistent with the notion that the body helps to influence mental representations (what we would now call core affective feelings; Barrett, 2006b) that are constitutive of the mind (see also Mowrer, 1960; Pribram, 1970).

*The Mind Influences the Body in Emotion*

The idea that the mind drives the body has also played a formative role in models of emotion. The majority of theories assume that different states of mind consistently produce different kinds of emotion embodied by distinct, coherent patterns of bodily changes. There is some variability in where the emotional reaction itself is said to be located: In some views, emotion is a mental state causing the body state; in others, emotion is the mental representation that is associated with bodily changes themselves.

One of the earliest modern examples of the Mind → Body approach can be found in Darwin (1859/1965), "The Expression of the Emotions in Man and Animals." Darwin's ideas about emotion were infused with the common-sense belief that certain states of mind seek expression in and therefore automatically cause behaviors. Darwin did not really craft a theory of emotion as much as make an argument for his theory of evolution and against creationism: If we are like other mammalian (particularly nonhuman primate) species with which we share a common ancestral heritage, then we should give evidence of homologous behaviors (like facial expressions) that are derived from a common origin. These behaviors become associated with certain states of mind (emotions) by force of habit. As a result, terror expresses itself as "hurried breathing," a "wildly beating heart," "pale skin," "bristled hair," secretions to kidneys, and "prostration" of the body (p. 77), whereas rage expresses itself as "labored respiration," "flow of nerve-force to the heart," a "reddened or deadly pale face," and "muscular exertion" (p. 74).

Later models built directly on this mind-body causality, and further developed the idea that mental states cause changes in body states. In these models, the mental state is described as a perception or conceptualization of not just an object but an entire stimulus situation. McDougall (1908, 1928) argued that an instinct, defined in mentalistic terms (as a disposition to perceive, attend to, and understand the meaning of particular objects in a particular way), produces a particular body state, which in turn produces a mental representation (feeling), which he identified as the emotion.[2] Wundt et al. (1894; Wundt, 1897) argued that emotions are mental representations (affective feelings) of pleasure/displeasure and arousal (tension-relaxation and excitement-depression) combined with additional ideational content deriving from perceptions of the stimulus situation. Wundt (1897) suggests that emotions can only be differentiated by their respective ideational contents,

---

[2]  In a sense, McDougall's view is similar to James, except that James describes body states as resulting reflexively from the mere identification of a stimulus, whereas McDougall sees them as the result of a more interpretation-infused mental state.

and it is this ideational content that produces changes in body state. The physical concomitants only serve to intensify the emotion (what is felt). Titchener (1921) agreed with Wundt that emotions are mental representations (feelings) deriving from basic affective feelings, but argued that such feelings could only be characterized as pleasant or unpleasant. For Titchener, as for Wundt, changes in body state were constituents of emotion evoked by mental states, but these body states were not in any way causally linked to the core of an emotional response (affective feeling).

Arnold (1960) directly implicated mental states in producing both body states and mental representations of emotion. Upon perceiving a stimulus, a person judges or appraises the personal significance of the object, as well as the object's value (good for me/bad for me) in an automatic, given fashion. The mental state (the appraisal of an object) initiates an "*action tendency that is felt as the emotion*, expressed in various bodily changes, and that eventually may lead to overt action" (p. 177, italics in the original). She also introduced the idea that the physical changes that come with an emotion are themselves sensed and appraised or evaluated as having some meaning for the person (what she called "secondary appraisal," p. 180), and in so doing foreshadowed the idea that there is a transactional relation between mind and body in emotion.

Several modern appraisal views take their lead from Arnold's notion that the mind produces both body states and mental representations that constitute an emotional response. Roseman (1984) and Scherer (1984) are the best examples of these views. Each type of emotion is characterized by a specific body and feeling state that is generated by a pattern of cognitive mechanisms or components (called cognitive appraisals) that make up the meaning of a situation. For example, Scherer (1984) proposed that emotions result most directly from an information processing subsystem (for basic perception and evaluation of the environment), where one of several types of stimulus appraisals – called "stimulus evaluation checks" (SEC)– cause a pattern of activity in other subsystems, such as a support subsystem (that controls neuroendocrine, somatic, and autonomic states), an executive subsystem (that plans and makes decisions), an action subsystem (that regulates neuromuscular states), and a monitoring subsystem (that is a control system that reflects on the states of other subsystems). Distinct pattern of SECs are thought to cause discrete emotions, which can be characterized by distinct body states.

Ortony, Clore, and Collins (1988) outlined an appraisal model based on the assumption that emotions arise from certain types of cognitions or perceptions about the world. Like Roseman and Scherer, their view rests on the idea that if an individual conceptualizes the situation in a particular way, then that person experiences a certain type of emotion. Ortony et al. can be distinguished from Roseman and Scherer in that they do not prescribe particular cognitive processes that produce patterns of situational construal. Theirs is a descriptive model that outlines a set of rules for which emotions are felt when.

Finally, Frijda (1986) suggested that certain situational meanings produce certain emotions in a law-like fashion. Like Arnold, Frijda characterized emotions as states of action tendency or readiness that are motivations to achieve or maintain a particular sort of relationship with the environment rather than a readiness to perform specific behaviors per se. The actual behaviors that are performed to realize any given action tendency will vary on the basis of contextual demands and other constraints. For example, "anger" is the urge to attack, but there are many different ways to implement an attack (one can yell, hit, withdraw, or be exceedingly kind). "Fear" is the urge to separate oneself from an aversive event, but there are many behaviors that can achieve this aim (one can freeze or flee).

### Mind and Body Interact in Emotion

Since the 1930s, many models of emotion have explicitly given a role to both the body and the mind in constituting an emotional response. In such views, the body plus some mental state (most typically, some ideation about the situation) together produce both an emotional state and its mental representation. Many of these theories are striking in how they foreshadow the major tenets of modern appraisal theories of emotion (in assuming the situation has a causal role in generating an emotional response). In some cases, ideational content about the situation is used to interpret the meaning of bodily states (an interactionist view), whereas in others the content merely coincides with the bodily states (an additive view).

Duffy (1934, 1941) may have been the first to put forth an interactionist view when she proposed that a mental representation of emotion emerges from the interaction of a body state and an awareness of the stimulus situation in which that state occurred. She suggested an emotion is a physiological event that is interpreted as having personal significance. The meaning of a stimulus event, expectations about how it might change, and knowledge about what set of responses typically occur in response, all guide the interpretation of felt bodily changes (Duffy, 1941). As a consequence, a mental representation of emotion occurs when basic affective states (pleasure, displeasure, and energy level) are interpreted as discrete emotional states. By introducing the psychological situation in this fashion, Duffy foreshadows the Schachter and Singer (1962) appraisal model of emotion. Young (1943) also foreshadows Schachter and Singer (1962) by suggesting that emotional responses are characterized by changes in body state (widespread visceral changes and behavior) that are interpreted in a "psychological situation" (i.e., a person's understanding of his or her relation to the immediate surroundings). According to Young, a person possesses primitive patterns of physical response (in more recent years called "behavioral stances" or "prepared responses"), but these are recognized as common-sense categories of emotion (e.g., anger, sadness, fear, and so on) only when a particular pattern is experienced in a particular type of psychological situation (e.g., fear exists when escape-related visceral and behavioral changes occur in a danger-related situation, but fear does not exist when the situation is not dangerous). The assumption is that some stimulus (or set of stimuli) triggers the primitive response, but the person must experience this response in the context of a meaningful psychological situation for an emotional event to have occurred.

Bull (1945) also foreshadows modern appraisal theories of emotion, particularly Frijda's (1986) idea that action readiness (a behavioral stance toward the environment) is a critical component in an emotional response. In Bull's view, a stimulus triggers a mental state called a "motor-attitude" which prepares the organism to act in a certain fashion (e.g., prepares the organism to strike in anger). The preparation for action inherent in this motor attitude engenders a feeling (i.e., a mental representation of emotion), which in turn leads to a behavior. Together, the motor attitude (i.e., a mental state), associated feelings (i.e., the mental representation of emotion) and actual bodily changes (i.e., body state), as well as an interpretation of the eliciting stimulus (i.e., ideation regarding a stimulus' meaning), produce an emotion state.

Schachter and Singer's famous (1962) theory of emotion proposes that mental representations of emotion arise from the interaction of cognitive interpretations (ideation) and perceived bodily arousal (bodily representation). An emotional episode occurs when a person attributes the cause of perceived arousal to some stimulus event. Attributing perceived arousal to a cause gives it meaning and transforms it into an intensional state. Mandler (1975) articulated a similar view, suggesting that a mental representation of emotion is an interaction between ideational processes and perceived bodily states. In Mandler's (1975) view, an individual performs a meaning analysis on feelings of arousal. The representation of this meaning analysis in consciousness is the emotion.

Finally, Brenner (1974) also outlined a theory whereby mental representation of emotion results from an interaction of bodily states and ideation. Brenner characterized emotions as complex mental phenomena that result from sensations of pleasure and displeasure and associated ideational content (i.e., beliefs, thoughts, memories). Unlike his predecessors, he specifically defined the physiological substrate of emotion to be feelings of pleasure or displeasure. Because pleasure and displeasure exist on a continuum, mental representations of emotion are really "constellations" of coordinated feelings and ideas. An emotion can be distinguished from another emotion in terms of the intensity of the pleasure or displeasure it involves and the ideas associated with it.

## A MODERN EMBODIMENT VIEW OF BODY AND MIND IN EMOTION

A modern embodiment view of the mind assumes a transactional, recursive relation between the body and the mind and, in so doing, does not rely on the Cartesian reductionism that treats the mind and the body as separable and independent causes of emotion, each with their own unique properties, structure, and function. Put simply: in a modern embodiment view the body helps to constitute the mind. Although the mind-body relationship is presumably recursive, for the purposes of this chapter, we focus on one direction in this dynamic relationship – where the body helps to constitute the mind. Specifically, we examine how the body might help to constitute the conceptual system for emotion, that is, which emotion categories we have concepts for, and how conceptual knowledge is constituted.

Modern embodiment views are based on three grounding assumptions. First, cognitive events derive from the types of experiences that come from having a body with particular sensorimotor capacities. As a result, the body allows the conceptual system to develop in relation to how the world is experienced. This is the idea of embodied realism (Lakoff & Johnson, 1999, p. 44): Concepts are not a mind-free, direct window on the external world because our own bodies, and our experience, have a hand in constructing them. The structure of the conceptual system for emotion would then be grounded in the structure of the physical events associated with emotion.

Second, the body helps to implement the mind in that the conceptual system (for emotion or for any set of categories) relies on sensorimotor simulations. An embodiment view of the mind assumes that knowledge, such as knowledge about categories of emotion like *anger*, *sadness*, and *fear*, is instantiated as modality specific sensorimotor (rather than abstract propositional) representations of prior events (Gallese, 2005), called *perceptual symbols* (Barsalou, 1999). Neurons in different modalities (e.g., vision, audition, interoception, motor behavior) capture different sensory and motor elements of a perceptual event, and neural representations accumulate to produce a "simulator" that serves as a toolbox for creating any future conceptual representation of a category. For example, a simulator for a category of knowledge, like *anger*, will develop as sensory, motor, and somatovisceral features that are integrated across contexts and settings where instances of anger are labeled. Sensory information about the object that is in the focus of attention (e.g., visual information about an interaction partner, auditory information about his or her voice), somatovisceral information about the emoter's internal state, motor programs for regulating the partner's and the emoter's own behavior, as well as the label "anger," and so on, would bind together (via conjunctive neurons; Simmons & Barsalou, 2003) to form an instance of *anger*. As instances of *anger* accumulate, and information is integrated across instances, a simulator for *anger* develops and conceptual knowledge about *anger* accrues. The resulting conceptual system is a distributed collection of modality-specific memories captured across all instances of a category. These establish the conceptual content for the basic-level category *anger*, and can be retrieved for later simulations of *anger*.

Not only does the body help to constitute the mind but so does the situation (for a review, see Robbins & Aydede, in press). In fact, an embodiment view of the mind assumes that cognition is situated. Perceptions of occurrences both inside and outside the body are captured by simulators and are seamlessly bound, so that perceptual symbols are situation-specific inferences for behavior that are tailored to a given situation. Context is particularly important in representing exemplars of abstract concepts (Barsalou & Weimer-Hastings, 2005) such as *anger, sadness, fear*, and so on. As a result, perceiving the situation in a particular way helps to constitute, not cause, a conceptualization of emotion.

## THE CONCEPTUAL SYSTEM FOR EMOTION

If the body and the situation help to constitute the mind, then the structure and content of the conceptual system for emotion should be grounded in the structure and content of emotional events as they naturally occur. A brief look at the scientific evidence on the structure and content of emotional responding provides a clear, but perhaps non-intuitive, set of hypotheses about the structure and content of the conceptual system for emotion.

The majority of the theories described previously, several of which serve as the most influential scientific models in the study of emotion, assume that emotions are biological categories imposed by nature, so that emotion categories are recognized, rather than constructed, by the human mind. This assumption is represented in the hypothesis that *anger*, *sadness*, and *fear*, as well as several other emotion words, reflect "natural kinds" of emotion that have distinctively coherent and consistent clusters of measurable properties, such as facial movements, autonomic activity, instrumental behavior, and so on (see Barrett, 2006a). Any two emotions (e.g., *anger* and *fear*) may have some overlap in one output or another (e.g., increased heart rate) but the patterns of outputs are presumed to be distinctive. Instances of *anger* must be sufficiently similar to one another in their profile of correlated properties, but sufficiently different from instances of *fear* so that people can clearly distinguish between the two, thereby "cutting nature at its joints." In this view, people would acquire simulators for *anger*, *sadness*, *fear*, and so on, that preserve the real, biological distinctiveness for these emotional responses. There are several recent embodiment models of emotion that rely explicitly on this assumption of distinctiveness (e.g., Damasio, Grabowski, Bechara, Damasio, Ponto, Parvizi, & Hichwa, 2000; Prinz, 2004).

A series of reviews spanning the course of the psychological literature call into question the idea that each emotion (e.g., fear) is a biologically distinct entity that can be distinguished from other emotions (e.g., happiness, sadness, etc) in some real and biologically observable way (Barrett, 2006a; Duffy, 1934, 1941; Hunt, 1941; Mandler, 1975; Ortony & Turner, 1990; Russell, 2003). In every domain of emotion research, studies finding biological distinctiveness between different emotions can be set against a larger backdrop of findings that fail to find it (for a review and discussion, see Barrett, 2006a). Mammals do many things in instances that are called "fear" – they freeze, they withdraw, they approach, they attack. What they do depends largely on the situation. Fear can occur in many different situations populated by many different objects. As a result, fear has yet to clearly and consistently reveal itself in the data on feelings, facial and vocal behaviors, peripheral nervous system responses, instrumental behaviors, and even neural correlates. The same can be said for instances called "anger" and "sadness," and for instances of other emotion categories that are typically considered to be biologically basic.

The implication of such findings is clear: the actual events that we call "fear" are really a heterogeneous set of instances that, thus far, seem not have a single, biological core that distinguishes them from instances of, say, "anger." Each instance called "fear" can vary in the physiological changes that occur, in facial and instrumental behaviors, in the objects that the response is attributed to, and so on. Such heterogeneity is very consistent with ideas originally proposed by William James, who argued that instances within each emotion category vary considerably, both across people and within a single person over time. According to James, there are variable sets of bodily symptoms associated with a single category of emotion, making each a distinct feeling state and therefore a distinct emotion. By the term *emotion*, James was referring to particular instances of feeling, not to discrete emotion categories. Different instances of an emotion, even if within the same category, will feel different if the somatovisceral activations are different. These observations suggest the hypothesis that the conceptual system for fear, or for any emotion category, will reflect this heterogeneity.

Amidst the variability in instances both within and across emotion categories, there exists elemental or core features of all emotional responses. Literally hundreds of studies point to *affect* as a fundamental element that occurs in every emotional response, be it experienced or observed. This is consistent with Wundt's idea, also present in interactionist theories, that emotions can be decomposed into more fundamental, psychologically basic elements (albeit, perhaps not in a linear fashion). Observations of subjective reports of emotion experience (e.g., Barrett, 2004; Barrett & Russell, 1999; Russell & Barrett, 1999), peripheral nervous system activation (Bradley & Lang, 2000; Cacioppo et al., 1997, 2000), facial muscle movements (Cacioppo et al., 1997, 2000; Messinger, 2002), vocal cues (Bachorowski, 1999) expressive behavior (Cacioppo & Gardner, 1999), and neural activations (Wager, Phan, Liberzon, & Taylor, 2003) are consistent in giving evidence of a general affect system (for a review, see Barrett, 2006b; Russell, 2003). Perceptions of other people's emotional states also contain inferences about affect (Russell, Bachorowksi, Fernandez-Dols, & 2003).

There are debates over the most scientifically viable way to represent this affective system (Cacioppo & Gardner, 1999; Russell & Barrett, 1999; Watson et al., 1999), but one candidate is a recently defined affective substrate called *core affect* (Barrett, 2006b, 2006c; Russell, 2003; Russell & Barrett, 1999). Core affect can be characterized as a neurophysiological state with the properties of pleasure/displeasure and activation/deactivation.[3] The fact that core affective

---

[3]  The term *core* signifies a form of affective responding that functions as a type of core knowledge (Spelke, 2000) about one's relation to the world that is supported by hardwiring that is present at birth (Bridges, 1932; Emde, Gaensbauer, & Harmon, 1976; Spitz, 1965; Sroufe, 1979), homologous in other mammalian species (Cardinal, Parkinson, Hall, & Everitt, 2002; Schneirla, 1959), and available to consciousness, where it is experienced as feeling good or bad (valence) and, to a lesser extent, as feeling activated or deactivated (arousal; for a review, see Russell & Barrett, 1999). The capacity to experience pleasure and displeasure is universal to all humans (Mesquita,

changes occur in all instances of emotion suggests that representations of pleasure and displeasure should be a fundamental feature in the conceptual system for emotion.

However, core affect does not give a sufficient account of the instances that we call "anger," "sadness," and "fear." As the brief historical analysis shows us, emotions are intensional states, meaning that they are about something in particular. People become angry *with* someone, afraid *of* something, sad *about* something. Core affective states become intensional, or about something, when they are linked to the perception and interpretation of an object (be it an event, a situation, or a person). Just as people interpret or imbue behavioral actions with "aboutness" by parsing them into discrete behavioral acts (Gilbert, 1998), so do they imbue core affect with intension or emotional "aboutness" when parsing it into discrete emotions (Barrett, 2006b). This observation suggests that object representations would also be a core feature of the conceptual system for emotion.

## Hypotheses Regarding the Conceptual System for Emotion

When viewed in light of an embodiment view of the mind, research on emotion suggests a distributed, flexible conceptual system for emotion that contains several distinctive properties.

### Core Affect

Situated conceptualizations of any emotion category will contain some neural representation of pleasure or displeasure and activation or deactivation. Because both core affect and conceptual representations share a representational format, they could be seamlessly integrated during an instance of perception. This may be especially true because emotion categories are abstract, and introspective state information is particularly important to abstract concepts (Barsalou & Wiemer-Hastings, 2005). The implication then is that conceptualizations of emotion should evoke the same neural circuitry as that involved with establishing an affective state and therefore have the potential to change a person's affective state.

A distributed set of functional circuits in the ventral portion of the human brain are thought to be involved with establishing a person's core affective

2003; Russell, 1983; Scherer, 1997). Core affect functions as a neurophysiological barometer of the individual's relation to an environment at a given point in time, with self-reported feelings as the barometer readings (Nauta, 1971), It may also form the core of experience more generally by selecting the contents of consciousness at any given point in time (for discussions, see Barrett, et al, 2007; Duncan & Barrett, 2007; Edelman & Tononi, 2000).

state (Barrett et al., 2007). One functional circuit, involving the basolateral (BL) complex of the amygdala, the central and lateral aspects of orbitofrontal cortex (OFC), and the anterior insula, establishes the sensory-based aspects of core affect. A second circuit, involving reciprocal connections between the ventromedial prefrontal cortex (VMPFC) (including the closely related subgenual anterior cingulate cortex, or ACC) and the central nucleus of the amygdala guides visceromotor control (i.e., autonomic, chemical, and behavioral). By virtue of a series of cascading routes, this ventral circuitry projects directly and indirectly (via ventral striatum) to hypothalamus and brainstem areas to quickly and efficiently influence the autonomic, chemical, and behavioral states in the body. Together, the resulting perturbations of the organism's somatovisceral state (or internal milieu) are integrated with information about the external world into an internal affective code or representation. These representations make up a person's core affective reaction to an object or stimulus, influencing a person's core affective state to resemble that which has resulted from prior experiences with the object and directing the body to prepare for some behavioral response toward that object. This view has elements in common with the somatic marker hypothesis (e.g., Bechara et al., 2000), with the view that the sensorimotor system is involved with emotion perception in others (Adolphs, 2002, 2003), and with recent findings that both producing facial depictions of emotion and watching them in others activates the amygdala, insula, and aspects of ventral premotor cortex (Carr et al., 2003).

### Object Representations

At its core, every situated conceptualization of emotion will also contain a representation of an object (what the emotion is perceived to be about). The ventral circuitry involved with establishing a core affective state not only musters attention toward an object (via the brainstem and basal forebrain; Mesulam 2000; Parvizi & Damasio, 2001) but also enhances visual processing of the object (Amaral et al., 2003; Freese & Amaral, 2005). Via re-entrant processing (Edelman & Tononi, 2000), the sensory features associated with an object, along with the associated affective state and motor consequences, will be perceptually bound together in a conceptualization of emotion. The implication is that perception of an object is instantiated, in part, by establishing an affective and behavioral stance toward the object.

In addition, object perception may be one way to prime emotion category knowledge in a bottom-up fashion (such that a simulation for the category will be launched). This hypothesis is consistent with the view that simulations can be embedded in one another (Barsalou et al., 2003) so that object representations (that is, simulations of physical objects) very likely contain inferences about the mental states likely to arise in conjunction with the object (Barsalou, 2003).

### Representations of Context

Situated conceptualizations will contain a representation of the psychological situation. Category instances are never represented in isolation. Tight couplings between object representations and situations have been observed (Yeh & Barsalou, 2006), and contextual information is even more important in simulating representations for abstract concepts (Barsalou & Wiemer-Hastings, 2005), like emotion concepts. Information about the relational context (Lazarus, 1991) or a situation's meaning to a person at a particular point in time (Clore & Ortony, 2000) may constitute some of the background information contained in situated conceptualizations of an emotion category that, like objects, may serve to launch a simulation. As a result, the psychological situation does not cause an emotion to be conceptualized – rather, it helps to constitute that conceptualization.

### Inferences about Behavior

Situated conceptualizations will also contain inferences about situated action (i.e., the actions that are needed in a given situation), making it possible, even likely, that conceptual knowledge about emotion can direct behavioral responses. Barsalou (2003) argues that "simulating is for doing," where "doing" might involve acting on the perceived cause of the emotion, or acting on your own body to manage your internal states and subsequent behaviors. For example, people may have learned that there are a host of different actions that have been associated with the category *anger*. Sometimes it works to yell, sometimes to pound a fist, sometimes to cry or walk away, sometimes to hit. Situated conceptualizations may be thought of as an inference about what will make for successful self-regulation or goal achievement. This is generally consistent with several existing ideas about emotion, including the idea that conceptual knowledge about emotion contains information about appropriate or effective forms of emotion regulation (Barrett & Gross, 2001), as well as the idea that emotions are functional for social behavior (Frijda, 1986; Keltner & Haidt, 1999).

### Emotion Words

Language most likely drives the acquisition of conceptual knowledge about emotion, and may therefore be a crucial element in any conceptualization of emotion. It is possible that people learn to represent emotion in the way that they learn about other abstract concepts for which there are no biological bases. Children acquire emotion categories that conform to their culture, not because there is some natural, biological reality to *anger* (or *fear*, or *sadness*) but because this level of categorization is socially functional. People may integrate in long-term memory two representations from the same emotion category, even when their surface similarities differ (see Barsalou, Simmons, Barbey & Wilson, 2003) because the label for the emotion links them in memory (see Gelman & Markman, 1987). The emotion words for *anger* (e.g., "angry," "hostile," "irritated," and so on) serve as the glue that integrates a variety of different sensorimotor states into one simulator for *anger*. This generative feature of situated conceptualizations may help to explain why people perceive prototypical emotion episodes even though they seem impossible to capture with the use of scientific instruments.

### Heterogeneity

Finally, situated conceptualizations for any emotion category, such as *anger*, will be heterogeneous, such that packets of conceptual knowledge will vary within a person over instances, as context and situated action demand. No single situated conceptualization for *anger* need give a complete account of the category *anger*. There is not one script for *anger*, but many. On any given occasion, the content of a situated conceptualization for *anger* will be constructed to contain mainly those properties of *anger* that are contextually relevant, and it therefore contains only a small subset of the knowledge available in long-term memory about the category *anger*. Heterogeneity in the perceptual symbols that issue from any emotion simulator will be further enhanced by the production of novel simulations, that is, representations of things that have never been encountered together (Barsalou, 2003). This is similar to what James (1884) originally proposed.

Heterogeneity in the conceptual system for emotion may explain why consistency and coherence is so difficult to find in actual instances of emotion. In the form of a perceptual symbol or simulation, the mind very likely helps to instantiate bodily responses. Once a simulator for an emotion category, such as *anger*, is established, it is available to re-enact subsets of its content when the conceptualization of anger is needed. All the experienced content for *anger* resides within the simulator for *anger*, so that different combinations can be simulated in a way that is tailored to the specific situation. The *anger* simulator might simulate a conceptualization of yelling on one occasion, running on another, and crying on yet another. In so doing, the conceptual system for cmotion (as an aspect of the mind) will yield a partial reenactment of sensorimotor events associated with some prior episode (or episodes) of anger, thereby changing the person's body state. In this account, observed heterogeneity in *anger* responses (or instances of any emotion category) may be a feature of the system, rather than a consequence of imprecise experimental methods or crude measurement tools.

## A CHANGE IN SCIENTIFIC PARADIGM FOR THE STUDY OF EMOTION

Much of scientific thinking in the 19th and 20th centuries was grounded in Descartes' machine metaphor. The computer analogy that launched the great cognitive revolution within psychology in the middle of the 20th century derived much of its explanatory power from the machine metaphor with great effect, but perhaps also with unfortunate constraints. Embodiment views of the mind relax some of these constraints, allowing us to question whether it is scientifically viable to reify boundaries between the mind and the body, and between what goes on inside a person's skull and what goes on outside. Furthermore, these views intrinsically question the notion that discrete emotions are preformed, stereotyped responses that are triggered within the individual and recognized from without. They allow for the possibility that emotion categories are constructed, not recognized, by the human mind, and that each conceptualization of emotion emerges from an intrinsic interplay between mind, body, and situation. Whether experienced in oneself or perceived in others, emotions may be conceptual acts, so that understanding the structure, content, and function of the conceptual system for emotion is central to understanding what emotions are and how they work.

Despite their Cartesian overtones, several older models of emotion, especially those published in the 1930s, 1940s, and 1950s (rarely cited anymore), contain insights that can be harvested to support such a view (e.g., Duffy, Young, Brenner). One insight is that any instance of emotion can be decomposed into more basic psychological elements (although the elements probably have a dynamic, interdependent relationship as opposed to a linear one). Like Wundt, many of these theorists specified affect (what some would now call "core affect") as one such component. A second insight is that ideational content proceeds in concert with the body, and may be what distinguishes an instance of one emotion category from an instance of another. Unlike these models (as well as the appraisal models they spawned), our suggestion is that ideational states help constitute, not cause, an emotional event, and that conventional notions of linear cause and effect are not useful for understanding emotion.

The view that we have outlined here, termed the *conceptual-act model*, is that discrete emotions are perceptual events that emerge in consciousness when core affect is conceptualized as an instance of (what English speakers call) fear, anger, sadness, etc. (Barrett, 2006b; Barrett, Lindquist, Bliss-Moreau, Duncan et al, 2007). Specifically, the experience of feeling an emotion, or the experience of seeing emotion in another person, occurs when conceptual knowledge about emotion is brought to bear to conceptualize a person's ongoing, momentary state of core affect. The conceptual knowledge that is called forth to conceptualize affect is thought to be tailored to the immediate situation, represented in sensorimotor terms, acquired from prior experience and supported by language. Conceptualizing the flux and flow of core affect as a discrete experience of emotion corresponds to the colloquial idea of "having an emotion."

Bodily states (as experienced in oneself or observed in others) and representations of psychological situations are very likely perceptually categorized and experienced as a single unified percept, much like color, depth, and shape are experienced together in object perception. In essence, a conceptualization of emotion may be an example of what Edelman (1989) calls "the remembered present." In this view, memory is not a neural representation that is stored someplace; it is the re-instantiation of a neural representation that has occurred in the past, so as to allow some replication of behavior or experience. Situated conceptualizations derive from a highly diversified and flexible conceptual system so that any instance of conceptualizing an emotion such as *anger* will entail a highly flexible package of conceptual knowledge that is tailored to the needs of the person in a given situation and is designed for action (Barsalou, Niedenthal et al., 2003; Niedenthal et al., 2005). It is the content of these acts of conceptualization that allow one to see anger or fear in another person, or that make one feeling of anger distinct from another feeling of anger, or different from any feeling of fear.

Together, core affect and conceptual knowledge about emotion constitute a highly flexible system that can account for the full richness and range of experience that makes up human emotional life. The ability to categorize confers some adaptive advantage, and so is likely evolutionarily preserved even if the specific categories are not. Many cultures have similar basic-level emotion concepts (such as anger, sadness, fear, and so on in Western culture), not because these categories have some biological priority but because these concepts are optimal tools for communicating in the type of social environment that humans typically occupy (living in large groups with complicated relational rules).

This view – that an experience of emotion is a state of mind whose content is at once affective and conceptual – is consistent with recent theoretical insights in the neurobiology of consciousness. There is a growing consensus that a conscious experience (e.g., seeing another person as angry, or feeling angry yourself) emerges when a selection of neuronal groups, coding for specific perceptual properties, fire together to form a temporary coalition or assembly of synchronous ("re-entrant") neural activity (Crick & Koch, 2004; Dehaene & Changeux, 2004; Edelman & Tononi, 2000; Engel & Singer, 2001; Llinas et al., 1998). Reverberating, globally coordinated neural activity of sufficient intensity and duration allows different sensorial features such as color, shape, sound, smell, interoceptive cues, and, as we now suggest, core affect, as well as other cognitive contents like beliefs or memories, to bind together into a single experience (but for a dissenting view, see Dennett, 1991; Zeki, 2003).

Neurobiological models of consciousness also imply that incoming sensory information (such as that which entails a core affective state) modulates a preexisting conscious field rather than generating it anew (Llinas et al., 1998). This stream of core affect can be a background or central feature (ground or figure) of consciousness, depending on where attention is applied. When people focus on some object or situation, they form a mental representation of something in the outside world. In such cases, core affect may be experienced as a property of the object (rather than as one's reaction to it), but presumably with the potential to influence behavior implicitly (Berridge & Winkielman, 2003; Winkielman et al., 2005). When core affect is foregrounded, pleasure or displeasure and sensory information from the world are bound in a meaningful way, yielding a mental representation of emotion. This mental event stands for a person's inference about how psychologically meaningful events in the world are causally linked to perceptions of affective feeling. Thus, we suggest that coordinated re-entrant neural activity of sufficient intensity and duration produces a unified conscious content, one type of which is the experience of seeing an emotion in another person, or "having" an emotion yourself.

Finally, an embodiment view not only questions the distinctions between body, mind, and situation, but between cognition and emotion more broadly. Although scientists are very used to thinking about cognitive events (such as thoughts, memories, and beliefs) as separate from emotional events, this distinction is probably phenomenological rather than causal, and may not be respected by the brain (for a discussion see Duncan & Barrett, 2007a;

Duncan & Barrett, 2007b). No one would ever mistake seeing for hearing (although one sensory representation might trigger another), but the same cannot be said for feeling and thinking, or even feeling and seeing.

## References

Adolphs, R. (2002). Neural systems for recognizing emotion. *Current Opinion in Neurobiology, 12,* 169–177.

Adolphs, R. (2003). Cognitive neuroscience of human social behavior. *Nature Reviews Neuroscience, 4,* 165–178.

Amaral, D. G., Capitanio, J. P., Jourdain, M., Mason, W. A., Mendoza, S. P., & Prather, M. (2003). The amygdala: Is it an essential component of the neural network for social cognition? *Neuropsychologia, 41,* 235–240.

Arnold, M. (1960). *Emotion and personality* (2 vols). New York: Columbia University Press.

Bachorowski, J. (1999). Vocal expression and perception of emotion. *Current Directions in Psychological Science, 8,* 53–56.

Bard, P. (1928). A diencephalic mechanism for the expression of rage with special reference to the sympathetic nervous system. *American Journal of Physiology, 84,* 490–515.

Barrett, L. F. (2004). Feelings or words? Understanding the content in self-report ratings of experienced emotion. *Journal of Personality & Social Psychology, 87,* 266–281.

Barrett, L. F. (2006a). Emotions as natural kinds? *Perspectives on Psychological Science, 1,* 28–58.

Barrett, L. F. (2006b). Solving the emotion paradox: Categorization and the experience of emotion. *Personality and Social Psychology Review, 10,* 20–46.

Barrett, L. F. (2006c). Valence as a basic building block of emotional life. *Journal of Research in Personality, 40,* 35–55.

Barrett, L. F., & Gross, J. J. (2001). Emotional intelligence: A process model of emotion representation and regulation. In T. J. Mayne & G. A. Bonanno (Eds.), *Emotions: Current issues and future directions* (pp. 286–310). New York: Guilford.

Barrett, L. F., Lindquist, K. A., Bliss-Moreau, E., Duncan, S., Gendron, M., Mize, J. & Brennan, L. (2007). Of mice and men: Natural kinds of emotion in the mammalian brain? *Perspectives on Psychological Science, 2,* 297–312.

Barrett, L. F., Mesquita, B., Ochsner, K. N., & Gross, J. J. (2007). The experience of emotion. *Annual Review of Psychology, 58,* 373–403.

Barrett, L. F., & Russell, J. A. (1999). The structure of current affect: Controversies and emerging consensus. *Current Directions in Psychological Science, 8,* 10–14.

Barsalou, L. W. (1999). Perceptual symbol systems. *Behavioral and Brain Sciences, 22,* 577–660.

Barsalou, L. W. (2003). Situated simulation in the human conceptual system. *Language and Cognitive Processes, 18,* 513–562. [Reprinted in H. Moss & J. Hampton, *Conceptual representation* (pp. 513–566). East Sussex, UK: Psychology Press].

Barsalou, L. W., Niedenthal, P. M., Barbey, A., & Ruppert, J. (2003). Social embodiment. In B. Ross (Ed.), *The psychology of learning and motivation* (pp. 43–92). San Diego, CA: Academic Press.

Barsalou, L. W., Simmons, W. K., Barbey, A. K., & Wilson, C. D. (2003). Grounding conceptual knowledge in modality-specific systems. *Trends in Cognitive Sciences, 7*, 84–91.

Barsalou, L. W., & Wiemer-Hastings, K. (2005). Situating abstract concepts. In D. Pecher & R. Zwaan (Eds.), *Grounding cognition: The role of perception and action in memory, language, and thought* (pp. 129–163). New York: Cambridge University Press.

Bechara, A., Damasio, H., & Damasio, A. R. (2000). Emotion, decision making and the orbitofrontal cortex. *Celebral Cortex, 10*(3), 295–307.

Bem, D. J. (1967). Self-perception: An alternative interpretation of cognitive dissonance phenomena. *Psychological Review, 74*, 183–200.

Bem, D. J. (1972). Constructing cross-situational consistencies in behavior: Some thoughts on Alker's critique of Mischel. *Journal of Personality, 40*, 17–26.

Berridge, K. C., & Winkielman, P. (2003). What is an unconscious emotion? (The case for unconscious "liking"). *Cognition & Emotion, 17*, 181–211.

Bloom, P. (2004). *Descartes' baby: How the science of child development explains what makes us human.* New York: Basic Books.

Bradley, M. M., & Lang, P. J. (2000). Measuring emotion: Behavior, feeling, and physiology. In R. D. L. L. Nadel (Ed.), *Cognitive neuroscience of emotion.* (pp. 242–276). New York: Oxford University Press.

Brenner, C. (1974). On the nature and development of affects: A unified theory. *Psychoanalytic Quarterly, 43*, 532–556.

Bridges, K. M. B. (1932). Emotional development in early infancy. *Child Development, 3*, 324–341.

Bull, N. (1945). Towards a clarification of the concept of emotion. *Psychosomatic Medicine, 7*, 210–214.

Cacioppo, J. T., & Gardner, W. L. (1999). Emotion. *Annual Review of Psychology, 50*, 191–214.

Cacioppo, J. T., Berntson, G. G., Klein, D. J., & Poehlmann, K. M. (1997). The psychophysiology of emotion across the lifespan. *Annual Review of Gerontology and Geriatrics, 17*, 27–74.

Cacioppo, J. T., Berntson, G. G., Larsen, J. T., Poehlmann, K. M., & Ito, T. A. (2000). The psychophysiology of emotion. In R. Lewis & J. M. Haviland-Jones (Eds.), *The handbook of emotion* (pp. 173–191). New York: Guilford.

Cannon, W. B. (1927). The James-Lange theory of emotions: A critical examination and an alternative theory. *American Journal of Psychology, 39*, 106–124.

Cardinal, R. N., Parkinson, J. A., Hall, J., & Everitt, B. J. (2002) Emotion and motivation: The role of the amygdala, ventral striatum, and prefrontal cortex. *Neuroscience and Biobehavioral Reviews, 26*, 321–352.

Carr, L., Iacoboni, M., Dubeau, M. C., Mazziotaa, J. C., & Lenzi, G. L. (2003). Neural mechanisms of empathy in humans: A relay from neural systems for imitation to limbic areas. *Proceedings of the National Academy of Sciences, 100*, 5497–5502.

Clore, G. L., & Ortony, A. (2000). Cognition in emotion: Always, sometimes, or never? In R. D., Lane & N. Lynn (Eds.), *Cognitive neuroscience of emotion* (pp. 24–61). London: London University Press.

Craig, A. D. (2002). How do you feel? Interoception: The sense of the physiological condition of the body. *Nature Neuroscience, 3*, 655–666.

Craig, A. D. (2003). Interoception: the sense of the physiological condition of the body. *Current Opinion in Neurobiology, 13*, 500–505.

Crick, F. C., & Koch, C. (2004). A framework for consciousness. In M. S. Gazzaniga (Ed.), *The cognitive neurosciences* (pp. 1133–1144). Cambridge, MA: MIT Press.

Damasio, A. R., Grabowski, T. J., Bechara, A., Damasio, H., Ponto, L. L. B., Parvizi, J., & Hichwa, R. D. (2000). Subcortical and cortical brain activity during the feeling of self-generated emotions. *Nature Neuroscience, 3*, 1049–1056.

Darwin, C. (1965). *The expression of the emotions in man and animals.* Chicago: University of Chicago Press. (Original work published 1859).

Dewey, J. (1894). The theory of emotion. I. Emotional attitudes. *Psychological Review, 1*, 553–569.

Dehaene, S., & Changeux, J. P. (2004). Neural mechanisms for access to consciousness. In M. S. Gazzaniga (Ed.), *The cognitive neurosciences* (pp. 1145–1158). Cambridge, MA: MIT Press.

Dennett, D. C. (1991). *Consciousness explained.* Boston: Little, Brown.

Duclos, S. E., Laird, J. D., Schneider, E., Sexter, M., Stern, L., & Van Lighten, O. (1989). Emotion-specific effects of facial expressions and postures on emotional experience. *Journal of Personality and Social Psychology, 57*, 100–108.

Duffy, E. (1934). Is emotion a mere term of convenience? *Psychological Review, 41*, 103–104.

Duffy, E. (1957). The psychological significance of the concept of "arousal" or activation. *Psychological Review, 64*, 265.

Duffy, W. (1941). An explanation of "emotional" phenomena without the use of the concept "emotion." *Journal of General Psychology, 25*, 283–293.

Duncan, S., & Barrett, L. F. (2007a). Affect as a form of cognition: A neurobiological analysis. *Cognition and Emotion, 21*, 1184–1211.

Duncan, S. L. & Barrett, L. F. (2007b). The amygdala in visual awareness. *Trends in Cognitive Sciences, 11*, 190–192.

Edelman, G. M. (1989). *The remembered present.* New York: Basic.

Edelman, G. M., & Tononi, G. (2000). *A universe of consciousness.* New York: Basic.

Ekman, P. (1972). Universals and cultural differences in facial expressions of emotion. In J. R. Cole (Ed.), *Nebraska Symposium on Motivation*, Vol. 19 (pp. 207–283). Lincoln, NE: University of Nebraska Press.

Emde, R. N., Gaensbauer, T. J., & Harmon R. J. (1976). Emotional expression in infancy: A biobehavioral study. *Psychology Issues, 10*, 1–200.

Engel, A. K., & Singer, W. (2001). Temporal binding and the neural correlates of sensory awareness. *Trends in Cognitive Sciences, 5*, 16–25.

Freese, J. L., & Amaral, D. G. (2005). The organization of projections from the amygdala to visual cortical areas TE and V1 in the Macaque monkey. *Journal of Comparative Neurology, 486*, 295–317.

Frijda, N. H. (1986). *The emotions.* Cambridge, UK: Cambridge University Press.

Gallese, V. (2005). Embodied simulation: From neurons to phenomenal experience. *Phenomenology and the Cognitive Sciences, 4*, 23–48.

Gelman, S. A., & Markman, E. M. (1987). Young children's inductions from natural kinds: The role of categories and appearances. *Child Development, 58*, 1532–1541.

Gilbert, D. T. (1998). Ordinary personology. In D. T. Gilbert & S. T. Fiske (Eds.), *The Handbook of Social Psychology*, Vol. 2, 4th ed. (pp. 89–150). New York: McGraw-Hill.

Hunt, W. A. (1941). Recent developments in the field of emotion. *Psychological Bulletin, 38*, 249–276.

James, W. (1884). What is an emotion? *Mind, 9*, 188–205.

James, W. (1950). The emotions. In *The principles of psychology*, Vol. II (pp. 442–485). New York: Dover. (Original work published 1890).

James, W. (1994). The physical basis of emotion. *Psychological Review, 101*, 205–210. (Original work published 1894).

Keltner, D., & Haidt, J. (1999). Social functions of emotion at four levels of analysis. *Cognition and Emotion, 13*, 505–522.

Laird, J. D. (1984). The real role of facial response in the experience of emotion: A reply to Tourangeau and Ellsworth, and others. *Journal of Personality and Social Psychology, 47*, 909–917.

Lakoff, G., & Johnson, M. (1999). *Philosophy in the flesh: the embodied mind and its challenge to Western thought.* New York: Basic Books.

Lange, C. (1922). The emotions. In K. Dunlap (Ed.), *The emotions.* Baltimore: Williams & Wilkins. (Original work published 1885).

Lazarus, R. S. (1991). Relational meaning and discrete emotions. In K. R. Scherer, A. Schorr, & T. Johnstone (Eds.), *Appraisal Processes in Emotion* (pp. 37–67). New York: Oxford University Press.

LeDoux, J. E. (1996). *The emotional brain: The mysterious underpinnings of emotional life.* New York: Simon & Schuster.

Llinas, R., Ribary, U., Contreras, D., & Pedroarena, C. (1998). The neuronal basis for consciousness. *Philosophical Transactions of the Royal Society of London B, Biological Sciences, 353*, 1841–1849.

MacLean, P. D. (1949). Psychosomatic disease and the "visceral brain"; recent developments bearing on the Papez theory of emotion. *Psychosomatic Medicine, 11*, 338–353.

MacLean, P. D. (1993). Cerebral evolution of emotion. In M. Lewis & J. M. Haviland (Eds.), *The Handbook of Emotion* (pp. 67–86). New York: Guildford.

Mandler, G. (1975). *Mind and emotion.* New York: John Wiley & Sons.

McDougall, W. (1908). *An introduction to social psychology.* New York: Methuen.

McDougall, W. (1928). Emotion and feeling distinguished. *Feelings and emotions: The Wittenberg symposium* (pp. 200–205). Worcester, MA: Clark University Press.

Mesquita, B. (2003). Emotions as dynamic cultural phenomena. In H. G. R. Davidson, & K. Scherer (Ed.), *Handbook of the affective sciences* (pp. 871–890). New York: Oxford.

Messinger, D. S. (2002). Positive and negative: Infant facial expressions and emotions. *Current Directions in Psychological Science, 11*, 1–6.

Mesulam, M. M. (2000). *Principles of behavioral and cognitive neurology.* New York: Oxford University Press.

Mowrer, O. H. (1960). *Learning theory and behaviour.* New York: Wiley.

Nauta, W. J. H. (1971). The problem of the frontal lobe: A reinterpretation. *Journal of Psychiatric Research, 8*, 167–187.

Niedenthal, P. M., Barsalou, L. W., Winkielman, P., Krauth-Gruber, S., & Ric, F. (2005). Embodiment in attitudes, social perception, and emotion. *Personality and Social Psychology Review, 9*, 184–211.

Ortony, A., Clore, G. L., & Collins, A. (1988). *The cognitive structure of emotions.* New York: Cambridge University.

Ortony, A., & Turner, T. J. (1990). What's basic about basic emotions? *Psychological Review, 97,* 315–331.

Panksepp, J. (1998). *Affective neuroscience: The foundations of human and animal emotions.* Oxford: Oxford University Press.

Parvizi, J., & Damasio, A. (2001). Consciousness and the brainstem. *Cognition, 79,* 135–159.

Pribram, K. H. (1970). Feelings as monitors: The Loyola symposium. In M. B. Arnold (Ed.), *Feeling and emotions* (pp. 41–53). New York: Academic Press.

Prinz, J. (2004). Embodied emotions. In R. C. Solomon (Ed.), *Thinking about feeling: Contemporary philosophers on the emotions* (pp. 44–59). New York: Oxford University Press.

Robbins, P., & Aydede, M. (Eds.) (in press). *Cambridge handbook of situated cognition.* Cambridge, UK: Cambridge University Press.

Roseman, I. J. (1984). Cognitive determinants of emotion: A structural theory. *Review of Personality & Social Psychology, 5,* 11–36.

Russell, J. A. (1983). Pancultural aspects of human conceptual organization of emotions. *Journal of Personality and Social Psychology, 45,* 1281–1288.

Russell, J. A. (2003). Core affect and the psychological construction of emotion. *Psychological Review, 110,* 145–172.

Russell, J. A., Bachorowski, J., & Fernandez-Dols, J. (2003). Facial and vocal expressions of emotion. *Annual Review of Psychology, 54,* 329–349.

Russell, J. A., & Barrett, L. F. (1999). Core affect, prototypical emotional episodes, and other things called emotion: Dissecting the elephant. *Journal of Personality and Social Psychology, 76,* 805–819.

Schachter, S., & Singer, J. E. (1962). Cognitive, social, and physiological determinants of emotional state. *Psychological Review, 69,* 379–399.

Scherer, K. R. (1997). Profiles of emotion-antecedent appraisal: Testing theoretical predictions across cultures. *Cognition & Emotion, 11,* 113–150.

Scherer, K. R. (1984). On the nature and function of emotion: A component process approach. In K. R. Scherer & P. Ekman (Eds.), *Approaches to emotion* (pp. 293–317). Hillsdale, NJ: Erlbaum.

Schneirla, T. C. (1959). An evolutionary and developmental theory of biphasic processes underlying approach and withdrawal. In M. R. Jones (Ed.), *Nebraska symposium on motivation* (pp. 1–42). Oxford: University of Nebraska Press.

Simmons, K., & Barsalou, L. W. (2003). The similarity-in-topography principle: Reconciling theories of conceptual deficits. *Cognitive Neuropsychology, 20,* 451–486.

Smith, C. A., & Ellsworth, P. C. (1985). Patterns of cognitive appraisal in emotion. *Journal of Personality and Social Psychology, 48,* 813–838.

Spelke, E. S. (2000). Core knowledge. *American Psychologist, 55,* 1233–1243.

Spitz, R. A. (1965). *The first year of life.* New York: International Universities Press.

Sroufe, L. A. (1979). Socioemotional development. In J. D. Osofsky (Ed.), *Handbook of infant development* (pp. 462–516). New York: Wiley.

Titchener, E. B. (1921). *A textbook of psychology.* New York: Macmillan.

Tomkins, S. S. (1962). *Affect, imagery, consciousness: The positive affects.* New York: Springer.

Tomkins, S. S. (1963). *Affect, imagery, consciousness: The negative affects.* New York: Springer.

Wager, T. D., Phan, K. L., Liberson, I., & Taylor, S. F. (2003). Valence, gender, and lateralization of functional brain anatomy in emotion: A meta-analysis of findings from neuroimaging. *NeuroImage, 19,* 513–531.

Watson, J. B. (1924). Behaviourism; the modern note in psychology. *Psyche, 5,* 3–12.

Watson, D., Wiese, D., Vaidya, J., & Tellegen, A. (1999). The two general activation systems of affect: Structural findings, evolutionary considerations, and psychobiological evidence. *Journal of Personal and Social Psychology, 76,* 1–52.

Winkielman, P., Berridge, K. C., & Wilbarger, J. L. (2005). Emotion, behavior, and conscious experience: Once more without feeling. In L. F. Barrett, P. M. Niedenthal, & P. Winkielman (Eds.), *Emotion and consciousness* (pp. 335–362). New York: Guilford.

Wundt, W. M. (1897). *Outlines of psychology.* Leipzig: Engelmann.

Wundt, W., Creighton, J. E., & Titchener, E. B. (1894). *Human and animal psychology.* London: Sonnenschein.

Yeh, W., & Barsalou, L. W. (2006). The situated nature of concepts. *American Journal of Psychology, 119,* 349–384.

Young, P. T. (1943). *Emotion in man and animal; its nature and relation to attitude and motive.* Oxford: Wiley.

Zeki, S. (2003). The disunity of consciousness. *Trends in Cognitive Sciences, 7,* 214–218.

# 11    The Embodied Emotional Mind

Piotr Winkielman, Paula M. Niedenthal,
and Lindsay Oberman

The environment is filled with emotionally significant information. On a walk in a forest, an individual might encounter a friendly dog or a disgruntled bear. In nearly every social interaction, an individual might be confronted with facial, vocal, and postural signs of emotion. Thus, spouses smile, colleagues frown, children pout, babies gurgle, and students tremble with anxiety or giggle with joy. Even computers deliver "just joking" faces by e-mail whereas stores and snacks lure with smiley faces. The importance of such information is now well documented: Emotionally charged objects can capture attention, bias perception, modify memory, and guide judgments and decisions (for an overview, see Eich, Kihlstrom, Bower, Forgas, & Niedenthal, 2000; Winkielman, Knutson, Paulus, & Trujillo, 2007).

Even abstract symbols that refer to emotional events, such as language, can rapidly shape an individual's behavior and trigger physiological responses. For example, most children learn through language rather than direct emotional experience that they should not put their fingers in electrical outlets or stand under a tree in a storm. Such information retains its heat in thought and language, and can be generalized to novel events (Olsson & Phelps, 2004). In adults, simple words like "the next tone will be followed by a shock" elicit a fear reaction (Phelps, O'Connor, Gateby, Grillon, Gore, & Davis, 2001) whereas terms of endearment trigger positive arousal (Harris, Ayçiçegi, & Gleason, 2003).

But how does this work? Just what happens when we see a smile, hear our partner say that special word, learn that an outlet can deliver a shock, or read about a wayward bear? In this chapter, we argue that new insights into how humans perceive, learn, understand, represent, and use emotionally significant information are offered by theories of embodied cognition. The structure of the chapter is roughly as follows. First, we place embodiment theories in the context of general debates about the nature of mental representation and discuss possible neural mechanisms. We then review evidence for the embodiment account in several domains of emotion processing. We cover research on emotional perception, comprehension, learning, influence, concepts, and language. Finally, we conclude with some observations about the strengths and limitations of the embodied theories of emotion and raise some questions for future research.

## THEORIES OF EMBODIED COGNITION AND EMOTIONAL PROCESSING

Until recently, mainstream psychologists and cognitive scientists have spent little time and resources on the development of models explaining how people acquire and use emotional information. For many scientists, the topic of emotion has seemed fraught with vexing issues including how emotion differs from cognition, how many emotions are there, the subjective nature of feelings, and how to elicit and measure emotion in laboratory experiments (Zajonc, 1980). There was also a general sense that emotions are somehow disruptive to "basic" mental processes such as perception, attention, decision making, and reasoning and thus perhaps best left to clinical experts (Damasio, 1994).

### Amodal Accounts

One way to avoid the problems with emotions is to make them trivial in the sense of being no different from cognition. Indeed, classic symbolic models of information processing in the cognitive sciences suggest that emotion is represented in an amodal fashion, devoid of its sensory and motor bases. Under these amodal accounts, emotional information, initially encoded in the different sense modalities (vision, olfaction, and audition), is represented and stored in a conceptual system that is functionally separated from its sensory origins. The resulting symbols bear no analogical relationship to the experienced event, and it is these symbols that enter into high-level cognitive processes such as thought and language (e.g., Fodor, 1975; Newell, 1980). Functionally, such amodal accounts of information processing render what individuals know about emotion equivalent to what they know about most other things. Just as people appear to know that *cars* possess the features engines, tires, and exhaust pipes, they know that *anger* involves the experience of a thwarted goal, a desire to strike out, and even that it is characterized by clenched fists and a rise in blood pressure.

## Embodied Accounts

The last decade and a half witnessed a surge of interest in alternative models of representation clustered under the label *embodied cognition theories* (Barsalou, 1999; Wilson, 2002; chapters in this volume). The basic tenets underlying those models are quite old, with philosophical predecessors in Merleau-Ponty and Heidegger, and psychological roots in Vygotsky and Piaget (for a broader perspective, see Clark, 1997; Prinz, 2002). An assertion common to modern instantiations of such theories is that high-level cognitive processes such as thought and language are *modal*, i.e., involve partial reactivations of states in modality-specific, sensorimotor systems. That is, the grounding for knowledge – what it refers to – is in the original neural states that occurred when the information was originally acquired. In such an embodied account, there is no need for states of activation in perceptual, motor, and introspective systems to be redescribed into abstract symbols that represent knowledge. Knowledge is in a sense partially "reliving" experience in its sensory, motor, and introspective modalities.

Recently, embodied accounts have been applied to understand the processing of emotional information (Barrett and Lindquist, this volume; Damasio, 1994; Decety & Jackson, 2004; Gallese, 2003; Niedenthal, Barsalou, Ric, & Krauth-Gruber, 2005; Niedenthal, Barsalou, Winkielman, Krauth-Gruber, & Ric, 2005). One such application proposes that sensorimotor and affective states triggered during the encounter with an emotion-eliciting stimulus (e.g., a bear) are captured and stored in modality-specific association areas (see Figure 11.1). Later, during recovery of the experience in consciousness (e.g., thinking about a bear), the original pattern of sensorimotor and affective states that occurred during the encounter can be reactivated. Critically for such an account, the reactivation can be partial and involves a dynamic, online use of modality-specific information. That is, what gets reactivated depends on how selective attention is allocated and what information is currently relevant to the individual (Barsalou, 1999). For embodied cognition theories, using knowledge – as in recalling memories, drawing inferences, and making plans – is thus called "embodied simulation" because parts of prior experience are reproduced in the originally implicated neural systems as if the individual were there in the very situation (Gallese, 2003). For example, an embodied simulation of anger could involve simulating the experience of anger,

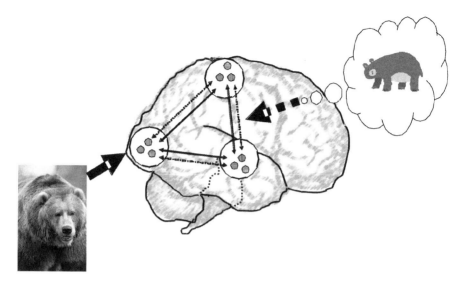

Figure 11.1. A schematic illustration of activation patterns in visual (left), affective (middle), and somatosensory (top) systems upon perception of a bear. Later, thinking about the bear reactivates parts of the original patterns.

including the activation of arm muscles that clench a fist or facial muscles that form a scowl.

## NEURAL BASIS OF EMBODIMENT

Many theories of embodied cognition suppose processes such as "re-experience" and "simulation." There is also a wide discussion of "mirroring" and "resonance." An in-depth review of the proposed neural architecture supporting these processes is outside the scope of this chapter. However, let us indicate some areas of current debate. We will also come back to the neural instantiation issues when reviewing specific findings.

One debate concerns the relative role of central and peripheral mechanisms. Early embodiment theories (e.g., James, 1896/1994). as well as some modern versions (Zajonc & Markus, 1984), highlight the role of input from the autonomic nervous system. However, starting with Cannon's (1927) rebuttal of James-Lange emotion theory, critics have argued that bodily feedback is too undifferentiated and slow to support emotional experience. In fact, some of these criticisms are misplaced. For example, facial musculature is refined and can respond quickly (Tassinary & Cacioppo, 2000). Further, recent research suggests that the autonomic feedback indeed contributes to emotional experience (Craig, 2002; Nicotra, Critchley, Mathias, & Dolan, 2006). More importantly, modern embodiment theories highlight that peripheral input works together with the brain's modality-specific systems, which can quickly simulate the necessary changes. For example, embodied states can be speedily and flexibly represented by "as-if loops" linking the ventromedial pre-frontal cortex, the limbic system, and the somatosensory and motor cortex (Damasio, 1994).

Another important debate concerns the exact substrates of the "simulation" mechanisms. Some researchers find it sufficient to assume that the brain represents information across a hierarchy of widely distributed associative areas, sometimes called *convergence zones* (Damasio, 1989). Those areas retain information about the modal (sensorimotor) features of the stimulus, with progressively "higher" areas tuned to more abstract aspects of the representation. This way of representing information preserves its modal contents and allows sensorimotor representations to be selectively reactivated, via attentional mechanisms, whenever the perceiver needs to construct a simulation (Barsalou, 1999). Note that on this account, there is no anatomically unique "simulation" or "mirroring" system. In a way, the whole brain can function as a simulation machine, with different modality areas being recruited depending on the goals in a particular task (Grush, 2004).

Others argue that simulation is supported by specialized *mirror neurons*, or even an entire *mirror neuron system*, which maps the correspondences between the observed and performed actions. However, there is much disagreement about the exact location of the mirror neurons, whether these neurons actually constitute a "system" (in the sense of interconnected elements), and whether there actually are specialized neurons dedicated to mirroring or whether regular neurons can simply perform a mirroring function. Some of the original work in monkeys emphasized a unique role of neurons located in the inferior parietal and inferior frontal cortex, which discharge both when a monkey performs an action and when it observes another individual's action (Gallese, Keysers, & Rizzolatti, 2004). The implications of this work were quickly extended to humans. Some scientists argue that humans have a dedicated "mirror neuron area," located around the Broadmann area 44 (human homologue of the monkey F5 region). This mirror area may compute complex operations such as mapping the correspondence between self and other, or differentiating between goal-oriented versus non-intentional action (Gallese et al., 2004). However, the empirical picture is a bit more complex, as we will discuss in more detail. Whereas there are some human studies that find activation in the putative mirror neuron area (which we discuss later), there are also many studies suggesting that mirror-like responses, in the sense of an area's involvement in both perception and action, can be observed in other regions of the brain. These may include a variety of emotion-related areas (insula, anterior cingulate), the somatosensory cortex, the superior temporal sulcus, the extrastriate body area, or the dentate of the cerebellum (for a review, see Decety & Jackson, 2004). Of course, this could suggest that the mirror neurons are scattered throughout the brain, perhaps forming a distributed mirror neuron system. However, it could also suggest that there is no "system," and mirroring is just a function that can be instantiated by many areas. In fact, one principle explaining these effects holds that neural coding generally tends to co-localize similar functions. For example, the neural representation of a visual image and linguistic concept of a "leg" is partially co-localized with the neural representation of the physical leg because of Hebbian learning (seeing one's leg move and moving it at the same time). Thus, it is not surprising that the same area can be active during perception and action (Buccino et al., 2001; Pulvermüller, this volume). We will come back to these issues throughout the chapter.

## EMOTION AND EMBODIMENT

Since the beginning of scientific psychology, writers have been fascinated by the tight connection between body, cognition, and emotion. In 1890, James observed that "Every representation of a movement awakens in some degree the actual movement which is its object." One hundred years later, Zajonc and Markus (1984, p. 74) wondered why "people engaged in an arithmetic problem often gnash their teeth, bite their pencils, scratch their heads, furrow their brows or lick their lips?" and "why do people who are angry squint their eyes and scratch their shoulders?"

There is now much systematic evidence for a link between emotion and embodiment. For example, merely thinking about emotional content elicits incipient facial expressions (Cacioppo, Petty, Martzke, & Tassinary, 1988) and brain activations similar to those accompanying encounters with real emotional objects (Damasio et al., 2000). Similarly, a large number of studies found that observers tend to overtly and covertly mimic behavior of those around them, including gestures and body postures (Chartrand & Bargh, 1999), facial expressions (Dimberg, Thunberg, & Elmehed, 2000; Wallbott, 1991) and even emotional tone of voice (Neumann & Strack, 2000). However, why do people make emotional faces and postures when thinking about emotion? Why do they activate similar neural circuitry? Why do they mimic other's expressions and gestures?

Some views, like the associative account, emphasize that the role of previously established stimulus-response links (Lipps, 1907). For example, people spontaneously smile when they observe another person smile because seeing and making a smile is frequently paired in the environment. Several studies have now clearly documented the role of experience in phenomena such as automatic imitation (e.g., Heyes, Bird, Johnson, & Haggard, 2005). This possibility makes some think that sensorimotor effects are causally inefficacious byproducts of higher-order processes (Fodor & Pylyshyn, 1988). Others think that a system based on associative learning can play a causal role in the recognition and understanding of action and emotion, but doubt there is a need for assumptions beyond the standard associative approach (Heyes, 2001).

In contrast, theories of embodied cognition suggest that the active engagement of sensorimotor processes is part and parcel of the process of emotional perception, understanding, learning, and influence. On that account, the vicarious re-creation of the other's state provides information about the stimulus meaning, and can go beyond the previously established associations. If so, manipulation (inhibition or facilitation) of somatosensory resources should influence the perception and understanding of emotional stimuli. Evidence for this interpretation has been now obtained in multiple domains, as we review next.

EMOTIONAL PERCEPTION

The evidence for the role of embodied simulation in emotion perception comes from a variety of behavioral and neuroscience studies (for a review, see Adolphs, 2006; Goldman & Sripada, 2005). Those studies examined the involvement of somatosensory resources by manipulating and measuring both peripheral and central mechanisms.

## Peripheral Mechanisms

Focusing on the role of feedback from facial muscles, Niedenthal and colleagues (2001) examined the possibility that mimicry (reproducing the observed stimulus using one's own muscles) is causally involved in the perception of the facial expression of emotion. Participants were asked to identify the point at which a morphed face changed from happy to sad and vice versa. During this task, some participants were free to move their faces naturally, whereas other were holding a pen sideways in their mouths, between their

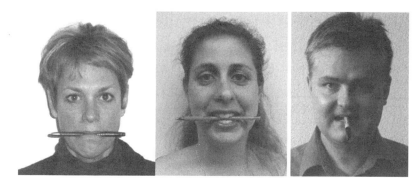

Figure 11.2. Different ways in which facial expressions relevant to happiness have been manipulated in behavioral experiments. From left to right, the authors demonstrate manipulations used by Niedenthal et al. (2001), Oberman, et al., (2007) and Strack et al. (1988). Note that the sideways pen manipulations (left and middle) prevent participants from differential responding using facial muscles, whereas the straight pen manipulation (right) allows additional smiling.

teeth and lips (see Figure 11.2, left panel). This manipulation prevents facial mimicry and thus reduces somatic feedback that supports the detection of change in the observed expressions. Participants whose facial movements were blocked by the pen detected the change in expression later in both directions (happy to sad and sad to happy) than those who were able to move their face freely, supporting the role of facial mimicry in the recognition of facial expressions.

Oberman, Winkielman, and Ramachandran (2007) extended this study by adding several controls and, more importantly, examining the specificity of the mimicry-blocking effect. Note that the embodiment account predicts that recognition of a specific type of facial expressions should be impaired by blocking mimicry in the group of facial muscles used in the production of this type of expression. The authors tested this hypothesis using four expressions (happy, disgust, fear, and sad) and four manipulations of facial mimicry: holding a pen sideways between the teeth, chewing gum, holding the pen just with the lips, and no task. Experiment 1 employed electromyography (EMG) and found that holding a pen sideways between the teeth selectively activates muscles involved in producing expressions of happiness (Figure 11.2, middle panel). In contrast, the gum manipulation broadly activates several facial muscles, but only intermittently (the lip manipulation had no effect on EMG). Testing for the accuracy of emotion discrimination, Experiment 2 found that the pen-biting manipulation selectively impaired the recognition of happiness, but had no effect on the recognition accuracy for disgust, fear, and sad expressions. This finding suggests that recognition of a specific type of facial expression involves the selective recruitment of muscles used to produce that expression, as predicted by embodiment accounts.

## Central Mechanisms

Several studies have investigated the role of central mechanisms underlying embodied simulation. In a pioneering study, Adolphs and colleagues (2000) asked 108 patients with a variety of focal brain lesions and 30 normal control participants to perform three visual emotion recognition tasks. In the first task, participants rated the intensity of basic emotional facial expressions. In the second task, participants matched a facial expression to its name. In the third task, participants sorted facial expressions into emotional categories. Though each task identified a slightly different group of regions, damage to primary and secondary somatosensory cortices impaired performance in all three tasks. This finding is consistent with the embodiment view in which emotion perception involves simulating the relevant state in the perceiver using somatosensory resources.

The previous lesion study did not report a particularly critical role of the classic mirror neuron areas (BA 44) in the recognition of facial expressions. However, such suggestions have been made in the functional magnetic resonance imaging (fMRI) literature. Carr, Iacoboni, Dubeau, Mazziotta, & Lenzi (2003) asked participants to just observe or to observe and imitate emotional facial expressions. Compared to rest, both observation and imitation tasks activated a similar group of regions, including the inferior frontal cortex (the mirror neuron area) as well as the superior temporal cortex, insula, and amygdala.

Finally, there is some evidence for the selectivity of central mechanisms in the embodied simulation of specific emotions. Wicker, Keysers, Plailly, Royet, Gallese, and Rizzolatti (2003) asked participants to inhale odors that generated strong feelings of disgust. The same participants then watched videos displaying other individuals expressing disgust. Results showed that the areas of the anterior insula and, to some extent, the anterior cingulate cortex were activated both when individuals experienced disgust themselves and when individuals observed disgust in others, presumably reflecting simulation. This interpretation is further supported by evidence that damage to the insula results in a paired impairment in the experience and recognition of disgust (Calder et al., 2000).

EMOTION COMPREHENSION

Going beyond the perception of specific emotional stimuli, such as facial expressions, the idea of embodied simulation can shed light on a more general process of emotional understanding and empathy. Social psychologists have long argued that empathy – "putting oneself in someone else's shoes" – can facilitate understanding (for review, see Batson, 1991). There is now evidence that this process might be supported by embodied simulation (Decety & Jackson, 2004). Much of the relevant data come from the perceiver's reaction to another person's pain.

One early study assessed activity in areas related to the experience of pain with a precise technique for neural mapping – single cell recording. This study found the activation of pain-related neurons when a painful stimulus was applied to the participant's own hand, and also when the patient watched the painful stimulus applied to the experimenter's hand (Hutchison, Davis, Lozano, Tasker, & Dostrovsky, 1999). This finding was extended by a recent fMRI study that revealed similar changes in pain-related brain regions (anterior cingulate and insula) of female participants while painful stimulation was applied to their own hand and to their partners' hand (Singer, Seymour, O'Doherty, Kaube, Dolan, & Frith, 2004). Further, the study showed that the change in relevant brain activations was related to the participants' level of empathy, suggesting the role of motivation to simulate. Indeed, this interpretation is consistent with recent studies from the same laboratory, which found an increase in activation of pain-related regions to the observation of a confederate receiving a painful stimulus, but only if the confederate had played fairly in a previous economic game (Singer et al., 2004). This finding highlights the goal- and context-dependent nature of simulation that is emphasized by modern embodiment theories. That is, the responses to another person are not simply automatic but are situated in a particular context that reflect the relationship with the person, or shared group memberships, and require active engagement of the perceiver in the process of constructing a simulation.

SOCIAL FUNCTIONING

If the ability to construct an embodied simulation is critical for emotion perception and understanding, one would expect that it would be related to social functioning. Evidence that this might indeed be the case comes from research on individuals with typical and atypical social functioning.

## Typical Individuals

One early suggestion comes from a study by Zajonc, Adelman, Murphy, and Niedenthal (1987), who investigated the facial similarity of couples at the time of their marriage compared to after 25 or more years of marriage. Zajonc and colleagues reasoned that if mimicry occurs in the service of empathy, then married partners should frequently mimic each other's facial expressions because they are particularly motivated to empathize with and understand each other. As a consequence of this frequent mimicry, the couple's facial morphology should grow more and more similar over time. After 25 years, the similarity of their faces should be greater than at the time of their marriage, and also more similar than random people of the same age. The researchers indeed found that facial similarity increased within couples over time, implicating the constant presence of facial mimicry. Furthermore, this effect was correlated with the quality of the marriage, and therefore presumably success in empathizing.

Recent research in social psychology suggests that one way embodiment relates to social functioning is because it modifies (and is modified by) self-other overlap. The idea here is that engaging in, say, mimicry, or even in a simple exchange of touch, can reduce the psychological distance with which the other is represented mentally to the representation of the self. Consistent with this idea, participants showed greater positivity toward a stereotyped group after being unobtrusively touched by a member of that group (Schubert, Waldzus, & Seibt, this volume; Smith, this volume). Interestingly, as highlighted by Semin and Cacioppo (this volume), a better match between the representation of the self and the other can promote social functioning because it facilitates "offloading" of social cognition across interaction participants.

## Individuals with Autism

A link between embodiment and social functioning is also suggested by the literature on autism – a disorder characterized by severe deficits in social and emotional understanding. Several authors have suggested that these deficits could result from reduced imitative abilities (for a review, see Williams, Whiten, & Singh, 2004). In fact, there is now substantial evidence that individuals with autism spectrum disorder (ASD) have deficits in the spontaneous imitation of both emotional and non-emotional stimuli (Hamilton, Brindley, & Frith, 2007). For example, McIntosh, Reichmann-Decker, Winkielman, and Wilbarger (2006) showed pictures of happy and angry facial expressions to adults with ASD and matched controls. In one condition, participants were simply asked to "watch the pictures as they appear on the screen." In another condition, participants were asked to "make an expression just like this one." Mimicry was measured by EMG, with electrodes placed over the cheek (smiling) and brow (frowning) regions. In the voluntary condition, there were no group differences, with ASD participants showing a normal pattern of voluntary mimicry (smile to a smile, frown to a frown). However, in the spontaneous condition, only typical participants mimicked, with ASD showing no differential responses.

It has been proposed that the imitation deficits of ASD individuals result from impairments in their mirror neuron system (Oberman & Ramachandran, 2007) and their inability to spontaneously map the mental representation of the self to the representation of the other (Williams et al., 2004). Evidence consistent with these proposals has been obtained by several research groups using different techniques. First, there are reports of anatomical differences in the mirror neuron system. For example, Hadjikhani and colleagues (2006) found that ASD individuals have local decreases of gray matter in the mirror neuron system areas, and that the cortical thinning of those areas was correlated with severity of ASD symptoms. Similarly, Villalobos et al. (2005) found that ASD individuals have reduced functional connectivity between the primary visual cortex and area 44, the prefrontal mirror neuron area. Second, several studies observed functional differences in the activity of the mirror neuron system. Most of this research focused on simple, non-emotional gestures. Nishitani et al. (2004) showed Asperger's syndrome (AS) and control participants pictures of a woman performing orofacial gestures and asked them to imitate these gestures. Cortical activations were recorded using magnetoencephalography (MEG), an electrophysiological technique that offers good temporal resolution. Compared to controls, the AS group showed weaker activations in the inferior frontal lobe and primary motor cortex, suggesting a reduced mirror neuron activity. Focusing on spontaneous imitation, Oberman et al. (2005) asked typical and ASD individuals to simply view videos of a person executing simple actions, or to perform the same actions. During these tasks, the experimenters recorded mu wave suppression, an electroencephalogram (EEG) index of activity in the primary motor cortex, and proposed it to be indicative of activity in the premotor "mirror neuron area" during the observation of action. The typically developing individuals showed mu wave suppression to both the execution and observation of action. However, individuals with ASD showed mu wave suppression when performing their own actual movement but not when observing movement (i.e., reduced mirror neuron activity).

Interestingly, and consistent with social psychological literature on the role of self-other overlap, there is evidence that autistic impairment in spontaneous mirroring might relate to a deficit in mapping the representation of the observed action to the self. Theoret et al. (2005) asked typical and ASD groups to view videos of index finger and thumb movements that were directed either toward or away from the participants. During these tasks, the experimenters recorded motor evoked potentials (MEP) induced by transcranial magnetic stimulation (TMS). In the typical group, both participant-directed and other-directed actions increased MEPs recorded from the participant's muscles, suggesting spontaneous mirroring. However, the ASD group showed increased MEPs (spontaneous mirroring) when viewing actions directed toward the participant, but not when viewing actions directed away from the participant. This suggests that ASD participants' mirroring failures might be due to a reduction in self-other mapping.

Finally, a recent fMRI study investigated the role of mirror neurons in the imitation of emotion stimuli in individuals with ASD and controls (Dapretto et al., 2005). Participants were asked to both imitate and observe emotional facial expressions. As compared to controls, ASD participants showed lower activation in a wide variety of regions, including visual cortices, primary motor, limbic, cerebellum, and the presumed "mirror neuron region" (inferior frontal gyrus). Though the group differences in brain activations were fairly broad, one intriguing finding is a negative correlation of the activity in the mirror neuron region with the severity of autism symptoms, measured by the Autism Diagnostic Observation Schedule (ADOS) and the Autism Diagnostic Interview (ADI). Again, these findings suggest that deficits in social and emotional understanding in autism could be due to a reduction in spontaneous simulation.

EMOTIONAL INFLUENCE

The embodiment perspective can also help explain how emotional stimuli influence behavior that is less automatic and immediate than spontaneous mimicry. Specifically, there is a large amount of evidence that salient emotional stimuli can shape how individuals act toward a variety of targets (for review, see Winkielman et al., 2007). This influence is often explored using an affective priming paradigm. In this paradigm, researchers first expose participants to emotional stimuli (e.g., emotional faces, scenes, or words) and then test the impact of these stimuli on a target behavior. For example, Winkielman, Berridge, and Wilbarger (2005) first exposed participants to a series of subliminal happy or angry faces and then asked them to perform a set of simple consumption behaviors (pour and drink a novel beverage). The results showed that participants poured and drank more after being exposed to happy than angry faces, especially when they were thirsty. But what is the mechanism of such an effect?

Many researchers treat affective priming in the same framework as any other type of "cold" semantic priming. Affective primes activate valence-congruent material in semantic memory, which then facilitates valence-congruent judgments and behaviors (Forgas, 2002). In contrast, the embodiment framework suggests that exposure to affective primes can elicit somatosensory reactions, which then bias and guide the processing of subsequent stimuli (e.g., Niedenthal, Rohman, & Dalle, 2002). These considerations generate an interesting prediction regarding the impact of affective primes on behavior. Stimuli that trigger an embodied response should have greater impact on subsequent behavior than stimuli that are comparable in semantic aspects of valence but do not trigger an embodied response. This should be particularly true for behaviors that require some form of evaluative engagement with the stimulus, rather than just simply associative responding (we will return to this point later).

Winkielman and Gogolushko (under review) tested these predictions in a study that compared the impact of emotional faces and scenes versus emotional words on consumption behavior (pouring and drinking a novel beverage). The priming stimuli were equated on valence and frequency, but emotional faces and scenes were more likely to trigger a physiological response than emotional words (Larsen, Norris, & Cacioppo, 2003). In Experiment 1, both subliminal and supraliminal emotional facial expressions influenced consumption behavior in a valence-congruent way, with happy primes leading to more pouring and drinking than angry primes. This effect was replicated in Experiment 2 with supraliminal pictures of high- and low-frequency emotional objects. In contrast, emotional words had no systematic effects on behavior in either study. There were also no differences between pictorial and word primes on more interpretive responses, such as ratings of the beverage. In sum, these studies suggest that to influence a somewhat complex hedonic behavior (like the consumption of a novel drink), an affective stimulus might need to first elicit an embodied response (for further discussion, see Winkielman et al., 2007).

## LEARNING AND EXPRESSION OF VALUE

Over the last two decades, social psychologists have conducted a series of ingenious experiments that reveal the role of embodiment in both the formation and expression of value, as expressed in people's preferences and attitudes.

## Attitude Formation

In an early demonstration of the role of embodiment, Wells and Petty (1980) instructed participants to nod their heads vertically or to shake their heads horizontally while wearing headphones, under the pretext that the research was designed to investigate whether the headphones moved around if listeners danced while listening to music. While nodding or shaking their heads, participants then heard either a disagreeable or an agreeable message about a university-related topic. Later, they rated how much they agreed with the message. Results suggested that the earlier head movements moderated their judgments. Specifically, participants who had nodded while hearing the message were more favorable than participants who had shaken their heads.

Researchers have also shown that one can enhance an attitude toward an object by covertly inducing individuals to smile (Strack, Martin, & Stepper, 1988). In the study, participants were asked to rate different novel cartoons while holding a pencil between their front teeth (Figure 11.2, right panel), making it easier for the participants to smile. Other participants were instructed to hold a pencil between their lips without touching the pencil with their teeth, making it more difficult to smile. Results revealed that cartoons were evaluated as higher by individuals with facilitated smiling rather than inhibited smiling.

Cacioppo et al. (1993) asked participants to view and evaluate neutral Chinese ideographs. During this task, the researchers manipulated the engagement of muscles involved in arm flexion and arm extension by having participants press against the bottom or the top of the table. Arm flexion was associated with higher rating of ideographs than muscle extension, presumably because of differential association of these actions with evaluative outcomes.

## Expression of Attitudes

One of the first studies that examined the role of embodied responses in attitude expressions was conducted by Solarz (1960). He asked participants to move cards with words that were mounted on a movable stage either toward or away from themselves. Participants responded faster with the pulling movement (typically associated with approach) to positive than to negative words, and faster with the pushing movement (typically associated with avoidance) to negative than to positive words (see also Chen & Bargh, 1999).

### Flexible Embodiment

Importantly, although findings like the ones we just discussed may suggest a relatively fixed link between valence and a specific muscle action or a specific direction of movement, this relationship is more complex. For example, Centerbar and Clore (2006) replicated the procedure of the Cacioppo at al. (1993) study with positively and negatively valenced ideographs and found that the impact of specific muscle movement on later evaluation depended on the initial stimulus valence. Thus, with initially negative stimuli, muscle extension (pushing away) led to more positive attitude than muscle flexion (pulling toward). Presumably, pushing away a bad stimulus is a more compatible action rather than pulling it toward oneself. As a result, this action might feel more fluent and pleasant (Winkielman, Schwarz, Fazendeiro, & Reber, 2003).

Further, the exact impact of action on valence depends on the meaning of the movement for the participant. For example, using a modified version of the Solarz/Chen and Bargh paradigm, Wentura et al. (2000) asked participants to respond to positive and negative words by either reaching out their hand to press a button or by withdrawing their hand from the button. Note that in this case, pressing the button (i.e., approaching it) required an extension movement (away from the body). In contrast, not pressing a button (avoiding it) required a flexion movement, withdrawing the hand toward the body. Consistent with the primacy of the functional meaning of movement (rather than a specific muscle movement), participants pressed the button faster for positive than for negative stimuli but withdrew their hand faster for negative than for positive stimuli. Similarly, Markman and Brendl (2005) demonstrated that the evaluative meaning of the movement does not depend on the relation to the "physical body," but rather the relation to the more abstract representation of the "self." Specifically, they found that positive valence facilitates any motor action (push or pull) that brings the stimulus closer to the self, even when the self is represented as the participants' name on a screen.

In summary, multiple studies suggest that bodily postures and motor behavior that are associated with positive and negative inclinations and action tendencies toward objects influence acquisition and expression of attitudes toward those objects. Thus, it seems that attitudes are in part grounded in embodied responses. Importantly, the link between these embodied responses and valence is flexible, and depends on features of the current situation, the initial value of the stimuli, and how participants interpret the meaning of the specific action. This flexibility is consistent with the modern theories of embodied cognition that view the use of somatosensory and motor responses as a constructive, online process, which dynamically uses relevant resources (Barsalou, 1999, this volume).

Thus far, most of our discussion has focused on relatively concrete emotional stimuli (e.g., faces or scenes). However, what about more symbolic forms of emotion knowledge? Can emotional words and sentences be embodied?

## Emotion Concepts

Recent findings from studies of emotion concepts suggest that embodied simulation is also involved in the representation of abstract emotion knowledge (Mondillon, Niedenthal, Vermeulen, & Winkielman, under review). In two experiments recently conducted in our laboratories, participants had to make judgments about whether concepts were associated with an emotion by providing a yes or no response. In the first study, the words referred to concrete objects (e.g., *party, vomit*) previously rated by other participants as being strongly associated with the emotions of joy, disgust, and anger, or as being very neutral. In a second study, the stimuli were abstract concepts, specifically, adjectives that referred to affective states and conditions (e.g., *delighted, nauseated*). During the judgment task, the activation of four different facial muscles was recorded with EMG. Previous research shows that the activity in the region of two muscles, the zygomaticus major and the orbicularis occuli, is elevated when an individual is smiling with happiness. The region of corrugator supercilli is activated when an individual is frowning with anger. The levator muscle is largely activated when an individual makes the grimace of disgust (Tassinary & Cacioppo, 2000).

Results of both of our studies suggest that in processing emotionally significant concepts, individuals simulated the relevant, discrete expressions of emotion on their faces. For example, the first study showed that in the very brief time (less than 3 seconds) it took participants to decide that, for example, *vomit* was related to an emotion, they activated disgust-related muscles on their faces. Similarly, the second study showed that when processing the concept *delighted*, individuals activated happiness-related muscles. Importantly, these EMG effects did not simply reflect an automatic response to the word but rather reflect a goal-dependent simulation of the word's referent (concrete objects for the first study and abstract emotional states for the second). Support for such a conclusion comes from an additional control condition of each study where participants were asked to simply judge (yes or no) whether the words were written in capital letters. To make such judgments, these participants would not have to simulate the emotional meaning of the words, and indeed findings revealed that they showed no systematic activation of the facial musculature. This finding suggests that emotional simulation does not occur when the judgment can be based on simpler features – a point that has been made in other research as well (Solomon & Barsalou, 2004; Strack, Schwarz, & Gescheidinger, 1985).

Further evidence for the embodiment of emotion concepts comes from extensions of research on the costs of switching processing between sensory modalities to the area of emotion. Previous research has shown that shifting from processing in one modality to another involves temporal processing costs (e.g., Spence, Nicholls, & Driver, 2001). For example, individuals take longer to detect the location of a visual stimulus after having just detected the location of an auditory rather then another visual stimulus. For the present concerns, it is of interest that similar "switching costs" are also found when participants engage in conceptual tasks: Individuals are slower to verify that typical instances of object categories possess certain features if those features are processed in different modalities (Pecher et al., 2003). For example, they are slower to verify that a *bomb* can be *loud* when they have just confirmed that a *lemon* can be *tart*, than when they have just confirmed that *leaves* can be *rustling*. This provides support for the general assertion made by theories of embodied cognition that individuals simulate objects in the relevant modalities when they use them in thought and language.

Vermeulen and colleagues examined switching costs in verifying properties of positive and negative concepts such as *triumph* and *victim* (Vermeulen, Niedenthal & Luminet, 2007). Properties of these concepts were taken from vision, audition, and the affective system. Parallel to switching costs observed for neutral concepts, the study showed that for positive and negative concepts, verifying properties from different modalities produced costs such that reaction times were longer and error rates were higher than if no modality switching was required. Importantly, this effect was observed when participants had to switch from the affective system to sensory modalities, and vice versa. In other words, verifying that a *victim* can be *stricken* was less efficient if the previous trial involved verifying that a *spider* can be *black* than if the previous trial involved verifying that an *orphan* can be *hopeless*. And verifying that a *spider* can be *black* was less efficient when preceded by the judgment that an *orphan* can be *hopeless* than that a *wound* can be *open*. This provides evidence that affective properties of concepts are simulated in the emotional system when the properties are the subject of active thought.

## Emotional Language

Finally, embodied cognition of language makes the claim that even the comprehension of complex sentences may involve embodied conceptualizations of the situations that language describes (Glenberg & Robinson, 2000; Zwaan, 2004). The first step in language comprehension then is to index words or phrases to embodied states that refer to these objects. Next, the observer simulates possible interactions with the objects. Finally, the message is understood when a coherent set of actions is created. Recently, Glenberg and colleagues provided some evidence for the simulation of emotions in sentence comprehension (Havas, Glenberg, & Rinck, in press; see Glenberg, this volume). Motivation for this research was the hypothesis that if the comprehension of sentences with emotional meaning requires the partial reenactment of emotional bodily states, then the simulation of congruent (or incongruent) emotions should facilitate (or inhibit) language comprehension. Participants had to judge whether the sentences described a pleasant or an unpleasant event while holding a pen between the teeth (again, to induce smiling) or between the lips (to induce frowning). Reading times for understanding sentences describing pleasant events were faster when participants were smiling than when they were frowning. Those that described unpleasant events were understood faster when participants were frowning than when they were smiling. The same effect was observed in a second experiment in which participants had to evaluate if the sentences were easy or difficult to understand. This research dovetails with other studies on comprehension of nonemotional language that have repeatedly demonstrated the role of embodied information (Glenberg, this volume; Zwaan, 2004).

### SUMMARY, OPEN ISSUES, AND FUTURE DIRECTIONS

In this chapter, we argued that theories of embodied cognition offer a fruitful approach to the processing of emotional information. We started by highlighting the weaknesses of symbolic models that reduce emotion processing to operations within an amodal semantic network. As an alternative account, we proposed that emotion processing is grounded in modality-specific systems, in which conceptual operations involve the partial reactivation or even recreation (simulation) of the actual emotion experience. We then reviewed supporting evidence from the literature on emotion perception, learning, and comprehension. Importantly, several of the studies suggest a causal rather than correlational relationship between embodiment and the processing of emotion. Our understanding of this relationship has also grown to be more sophisticated, with researchers now appreciating that simulation is a dynamic, goal-dependent processes, and that the exact impact of the particular sensorimotor input depends on situated conceptualizations. There also has been remarkable progress in understanding the neural basis of embodiment and the specific peripheral and central mechanisms supporting processes of simulation. Finally, and perhaps most critically, the embodiment approach has been able to generate exciting and counterintuitive predictions across a variety of areas in psychology and neuroscience, including affective perception, influence, social functioning, and language comprehension.

Of course, open issues remain. One theoretical challenge for the embodiment account in general, not only of emotion, is the representation and processing of abstract information. For example, how do people understand social concepts, such as status, legal concepts, such as eminent domain, or logical concepts, such as recursion? There are some promising attempts to solve this issue (Barsalou, 2003), even for such abstract domains as mathematics, though some of these solutions assume fairly powerful abilities to process metaphorical information (Lakoff & Núñez, 2000). A similar challenge applies to emotion concepts. For example, how do people understand the differences between shame, embarrassment, and guilt? Such understanding certainly involves the ability to simulate a relevant experience, but also requires the ability to connect the simulation to a more abstract knowledge about respective eliciting conditions and consequences (e.g., understanding that shame and guilt, but not necessarily embarrassment, involve norm violation, and that guilt, but not shame, implies recognition of responsibility). Recently, in our laboratories we have begun to explore the idea that depending on their current goal, people represent an emotional concept (e.g., anger) in more modal or amodal fashion, and thus engage in different amounts of perceptual simulation. These differences in representation can then change how the concept is used to interpret novel behaviors. For example, the activation of a modal, rather than amodal, representation of anger should invite different inferences about the causes of a target's violent behavior, perhaps leading to different judgments of responsibility.

Another challenge for emotional embodiment theory is clarifying the difference between emotion and non-emotion concepts. That is, embodiment effects have been shown in a variety of modalities, including the motor system (Tucker & Ellis, 1998), visual, auditory, and gustatory systems (Barsalou, this volume), so a legitimate question is whether there is anything unique about emotion concepts. One difference is that emotion concepts recruit a unique modality – internal representation of bodily state – and are tightly connected to motivation. A related difference is that emotion concepts organize information across modalities according to principles of subjective value, rather than relation to the objective external world (see also Barrett & Lindquist, this volume). Finally, emotion concepts have a unique function and power in cognitive processing (e.g., they can prioritize processing according to the perceivers' internal goals, interrupt ongoing processing streams, and so on). In any case, exploring the differences between the embodiment of emotional and non-emotional concepts offers an exciting direction for future research.

Further, now that many emotion embodiment effects have been demonstrated, it is time to develop systematic models of their boundary conditions. For example, as we have discussed, there are now several demonstrations that peripheral manipulations of facial mimicry can influence emotion perception and judgment. However, there is little research directly contrasting inhibitory effects, such as impairment in the detection of happiness observed by Oberman et al. (2007) and Niedenthal et al. (2001) versus facilitatory effects, such as the enhancement of cartoon judgments observed by Strack et al. (1988). One possible explanation is that forcing a participant's face into a permanent smile (i.e., creating a constant level of muscular feedback) or immobilizing the face (i.e., removing muscular feedback) lowers a participant's sensitivity to the presence versus absence of happy expressions by cutting out the differential information from the muscles (see left and middle panels of Figure 11.2). On the other hand, forming a half-smile (see right panels of Figure 11.2) creates a positivity bias – tendency toward happy responding toward ambiguous stimuli. Incidentally, some related cognitive research reports that similar embodiment manipulations can have both facilitatory and inhibitory effects, with subtle differences in timing and task requirements leading either to resource priming or resource competition (Reed & Farah, 1995; Reed & McGoldrick, 2007).

Though challenges remain, it is clear that recent years have seen remarkable progress in understanding the nature of emotion. Emotion is no longer ignored by psychology and cognitive science but, in fact, is one of the most studied topics. The embodiment account has inspired and is continuing to generate research that advances the understanding of emotional perception, learning, comprehension, attitudes, prejudice, empathy, and even certain behavioral deficits. So even if we restrict our judgment of the embodiment account of emotion purely to its generative value, it has served us extremely well and should continue to do so in the foreseeable future.

### References

Adolphs, R. (2006). How do we know the minds of others? Domain-specificity, simulation, and inactive social cognition. *Brain Research, 1079*, 25–35.

Adolphs, R., Damasio, H., Tranel, D., Cooper, G., & Damasio, A. (2000). A role for somatosensory cortices in the visual recognition of emotion as revealed by three-dimensional lesion mapping. *Journal of Neuroscience, 20,* 2683–2690.

Barsalou, L. W. (1999). Perceptual symbol system. *Behavioral and Brain Sciences, 22,* 577–660.

Barsalou, L. W. (2003). Abstraction in perceptual symbol systems. *Philosophical Transactions of the Royal Society of London: Biological Sciences, 358,* 1177–1187.

Batson, C. D. (1991). *The altruism question: Toward a social-psychological answer.* Hillsdale, NJ: Erlbaum.

Buccino, G., Binkofski, F., Fink, G. R., Fadiga, L., Fogassi, L., Gallese, V., et al. (2001). Action observation activates premotor and parietal areas in somatotopic manner: An fMRI study. *European Journal of Neuroscience, 13,* 400–404.

Cacioppo, J. T., Petty, R. E., Martzke, J., & Tassinary, L. G. (1988). Specific forms of facial EMG response index emotions during an interview: From Darwin to the continuous flow model of affect-laden information processing. *Journal of Personality and Social Psychology, 54,* 592–604.

Cacioppo, J. T., Priester, J. R., & Berntson, G. G. (1993). Rudimentary determinants of attitudes. II. Arm flexion and extension have differential effects on attitudes. *Journal of Personality and Social Psychology, 65,* 5–17.

Calder, A. J., Keane, J., Cole, J., Campbell, R., & Young, A. W. (2000). Facial expression recognition by people with Mobius syndrome. *Cognitive Neuropsychology, 17,* 73–87.

Cannon, W. B. (1927). The James-Lange theory of emotions. *American Journal of Psychology, 39,* 115–124.

Carr, L., Iacoboni, M., Dubeau, M. C., Mazziotta, J. C., & Lenzi, G. L. (2003). Neural mechanisms of empathy in humans: A relay from neural systems for imitation to limbic areas. *Proceedings of the National Academy of Science USA, 100,* 5497–5502.

Centerbar, D., & Clore, G. L. (2006). Do approach-avoidance actions create attitudes? *Psychological Science, 17,* 22–29.

Chartrand, T. L., & Bargh, J. A. (1999). The chameleon effect: The perception-behavior link and social interaction. *Journal of Personality and Social Psychology, 76,* 893–910.

Chen, S., & Bargh, J. A. (1999). Consequences of automatic evaluation: Immediate behavior predispositions to approach or avoid the stimulus. *Personality and Social Psychology Bulletin, 25,* 215–224.

Clark, A. (1997). *Being there: Putting brain body and world together again.* Cambridge, MA: MIT Press.

Craig, A. D. (2002). How do you feel? Interoception: The sense of the physiological condition of the body. *Nature Reviews Neuroscience, 3,* 655–666.

Damasio, A. R. (1989). Time-locked multiregional retroactivation: A systems-level proposal for the neural substrates of recall and recognition. *Cognition, 33,* 25–62.

Damasio, A. R. (1994). *Descartes' error: Emotion, reason, and the human brain.* New York: Grosset/Putnam.

Damasio, A. R., Grabowski, T. J., Bechara, A., Damasio, H., Ponto, L. L. B., Parvizi, J., Hichwa, R. D. (2000). Subcortical and cortical brain activity during the feeling of self-generated emotions. *Nature Neuroscience, 3,* 1049–1056.

Dapretto, M., Davies, M. S., Pfeifer, J. H., Scott, A. A., Sigman, M., Bookheimer, S. Y., et al. (2005). Understanding emotions in others: Mirror neuron dysfunction in children with autism spectrum disorders. *Nature neuroscience, 9*(1), 28–30.

Decety, J., & Jackson, P. L. (2004). The functional architecture of human empathy. *Behavioral and Cognitive Neuroscience Reviews, 3*, 71–100.

Dimberg, U., Thunberg, M., & Elmehed, K. (2000). Unconscious facial reactions to emotional facial expressions. *Psychological Science, 11*, 86–89.

Eich, E., Kihlstrom, J., Bower, G., Forgas, J., & Niedenthal, P. (2000). *Cognition and Emotion*. New York: Oxford University Press.

Fodor, J. (1975). *The language of thought*. Cambridge, MA: Harvard University Press.

Fodor, J., & Pylyshyn, Z. (1988). Connectionism and cognitive architecture: A critical analysis. *Cognition, 28*, 3–71.

Forgas, J. P. (2002). Feeling and doing: The role of affect in social cognition and behavior. *Psychological Inquiry, 9*, 205–210.

Gallese, V. (2003). The roots of empathy: The shared manifold hypothesis and the neural basis of intersubjectivity. *Psychopathology, 36*, 71–180.

Gallese, V., Keysers, C., & Rizzolatti, G. (2004). A unifying view of the basis of social cognition. *Trends in Cognitive Sciences, 8*, 396–402.

Glenberg, A. M., & Robinson, D. A. (2000). Symbol grounding and meaning: A comparison of high-dimensional and embodied theories of meaning. *Journal of Memory and Language, 43*, 379–401.

Goldman, A. I., & Sripada, C. S. (2005). Simulationist models of face-based emotion recognition. *Cognition, 94*, 193–213.

Grush, R. (2004). The emulation theory of representation: Motor control, imagery, and perception. *Behavioral Brain Sciences, 27*, 377–96.

Harris, C. L., Ayçiçegi, A., & Gleason, J. B. (2003). Taboo and emotion words elicit greater autonomic reactivity in a first language than in a second language. *Applied Psycholinguistics, 4*, 561–578.

Hadjikhani, N., Joseph, R. M., Snyder, J., & Tager-Flusberg, H. (2006). Anatomical differences in the mirror neuron system and social cognition network in autism. *Cerebral Cortex, 9*, 1276–1282.

Hamilton, A., Brindley, R. M. & Frith, U. (2007). Imitation and action understanding in autistic spectrum disorders: How valid is the hypothesis of a deficit in the mirror neuron system? *Neuropsychologia, 45*, 1859–1868.

Havas, D. A., Glenberg, A. M., & Rinck, M. (in press). Emotion simulation during language comprehension. *Psychonomic Society Bulletin and Review*.

Heyes, C. M. (2001). Causes and consequences of imitation. *Trends in Cognitive Sciences, 5*, 253–261.

Heyes, C. M., Bird, G., Johnson, H., & Haggard, P. (2005). Experience modulates automatic imitation. *Cognitive Brain Research, 22*, 233–240

Hutchison, W. D., Davis, K. D., Lozano, A. M., Tasker, R. R., & Dostrovsky, J. O. (1999). Pain related neurons in the human cingulate cortex. *Nature Neuroscience, 2*, 403–405.

James, W. (1896/1994). The physical basis of emotion. *Psychological Review, 101*, 205–210.

Lakoff, G., & Núñez, R. (2000). *Where mathematics comes from: How the embodied mind brings mathematics into being*. New York: Basic Books.

Larsen, J. T., Norris, C. J., & Cacioppo, J. T. (2003). Effects of positive affect and negative affect on electromyographic activity over zygomaticus major and corrugator supercilii. *Psychophysiology, 40*, 776–785.

Lipps, T. (1907). Das Wissen von fremden Ichen. In T. Lipps (Ed.), *Psychologische Untersuchungen (Band 1)* (pp. 694–722). Leipzig: Engelmann.

Markman, A. B., & Brendl, C. M. (2005). Constraining theories of embodied cognition. *Psychological Science, 16*, 6–10.

McIntosh, D. N., Reichmann-Decker, A., Winkielman, P., & Wilbarger, J. (2006). When mirroring fails: Deficits in spontaneous, but not controlled mimicry of emotional facial expressions in autism. *Developmental Science, 9*, 295–302.

Mondillon, L., Niedenthal, P. M., Winkielman, P., & Vermeulen, N. (under review). Embodiment of emotion concepts: Evidence from EMG measures.

Neumann, R., & Strack, F. (2000). "Mood contagion": The automatic transfer of mood between persons. *Journal of Personality and Social Psychology, 79*, 211–223.

Newell, A. (1980). Physical symbol systems. *Cognitive Science, 4*, 135–183.

Nicotra, A., Critchley, H. D., Mathias, C. J., & Dolan, R. J. (2006). Emotional and autonomic consequences of spinal cord injury explored using functional brain imaging. *Brain, 129*, 718–728.

Niedenthal, P. M., Barsalou, L. W., Ric, F., & Krauth-Gruber, S. (2005). Embodiment in the acquisition and use of emotion knowledge. In L. F. Barrett, P. M. Niedenthal, & P. Winkielman (Eds.), *Emotion: Conscious and unconscious* (pp. 21–50). New York: Guilford.

Niedenthal, P. M., Barsalou, L. W., Winkielman, P., Krauth-Gruber, S., & Ric, F. (2005). Embodiment in attitudes, social perception, and emotion. *Personality and Social Psychology Review, 9*, 184–211.

Niedenthal, P. M., Brauer, M., Halberstadt, J. B., & Innes-Ker, Å. (2001). When did her smile drop? Facial mimicry and the influences of emotional state on the detection of change in emotional expression. *Cognition and Emotion, 15*, 853–864.

Niedenthal, P. M., Rohman, A., & Dalle, N. (2002). What is primed by emotion words and emotion concepts? In J. Musch & K. C. Klauer (Eds.) *The psychology of evaluation: Affective processes in cognition and emotion.* Mahwah, NJ: Erlbaum.

Nishitani, N., Avikainen, S., & Hari, R. (2004). Abnormal imitation-related cortical activation sequences in Asperger's syndrome. *Annals of Neurology, 55*, 558–62.

Oberman, L. M., Hubbard, E. M., McCleery, J. P., Ramachandran, V. S., & Pineda, J. A. (2005). EEG evidence for mirror neuron dysfunction in autism. *Cognitive Brain Research, 24*, 190–198.

Oberman, L. M., & Ramachandran, V. S. (2007). The simulating social mind: The role of simulation in the social and communicative deficits of autism spectrum disorders. *Psychological Bulletin, 133*, 310–327.

Oberman, L. M., Winkielman, P., & Ramachandran, V. S. (2007). Face to face: Blocking expression-specific muscles can selectively impair recognition of emotional faces. *Social Neuroscience, 2*, 167–178.

Olsson, A., & Phelps, E. A. (2004). Learned fear of "unseen" faces after Pavlovian, observational, and instructed fear. *Psychological Science, 15*, 822–828.

Pecher, D., Zeelenberg, R., & Barsalou, L. W. (2003). Verifying different-modality properties for concepts produces switching costs. *Psychological Science, 14*, 119–124.

Phelps, E. A., O'Connor, K. J., Gateby, J. J., Grillon, C., Gore, J. C., & Davis, M. (2001). Activation of the amygdala by cognitive representations of fear. *Nature Neuroscience, 4*, 437–441.

Prinz, J. J. (2002). *Furnishing the mind: Concepts and their perceptual basis.* Cambridge, MA: MIT Press.

Reed, C. L., & Farah, M. J. (1995). The psychological reality of the body schema: A test with normal participants. *Journal of Experimental Psychology: Human Perception and Performance, 21,* 334–343.

Reed, C. L., & McGoldrick, J. E. (2007). Action during body perception: Processing time affects self-other correspondences. *Social Neuroscience, 2,* 134–149.

Singer, T., Seymour, B., O'Doherty, J., Kaube, H., Dolan, R. J., & Frith, C. D. (2004). Empathy for pain involves the affective but not sensory components of pain. *Science, 303,* 1157–1162.

Solarz, A. K. (1960). Latency of instrumental responses as a function of compatibility with the meaning of eliciting verbal signs. *Journal of Experimental Psychology, 59,* 239–245.

Solomon, K. O., & Barsalou, L. W. (2004). Perceptual simulation in property verification. *Memory & Cognition, 32,* 244–259.

Spence, C., Nicholls, M. E., & Driver, J. (2001). The cost of expecting events in the wrong sensory modality. *Perception & Psychophysics, 63,* 330–336.

Strack, F., Martin, L. L., & Stepper, S. (1988). Inhibiting and facilitating conditions of the human smile: A nonobtrusive test of the facial feedback hypothesis. *Journal of Personality and Social Psychology, 54,* 768–777.

Strack, F., Schwarz, N., & Gschneidinger, E. (1985). Happiness and reminiscing: The role of time perspective, mood, and mode of thinking. *Journal of Personality and Social Psychology, 49,* 1460–1469.

Tassinary, L. G., & Cacioppo, J. T. (2000). The skeletomuscular system: Surface electromyography. In J. T. Cacioppo, L. G. Tassinary, & G. G. Berntson (Eds.), *Handbook of psychophysiology,* 2nd ed. (pp. 163–199). New York: Cambridge University Press.

Theoret, H., Halligan, E., Kobayashi, M., Fregni, F., Tager-Flusberg, H., & Pascual-Leone, A. (2005). Impaired motor facilitation during action observation in individuals with autism spectrum disorder. *Current Biology, 15,* R84–R85.

Tucker, M., & Ellis, R. (1998). On the relations between seen objects and components of potential actions. *Journal of Experimental Psychology: Human Perception and Performance, 24,* 830–846.

Vermeulen, N., Niedenthal, P. M., & Luminet, O. (2007). Switching between sensory and affective systems incurs processing costs. *Cognitive Science, 31,* 183–192.

Villalobos, M. E., Mizuno, A., Dahl, B. C., Kemmotsu, N., & Muller, R. A. (2005). Reduced functional connectivity between V1 and inferior frontal cortex associated with visuomotor performance in autism. *Neuroimage, 25,* 916–925.

Wallbott, H. G. (1991). Recognition of emotion from facial expression via imitation? Some indirect evidence for an old theory. *British Journal of Social Psychology, 30,* 207–219.

Wells, G. L., & Petty, R. E. (1980). The effects of overt head movements on persuasion: Compatibility and incompatibility of responses. *Basic and Applied Social Psychology, 1,* 219–230.

Wentura, D., & Rothermund, K., & Bak, P. (2000). Automatic vigilance: The attention-grabbing power of approach- and avoidance-related social information. *Journal of Personality and Social Psychology, 78,* 1024–1037.

Williams, J. H. G., Whiten, A., & Singh, T. (2004). A systematic review of action imitation in autistic spectrum disorder. *Journal of Autism & Developmental Disorders, 34,* 285–299.

Wilson, M. (2002). Six views of embodied cognition. *Psychonomic Bulletin & Review, 9,* 625–636.

Wicker, B., Keysers, C., Plailly, J., Royet, J. P., Gallese, V., & Rizzolatti, G. (2003). Both of us disgusted in My insula: the common neural basis of seeing and feeling disgust. *Neuron, 40,* 655–664.

Winkielman, P., Berridge, K. C., & Wilbarger, J. L. (2005). Unconscious affective reactions to masked happy versus angry faces influence consumption behavior and judgments of value. *Personality and Social Psychology Bulletin, 1,* 121–135.

Winkielman, P., & Gogolushko, K. (under review). How does emotion influence motion? Pictures, but not words, elicit valence-congruent changes in hedonic behavior.

Winkielman, P., Knutson, B., Paulus, M. P. & Tujillo, J. T. (2007). Affective influence on decisions: Moving towards the core mechanisms. *Review of General Psychology, 11,* 179–192.

Winkielman, P., Schwarz, N., Fazendeiro, T., & Reber, R. (2003). The hedonic marking of processing fluency: Implications for evaluative judgment. In J. Musch & K. C. Klauer (Eds.), *The psychology of evaluation: Affective processes in cognition and emotion* (pp. 189–217). Mahwah, NJ: Erlbaum.

Zajonc, R. B. (1980). Feeling and thinking: Preferences need no inferences. *American Psychologist, 35,* 151–175.

Zajonc, R. B., Adelmann, P. K., Murphy, S. T., & Niedenthal, P. M. (1987). Convergence in the physical appearance of spouses. *Motivation and Emotion, 11,* 335–346.

Zajonc, R. B., & Markus, H. (1984). Affect and cognition: The hard interface. In C. Izard, J. Kagan, & R. B. Zajonc (Eds.), *Emotions, cognition and behavior* (pp. 73–102). Cambridge, UK: Cambridge University Press.

Zwaan, R. A. (2004). The immersed experiencer: Toward an embodied theory of language comprehension. In B. H. Ross (Ed.). *The psychology of learning and motivation, 44,* 35–62.

## 12 Expression Entails Anticipation

*Toward a Self-Regulatory Model of Bodily Feedback Effects*

Jens Förster and Ronald S. Friedman

Expressive behavior represents more than merely a reaction to stimuli in the external world. Obviously, individuals nod when they are in agreement and embrace when they like one another; however, because the link between information processing and expressive behavior is overlearned, over the course of a lifetime, even innate expressive behavior comes to reciprocally influence the way that individuals process information. Accordingly, research on the impact of bodily feedback has repeatedly demonstrated that unobtrusively induced expression patterns can unintentionally influence cognition, emotion, and behavior.

In this chapter, we will argue that models accounting for such effects largely overlap with models predicting affective influences on cognition and behavior because they focus on the affective meaning of the bodily patterns. However, some bodily cues can activate systems of approach or avoidance, triggering strategic inclinations that operate independent of affect. We will introduce a self-regulatory model to explain such effects. Let us first summarize some of the pertinent findings.

### FACIAL AND BODILY FEEDBACK EFFECTS: SUMMARY OF RESEARCH FINDINGS

Effects of bodily expression patterns have been found on feelings, evaluative judgments, memory, and behavior. For example, several experiments have shown that unobtrusively induced expression patterns influence participants' reported *feelings* (e.g., Zajonc, Murphy, & Inglehart, 1989). Prominently, Stepper and Strack (1993) found that participants feel pride more intensely if they experience positive feedback while maintaining a positive, upright body position than if they receive the same feedback while in a negative, slouched position.

Bodily feedback can also influence the *evaluation of external stimuli* (e.g., Strack, Martin, & Stepper, 1988; Wells & Petty, 1980). For example, in a series of experiments by Cacioppo, Priester, and Berntson (1993), participants performed rudimentary components of expression patterns, specifically, arm flexor contraction (by pressing their palms upward on the back of a tabletop) and arm extensor contraction (by pressing their palms downward on it). According to the authors, the sensory feedback produced by arm flexion is associated with approaching positive stimuli, whereas the feedback produced by arm extension is associated with avoiding negative stimuli. Over the course of a lifetime, arm flexion (in which the motor action is directed toward the self) is repeatedly associated with acquiring or consuming desired objects (i.e., approach motivation), whereas arm extension (in which the motor action is directed away from the self) is repeatedly associated with rejecting undesired objects (i.e., pushing an object away). Consistently, results showed that unknown Chinese ideographs were rated more positively when participants flexed their arms during evaluation than when they extended their arms during evaluation. Importantly, these arm positions did not affect self-reported mood, nor could they have activated different semantic constructs, allowing self-perception processes to operate (e.g., "I feel good/I flex therefore I must like the object!") because cover stories prevented participants from inferring the meaning of their expressions.

Förster (1998, 2004) extended these results, showing that even evaluations of strong attitude objects (beef lung and unattractive strangers as negative stimuli versus a candy bar and attractive strangers as positive stimuli) were affected by the respective arm positions. However, here arm flexion led positive stimuli to be judged more favorably than both arm extension and no arm movement (participants in a control group were asked to place their arms on their laps) but had no influence on judgments of negative stimuli. Similarly, arm extension only affected judgments of negative stimuli. Thus, it seems that with valenced stimuli, movements must be congruent with the valence of the stimulus to have an effect (for a related point, see Clore & Schnall, this volume; Neumann, Förster & Strack, 2003). In a similar vein, it was shown that arm flexion and extension differentially influenced behavior but only if they were valence-compatible: participants that were asked to flex their arms consumed a larger quantity of highly palatable orange juice than participants who extended their arms. However, there was no effect on (neutral) water.

Other research has shown effects on the encoding of valenced information. Using a paradigm employed by Wells and Petty (1980), Förster and Strack (1996) have demonstrated that participants who performed vertical head movements while listening to positive and negative words had better memory for the positive words than negative words, whereas the reverse was true for participants who performed horizontal head movements. To demonstrate that learning information incompatible with an expressive motor pattern requires more cognitive capacity than learning compatible information, participants in one experiment (Förster & Strack, 1996; Experiment 3) performed a secondary task (placing pegs into holes on a board) while learning positive or negative words. Participants performed more poorly on the secondary task when their head movements were incompatible with the words than when they were compatible. Later studies replicated these findings with upright (dominant, and thereby positive) and kneeling (submissive, and thereby negative) body postures (Förster & Stepper, 2000).

What is the driving factor behind all these effects? Because similar mechanisms have been invoked to account for these sundry effects, let us now review some of these explanations.

## EXPLANATIONS FOR BODY FEEDBACK EFFECTS

On the basis of Cacioppo et al.'s (1993) research, one may classify manipulations in body feedback experiments as either approach or avoidance related. Because mood also entails valenced or approach versus avoidance related components, it is not surprising that both phenomenologically and theoretically these two research fields share vast overlaps. Thus, influences of full-blown moods have been shown on memory (Blaney, 1986), evaluations (Schwarz & Clore, 2007), and consumer's behavior (Shiv & Fedorikhin, 1999), to name only a few. From this point of view, body feedback effects seem to be like mood effects without evaluative semantics because they lack the phenomenal experiences characteristic of mood effects.

Models of bodily feedback effects are typically based on models of mood. As such, they contribute to the understanding of what is needed to obtain effects of emotional and unemotional experiences on feelings, behavior, and cognition (Strack, 1992). Thus, explanations focus on affect-like representations (see Zajonc & Markus, 1984) or modal representations (Barsalou, Niedenthal, Barbey, & Ruppert, 2003), processes that translate affect into propositional codes (see Bower, 1981) or compatibility between motor and conceptual representations (see Förster & Strack, 1996) that can additionally lead to experiences of fluency (Centerbar & Clore, 2006) and that typically entail learning-theoretical notions (Cacioppo et al., 1993).

Furthermore, processes such as misattribution of experiences are commonly used to explain both influences of moods and body movements on attitudes. Förster & Strack's (1996) *conceptual-motor compatibility* model (for more detail, see Förster, 1995, 2004) basically predicts that if both approach and avoidance reactions are compatible with the valence of stimuli, both affective reactions to the stimulus and the feedback elicited by the bodily movement may contribute to judgments (see Clore & Schnall, this volume). In these conditions, encoding is "easy," the two influences are difficult to distinguish, and the evaluative responses combine with one another. However, when the two sources of stimulation are incompatible, participants may be able to distinguish between relevant and irrelevant sources of information and, therefore, do not misattribute the behavior-induced subjective experience to the object they are judging.[1] Support for such models comes from the aforementioned research on processing fluency (Förster & Strack, 1996) and evaluation of valenced attitude objects (Förster, 2004).[2] To repeat, such models have been borrowed from mood theories (see Schwarz & Clore, 1983).

Recently, research shows that body feedback has even more far-reaching effects on people's processing styles, influencing such higher-order processes as creative and analytic thinking. Again, these effects on processing styles show a close resemblance to affect-driven effects, and we will now summarize some of this research.

BODY FEEDBACK AND PROCESSING STYLES

The influence of approach versus avoidance-related affect on processing styles such as those involved in creative and analytical thinking was first shown with full-blown mood inductions. Most prominently, Isen and her associates (for a review, see Isen, 2000) have amassed an extensive array of

---

[1]   Note that whereas the inferential component is a more conscious process, which can develop as a heuristic over time (e.g., "do not use your bodily experiences if your reaction is odd"), the subjective responses that are used as a basis for inference may be stimulated by factors of which participants are not clearly aware. This is the case in the body feedback experiments and in situations where people simply do not know that their behavior was influenced by external factors (e.g., seating arrangements that cause slouched postures).

[2]   The fluency with which positive versus negative information is processed in approach versus avoidance settings can also sometimes lead to positive feelings so that negative objects gain value if they are performed under avoidance behavior (Centerbar & Clore, 2006). This misattribution effect of the ease of processing toward the attitude object is also known from research on the influence of full- blown mood on information processing (see Schwarz & Clore, 1983).

evidence suggesting that positive mood bolsters creativity, for instance, showing that transient happiness facilitates insight problem solving (Isen, Daubman, & Nowicki, 1987) and enhances the unusualness of free associations (Isen, Johnson, Mertz, & Robinson, 1985; see also Hirt, McDonald, & Melton, 1996). Because solving insight problems and generating unusual associations both presumably demand recruiting relatively inaccessible cognitive material from long-term memory (Schooler & Melcher, 1995), these results have been broadly interpreted to reflect the fact that approach-related motivational states expand the focus of conceptual attention, enabling internal targeting and activation of relatively remote cognitive representations. Consistently, Isen and Daubman's (1984) study demonstrated that experimentally induced positive mood engenders more, rather than less, inclusive categorization on an exemplar rating task. For example, participants were more likely to accept the unusual exemplar "camel" as a member of the category "vehicles" when in a good mood compared to when in bad mood. These findings suggest that positive mood or approach-related states expand the breadth of conceptual attention, enhancing working memory access to shared exemplar features and thereby facilitating the construction of broader mental categories.

In line with this research, Friedman and Förster (2000, 2001, 2002; Förster, Friedman, Özelsel, & Denzler 2006) have recently put forth evidence suggesting that the aforementioned arm positions (flexion versus extension) that are associated with approach and avoidance states, yet which do not themselves elicit conscious affective experience, influence components of creative and analytic thinking as well. For instance, Friedman and Förster (2002) manipulated the aforementioned arm motor actions and then gauged both the ability to solve insight problems (Experiment 1) and to generate creative alternatives (Experiment 2). To reiterate, insight problem solving calls for recruiting relatively inaccessible information from memory to restructure the problem or at least reconstrue its component features (Ohlsson, 1984; Schooler & Melcher, 1995). Similarly, generating creative alternatives entails "going beyond the information given" and retrieving comparatively remote associates and schematic representations (e.g., Smith, 1995; Smith, Ward, & Schumacher, 1993). As such, tasks of this ilk may be understood as requiring an expansion of the conceptual scope of attention. It seems that in generating effects of affect on creativity, simple rudimentary approaches, relative to avoidance cues, broaden conceptual scope. In both experiments at issue, arm flexion enhanced creativity relative to arm extension.

In other studies, Friedman and Förster administered tasks in which performance may be understood as benefiting from narrowed attention. For example, in one experiment (Friedman & Förster, 2000; Experiment 7), participants performing either arm flexor or extensor contraction completed a number of logical reasoning problems borrowed from the GRE Analytical test. Problems of this sort have been understood to require narrowed conceptual attention upon and manipulation of the information given (e.g., Fiedler, 1988). Here, consistent with the notion that rudimentary avoidance (relative to approach motivational) cues narrow the conceptual scope of attention, arm extension bolstered performance relative to arm flexion.

Replications have also been performed with tasks assessing participants' perceptual scope. For instance, in several experiments, Friedman and Förster (2000; Experiments 1–4; Förster et al., 2003) manipulated arm flexion versus arm extension, and while performing these arm contractions, participants completed several different measures of perceptual disembedding (e.g., the Embedded Figures Test; Witkin, Oltman, Raskin, & Karp, 1971) and visual restructuring (e.g., the Gestalt Completion Test; Ekstrom, French, Harman, & Dermen, 1976). Such tasks are designed so as to initially train attention upon misleading stimulus configurations (Schooler & Melcher, 1995) and demand a broadening of perceptual focus to encompass visual cues that fall outside this initial range of fixation. In short, Friedman and Förster (2000; Förster et al., 2003) found that arm flexion, relative to arm extension, facilitated performance on the full complement of these visual tasks, suggesting that rudimentary approach motivational cues, relative to avoidance motivational cues, expand the scope of perceptual attention. Again the question arises: How can one explain such effects? Recently, we suggested the following model, which we will now summarize in more detail (see Friedman & Förster, 2005, 2007; Förster et al. 2006).

EXPLAINING BODY FEEDBACK EFFECTS ON CONCEPTUAL SCOPE

Our model is based on the classic Easterbrook hypothesis (Easterbrook, 1959) suggesting that " ... arousal acts ... to reduce the range of cues that an organism uses. ... " Recent findings and theorizing have led to the reinterpretation of this classic notion to suggest that arousal narrows the scope of perceptual attention, engendering visual focus upon peripheral and local, as opposed to central and global, details (Derryberry & Tucker, 1994; Cacioppo, Berntson, & Crites, 1996; Burke, Heuer, & Reisberg, 1992). Notably, researchers have typically interpreted Easterbrook's notion as referring to stimulation due to aversive motivational states such as anxiety or stress. As such, they have demonstrated that such states undermine the ability to detect visually peripheral targets, such as flickering lights (e.g., Weltman, Smith, & Edstrom, 1971; Reeves & Bergum, 1972), and enhance attention to component features of visual stimuli as opposed to their global form (e.g., Tyler & Tucker, 1982). More recent findings and theorizing by Derryberry, Tucker, and their research group (1994; see also Luu, Tucker, & Derryberry, 1998; Derryberry & Reed, 1998) have supported this view.

Because the Easterbrook hypothesis only makes predictions regarding the scope of perceptual attention, and it is silent regarding how motivational states may impact performance on conceptual tasks (e.g., word problems) that are insensitive to variations in perceptual scope, the authors suggest a model that encompasses conceptual scope as well. More specifically, Derryberry and Tucker (1994) propose that motivational states not only influence the scope of perceptual attention (i.e., the extent to which attention is focused upon central as opposed to peripheral environmental cues) but analogously influence the scope of conceptual attention. Conceptual attention refers to internal attention to mental representations as opposed to external percepts (Anderson & Neely, 1996). A narrower scope of conceptual attention is conceived of as restricting activation of mental representations to those with the highest accessibility in a given context (e.g., dominant semantic associates to a contextually primed word), whereas a broader scope of conceptual attention is conceived of as expanding the range of activation to additionally target representations with lower a priori accessibility (e.g., subordinate semantic associates).

Second, Derryberry and Tucker (1994) also significantly extend the Easterbrook hypothesis by proposing that different types of motivational states will yield different effects on attentional scope. In short, Derryberry and Tucker (1994) additionally imply that approach-related states or elated arousal broaden the focus of attention, leading to the increased responsiveness to peripheral cues on the perceptual level and the increased activation of relatively inaccessible mental representations on the conceptual level (cf. Fredrickson, 2001).

Third, the research group proposes that the attentional "tuning" effects of "elated" and "tense" arousal states flow from their origins in distinct brain systems (Tucker & Williamson, 1984; Derryberry & Tucker, 1994). The *phasic* system associated with appetitive arousal is conceived of as right-lateralized. In the face of approach-worthy incentives, it automatically elicits a *habituation bias*, expanding attentional scope and enabling access to perceptually peripheral or cognitively inaccessible information. In contrast, the *tonic* system associated with aversive arousal is proposed to reside in the left hemisphere. Upon exposure to threat cues, it automatically elicits a *redundancy bias*, constricting the scope of attention and "choking off" access to "remote" stimuli and constructs. It is suggested that the connection between appetitive and aversive arousal states and these information processing biases is hard-wired.

Upon examination, a great deal of empirical evidence may be construed as consistent with this model. Regarding Derryberry and Tucker's (1994) prediction that approach-related states broaden the scope of perceptual atten-tion, at least two recent studies (Gasper & Clore, 2002; Gasper, 2004) have experimentally demonstrated that happiness (an affective concomitant of approach motivation; Carver, Sutton, & Scheier, 2000; Higgins, 2000; Rose-man, 1984) engenders a perceptual focus on global form as opposed to local details. Similar results were obtained with trait happiness rather than mood inductions (Basso, Schefft, Ris, & Dember, 1996).

Influences of affect on scope of conceptual attention have also been revealed. For example, Mikulincer, Kedem, and Paz (1990a; see also, Mikulin-cer, Paz, & Kedem, 1990b) replicated the aforementioned studies by Isen and Daubman (1984) on inclusion of atypical exemplars into a given category with assessments of participants' trait and state anxiety. In sum, those stud-ies suggest that anxiety narrows the scope of conceptual attention, preventing participants from seeing similarities between fringe exemplars and the pro-totype of a category.

Notably, studies using body feedback as a manipulation instead of mood manipulations show that the mere enactment of approach or avoidance behaviors, actions or procedures typically associated with acquiring rewards or evading punishment, may independently tune the scope of attention, even when such behaviors are not explicitly performed in the service of personal goals and even if they do not elicit feelings or associations that could give rise to semantic or affective priming effects or conscious inferences via self perception. It seems that over the course of a lifetime, mental representations of responses that are chronically activated in the face of incentive or threat cues may come to serve as associative primes, eliciting the attentional broad-ening or narrowing that is otherwise triggered by "full-blown" approach or avoidance motivational states. In other words, enactment of approach or avoidance behavior is posited to develop into a conditioned signal that the current situation is potentially rewarding or punishing and thereby tune attention in a manner that is best suited to rewarding or punishing situations (cf. Schwarz, 1990; Clore, Schwarz, & Conway, 1994). As such, the mere enact-ment of approach or avoidance behaviors may lead to attentional broadening or narrowing, even when the enacted behaviors are divested of any relevance to personal concerns.

Again, it seems that body feedback and mood effects share similarities both on the phenomenal and the theoretical level when it comes to bodily feedback effects on processing styles. However, there is some reason to believe that looking at approach/avoidance movements as mere "rudimentary components" of approach versus avoidance or mood is missing an important aspect of bodily expression patterns that moods may not necessarily have. It is possible that approach/avoidance expression patterns are especially prone to prepare a certain action and anticipate a certain outcome. People may approach positive end states and they may avoid negative end states. While doing so, little or no actual feeling or experience may be involved.

The difference between approach and avoidance anticipation and positive versus negative feelings or arousal states have recently received some attention because it was able to account for discrepancies with respect to neuropsychological predictions of Tucker's model and leading views regarding the hemispheric substrates of arousal (with constriction of attention scope and tense arousal relying on left hemispheric processing and with expansion of scope and elated arousal relying on right hemispheric processing). However, most research has suggested that these arousal states are associated with the very opposite pattern of relative hemispheric activation.

To address such differences, Heller has recently theorized that tense arousal (i.e., anxiety) may be subdivided into a somatic component, reflecting the physiological excitation associated with avoidance motivational states (i.e., panic), as well as a cognitive component, reflecting the anticipation of threats (i.e., worry). Moreover, she and her colleagues provided evidence for the notion that the cognitive component is associated with greater relative left hemispheric activation than is the somatic component (e.g., Heller, Koven, & Miller, 2003; Nitschke, Heller, Palmieri, & Miller, 1999; Heller & Nitschke, 1998; Heller, Nitschke, Etienne, & Miller, 1997). Assuming that the cognitive component of anxiety to which Heller refers is akin to a focus on the anticipation of undesired outcomes, it is therefore possible that avoidance motivational states may indeed shunt activation toward the left hemisphere as proposed by Derryberry and Tucker's model (for an analogous proposition, see Derryberry & Reed, 1998). Following this reasoning, it is likewise possible that approach-related bodily expressions engender increased relative right hemispheric activation if body expressions include the anticipation of outcomes. Notably with respect to hemisphere activation, expression patterns then could lead to opposite results compared to arousal because we assume that negative arousal would activate the right and positive arousal the left hemisphere.

Interestingly, recent theorizing on self regulation made a similar distinction between arousal and anticipation that may accompany motivational orientations of approach versus avoidance (for more details, see Friedman

& Förster, 2007). Most prominently, Higgins (1997; Higgins, Shah, & Friedman, 1997), in his Regulatory Focus Theory (RFT), argued that discrepancies between ideal and actual states lead to a promotion focus on gains and non-gains, whereas discrepancies between oughts and actual states lead to a prevention focus on losses and non-losses. Promotion focus concerns entail ideals, hopes, and aspirations whereas prevention focus concerns consist of oughts, responsibilities, and obligations. Thus, when people are pursuing an ideal goal (such as sharing a life with a person), they focus on whether they can attain or not attain it, whereas when people are pursuing ought goals (such as not disturbing others) they focus on whether they fail or not fail to attain it. These different motivational orientations lead to approach orientations when in a promotion focus and to avoidance orientations when in a prevention focus.

RFT also makes predictions regarding emotional experience, suggesting and showing that success and failure are felt differently in a promotion versus a prevention focus. For example, when people successfully attain their ideal goals, they feel cheerful and happy, whereas when they successfully attain their ought goals, they feel relaxed and calm. With respect to negative emotions, people feel sad or depressed after failure to attain their ideals, whereas they feel anxious and nervous after failure to attain their oughts. Most relevant for the current argument, the theory decouples the arousal or feeling component in goal pursuit and attainment from the anticipation or strategic part. Thus, even though feelings can accompany goal pursuit, the mere focus on or anticipation of desired or undesired outcomes can drive people's behavior without concomitant involvement of affective experience.

Meanwhile, it has been shown in an impressive series of experiments that people can adopt approach versus avoidance strategies when in a promotion versus prevention focus without concomitant feelings. For example, it has been shown that when participants were asked to work on a signal detection task that was framed in terms of gains and non-gains (eliciting a promotion focus), they adopted an "eager" strategy of ensuring hits at the expense of false alarms, whereas when the task was framed in terms of losses and non-losses (eliciting a prevention focus), they adopted a vigilant strategy of ensuring correct rejections at the expense of misses (Crowe & Higgins, 1997). Notably, these approach versus avoidance strategies were not accompanied by moods or arousal states.

One may then suggest that in situations with a prevention focus, in which individuals focus on security and are vigilant, they should concentrate on their concrete surroundings to maintain security and narrow attention (see Förster & Higgins, 2005). In case of a threat, an individual may screen the environment to identify and eliminate obstacles to the fulfillment of this goal.

Concrete means are instrumental to attain the goal, and the vigilant encoding of local details is crucial. In contrast, in situations with a promotion focus, in which concerns of security are replaced by an emphasis on self-fulfillment, growth, and accomplishment, and vigilance is replaced by eagerness, processing the concrete surroundings would be insufficient or even detrimental for effective goal pursuit. Fulfillment of growth needs might profit from abstract rather than concrete construals, that is, from construals that go beyond the given information and that lead to an explorative and global processing style. One may suggest then that these strategies may become proceduralized over time so that even subtle cues of (threatened) security may narrow perceptual and conceptual attention, whereas cues of ideals, hopes, and aspirations may broaden perceptual and attention automatically.

There is some evidence for the influence of regulatory focus on local versus global processing and creative versus analytic thinking. For example, Förster and Higgins (2005) measured participants' chronic promotion versus prevention focus and gauged their perceptual scope in the Navon (1977) letter task. Specifically, participants were shown large letters made up of small letters and decided if either a large letter (global) or a small letter (local) had appeared on the screen. They found that the strength of promotion focus was positively correlated with the speed of processing global letters (presumably reflecting a broader perpetual scope) and negatively correlated with the speed of processing local letters (presumably reflecting a narrower perpetual scope), whereas the reverse was true for the strength of prevention focus.

There is also some support for the influence of regulatory foci on creative versus analytic thinking. Friedman and Förster (2001, Experiments 1–4; Förster et al., 2003) have conceptually replicated a number of the aforementioned findings on creative task performance, using a manipulation of external (as opposed to interoceptive) approach and avoidance motivational cues. In these experiments, participants completed an initial task that was ostensibly unrelated to the dependent measures that followed. In this task, participants worked through a paper-and-pencil maze in which they had to lead a cartoon mouse from the center of the maze to the exit. In the approach condition, a piece of cheese was depicted as lying at the exit. In the avoidance condition, instead of cheese, a cartoon owl was portrayed as hovering over the maze, ready to capture the mouse if it could not escape the labyrinth. Friedman and Förster (2001; Förster et al., 2003) posited that by priming the cognitive representation of "seeking reward" versus "avoiding punishment," completion of these mazes would subtly activate the approach versus avoidance motivational systems, respectively. As predicted, Friedman and Förster (2001) found that completion of the "cheese" maze, relative to

the "owl" maze, enhanced both perceptual disembedding and creative generation, suggesting that external approach cues broaden the scope of both
perceptual and conceptual attention, bolstering performance on tasks that
profit from expanded attentional focus. Friedman and Förster (2003) have
also found that the owl maze, relative to the cheese maze, enhances logical
problem solving, suggesting that external avoidance cues constrict the scope
of conceptual attention, facilitating performance on tasks that profit from
restricted conceptual activation. Unsurprisingly, these effects were all independent of any changes in conscious affective experience, none of which were
elicited by the maze tasks that asked participants to "help" a cartoon rodent.

Friedman and Förster (2005) also collected preliminary evidence that the
mazes engendered a different pattern of cerebral hemispheric activation than
full-blown mood. In one study, anticipation and emotional arousal were
separately manipulated and relative hemispheric activation was behaviorally
assessed (Friedman & Förster, 2005; Experiment 3). Specifically, participants
were either administered the "standard" cheese or owl mazes, or a variant
of the maze tasks meant to elicit affective arousal. In the appetitive arousal
group, participants were asked to look at the cheese maze and imagine the
mouse gradually approaching the cheese and eventually eating it. They were
then given 10 minutes to write a vivid story from the perspective of the mouse,
to be entitled, "The Happiest Day in the Life of the Mouse." Those in the
aversive arousal group were asked to look at the owl maze and to imagine
the mouse attempting to escape the owl but eventually getting caught, killed,
and eaten. The title of their story was to be, "The Terrible Death of the
Mouse." A manipulation check revealed a significant effect of this writing
manipulation on affective arousal (i.e., current mood), whereas in line with
earlier studies, there was no effect of the standard maze manipulation on
self-reported affectivity.

Following these manipulations, participants completed a variant of the
Milner line bisection task (Milner, Brechmann, & Pagliarini, 1992). In this
task, participants are presented with a series of horizontal lines and asked
to mark the center of each line. On average, participants commit a leftward
error in bisection. This indicates an attentional bias toward the left visual
field (LVF), engendering attentional neglect of the rightward extension of
the line. Theoretically speaking, this LVF bias reflects greater relative right
hemispheric activation; however, the extent of the bias varies, enabling assessment of transient differences in the relative activation of the right versus left
hemispheres (e.g., Baumann, Kuhl, & Kazén, 2005; Milner, Brechmann, &
Pagliarini, 1992; see also Bowers & Heilman, 1980; Bisiach, Geminiani, Berti,
& Rusconi, 1990; Morton, 2003).

In terms of results, consistent with scores of previous findings (for a review, see Coan & Allen, 2003) within the emotional arousal condition, those in whom appetitive arousal was induced demonstrated significantly greater relative left hemispheric activation than those in the aversive arousal group. In multiple regression analyses, the reliability of this effect was reduced by the participants' current mood. This reinforces the assumption that this effect was mediated by induced differences in emotional arousal. In contrast, following predictions, within the standard maze conditions, the owl maze (avoidance) was associated with greater relative left hemispheric activation than was the cheese maze (approach). This suggests that the sheer cognitive orientation toward desired versus undesired end states may indeed entail a pattern of hemispheric activation that is essentially the opposite of that associated with appetitive versus aversive emotional arousal.

Previously, we suggested that expression patterns have an anticipatory element that drives body feedback effects. If this is true, one would expect that rudimentary approach expression patterns activate the right hemisphere, whereas rudimentary avoidance expression patterns should activate the left hemisphere. However, if it is the feeling component that drives the effects, one may expect the opposite pattern.

In a series of experiments, we examined the relation between arm extension and arm flexion and relative hemispheric activation with different behavioral measures (Förster & Friedman, 2007). In a first set of studies, we asked participants to work on the aforementioned line bisection task while performing arm flexion or arm extension with their right arms; a control group was asked to place their right arms in their laps. We predicted and found that arm flexion, relative to arm extension, engenders a more pronounced leftward line bisection error, suggesting that approach, compared to avoidance cues, engender intensified relative right hemispheric activation.

In a different experiment, we replicated these findings using a different measure of relative activation, namely, the chimeric faces task (Levy, Heller, Banich, & Burton, 1983a, 1983b) and additionally checked for mood as mediator. In the task, participants were presented on the computer with 40 pictures of faces, specifically, 10 sad, 10 happy, and 20 "chimeric" faces, whose left and right sides displayed different emotional expressions (e.g., happy on the left and sad on the right). Each face appeared on screen for 200 msec and participants were asked to judge as quickly as possible whether each looked "happy" or "sad." The tendency to perceive the chimeric faces as having the expression displayed on the left side is posited to indicate an LVF bias, suggesting increased relative right hemispheric activation. In sum, the results replicated results with the line bisection task, providing additional behavioral evidence that approach, relative to avoidance, motivational cues elicit greater relative activation of the right hemisphere.

Inasmuch as Heller's theory on anticipation versus arousal is correct, one may now speculate that arm flexion versus arm extension entails an anticipation component that drives body feedback effects independent of arousal or feelings. One would have expected the opposite pattern if the arousal accompanying the arm positions were responsible for the effects. To be sure, these preliminary data sets must be validated by employing measures with far greater spatiotemporal resolution (e.g., functional magnetic resonance imaging, fMRI). However, if these findings are replicated, what does this mean for bodily feedback research?

## IMPLICATIONS FOR BODILY FEEDBACK EFFECTS

For body feedback research in general, it would mean that using models of mood to explain body feedback effects, simply on the basis of an apparent similarity between paradigms, is insufficient. Rather, one may adopt models of self regulation that could explain the effects without necessarily referring to arousal states. By doing so, one may derive original predictions that cannot easily be made on the basis of affect based models. For example, one may assume that approach and avoidance expression behavior may increase the closer one is to attaining a goal to complete a certain task (i.e., Lewin, 1935; Miller, 1944; see also Förster, Higgins, & Idson, 1998; Förster, Grant, Idson, & Higgins, 2001). Thus, one may conclude that expression behavior is stronger the closer people are to a current goal. If intensity of such expression patterns plays a role in body feedback effects, one may expect stronger effects the closer people are working toward a certain goal.

So far, our analysis has focused on arm flexion versus arm extension as examples of approach versus avoidance expressive components. The question would then be whether other expression patterns manipulated in the literature also relate to approach or avoidance.

Research on RFT actually shows that promotion-focused participants exhibited a yea-saying bias leading to a greater number of hits as well as false alarms in recognition, whereas prevention-focused participants exhibited a nay-saying bias, leading to a greater number of correct rejections and misses (Crowe & Higgins, 1997; Friedman & Förster, 2001). Thus, it may well be the case that nodding is more likely to be related to a promotion focus whereas head shaking is related to a prevention focus, respectively. Similarly, smiling may be an expression of cheerfulness-related (promotion-focus) emotions rather than quiescence related moods (prevention-focus), whereas frowning may express doubts and concerns that may further lead to a need to focus on the details of the matter at hand (prevention-focus emotion). Finally, a slumped position, which often expresses submission, may be related to security seeking. In sum, additional research regarding the connection between bodily expressions and regulatory foci will be needed to forge a comprehensive appreciation of the functional utility of embodied cognition.

AUTHOR NOTE

Preparation of this article was supported by grants from the Research Board of the University of Missouri-Columbia as well as the National Institute of Mental Health (MH72669–01) to Dr. Friedman and by two grants from the Deutsche Forschungsgemeinschaft to Dr. Förster (FO 244/6–1, FO244/8–1). We thank Konstantin Mihov for editing the manuscript.

### References

Anderson, M. C., & Neely, J. H. (1996). Interference and inhibition in memory retrieval. In E. L. Bjork & R. A. Bjork (Eds.), *Memory* (pp. 237–313). New York: Academic Press.

Barsalou, L. W., Niedenthal, P. M., Barbey, A. K., & Ruppert, J. A. (2003). Social embodiment. In B. H. Ross (Ed.), *The Psychology of Learning and Motivation*, Vol. 43 (pp. 43–92). San Diego, CA: Academic Press.

Basso, M. R., Schefft, B. K., Ris, M. D., & Dember, W. N. (1996). Mood and global-local visual processing. *Journal of the International Neuropsychological Society, 2,* 249–255.

Baumann, N., Kuhl, J., & Kazén, M. (2005). Left-hemispheric activation and self-infiltration: Testing a neuropsychological model of internalization. *Motivation and Emotion, 29,* 135–163.

Bisiach, E., Geminiani, G., Berti, A., & Rusconi, M. L. (1990). Perceptual and premotor factors of unilateral neglect. *Neurology, 40,* 1278–1281.

Blaney, P. H. (1986). Affect and memory: A review. *Psychological Bulletin, 99,* 229–246.

Bower, G. H. (1981). Mood and memory. *American Psychologist, 36,* 129–148.

Bowers, D., & Heilman, K. M. (1980). Pseudoneglect: Effects of hemispace on a tactile line bisection task. *Neuropsychologia, 18,* 491–498.

Burke, A., Heuer, F., & Reisberg, D. (1992). Remembering emotional events. *Memory & Cognition, 20,* 277–290.

Carter, W. R., Johnson, M. C., & Borkovec, T. D. (1986). Worry: An electrocortical analysis. *Advances in Behavioral Research and Therapy, 8,* 193–204.

Cacioppo, J. T., Berntson, G. G., & Crites, S. L. (1996). Social neuroscience: Principles of psychophysiological arousal and response. In E. T. Higgins & A. W. Kruglanski (Eds). *Social psychology: Handbook of basic principles* (pp. 72–101). New York: Guilford.

Cacioppo, J. T., Priester, J. R., & Berntson, G. G. (1993). Rudimentary determinants of attitudes II: Arm flexion and extension have differential effects on attitudes. *Journal of Personality and Social Psychology, 65,* 5–17.

Carver, C. S., Sutton, S. K., & Scheier, M. F. (2000). Action, emotion, and personality: Emerging conceptual integration. *Personality and Social Psychology Bulletin, 26*, 741–751.

Centerbar, D. B., & Clore, G. L. (2006). Do approach-avoidance actions create attitudes? *Psychological Science, 17*, 22–29.

Clore, G. L., Schwarz, N., & Conway, M. (1994). Affective causes and consequences of social information processing. In R. S. Wyer & T. Srull (Eds.), *Handbook of social cognition*, 2nd ed. (pp. 323–417). Mahwah, NJ: Erlbaum.

Coan, J. A., & Allen, J. J. B. (2003). The state and trait nature of frontal EEG asymmetry in emotion. In K. Hugdahl and R. J. Davidson (Eds.), *The asymmetrical brain* (pp. 565–615). Cambridge, MA: MIT Press.

Crowe, E., & Higgins, E. T. (1997). Regulatory focus and strategic inclinations: Promotion and prevention in decision making. *Organizational Behavior and Human Decision Processes, 69*, 117–132.

Derryberry, D., & Reed, M. A. (1998). Anxiety and attentional focusing: Trait, state and hemispheric influences. *Personality and Individual Differences, 25*, 745–761.

Derryberry, D., & Tucker, D. M. (1994). Motivating the focus of attention. In P. M. Niedenthal and S. Kitayama (Eds.), *Heart's eye: Emotional influences in perception and attention* (pp. 167–196). New York: Academic Press.

Easterbrook, J. A. (1959). The effect of emotion on cue utilization and the organization of behavior. *Psychological Review, 66*, 183–201.

Ekstrom, R. B., French, J. W., Harman, H. H., & Dermen, D. (1976). *Manual for kit of factor-referenced cognitive tests*. Princeton, NJ: Educational Testing Service.

Fiedler, K. (1988). Emotional mood, cognitive style, and behavior regulation. In K. Fiedler & J. Forgas (Eds.), *Affect, cognition, and social behavior* (pp. 100–119). Toronto: Hogrefe International.

Förster, J. (1995). *Der Einfluß von Ausdrucksverhalten auf das menschliche Gedächtnis: Theoretische Überlegungen und Experimente zu Motor-Kongruenzeffekten [The influence of expression behavior on human memory: Theoretical reflections and experiments on motor-congruency effects]*. Bonn: Holos.

Förster, J. (1998). The influence of motor perception on likeability judgments of attractive and unattractive portraits. *Zeitschrift für Experimentelle Psychologie, 45*, 167–182.

Förster, J. (2003). The influence of approach and avoidance motor actions on food intake. *European Journal of Social Psychology, 33*, 339–350.

Förster, J. (2004). How body feedback influences consumers' evaluation of products. *Journal of Consumer Psychology, 14*, 416–426.

Förster, J., Friedman, R. S., Özelsel, A., & Denzler, M. (2006). The influence of approach and avoidance cues on the scope of perceptual and conceptual attention. *Journal of Experimental Social Psychology, 42*, 133–146.

Förster, J., Grant, H., Idson, L. C., & Higgins, E. T. (2001). Success/failure feedback, expectancies, and approach/avoidance motivation: How regulatory focus moderates classic relations. *Journal of Experimental Social Psychology, 37*, 253–260.

Förster, J., & Higgins, E. T. (2005). How global versus local perception fits regulatory focus. *Psychological Science, 16*, 631–636.

Förster, J., Higgins, E. T., & Bianco, A. T. (2003). Speed/accuracy decisions in task performance: Built-in trade-off or separate strategic concerns? *Organizational Behavior and Human Decision Processes, 90*, 148–164.

Förster, J., Higgins, E. T., & Idson, L. C. (1998). Approach and avoidance strength as a function of regulatory focus: Revisiting the "goal looms larger" effect. *Journal of Personality and Social Psychology, 75*, 1115–1131.

Förster, J., & Stepper, S. (2000). Compatibility between approach/avoidance stimulation and valenced information determines residual attention during the process of encoding. *European Journal of Social Psychology, 30*, 853–871.

Förster, J., & Strack, F. (1996). Influence of overt head movements on memory for valenced words: A case of conceptual-motor compatibility. *Journal of Personality and Social Psychology, 71*, 421–430.

Fredrickson, B. L. (2001). The role of positive emotions in positive psychology: The broaden-and-build theory of positive emotions. *American Psychologist, 3*, 218–226.

Friedman, R. S., & Förster, J. (2000). The effects of approach and avoidance motor actions on the elements of creative insight. *Journal of Personality and Social Psychology, 79*, 477–492.

Friedman, R. S., & Förster, J. (2001). The effects of promotion and prevention cues on creativity. *Journal of Personality and Social Psychology, 81*, 1001–1013.

Friedman, R. S., & Förster, J. (2002). The influence of approach and avoidance motor actions on creative cognition. *Journal of Experimental Social Psychology, 38*, 41–55.

Friedman, R. S., & Förster, J. (2003). The influence of approach and avoidance cues on analytical problem solving. Unpublished manuscript, Universität Würzburg.

Friedman, R. S., & Förster, J. (2005). Effects of motivational cues on perceptual asymmetry: Implications for creativity and analytical problem solving. *Journal of Personality and Social Psychology, 88*, 263–275.

Friedman, R. S., & Förster, J. (2007). Activation and measurement of motivational states. In A. J. Elliott (Ed.), *Handbook of approach and avoidance motivation*. New York: Guilford.

Gasper, K. (2004). Do you see what I see? Affect and visual information processing. *Cognition and Emotion, 18*, 405–421.

Gasper, K., & Clore, G. (2002). Attending to the big picture: Mood and global versus local processing of visual information. *Psychological Science, 13*, 34–40.

Heller, W., Koven, N. S., & Miller, G. A. (2003). Regional brain activity in anxiety and depression, cognition/emotion interaction, and emotion regulation. In K. Hugdahl & R. J. Davidson (Eds.), *The asymmetrical brain* (pp. 533–564). Cambridge, MA: MIT Press.

Heller, W., & Nitschke, J. B. (1998). The puzzle of regional brain activity in depression and anxiety: The importance of subtypes and comorbidity. *Cognition and Emotion, 12*, 421–447.

Heller, W., Nitschke, J. B., Etienne, M. A., & Miller, G. A. (1997). Patterns of regional brain activity differentiate types of anxiety. *Journal of Abnormal Psychology, 106*, 376–385.

Higgins, E. T. (1997). Beyond pleasure and pain. *American Psychologist, 52*, 1280–1300.

Higgins, E. T. (2000). Beyond pleasure and pain. In E. T. Higgins & A. W. Kruglanski (Eds.), *Motivational science: Social and personality perspectives* (pp. 231–255). Philadelphia: Taylor & Francis.

Higgins, E. T., Shah, J., & Friedman, R. (1997). Emotional responses to goal attainment: Strength of regulatory focus as moderator. *Journal of Personality and Social Psychology, 72*, 515–525.

Hirt, E. R., McDonald, H. E., & Melton, R. J. (1996). Processing goals and the affect-performance link: Mood as main effect or mood as input? In L. L. Martin & A. Tesser (Eds.), *Striving and feeling: Interactions among goals, affect, and self-regulation* (pp. 303–328). Hillsdale, NJ: Erlbaum.

Isen, A. M. (2000). Positive affect and decision making. In M. Lewis & J. Haviland-Jones (Eds.), *Handbook of emotions*, 2nd ed. (pp. 417–435). New York: Guilford.

Isen, A. M., & Daubman, K. A. (1984). The influence of affect on categorization. *Journal of Personality and Social Psychology, 47*, 1206–1217.

Isen, A. M., Daubman, K. A., & Nowicki, G. P. (1987). Positive affect facilitates creative problem solving. *Journal of Personality and Social Psychology, 52*, 1122–1131.

Isen, A. M., Johnson, M. M. S., Mertz, E., & Robinson, G. F. (1985). The influence of positive affect on the unusualness of word associations. *Journal of Personality and Social Psychology, 48*, 1413–1426.

Levy, J., Heller, W., Banich, M. T., & Burton, L. A. (1983a). Are variations among right-handed individuals in perceptual asymmetries caused by characteristic arousal differences between hemispheres? *Journal of Experimental Psychology: Human Perception and Performance, 9*, 329–359.

Levy, J., Heller, W., Banich, M. T., & Burton, L. A. (1983b). Asymmetry of perception in free viewing of chimeric faces. *Brain & Cognition, 2*, 404–419.

Lewin, K. (1935). *A dynamic theory of personality*. New York: McGraw-Hill.

Luu, P., Tucker, D. M., & Derryberry, D. (1998). Anxiety and the motivational basis of working memory. *Cognitive Therapy and Research, 22*, 577–594.

Mikulincer, M., Kedem, P., & Paz, D. (1990a). Anxiety and categorization – 1. The structure and boundaries of mental categories. *Personality and Individual Differences, 11*, 805–814.

Mikulincer, M., Paz, D., & Kedem, P. (1990b). Anxiety and categorization – 2. Hierarchical levels of mental categories. *Personality and Individual Differences, 11*, 815–821.

Miller, N. E. (1944). Experimental studies of conflict. In J. M. Hunt (Ed.), *Personality and the behavior disorders* (pp. 431–465). Oxford: Ronald Press.

Milner, A. D., Brechmann, M., & Pagliarini, L. (1992). To halve and to halve not: An analysis of line bisection in normal subjects. *Neuropsychologia, 30*, 515–526.

Morton, B. E. (2003). Two-hand line-bisection task outcomes correlate with several measures of hemisphericity. *Brain and Cognition, 51*, 305–316.

Navon, D. (1977). Forest before trees: The precedence of global features in visual perception. *Cognitive Psychology, 9*, 353–383.

Neumann, R., Förster, J., & Strack, F. (2003). Motor compatibility: The bidirectional link between behaviour and evaluation. In J. Musch & K. C. Klauer (Eds.), *The psychology of evaluation: Affective processes in cognition and emotion* (pp. 371–391). NJ: Erlbaum.

Nitschke, J. B., Heller, W., Palmieri, P. A., & Miller, G. A. (1999). Contrasting patterns of brain activity in anxious apprehension and anxious arousal. *Psychophysiology, 36*, 628–637.

Ohlsson, S. (1984). Restructuring revisited: II. An information processing theory of restructuring and insight. *Scandinavian Journal of Psychology, 25*, 117–129.

Reeves, F. B., & Bergum, B. O. (1972). Perceptual narrowing as a function of peripheral cue relevance. *Perceptual and Motor Skills, 35*, 719–724.

Roseman, I. J. (1984). Cognitive determinants of emotions: A structural theory. In P. Shaver (Ed.), *Review of personality and social psychology*, Vol. 5 (pp. 11–36). Beverly Hills, CA: Sage.

Schooler, J. W., & Melcher, J. (1995). The ineffability of insight. In S. M. Smith, T. B. Ward, & R. A. Finke (Eds.), *The creative cognition approach* (pp. 97–134). Cambridge, MA: MIT Press.

Schwarz, N. (1990). Feelings as information: Informational and motivational functions of affective states. In E. T. Higgins & R. M. Sorrentino (Eds.), *Handbook of motivation and cognition: Foundations of social behavior*, Vol. 2 (pp. 527–561). New York: Guilford.

Schwarz, N., & Clore, G. L. (1983). Mood, misattribution, and judgments of well-being: Informative and directive functions of affective states. *Journal of Personality and Social Psychology, 45*, 513–523.

Schwarz, N., & Clore, G. L. (2007). Feelings and phenomenal experiences. In E. T. Higgins & A. Kruglanski (Eds.), *Social psychology. Handbook of basic principles*, 2nd ed. (pp. 385–407). New York: Guilford.

Shiv, B., & Fedirikhin, A. (1999). Heart and mind in conflict: The interplay between affect and cognition in consumer decision making. *Journal of Consumer Research, 26*, 278–292.

Smith, S. M. (1995). Fixation, incubation, and insight in memory, problem solving, and creativity. In S. M. Smith, T. B. Ward, & R. A. Finke (Eds.), *The creative cognition approach* (pp. 135–155). Cambridge, MA: MIT Press.

Smith, S. M., Ward, T. B., & Schumacher, J. S. (1993). Constraining effects of examples in a creative generation task. *Memory & Cognition, 21*, 837–845.

Stepper, S., & Strack, F. (1993). Proprioceptive determinants of emotional and nonemotional feelings. *Journal of Personality and Social Psychology, 64*, 211–220.

Strack, F. (1992). The different routes to social judgments: Experiential versus informational strategies. In L. L. Martin & A. Tesser (Eds.), *The construction of social judgment* (pp. 249–275). Hillsdale, NJ: Erlbaum.

Strack, F., Martin, L. L., & Stepper, S. (1988). Inhibiting and facilitating conditions of the human smile: A nonobtrusive test of the facial feedback hypothesis. *Journal of Personality and Social Psychology, 54*, 768–777.

Tucker, D. M., & Williamson, P. A. (1984). Asymmetric neural control systems in human self-regulation. *Psychological Review, 91*, 185–215.

Tyler, S. K., & Tucker, D. M. (1982). Anxiety and perceptual structure: Individual differences in neuropsychological function. *Journal of Abnormal Psychology, 91*, 210–220.

Wells, G. L., & Petty, R. E. (1980). The effects of overt head movements on persuasion: Compatibility and incompatibility of responses. *Basic and Applied Social Psychology, 1*, 219–230.

Weltman, G., Smith, J. E., & Edstrom, G. H. (1971). Perceptual narrowing during pressure-chamber exposure. *Human Factors, 13*, 99–107.

Witkin, H. A., Oltman, P. K., Raskin, E., & Karp, S. A. (1971). *A manual for the embedded figures test.* Palo Alto, CA: Consulting Psychologists Press.

Zajonc, R. B., & Markus, H. (1984). Affect and cognition: The hard interface. In C. Izard, J. Kagan, & R. B. Zajonc (Eds.), *Emotions, cognition, and behavior* (pp. 73–102). Cambridge, UK: Cambridge University Press.

Zajonc, R. B., Murphy, S. T., & Inglehart, M. (1989). Feeling and facial efference: Implications of the vascular theory of emotion. *Psychological Review, 96*, 395–416.

# Index